ANATOMY OF A BUSINESS: WHAT IT IS, WHAT IT DOES, AND HOW IT WORKS

Sasha Galbraith

GREENWOOD PRESS
Westport, Connecticut • London

Library of Congress Cataloging-in-Publication Data

Galbraith, Sasha.
   Anatomy of a business : what it is, what it does, and how it works /
   by Sasha Galbraith.
     p. cm.
   Includes bibliographical references and index.
   ISBN 0–313–33793–4 (alk. paper)
   1. Business enterprises.   2. Industrial management.   3. Business.   4. Commerce.
   I. Title.
 HF1008.G35   2007
 338.7—dc22   2006026199

British Library Cataloguing in Publication Data is available.

Library of Congress Catalog Card Number: 2006026199
ISBN–13: 978–0–313–33793–2
ISBN–10: 0–313–33793–4

First published in 2007

Greenwood Press, 88 Post Road West, Westport, CT 06881
An imprint of Greenwood Publishing Group, Inc.
www.greenwood.com

Printed in the United States of America

The paper used in this book complies with the
Permanent Paper Standard issued by the National
Information Standards Organization (Z39.48–1984).

10 9 8 7 6 5 4 3 2 1

Screen Beans art is used with permission of A Bit Better Corporation.
Screen Beans is a registered trademark of A Bit Better Corporation.

Mike Keefe cartoons are copyrighted material and are used with the permission of
Mike Keefe and dePIXion Studios, Inc..

Dilbert cartoons are copyrighted by Scott Adams and distributed by United Feature
Syndicate, Inc. They are used with permission.

For my mentor, best friend, toughest critic, and
most valiant supporter, Jay.

Contents

List of Illustrations

FIGURES

Preface

When I was approached by the publisher to write this book, I couldn't believe that a basic business reference book didn't exist. On top of that, I couldn't believe that high school and undergraduate college students still read books. Isn't that what the Internet is for? No, no, no, said my editor, we want a book with some "attitude," a business book that will teach the principles of business in an entertaining manner. Well, that's what they got. My mother says that I have a wicked sense of humor, and I did honestly try to hold it back.

HOW TO USE THIS BOOK

Dive in! If you've got a question on a particular area of business, then go to that chapter—they're arranged by function. Hopefully you'll find the answer you're after. If not, then check the Internet resources at the end of each chapter for more information, or you can go to print resources (books) listed in the annotated bibliography.

There are some unique (and not so unique) features of this book. First, we have a section in each chapter called "A Day in the Life." These sections spotlight real executives telling you what they do: the fun, the boring, and the exhilarating parts of their job. They'll also tell you what it takes to work your way up to a job like theirs. And speaking of getting a job ... the Appendix includes a career guide that gives you some ideas on where to look for guidance, learn about the types of jobs available, and how to go about getting a job. (It's not meant to be exhaustive, but it should give you a start.) At the end of the book the glossary defines several key terms and will help reinforce the concepts presented here.

I've used the terms him, her, he, she, his, hers, etc., all interchangeably in an effort to wake you up to the fact that women can do all the same jobs as men can (and, I might add, often better).

This is not meant to be an encyclopedia of business. So there are crucial bits of information that aren't contained in this book (hey, I had a word count limit). But I've tried to give you the basics of business in a way that awakens your desire to learn much more. Business is a fun career and you can earn heaps of money at it if you do good (and legal) work.

THANK YOUS

I won't drone on about who did what here … but I do have a few folks who helped make this book what it is.

First, my "A Day in the Life" contributors. Without them this book would not be nearly as interesting (or educational) to read. They gave freely of their time and did it for free. Thank you, thank you all!

Second, my husband, Jay. He helped me enormously with the topics on organization design and structure, R&D, and sales. He also put up with many pizza delivery nights when I was too busy to cook.

Third, Niamh McGoff, our assistant and lifesaver. She took over much of my "day job" of running our consulting business so I could focus on writing a book. She also walked our dogs (Belgian Malinois) when I was chained to my computer (a Mac).

Fourth, I had some expert help from industry experts like Lynn Magrath (head librarian at Summit County High School), Crista Peters (MIS), Joe Glasman (Finance), Traci Hilliard (Accounting), Mr. Wind at His Back and Bill Goodwin (HR), who gave me some very good tips, comments, and critiques on the stuff I wrote.

And last, a good writer should always thank her editor. Mine, Nick Philipson, was MIA most of the time, which was probably good. Who needs the extra pressure? But he gave me very uplifting positive feedback, which helped tremendously at key moments.

May 2006
Breckenridge, Colorado

Abbreviations

BU	Business Unit
CEO	Chief Executive Officer
CFO	Chief Financial Officer
CIO	Chief Information Officer or Chief Innovation Officer
CMO	Chief Marketing Officer
COO	Chief Operating Officer
CRM	Customer Relationship Management
CSO	Chief Sales Officer or Chief Strategy Officer
CTO	Chief Technology Officer
EBIT	Earnings Before Interest and Taxes
EBITDA	Earnings Before Interest, Taxes, Depreciation, and Amortization (or Earnings Before I Tricked the Dumb Auditor)
EDI	Electronic Data Interchange
ERP	Enterprise Resource Planning
EVA	Economic Value Added
FICA	Federal Insurance Contributions Act (Social Security Taxes)
HR	Human Resources
IS	Information Systems
IT	Information Technology
JIT	Just-in-Time (manufacturing)
MIS	Management of Information Systems
MPC	Manufacturing Planning and Control systems
MRP-II	Manufacturing Resources Planning
P&L	Profit and Loss
PE Ratio	Price to Earnings Ratio
PERT	Program Evaluation and Review Technique (or Problems Eventually Resolve Themselves)
R&D	Research and Development
ROA	Return on Assets
ROI	Return on Investment
ROIC	Return on Invested Capital

SBU	Strategic Business Unit
SCM	Supply Chain Management
SOP	Standard Operating Procedure
SWOT	Strengths, Weaknesses, Opportunities, and Threats
TQM	Total Quality Management
USP	Unique Selling Proposition
VAR	Value-Added Reseller
WIP	Work in Progress, or Work in Process

1

Introduction

People always overestimate how complex business is. This isn't rocket science; we've chosen one of the world's more simple professions.
                                                —Jack Welch, CEO of General Electric (retired)

Work is the curse of the drinking classes.

                                                —Oscar Wilde

WHAT IS BUSINESS?

The economic definition of business is the purchase and sale of goods in an attempt to make a profit. It can also mean the actual enterprise or establishment, which is used to create profits. In each case, the idea is to make more money than one spends in generating the sales. Business is also sometimes referred to as commerce. Commerce, another word for business, is defined in the *American College Dictionary* as the "interchange of goods or commodities, especially on a large scale between different countries or between different parts of the same country; trade; business."[1]

At its simplest, let's take the lemonade stand. Joey buys a case of lemons for $5.00, a pound of sugar for $1.50, and his "secret ingredient" for $2.00. He borrows some boards and a chair from his parents, sets up his stand, and paints a sign announcing lemonade for sale at $0.50 per cup. Meanwhile he makes the lemonade by squeezing the lemons by hand, adding some water and ice, and stirring in some sugar. Joey ends up with about fifty cups of lemonade. Joey figures that his cost for each cup of lemonade is 17 cents (the price of all the ingredients divided by fifty cups). If he sells a cup of lemonade, he will earn a profit of 33 cents on that cup. But Joey has not included the cost of his own time, the cost of the water, or the energy costs to produce the ice in the equation. If he added those in, his cost per cup of lemonade would increase and his profits would decrease.

Joey's lemonade stand is doing a brisk business because he set it up on the sidewalk outside his house, which happens to be opposite the entrance to the city's football stadium. When he needs to refill his supply of lemonade, he can run into the house, open the refrigerator, and get another pitcher of lemonade for his stand. But an inspector from the Department of Health has just arrived and told Joey that he needs a permit to set up a business on city property (the sidewalk). And furthermore, he needs to have his kitchen inspected for sanitary conditions in order to obtain a permit to sell beverages. The tax inspector is not far behind and claims that Joey needs to file an income tax statement and pay tax of 20 percent on all cups of lemonade that he has sold. The city treasurer then comes along and wants to charge Joey rent for the 4 square feet of city property that Joey is using to promote his business, but the zoning board needs to first approve the retail use of the sidewalk in his neighborhood and ensure that he has provided handicapped access. Meanwhile, the concessionaire at the football stadium is complaining because her contract with the city has a non-compete clause. This guarantees that she will have no competition from other vendors (sellers) of food or beverages within a 1-mile radius. She wants Joey to compensate her for the loss of business she has suffered because people have bought Joey's lemonade instead of hers. Joey points out that if her lemonade were as good as his, she wouldn't lose the business. Joey's 33-cent profit on each cup is rapidly diminishing, to the point where there will be no profit. Joey starts to rethink this lemonade business. . . . Maybe opening a snowboard shop would be more fun (see Chapter 5).

Hotspot Lemonade Stand by Mike Keefe
© Mike Keefe, Reprinted with permission.

HISTORY OF BUSINESS

How did business start? Who were the first businesspeople? What did they sell and buy? No one knows. There's evidence that people conducted business as much as 10,000 years ago in China as well as in Mesopotamia, the "cradle of civilization," which is now known as Iraq and Iran. Business probably arose as one caveman traded his extra brontosaurus teeth for saber-tooth cat skins. By trading one thing for another, both cavemen came out ahead. The caveman who lived in an area with lots of brontosaurus had plenty of meat to eat and bones to make weapons with, but getting tiger skins to keep him and his family warm was more problematic. The other caveman, who lived in an area full of saber-toothed tigers, needed the leather from brontosaurus for shoes. By trading, each man got what he could not otherwise kill for himself.

The next sections will give you a summary of the origins and development of business. We'll also describe the basic nature of business: trade, and how trade has changed over the millennia.

Business as Trade

Trading is at the root of all business transactions. What first started as an exchange of natural resources grew to become a worldwide explosion of commerce. "Commerce originated when a human demand was first supplied by some other person than the one demanding it."[2] The first traders probably spoke cave language and exchanged goods such as furs and rudimentary tools made of bones or stones. But because there was no written record until biblical times, very little is known about early, early trade. Generally speaking, in order to have trade or commerce, some sort of organized civilization must be present. That is, there must be a group of people who have an established social hierarchy, practice agriculture, have developed specialization of labor, and, thus, have identified gaps in their natural resources and are interested in trading with other groups who have resources that they do not.

The Barter System

The earliest notion of business was built around trade. This is also called barter. One person who has a product or good that someone else wants is in a position to trade that good for something she wants in exchange. Some of the first items that were bartered were domesticated animals—cattle, sheep, goats, and camels. As societies became less nomadic and settled down to grow crops, grain and vegetable products were also traded.

The biggest problem with the barter system was that it depended on the mutual coincidence of wants and needs. That is, if you had a surplus of beef filets and you needed your shoes repaired, you would have to find a cobbler who wanted beef filets. The local cobbler, you discover, has the time and talent to repair your shoes, but he is a vegetarian who would rather have a bushel of apples. Now you have to find an apple grower who would like to trade apples for beef so you can get your shoes fixed. This is where money came into play. People needed an intermediate store of value, or currency, that facilitated trade. Ideally, that intermediate form of currency had to be durable, easy to transport, and intrinsically valuable (such as made of a semi-precious metal or otherwise difficult to create by oneself). Over the years, currency has taken several different forms (see box).

Today, bartering still exists. Friends trade their services among one another. Some people trade products and services in an effort to get around the taxman. The following web sites help people to arrange barter transactions:

www.dotcombarter.com
www.metrotrading.com
www.u-exchange.com
www.ucanbarter.com

Currency through the Ages

9000–6000 BC: Livestock

Livestock (cattle, sheep, goats, camels, water buffalo, etc.) was edible protein, could work a farm, and could produce milk. It was an excellent store of value and one of the earliest bartered goods. Around 6000 BC people also traded produce, grains, barley beer, and wine.

1200 BC: Cowrie Shells (Puka Shells)

These are the shells of mollusks that proliferated in the Pacific and Indian Oceans. It is the earliest and most widely used form of an intermediate currency.

1000—500 BC: Coins

The first coins were bronze and copper cowrie shell imitations found in China. Eventually these coins were flattened and had holes punched in the middle of them so that they could be strung on a chain or string. In other areas of the world (Turkey, Greece, Persia, Macedonia, and later, the Roman Empire), lumps of silver, bronze, and gold were used. These lumps eventually became round and were stamped with pictures of gods and emperors to guarantee their value.

500 BC: Gold and Silver Coins

Darius I introduced gold and silver coins which vastly expanded the economy of the Achaemenid Empire (parts of present day Iran, Iraq, Turkey, Bulgaria, Greece, Egypt, Syria, Pakistan, Jordan, Israel, Lebanon, Central Asia, Arabia, and Libya).

118 BC: Leather Money

The first attempt at a banknote was one-foot square pieces of deerskin leather in China. It was painted with colorful borders.

AD 900: Paper Currency

The first banknotes appeared in China during the Tang Dynasty. Merchants exchanged deposit notes for deposit currency to satisfy their payment obligations.

AD 800–900: The Nose

Folklore has it that Irish people would have to "pay through the nose" if they refused to pay taxes levied by the Danish Vikings who had raided their territories. These recalcitrant taxpayers had their noses slit by the Vikings.

1500s: Paper Promises

Merchants in Europe issued receipts in return for deposits. This became the first form of true banking operation where financial intermediaries exchanged different forms of receipts and payment orders, including the promissory note, the check, and the bill of exchange.

1661: Banknotes

The Bank of Stockholm issued the first government-backed currency in Europe.

1816: The Gold Standard

The problems of inflation that accompanied government-issued notes led Britain to adopt gold as its standard of value for the British pound (which was based on a pound of silver to denominate its value). Other European countries followed and the United States adopted the Gold Standard Act in 1900. However, by the 1970s most countries had abandoned gold.

2002: The Euro

The largest consolidation of national currencies in modern history took place on January 1 with the introduction of new banknotes and coins in the European Union.

Today: Intangible Money

Wire transfers, electronic payments, and other forms of electronic money are becoming more prevalent and probably will grow, especially with the introduction of "smart cards" (credit cards with microchips embedded within that facilitate smaller transactions).

Sources: Glyn Davies. *A History of Money from Ancient Times to the Present Day*, 3rd ed. Cardiff: University of Wales Press, 2002; and Wikipedia, taken from http://en.wikipedia.org/wiki/Achaemenid on June 28, 2005.

The Haves and the Have-nots: Natural Resources and Where's the Beef?

Trade or barter could not exist without natural resources—the things provided by Mother Nature, such as stones, metals, fruits, vegetables, grains, spices, fish, cattle, goats, pigs, horses, water, products from trees (wood, bark, rubber, coconut oil, palm oil, fences, etc.), products from animals (wool, leather, tallow, eggs, fur, etc.), and, later on, oil, natural gas, hydropower, and ethanol. As a result, the people who had the early advantage in trade were those who had an abundance of natural resources. As societies grew more specialized, people learned to take some of the natural resources at their disposal, manipulate, and/or add services to them and turn them into something more valuable. This is also known as the "value chain" and will be discussed more in Chapter 2. An early example of a value chain is Chinese families who knew how to raise silk worms, harvest their silk threads, boil and color the threads, and weave the threads into beautiful fabrics that could then be turned into clothing, upholstery, bags, carpets, and numerous other products. The Chinese received a premium for these products over and above the price of a silk worm or its raw silk. In fact, these silk products were so highly valued that a huge trading network was later named after the prize: the Silk Road, which was active from about 200 BC to AD 1400.

What were historically the most sought after natural resources?

Pepper, nutmeg, and mace (the outer layer of a nutmeg).

Early Traders

The area known as the Fertile Crescent (Israel, Jordan, Lebanon, and parts of Syria, Iraq, and southeastern Turkey) is thought to be the birthplace of agriculture. The Sumerians, an ancient culture that occupied the southern part of Mesopotamia in about 5000–4000 BC were the world's first farmers, writers, and astronomers. They invented numerous military items along with the wheel, the hammer, nails, sandals, and beer brewing. They invented a picture type of writing that later evolved into cuneiform and predated Egyptian hieroglyphics by 75 years. The Sumerians also correctly identified twelve planets in the solar system and the distance between them (Pluto wasn't "discovered" by our modern astronomers until 1930). We have the Sumerians to thank for the 60-second minute and the 60-minute hour. Discoveries of obsidian and lapis lazuli from faraway places suggest that the Sumerians were early traders.

There is some evidence that people in the Neolithic period (8500–4000 BC) were making wine in present-day Syria and Egypt. Ancient pottery, texts, and letter seals suggest that wine was actively traded and enjoyed in the region now known as Iran, Iraq, and Syria back in 3500–3100 BC[3] — ironically, these are countries that today ban alcohol because of their Islamic beliefs. These communities were year-round settlements housing domesticated animals and some agriculture. The neoliths were also credited with producing bread, beer, and various meat and grain dishes. It's very possible that residents traded among themselves and passing nomads during this time.

Meanwhile in China, the Peiligang culture in Henan Province comprised a group of Neolithic communities in 8000–5000 BC that grew millet and raised pigs. This group is believed to be among the first pottery producers in China. In South Asia, a group of people in Mehrgarh (established in 7000 BC between present-day Quetta, Kalat, and Sibi, Pakistan) started domesticating cattle, sheep, and goats, and grew wheat and barley.

The earliest historical mention of trading and commodities came at about 2600 BC when the Egyptians bought spices from Asia to feed to workers on the Cheops Pyramid, in the belief that the spices gave them extra strength. Additionally, the Egyptians needed cassia and cinnamon, which were necessary for embalming the dead. Soon after, the Syrians procured cloves from the Spice Islands in Indonesia. In fact, 2000 BC was a very busy time. The Babylonian Empire (present-day Iraq) was just getting started and, by some accounts, the Egyptian monarchy had already been in place for a few hundred years. The first bankers wore togas back around 2000 BC and spoke Phoenician or Assyrian in the Tigris River valley (present-day Iran/Iraq). The Chinese were already making silks in 2000 BC and trading them from their homes. At about the same time, Sidon (present-day Lebanon) was known for fine textiles. The descendants of the Canaan Settlement (present-day Israel and Lebanon) settled Phoenicia and became renowned as excellent navigators and traders of antiquity. The Phoenicians are responsible for the original Roman alphabet. In addition, the Phoenicians discovered a local source for murex, a shellfish that produced a rare and valuable purple dye. At the height of Phoenician power, they controlled trade throughout the Mediterranean — from North Africa and Spain through Egypt, Italy, and on to the far eastern shores of the Black Sea.

On the other side of the world during this time, Fohi (or Yao) — called by some "the Noah of the Bible" — founded the first dynasty (Hiah) of China. According to Chinese historians, Fohi invented a style of writing that used pictures. He is also credited with inventing music, dressmaking, and the custom of sacrificing during the solstices. Fohi's son, Shin-Nong, thought by some to be the Shem of the Bible, is said to have taught the art of farming (husbandry), making bread from wheat, and wine from rice.

Ancient Persia was probably the earliest geographical location of formal business. Many words in the English language come from typical trade-related items in the Persian language, like asparagus, bazaar, lemon, melon, orange, peach, sash, shawl, spinach, tiara, and turquoise. Nineveh on the Tigris River (today's Mosul, Iraq) under the Assyrian domination was a long-time center for trade between Armenia, the Persian Gulf, India, and China. Nineveh was eclipsed by Babylon (60 miles from present-day Baghdad) due to her strategic location on the more international river, Euphrates. Gold, ivory, jewels, silks, cotton, wool, tapestries, spices, fine woods, and hunting dogs came from India, Bactria (the Hindu Kush in northern Afghanistan and Pakistan), and China. Ceylon (Sri Lanka) and the Persian Gulf countries produced pearls while Arabia traded frankincense, myrrh, and various other perfume and incense ingredients. The eastern Mediterranean countries contributed lumber and stone; Armenia and Asia Minor supplied wine and oils; Egypt had flax, grains, cattle, and horses; and Scythia (exact location is disputed; some claim it is the Altai region where Mongolia, China, Russia, and Kazakhstan intersect) traded furs and hides. When Babylon fell, the trading center moved to Susa (in southwestern Iran—also known as Shush).

Trade became impossible to extinguish and entire governments rose and fell on the basis of abundance or lack of natural resources necessary for trade—and their ability to control those resources. As the Phoenician's influence waned, their students, the Greeks, gained power in commerce, with cities like Athens and Corinth becoming the international trade centers (400 BC). Alexander the Great (a Macedonian native) gave a huge boost to many cities in the eastern Mediterranean by founding Alexandria, planning a canal between the Black Sea and the Caspian Sea, and reopening the sea route between Babylon and India. As commerce in key civilizations rose, so did contributions to the foundations of philosophy, art, literature, architecture, and politics.

In addition to the Greeks, the Etruscans (centered in the Po Valley, northern Italy) gained influence. With their iron mines in Elba they provided hardware and foreign exchange. The orange-and-black Etruscan pottery is second to none in elegance over the ages. However, the Etruscans lost dominance after a battle between the Greeks and Carthaginians (ninth century BC) with whom they were allied; all were later eclipsed by the Roman Empire.

The Roman Empire was one of the most important in ancient history as is documented numerous places elsewhere. From the standpoint of trade, the Romans imported vast quantities of agricultural products, wine, and manufactured goods (silks, spices, tapestries, and other luxuries) from all corners of the empire. However, the Romans were poor at exporting goods. The Roman contribution to trade was principally in roads and upgraded infrastructure. Ultimately high taxation, political instability, and "such physical vices as drunkenness, gluttony and licentiousness"[4] resulted in the commercial decline of the empire two centuries later (AD 476). Of course, it did not help Rome that Atilla and his Huns thrashed the Roman army in AD 443.

The Silk Road

Europe gradually declined into the "Dark Ages" (roughly 800–1100 AD) known for high banditry, serfdom, oppression of the masses by the moneyed class, and rampant epidemics. Trade and commerce were reduced but not eliminated. Due to the lack of a stable monetary currency, the wealthy preferred to hold their assets in the form of gold, silver, rare pottery, ornaments, fine tapestries, and precious stones. Paradoxically, conditions in the Middle East and Asia were luxurious and trade there flourished. The Persians were living in splendor greater than any European king or queen. Constantine had founded Constantinople (modern day Istanbul) that provided a central entrepôt for Greek merchant ships and luxury goods from the east.

The Silk Road reached its apogee of commerce and culture at this point. Marco Polo spent 24 years traveling through Asia along the Silk Road, which was in fact a network of routes between China, India, the Middle East, and Europe. The importance of the Silk Road to trade, political integration, religion, and culture cannot be overstated. Every nation that was connected to the Silk Road benefited in some way. Trade increased the standard of living for citizens of all nations that participated. Buddhism was spread from China to Southeast Asia, Hinduism from India to Asia, Islam from Persia to Africa, Central and Southeast Asia, and so on. Governments levied tariffs on goods that passed through their territories in exchange for protection of the traveling caravans. Many of these tariffs, particularly in Europe, were exorbitant and dampened trade.

A group of multilingual Jewish merchants, known as Radhanites, arose as trusted brokers between the Middle Eastern and European buyers. The Radhanites generally brought high-value, low-bulk items like spices, perfumes, jewelry, and silk to European buyers in exchange for eunuchs, female slaves, boys, swords, and furs. However, in AD 908 the trading routes became unsafe in the Middle East and China and the Radhanite network dissolved.

At the same time that the Radhanites became influential in Europe, Mohammed, founder of Islam, unified the warring Arab tribes into one state and told them that commerce is good. Arabs soon produced some of the highest valued silks, brocade, tapestries, rugs, and tempered swords known anywhere. Arabs were responsible for two important contributions to commerce. First, their skills in art and manufacture of fine goods (leather, glassware, pottery, paper, perfumes, etc.) escalated the entire Western notion of quality to a new level. Second, they instituted scientific agriculture and practiced systematic irrigation and crop rotation, utilized fertilizers, and produced entirely new crops using grafts of various fruits and flowers.

Trader as Raider

Many raiders or pirates throughout history have been associated with conquest. Several of them, like Attila the Hun, the Visigoths, and others sought territorial claims over generally stationary and agrarian societies (otherwise known as colonization). However, some raiders (probably unwittingly) fostered trade in the process.

From the eighth to the eleventh century, the Vikings roamed northern Europe, Russia, and even as far west as Newfoundland. Their legacy is mixed as some see them as heroes and others as raiders and rabble-rousers. They were colonizers, pirates, businessmen, and explorers. For the most part they distributed fear, but they did eventually develop commerce in the countries they settled (England, Russia, and Iceland). During their plundering, they did, however, resurrect trade, which had languished throughout most of Europe.

Meanwhile several Italian cities rose in prominence as major trading venues. Venice, founded by refugees fleeing Attila the Hun, became the new capital of commerce with its strategic location offering access to western Europe, Egypt, Syria, Greece, Constantinople, and the Far East. In addition, Venice produced two key products that were in high demand: fish and salt. The Venetians are also credited with inventing the discipline of international merchant financing, although the Radhanites, who frequently used letters of credit, would probably dispute that claim. (The English term *bank* comes from the Italian word for bench, *banco*, which is where the money changers operated.)

Commerce is at the heart of the precipitation of the Crusades (eleventh to thirteenth centuries). The pope told his subjects that they were not allowed to engage in business with "the infidels" (non-Christians) who were occupying parts of Europe (notably southern Spain and southern Italy) as well as Byzantium (Turkey). Nonetheless, the merchant class—especially the Italian city-states of Venice, Genoa, and Pisa—continued to trade with the East. As the Abbasids (precursors to Iraq's Sunni tribes) gained power in the Middle East and began to pursue domination of Byzantium, they also instilled a more strict form of Islam (some have called it "despotic tyranny.")[5] The pope then sanctioned a Holy War against the Islamic populations to the East. European traders, believing that their business activities were threatened, wholeheartedly supported the Crusades with financing and logistical support. In return, the merchants were rewarded with tax exemptions, commercially strategic land grants, retail concessions in far outposts, and monetary payments. Two important results came from the Crusades: feudalism ended because so many nobles had been financially ruined or killed, and the West learned many invaluable lessons in manufacturing (textiles, glassware, leather), agriculture (new crops and farming techniques), technology (windmills and navigation), and the art of living (the use of underclothes, showering more than once a year, refined manners, table and bed linens, soaps, perfumes, spices, wall paper, tiles, carpets, etc.) from the Islamic societies. Commoners returned from their tour of duty with stories and examples of the luxuries that these Eastern people cultivated and, in many cases, sought to replicate such items in their European cities. As a result, commerce between East and West grew and became even more interconnected.

As Europe emerged from the Dark Ages and put the Crusades behind her, Asia and the Middle East were being absorbed into the Mongol Empire—the world's second largest after the British Empire. At its height in 1290 the empire stretched from Korea to Hungary and Russia to Iran. It comprised 13.8 million square miles (35 million square kilometers) and over 100 million people (that's not counting the 30 million who were killed in its creation). Genghis Khan, the founder, installed a number of principles and practices that enhanced trade throughout the empire:

- Stiff discipline
- Merit-based promotions
- Religious tolerance
- Strict punishment (death) for thievery and vandalism of civilian property
- Tax exemptions for teachers, lawyers, and artists
- Development of an extensive postal system
- Active protection of trade routes and commercial relationships

In fact, the Silk Road became more prosperous and well traveled than ever under the protection of the Mongols. The postal system was an enhancement over the first "pony express" nearly 2,000 years earlier (see "Pony Express").

But the Mongol Empire declined in 1400 because Ghengis' sons and grandsons weren't quite the man he was. The Silk Road closed shortly thereafter due to political instability along the territories, and the Ming Dynasty in China closed its borders. The Ottoman Empire rose from the disarray. This period spelled a decline in products originating from the East and tipped the balance and power of trade back to the West, and Italy in particular.

In Europe the Renaissance was taking hold, fueled in large part by the Medici family in Florence. While the Mongol Empire facilitated trade over land, it was sea trade that held the greatest profits and possibilities for expansion. As the Silk Road trade declined, sea trade took off somewhat simultaneously in Europe (principally from Venice) and China. The eunuch admiral Zheng He visited thirty-seven countries over seven journeys to the Persian Gulf, the Red Sea, and the East African coast. The Venetian government controlled almost all aspects of sea trade, including the routes, schedules, ports of call, arrival and departure times, number of sailors and commanders per vessel, specific cargoes to be traded, and the prices for each item. A consul was stationed at each port. He reported on the local political and economic conditions, including the status of agricultural and manufactured products. These Venetian consuls were instrumental in developing intergovernmental international relations as well as codes of maritime law. At the end of the fifteenth century, Venice had 3,000 merchant ships, which were protected by more than 300 warships. The value of all commercial trade back then was estimated at $25 million (that's more than $600 million in 2003 dollars). And the annual income of the average Venetian merchant prince was about $14,000 ($308,000 in 2003 dollars).

If Venice was the epicenter for commercial shipping, Florence had become the international banking center. The Medici family established large banks throughout Italy and even maintained branches in London and Geneva. Florentine banks took deposits, made loans, handled foreign exchange transactions, and developed an extensive credit network including certificates of deposit and international letters of credit. This meant that merchants did not have to haul around sacks of gold and the various oddball coins that were required to conduct commerce in each fiefdom. Deposit accounts and letters of credit (these are like today's debit and credit cards) greatly facilitated international trade and enabled several governments to finance their foreign expeditions.

Colonialism—The Sun Never Sets on the British (French, Portuguese, Spanish) Empire

The Renaissance awakened Europe to life's possibilities beyond serfdom, poverty, piety toward the church, and an ascetic lifestyle. Three important inventions changed the world of commerce for good: gunpowder, the printing press, and the compass. Gunpowder facilitated the overthrow of feudalism, which had hindered trade during the Middle Ages. The printing press led to cheaper books and the wider dissemination of knowledge among all classes of people, which in turn fueled desires for exploration and further knowledge. The compass revolutionized sea travel and led directly to the "discovery" of America and the Cape of Good Hope as well as the circumnavigation of the globe. These new geographical discoveries opened the field of commerce beyond the Mediterranean and the North Sea and led to an increasing appetite among several European governments to expand their territories throughout the world.

It was predominantly the Europeans who had a taste for exploration and subsequent colonization of foreign lands. The Portuguese sailor, Vasco de Gama, started it off by rounding the Cape of Good Hope and charting a sea route to Calcutta and the highly sought-after center of the pepper trade, Kerala. Other Portuguese explorers followed (sixteenth century) and claimed title on behalf of Portugal to several countries including India, the Straits of Hormuz, Oman, Malacca (the southern part of Malaysia), the Moluccas and Bandas (Spice Islands in Indonesia), the Philippines, the western and eastern coastal areas of Africa, and the eastern part of present-day Brazil. The Portuguese government practiced a form of monopoly trade: they controlled all of the strategic shipping outposts and only allowed Portuguese merchants to bring goods from India and Asia to Europe. In addition, the government completely controlled the sale of certain spices (like vanilla, pepper, cloves, and nutmeg) and strictly regulated trade between intermediate countries by giving the right to trade goods in specific regions to certain groups of people. But Portugal's fledgling empire declined quickly for a number of reasons. First, the government tended to focus its trade on bringing goods back from its colonies to Portugal, and from there offloaded the ships to European (mostly Dutch) traders. Thus the Portuguese played the middleman and did not gain the additional income from freight forwarding. Second, their monopolistic practices in Africa and Asia, coupled with a cruel policy toward the natives, led other countries, notably the Dutch, English, and French, to aggressively pursue their own trade at the expense of the Portuguese. Third, Lisbon has the unenviable reputation of having been the first and largest market for African slave trade—the Portuguese government so antagonized the natives of Africa that they actively worked to rid themselves of Portuguese control, even fleeing to the arms of other colonial powers. And fourth, the Portuguese had a "take" mentality whereby they pillaged the colonies. They did not invest in any of the countries that they took over. The Portuguese could have attempted to make their colonies productive trade-supplying nations by fostering agricultural or manufacturing industries, but they did not.

The Spaniards were the next great empire builders. Starting with Columbus (1492) through Cortez, Pizarro, Almagro, Magellan, and Urdaneta (1565), Spain grew to encompass most of South and Central America, Mexico, the Caribbean nations (Cuba, San Domingo, Puerto Rico, etc.), and the Philippines. But while the Spanish explorers went looking for land and gold, their interests were less in building trading outposts. Two principal outcomes resulted from Spain's conquests: (1) the annihilation of many native cultures and arts while attempting to convert them to Catholicism, and (2) the spread of the Spanish language throughout the Americas. Spain practiced the same monopolistic practices that Portugal did in its colonies. They could have had the natives manufacture many articles (thereby adding value to the natural resource and benefiting Spain with cheap labor), but the Spanish government forbade the manufacture of many articles so that the Spanish merchants could extort high prices for the raw goods (ship captains could expect a profit of 100–300% on their cargo). Spaniards held all of the senior positions in the colonies, foreigners were not allowed to trade or settle in the countries, and very high taxes and customs duties were imposed on all imports and exports.

By 1648, Spain's empire had collapsed. Spain was one of the most culturally and technologically advanced countries in all of Europe, having learned about mathematics, arts, agriculture, and manufacturing from the presence of the Moors in southern Spain. But Spain did not capitalize on that knowledge and constantly persecuted the Moors until they moved back to Africa. In addition, by importing huge quantities of silver (coins) the government unwittingly caused inflation and attempted to solve it by putting in price controls, restricting industry, and prohibiting exports. Spain seemed to be almost singularly focused on spreading Catholicism. Philip II ruled the Netherlands, which had become a prosperous trading nation. But in his mania to convert the Protestants to Catholics, he destroyed most of the southern part of the country (now known as Belgium). The northern part (Amsterdam, Rotterdam, etc.) escaped much of Philip's misrule and continued to prosper. Dutch shipbuilders and sailors became known as the best and most daring in the world. Meanwhile, back in Spain, the Inquisition (1481–1492) served to chase away or kill many productive and knowledgeable members of her society. And finally, the English defeated Spain's *Invincible Armada* in 1588, thus putting an end to Spain's maritime dominance.

France and Holland also pursued trade in foreign colonies, mostly in Africa and Asia. The Dutch took over Indonesia and the Spice Islands as the Portuguese influence there waned. The French colonized many African nations and became a welcome "protector" from other colonial powers by virtue of France's policy of protecting all oriental Catholics. France signed a treaty with Turkey's Solyman II that gave her the right to trade with the Ottoman Empire. But as France imported more gold and silver from America, her economy suffered from inflation and France followed the same choking economic policies as Spain. At the end of the sixteenth century, France was embroiled in internal wars and faced with stiff competition in international trade from the English and the Dutch.

The First Corporation

The Dutch, 'having rid themselves of Spanish misrule, rebuilt their economy with unparalleled zeal. They pursued fishing, farming, manufacturing, banking, trading, and exploration. Amsterdam became the world merchant and banking capitol. Philip II had prohibited all trade between Spain and the Netherlands, thus forcing Dutch merchants to go directly to the East Indies for products. From this rose the Dutch East and West India Companies, two of the earliest corporate entities. The Dutch East India Company, founded in 1602 by the government of the Netherlands, was the world's first multinational company and the first company to issue ownership shares, or stock. Several Dutch cities and private citizens, including Dutch, Germans, and Belgians, held stock in the companies and received a share of the profits. The Dutch East India Company succeeded in expelling the Portuguese from Malacca, the Moluccas, Java, Ceylon, the Celebes, and the Malay Peninsula. The company established a headquarters in Batavia (present-day Jakarta), which became the capital of the Dutch colonial empire. The Dutch East India Company was one of the first quasi-government and quasi-corporate entity that both governed the empire and maintained a virtual monopoly on precious natural resources (pepper, nutmeg, mace, cloves, sugar, rice, cotton, silks, hard woods, and precious stones) that were shipped back to Europe. The company was immensely profitable and annual dividends ranged from 12.5 percent to as much as 75 percent. By 1669 the Dutch East India Company was the richest in the world, and by 1799 it ceased to exist, the result of mismanagement, corruption, and excessive debt.

The Dutch West India Company was founded in 1621 by merging a number of individual and small enterprises that were all pursuing trade in the New World (America, Brazil, and the Caribbean). Henry Hudson, working for the Dutch East India Company, was trying to find a northwest passage to the East Indies and discovered the river that bears his name. He didn't find Asia through this route, but he did claim the region on behalf of the Dutch while he was there. The Dutch traded with the natives and later built forts in New Amsterdam (now New York City), Orange, Hartford, and Good Hope. The Dutch West India Company was not as successful as its sister. Although it paid high dividends, the company's profits

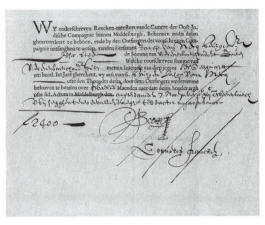

World's oldest stock certificate.

came from the slave trade, smuggling, and piracy. The Peace of Westphalia (1648), which among other achievements decreed the independence of the Netherlands from Spain, also curtailed Dutch smuggling and thus diminished the Dutch West India Company's profits. In addition, the Dutch West India Company was not very good at keeping hold of its colony in America, soon ceding it to the English.

Meanwhile, during the sixteenth century, England had been expanding her horizons. Queen Elizabeth I reigned over the longest peacetime economy in the era and encouraged international commerce and exploration. The English privateers (pirates or raiders) gave way to state-sanctioned enterprises that pursued trade with other nations under the backing of the English flag. Organizations such as the Russian Company and the Levant Company negotiated contracts to trade with Russia over the Volga River, and with Turkey, Syria, and Asia Minor. Queen Elizabeth also encouraged immigration of workers and artisans from France, Germany, Belgium, and the Netherlands, where they faced religious and civil persecution.

The English were the last to pursue colonization, but the most successful. Part of the reason is that the pope had extraordinary power over European nations, and issued proclamations (papal bulls) that decreed who could control various areas of the world (for example, the Portuguese were given exclusive possession of the East Indies). This ended with the Peace of Westphalia, and the pope was demoted to his current position of head of the Catholic Church. As the Portuguese influence waned in Asia, Queen Elizabeth chartered the East India Company. The two East India Companies (Dutch and English) clashed but worked out an agreement whereby the English controlled the Indian subcontinent and the Dutch controlled Southeast Asia. Gradually the Dutch, hobbled by events back in Europe, ceded control of many of their spheres of influence (Ceylon, Malaysia, Burma) in Southeast Asia to the British, who by this time had allied with the Scottish and Welsh kingdoms.

English activities in the New World were less organized and depended largely on the activities of independent, sober, pious, and hardworking pioneers who emigrated to America and built up an existence. The mother country did little to help these colonists and, in fact, actively went around them. England imported more sugar and tobacco at better terms from her island colonies in the Caribbean than from the East Coast colonies.

Business as Communication

Communication is at the heart of every business transaction; whether it is trading two saber-tooth tiger furs for six stone tools or negotiating a complex international corporate merger. At the least, people have to be able to indicate to each other what they are willing to buy or sell and for what price. Today, communication seems effortless with e-mail, cell phones, and the Internet. But back in the day when it took days or even months on foot, horseback, or sailboat to trade with the next village, communication was much more arduous. As we have seen throughout the history of business, whenever a civilization or empire fell into disrepair, the transportation and communication networks usually suffered, and so did the volume of trade. Thus, business is highly dependent on a good communication and transportation infrastructure.

Pony Express

The very first "pony express" or horse relay system was established about 500 years BC between what is now Izmir, Turkey, and Shush, Iran. The horses and riders were stationed along a 1,500-mile (2,500-km) long highway that joined twenty administrative units, or *satrapies*. It took 15 days to go from one end of the highway to the other.

By the time of Herodotus (c. 475 BC), the Persian Royal Road ran some 2,857 km from the city of Susa on the lower Tigris to the port of Smyrna (modern Izmir in Turkey) on the Aegean Sea. It was maintained and protected by the Achaemenid empire (c. 700–330 BC) and had postal stations and relays at regular intervals. By having fresh horses and riders ready at each relay, royal couriers could carry messages the entire distance in 9 days, though normal travelers took about 3 months. This Royal Road linked into many other routes. Some of these routes, such as the passages to India and Central Asia, were also protected by the Achaemenids and facilitated regular contact between India, Mesopotamia, and the Mediterranean. At first, the Royal Road was used only for official administrative messages between the satrapies. But later on it carried personal and business communications, including price information on goods trading elsewhere.

During the Mongol Empire (1206–1368), the postal system was open to all. There were three types of service: second class, first class, and top priority, the last of which was reserved for imperial messages. Second-class service was carried out on foot, with runners who ran between relay stations that were 3 miles apart. Each runner wore a belt with bells on it so that upon his approach to the relay station, his replacement would be ready to run to the next station. This second-class postal system enabled a message to travel in 24 hours a distance that would normally take 10 days to walk. Each relay station kept records of the messages coming through, and inspectors patrolled the routes regularly. First-class mail was carried on horseback with relay stations every 25 miles. Top-priority class was used only for the Khan's (the ruler's) business. Special riders who carried the official tablet of the empire galloped between relay stations. The messenger sounded a horn upon his approach and a fresh horse was ready and waiting for him to mount. This express service could cover 250–300 miles in 1 day.

Mongolian horseman.

In addition, the postal stations offered hospitality to visiting officials and were used as military outposts. Furthermore, regular travelers could stay at the postal stations for a small fee. (Imagine your local post office as a hotel!)

Business as Economic Development

Although history is littered with bad apples in business, trade between societies is undisputedly the engine that drives economic development. The cultural groups that engaged in free trade with other groups inevitably came out ahead. One theory posits that *Homo sapiens* displaced *Homo neanderthalensis* (Neanderthals) because the *Homo sapiens* had developed a better economic system. About 40,000 years ago the two groups coexisted in Europe, but some evidence suggests that *Homo sapiens* engaged in trade with other distant groups and they developed labor specialization. That is, the bad hunters were left home to make tools and clothes, while the good ones went out to bring home the bacon. This made the *Homo sapiens* more efficient and their families got more meat. Since the supply of meat was limited, the Neanderthals (who were less efficient hunters) didn't get as much and they eventually became extinct.

Throughout history we've seen that as trade in a society declines, so does the general health and welfare of the population. Persia was once a font of scientific knowledge and luxurious living, but as that society closed its borders, it lost its edge in scientific thought and cultural advancement. The same can be said of China. In the modern age, countries that practice free trade (that is, they keep the trade barriers and tariffs to a minimum) do better economically in the long run than those countries that limit trade.

SUMMARY

In this chapter we learned what a business is and the history of business. One of the fundamental principles of business is that it revolves around trading a good or service for something of equal perceived value (either another good or service, which means barter, or money). We learned that governments and merchants would go to great lengths, spending lots of money and enduring high personal risk to obtain goods that were highly valued at the time. In many ways this has not changed. Communication is another essential element of business, and the better the communication network (roads, postal system, verbal), the more efficient and beneficial the business transactions.

2

Business Basics

We don't have a monopoly. We have market share. There's a difference.
—Steve Balmer, CEO of Microsoft

If you can run one business well, you can run any business well.
—Sir Richard Branson, founder of Virgin Group

This chapter will give you some of the basics you need to know to understand how business works. We'll discuss the types of businesses, some basic economic forces that drive businesses, and the structural parts of a business.

TYPES OF BUSINESSES

In order to sign contracts and conduct commerce in the modern world, a business must be established as a legal entity. There are several types of legal entities to choose from. Each type has benefits and weaknesses and the choice of the type of business entity depends on the owners, their motivations, and often their tax status. The main reasons for adopting one type of legal status over another is to manage the liability that can be associated with various business activities, and to avoid personal harm in the event of a lawsuit.

U.S. Businesses

Men own 57 percent; Women own 28 percent; 12 percent are equally male-female owned; 3 percent are publicly owned

- Most owners (71 percent) have some college education—about a quarter have a bachelor's degree and one in five have a graduate degree.
- Asian and African-American business owners are more likely to hold graduate degrees.
- Women start new businesses at twice the rate of men, and their revenues grow faster (39 percent versus 34 percent for male-owned firms).
- Hispanics start new businesses at three times the national average.

Source: US Census Bureau 2002 Survey of Business Owners and U.S. Department of Commerce

Sole Proprietorship

A sole proprietorship is a business that is owned by one person, like Joey's Lemonade Stand. Joey is the sole proprietor, or owner, of his business. In most cases, a sole proprietorship is the same as the person who runs the business. So if Joey wants to buy a new table for his business, he would buy it using his own money and the ownership of the table would probably be in Joey's own name. The benefit of this type of legal entity is that it is the simplest to manage (often no paperwork or lawyers are required). The drawback of this type of business entity is that there is no difference between Joey's personal assets (such as his train set, his bike, or his piggy bank) and the assets of the business (Joey's lemonade stand table). So if Joey gets sued by someone who claims he got sick from drinking Joey's lemonade, Joey's train set might be used to compensate the person who got sick.

Partnership

A partnership is a business where two or more people, companies, or groups get together and form a team that together conducts business. Two well-known partnerships in business started when (1) William Hewlett and David Packard got together to design a test instrument in a garage, and (2) Bill Gates and Paul Allen cobbled together the MS-DOS operating system, which later morphed into today's Microsoft Windows. Both of these partnerships later became huge corporations, but they started when two people had a good idea and worked together to turn it into a profitable business. A partnership can be very small (two people) or huge (like McKinsey & Company, a global management consulting firm of nearly 900 partners worldwide). In a partnership, all partners share in the profits and losses, usually at a rate commensurate with their initial investment (or tenure) in the business. One can imagine that in the case of Hewlett-Packard, both Mr. Hewlett and Mr. Packard were equal partners, so they each owned 50 percent of the business. Partnership shares can be determined through a number of different formulas: the amount of money (start-up or investment capital) one puts in, "sweat equity" or hours of hard work, the implicit value of an idea or specific technology contributed, some other type of tangible asset (like a house or garage) contributed to the business, or access to a market (such as an Indonesian company that knows how to sell products to Indonesian customers).

In partnerships the partners can be equal or unequal. One partner could be a general partner, who has the most at risk if the business loses a lawsuit against it and is forced to pay a penalty. Usually the general partner runs the business and has the most knowledge about the business. Other partners in this case would be limited partners, who would lose only the amount of money or other assets they contributed to the partnership. There are also silent partners who do not have anything to do with the operation of the business but share in the profits and losses.

The benefit of a partnership is that it engenders a team spirit working toward a common goal, a certain degree of collegiality, and a sense of "first among equals" that can foster a sense of pride to belong to an elite group. There are a couple of downsides to a partnership. First, a partnership depends on the mutuality of purpose; that is, if one partner loses interest or is not perceived to be contributing the effort it originally committed to, the relationship sours.

In these cases, the partnership is often much more difficult to unwind than in a corporate-type of entity because it is usually the unique contributions of the partners that make the business successful. And second, like a sole proprietorship, the partners are personally liable for any transgressions or mistakes that the partnership makes in conducting business. Thus the partners could end up losing considerably more of their personal assets than they contributed to starting and growing the business.

Doctors, attorneys, and management consultants frequently organize themselves as a partnership. These kinds of partnerships often operate under a leveraged model where there are a few senior partners, a few more junior partners, several associates, and lots of worker bees. Leverage is gained by billing out the various people at different rates to clients, so that the efforts of many worker bees support the more senior people in the group.

Other partnerships are formed between two companies. These are often called joint ventures. You'll see these partnerships between a large company with established technology and another company or person who has something that the company needs (technology or market access or both). One example is when the 3M Corporation (maker of Post-It® Notes among other things) wanted to break into a new market, such as Indonesia. The company didn't know how to sell its products to Indonesians. So it formed a joint venture with a local Indonesian company that knew the market. Another example is Corning Glass, which has formed partnerships with Dow Chemical (Dow-Corning, maker of silicones), Owens-Illinois (Owens-Corning, maker of fiberglass, roofing material, and insulation), and Samsung (Samsung Corning Precision Glass, maker of specialty glass substrates used in thin film transistor LCDs).

Corporation

A corporation is one of the few business entities that actually takes on a separate legal persona. Although a corporation is not a living being, like Joey, or Hewlett and Packard, it has legal rights like a person. A corporation is considered a "legal or fictional person" that has a perpetual lifetime. It can own property, sign contracts, pay taxes, and otherwise participate in society (but a corporation cannot vote for mayor or the president of the United States like a human citizen can). A corporation usually has a board of directors who supervise and advise the chief executive officer (the CEO, who is often a member of the board of directors). The board of directors has a fiduciary duty to protect the corporation's interests and livelihood, as well as the interests of the shareholders (sometimes those are not the same). Corporations sell ownership shares to people, trusts, and other corporations. Unlike a proprietorship or partnership, owners of the corporation are not personally liable for actions of the corporation, and their personal losses are only as large as their investment in corporate stock (shares). But officers of a corporation are increasingly being held accountable for corporate misdeeds. The Sarbanes-Oxley Act of 2002 now requires corporate officers to sign off on the financial statements and guarantee that no one has been cooking the books.

Most corporations are publicly traded corporations whose shares are bought and sold on an exchange, like the New York Stock Exchange or NASDAQ. Some corporations are private or closely held, and the stock of these entities is rarely traded, and if so, only directly when a seller has a ready buyer (that is, not on an open and public stock exchange).

There are several benefits to a corporation: limited liability, perpetual life-time, the idea that it is a separate entity or "fictional person," and the ability to raise large amounts of capital (cash) from a wide variety of places. There are also some downsides to incorporation (the act of turning a business into a corporation): lots of paperwork (a corporation, especially one that is publicly traded, must produce reams of paper for government regulators, stockholders, and anyone else who is interested), double taxation (the corporation is taxed on its profits, and shareholders are taxed again on any dividends they earn), and market oversight (the company's value will vary day to day depending on the price of the shares).

Limited Liability Company (LLC)

A limited liability company (LLC) is sort of a cross between a corporation and a sole proprietorship or partnership. It is a relatively recent invention in the United States, and is patterned after its older German cousin, the GmbH (*Gesellschaft mit beschränkter Haftung*). Most LLCs are formed by professionals, such as accountants, doctors, lawyers, interior designers, and so forth.

The main benefits are that there is much less paperwork to establish and maintain an LLC, and like a corporation, the liability of the owners is limited to the amount of capital put into the LLC (which is often very low in the case of professionals) and the owners avoid double taxation since the profits are taxed on the owners' personal tax returns. Another benefit of the LLC is that it can choose how it wants to operate for U.S. tax purposes. In the early years, when it has more losses than profits, it can be a sole proprietorship and the losses will go against the owner's personal income statement. In later years, the LLC can choose to operate and report its profit as a corporation so that the owner avoids self-employment taxes.

The disadvantages of an LLC are that some states levy high fees or franchise taxes on these entities, the LLC can end up with a short lifespan due to the death of one of the owners, it can be difficult to raise money from investors, and the accounting requirements of an LLC are greater than those for sole proprietorships and partnerships.

Nonprofit Organization

A nonprofit organization or not-for-profit corporation (nonprofit) is a company that is organized under the jurisdiction of a government authority and has no shareholders. It does not issue stock. A nonprofit organization usually engages in some sort of societal good, such as charity work, a homeowners' association, a foundation to explore research, and so on. Sometimes nonprofits are incorporated, but they are exempt from taxation by government law. The idea of a nonprofit organization is that its goal is not to make a profit, but to pour any and all money into the primary purpose of the organization (funding cancer research, operating a boy scout troop, providing wheelchairs for the physically challenged, building a clean water supply for a Malaysian village, etc.). Most nonprofits are funded by donations from individuals and/or corporations or by grants from governments.

The benefit of a nonprofit is that it does not pay income or sales taxes, and it may qualify for reduced rates on goods and services that it purchases. The drawback is that it must comply with strict rules and reporting requirements

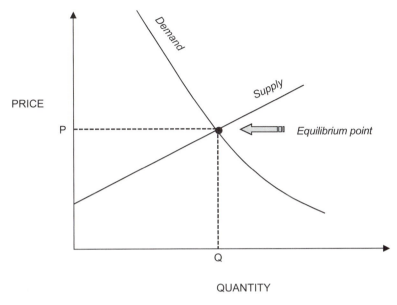

Figure 2.1. Supply and demand curves.

on how it generates and disposes of its income. Some nonprofits have financing restrictions as well (that is, they cannot borrow money). The largest nonprofit in the world is the Bill and Melinda Gates Foundation, which has an endowment, or pile of cash, of $61 billion. (Bill Gates is one of the founders of Microsoft.)

SOME BASIC ECONOMICS

In order to better understand the elements that go into making a business become profitable, we need to discuss some basic economic laws that underpin every business decision. Every business, no matter what type, is subject to the laws of supply and demand and to the concepts of fixed and marginal costs. Most businesses also have a value chain that can be exploited in different ways to make more money. These concepts are outlined below.

Supply and Demand

Supply and demand are the core concepts of any business proposition and there is usually a predictable relationship between the two, as shown in Figure 2.1.

The demand curve, shown in Figure 2.1 plotted against price and quantity, usually slopes downward. This means that a customer might be willing to pay 50 cents for a cup of lemonade—and at that price, she might even buy an additional two cups of lemonade for her kids. But if the price for a cup of lemonade goes up to $1.00, then the customer will only buy one cup of lemonade and probably not share it with her kids. That is, the cheaper the lemonade, the more she will buy.

The supply curve, also shown plotted against price and quantity in Figure 2.1, slopes upward. The idea is that a producer would set a price for a good—say a cup of lemonade—that reflects his costs to make that good and also provide him with a fair profit. As the price goes up, the producer (Joey)

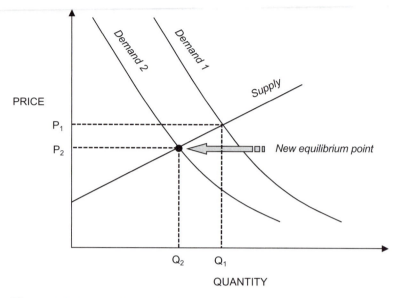

Figure 2.2. Shifting demand curve.

is willing to make more lemonade—but the question is, how much lemonade would people buy at such a high price? The place on the chart where supply and demand intersect is called the equilibrium point. At this point, the market for the good in question is said to be in equilibrium. That is, people will buy enough lemonade at 50 cents per cup to satisfy Joey and allow him to make a fair profit.

But what happens if demand changes? What if a government study shows that lemons are harmful to your health? Those people who used to buy lemonade but are health conscious, will no longer buy lemonade. The demand curve will shift as shown in Figure 2.2. When there is less demand, but Joey still makes as much lemonade as he always has, it will result in an oversupply of lemonade. The supply–demand equation is fixed and the market (all the people who buy lemonade and all the lemonade producers) will revert to equilibrium.

This means that people will only buy lemonade if the price is lower, and because the price is lower, some of the producers will either stop making lemonade altogether, or they will make less. Joey has two choices: either lower the price for his lemonade or reduce the amount he makes. His choice will probably depend on other factors, which we will discuss later, such as whether there are substitutes for Joey's lemonade (diet coke, orange juice?) and what the competing lemonade producers are doing in reaction to the reduced demand. Joey actually has a third choice: he could try to increase the demand for lemonade by combining it with a charity, like Alexandra "Alex" Scott did for cancer research (see http://www.alexslemonade.com/).

As you might have guessed, the supply curve can shift too. Say that someone has come up with a way to grow more lemons at the same cost. The supply curve will shift down along the demand curve as shown in Figure 2.3. The new equilibrium point (when the market is in balance) is at a lower price and larger quantity (as lemonade becomes cheaper, people will buy more).

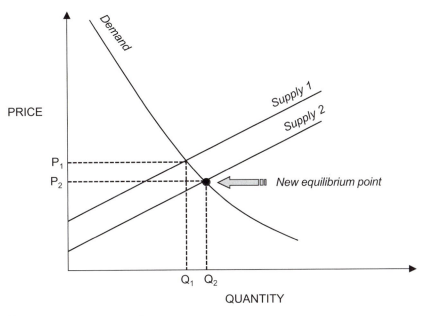

Figure 2.3. Shifting supply curve.

But what happens if Joey (an individual producer) tries to raise his prices? This is shown in Figure 2.4. Unless Joey's lemonade is much better than his competitor's lemonade, he will encounter an oversupply, because customers will decide that all lemonade is basically the same and choose to pay the lower price. Joey will then have to reduce the price of his lemonade to match that of his competitors. In the end, prices will settle back to an equilibrium point where supply and demand are in balance.

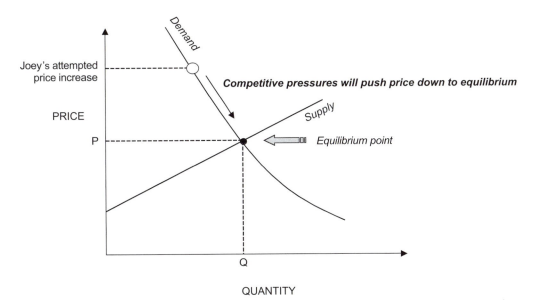

Figure 2.4. Attempted price increase.

An example: Supply and demand in a 6-person economy (from http://en. wikipedia.org/wiki/Supply_and_demand)

Supply and demand can be thought of in terms of individual people interacting at a market. Suppose the following 6 people participate in this simplified economy:

> Alice is willing to pay $10 for a sack of potatoes.
> Bob is willing to pay $20 for a sack of potatoes.
> Cathy is willing to pay $30 for a sack of potatoes.
> Dan is willing to sell a sack of potatoes for $5.
> Emily is willing to sell a sack of potatoes for $15.
> Fred is willing to sell a sack of potatoes for $25.

There are many possible trades that would be mutually agreeable to both people, but not all of them will happen. For example, Cathy and Fred would be interested in trading with each other for any price between $25 and $30. If the price is above $30, Cathy is not interested, since the price is too high. If the price is below $25, Fred is not interested, since the price is too low. However, at the market Cathy will discover that there are other sellers willing to sell at well below $25, so she will not trade with Fred at all. In an efficient market, each seller will get as high a price as possible, and each buyer will get as low a price as possible.

Imagine that Cathy and Fred are bartering over the price. Fred offers $25 for a sack of potatoes. Before Cathy can agree, Emily offers a sack of potatoes for $24. Fred is not willing to sell at $24, so he drops out. At this point, Dan offers to sell for $12. Emily won't sell for that amount, so it looks like the deal might go through. At this point Bob steps in and offers $14. Now we have two people willing to pay $14 for a sack of potatoes (Cathy and Bob), but only one person (Dan) willing to sell for $14. Cathy notices this and doesn't want to lose a good deal, so she offers Dan $16 for his potatoes. Now Emily also offers to sell for $16, so there are two buyers and two sellers at that price (note that they could have settled on any price between $15 and $20), and the bartering can stop. But what about Fred and Alice? Well, Fred and Alice are not willing to trade with each other, since Alice is only willing to pay $10 and Fred will not sell for any amount under $25. Alice can't outbid Cathy or Bob to purchase from Dan, so Alice will not be able to get a trade with them. Fred can't underbid Dan or Emily, so he will not be able to get a trade with Cathy. In other words, a stable equilibrium has been reached.

A supply and demand graph could also be drawn from this. The demand would be:

> 1 person is willing to pay $30 (Cathy).
> 2 people are willing to pay $20 (Cathy and Bob).
> 3 people are willing to pay $10 (Cathy, Bob, and Alice).

The supply would be:

> 1 person is willing to sell for $5 (Dan).
> 2 people are willing to sell for $15 (Dan and Emily).
> 3 people are willing to sell for $25 (Dan, Emily, and Fred).

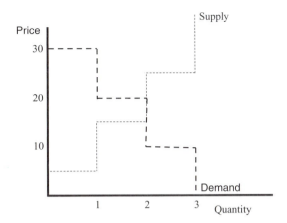

Supply and demand match when the quantity traded is 2 sacks and the price is between $15 and $20. Whether Dan sells to Cathy, and Emily to Bob, or the other way round, and what precisely is the price agreed cannot be determined. This is the only limitation of this simple model. When considering the full assumptions of perfect competition the price would be fully determined, since there would be enough participants to determine the price. For example, if the "last trade" was between someone willing to sell at $15.50 and someone willing to pay $15.51, then the price could be determined to the penny. As more participants enter, the more likely there will be a close bracketing of the equilibrium price.

It is important to note that this example violates the assumption of perfect competition in that there are a limited number of market participants. However, this simplification shows how the equilibrium price and quantity can be determined in an easily understood situation. The results are similar when unlimited market participants and the other assumptions of perfect competition are considered.

Market Forms

The examples above regarding supply and demand all assume that you have a balanced and open market in which there are lots of buyers and lots of sellers, and no one player has more power than anyone else. This is the case in most markets and it's called perfect competition. However, there are some situations where you have a market with only one seller, called a monopoly, or a few sellers, called an oligopoly. The other side of the supply–demand equation, where you have only one buyer, called an monopsony, or a few buyers, called an oligopsony, also exists but it's less common.

In a monopoly, the one seller can set whatever price it wants along with purchase or licensing terms for the products or services it sells. In a true monopoly there are no close substitutes for the unique product or service being sold, and it is very difficult, if not impossible, for a competitor to enter the market. Microsoft is an example of a company that has for many years held a monopoly on PC operating systems. Unless you use an Apple computer, you probably have a Microsoft-produced Windows operating system on your PC. Many of the pharmaceutical companies hold monopolies over the sale of certain products while they are still protected by patents. As you can see, monopolies are a good thing to be in if you're the one seller (you can name your price and profits are usually very high). But monopolies are not so good if you're a buyer. So the risk for a monopolist is that a government will intervene and clamp down on the company's ability to charge unreasonably high prices or set onerous sales terms (this is why Microsoft has had many legal battles with the U.S. government and more recently, the European Union).

There are several ways monopolies can come into being, but the most common way is by government edict. The power company that supplies electricity and/or gas to your house is most likely a government-sanctioned monopoly. The same is true of your local phone company, which provides the land line (copper wire) into your house. The reason these monopolies exist is because it's more efficient for one company to build and maintain the electrical grid or the phone wiring system in a particular region, than it is for several companies to compete and tear up the landscape while installing their own networks. In these cases, the government regulates the companies and makes sure that they do not charge exorbitant fees for the services they provide. Another way monopolies can arise is by law. The patent process is a legal way to gain monopoly power over the sale of a product (like a proprietary drug or technology).

An oligopoly is a market form where there are a few big sellers who wield a great deal of power over pricing and sales terms. In oligopolies, the handful of sellers are very aware of what their competitors are doing and react quickly to meet or beat strategic marketing tactics. Oligopolists rarely compete strictly on price because a price reduction usually just hurts everyone (except, of course, the buyers). Some examples of industries with oligopolies are oil, cigarette, beer, diamond, airline, aircraft, and aircraft engine. If the major sellers in a particular industry collude to set prices and sales terms, this is called a cartel. Cartels are illegal in most countries, but they can exist across countries and outside the jurisdiction of national governments. Two prominent cartels are the Organization of Petroleum Exporting Countries (OPEC) and the De Beers diamond cartel.

Fixed and Marginal Costs

In order to make a profit in business, you have to know what your costs or expenses are. Ideally, you would price your product such that you make money on every item that sells. There are two main types of costs: fixed and marginal. A fixed cost is a large onetime amount of cash you need to spend in order to get into business before you have even made your first product. It usually goes to buying the equipment you need to make your product. A fixed cost can also be something that you need to spend in order to upgrade your product, like a faster computer, or to increase your production capacity, like another factory. A marginal cost is what it will cost you to produce one more unit of your product. In the case of Joey's lemonade stand, Joey's fixed cost is the money he spent on a pitcher, his lemonade stand sign, and his lemonade stand table (keep in mind that we're not counting the cost of the refrigerator to keep the lemonade cool). This is what is often called a "sunk cost" because the money is gone (sunk) before he has even sold one cup of lemonade. Joey's marginal cost is what he will have to spend in order to make another cup of lemonade. This includes the lemons, sugar, the secret ingredient, and serving cups. Using the numbers from Chapter 1, Joey's marginal cost to make one single cup of lemonade is about

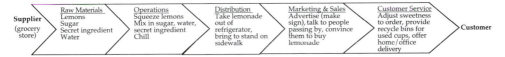

Figure 2.5. Value chain for Joey's Lemonade Stand.

17 cents. If he decides to invest in a lemon squeezing machine, his marginal costs will drop even more because he can make larger batches much faster, and he can get discounts when he buys larger quantities of ingredients.

Knowing your marginal cost can help you determine what price you need to charge for your product. In a competitive market, you generally want to price your product at or above the marginal cost, so that you don't lose money. If the market is not competitive and you can name your price, then the sky's the limit! (But that rarely happens, unless you happen to be Microsoft.)

In a large company with many products, services, employees, and markets, marginal and fixed costs are a little more complex, but the principles are the same.

The Value Chain

The value chain is a model that explains how businesses receive raw materials and, through various processes, convert those materials to products and/or services to sell to customers. The idea is that you can create more value for both yourself (profits) and your customers (product features, use, convenience, etc.) by doing something to a raw material and converting it to something that people can use. For example, a teak tree is not very useful to someone who lives in a small apartment in New York, but a teak chair is. The value chain for the person who makes the chair would start with teak wood, either as a log, or as several pre-sawn boards. The chair maker then adds value to the wood by carving it or cutting and nailing the boards together to make a chair. She might also paint or lacquer the chair to make it match modern furniture designs, and possibly add a custom-made cushion. At each step of the process, the chair maker adds value to the original piece of teak. The next step is to decide on a sales price and tell people in New York that the chair is available for sale. Then, when orders for chairs arrive, the chairs need to be shipped to the customer. The final step in the value chain is to provide after sales customer service (what if one of the legs is shorter than the rest?) to make sure that the customer receives a good product (and presumably comes back for more chairs, a table, and/or recommends that particular chair manufacturer to their friends).

Similarly, a bag of sugar, some water, and a lemon isn't very useful to someone who is thirsty (but doesn't want plain water) and in a hurry. Therefore, the thirsty, busy person might be willing to pay more for a cup of lemonade because he is paying for Joey's service (value added) of turning lemons into lemonade. In the case of Joey's lemonade stand, the value chain would look like the chart shown in Figure 2.5.

At each step of the value chain, Joey applies a process and adds value to the previous input. From raw materials, Joey mixes lemon juice and sugar water (plus his secret ingredient) and chills the liquid. This takes energy (both human and electric) and knowledge. Joey adds more value by bringing his mixture to the lemonade stand and actively encouraging people to buy a cup. Once he has steady customers, Joey can add even more value by offering to deliver the lemonade to their home or office (for an additional fee, of course).

Every type of business has a value chain, whether it makes something tangible (like chairs or lemonade) or provides a service (like a dentist). The key to making a business profitable is to understand the value chain for the business and find ways to make it more profitable. There are two main ways to manipulate the value chain to gain more profit: cost advantage and product/service differentiation. If a business can process the raw materials and deliver the finished product for less, then there is more money left over. Similarly, if a business can find a way to make its product superior to those offered by competitors or substitutes, then the business will command a higher price. Ideally, all parts of the business (organizational structure, control systems, human resources management, operations, research and development, finance, accounting, marketing, sales, distribution, logistics, and so on) should support the value chain with the lowest cost and the highest degree of innovation possible. The role of strategy in the value chain is to figure out how to make each step work at peak efficiency so that together, all the steps produce a superior product at the lowest possible cost and, thus, deliver a high profit.

BASIC ORGANIZATION TYPES

Small businesses (less than 10 people) generally don't worry too much about organization structure, since often, the people working in them "wear many hats" and perform a multitude of jobs. The only hierarchy in a small business is normally that of the boss/owner and workers. But as a business grows, two things happen. The size of the business grows as more people are hired. And increased size allows a business to take advantage of the division of labor by employing specialists. Let's see how Joey would have done it.

> You can build a lasting competitive edge through the excellence of your organization structure.
>
> —Percy Barnevik, former CEO of ABB

Functional Organization

The success of Joey's Lemonade Stand led him to add new locations. The expansion required him to hire people to run the new stands. Very soon Joey discovers the first kind of division of labor—the vertical division. Joey must become a manager and not a doer. He must choose new locations for expansion. He must recruit, select, and train people to work the stands. And when some of the new people do not sell as much as he did, he must supervise and coach them. And when two new recruits both want the same location, he must settle disputes. So Joey replaced himself at his original stand and became a full time manager. In this new role, Joey has authority and becomes the boss of the others. In our society he has the right to hire and fire. He has the power to assign locations to people and reward the top performers. This vertical division of labor creates leaders who have different roles and authority than the followers.

In his new role as manager, Joey discovers ways to improve the business. For example, he asks if every stand should make its own lemonade. He notices varying quality across the stands. So why not let the person who makes the best lemonade, make it for all the stands? In this way the top lemonade maker specializes in the operations function. The people at the stands can now spend more time with customers. By centralizing the preparation, larger and lower cost batches can be made. Joey can buy specialized equipment (such as a lemon squeezing machine) to lower costs even more. With larger batches, Joey can purchase materials in larger quantities and qualify for quantity discounts. This is called "economies of scale." So by specializing some people in the operations function, the total preparation is concentrated in one place, economies of scale are achieved, cost reductions are obtained, consistent high quality is achieved, and sales people can concentrate on customers. These are the benefits that are achieved through the horizontal division of labor. Joey's Lemonade Company has a sales function selling lemonade at the stands and an operations function that produces the lemonade.

Further increases in volume are matched with further increases in the division of labor. When volume is sufficient, Joey can hire a person to distribute the lemonade from the factory to the stands. Another person can handle the purchasing. The purchasing function can search for and qualify the best suppliers, decide whether to hold a raw material inventory to prevent running out of lemonade on a hot day, negotiate long-term contracts to guarantee supply, and so on. The division of labor creates specialists and these specialists then form functions. Joey now has functions for sales, distribution, operations, and purchasing.

What Color Is Your Collar?

White collar = management or "exempt" employee. Usually someone on a fixed salary. It relates back to the day when managers were required to wear a white shirt and tie.

Blue collar = worker or "nonexempt" employee. Usually someone who is paid hourly with an increased hourly rate for any hours worked over 40 per week (overtime) or on Sundays or holidays. It relates back to the day when factory workers wore blue coveralls.

Pink collar = women employed in the "velvet ghetto" of human resources, public relations, government relations, investor relations, communications, and other staff functions.

No collar = Silicon Valley workers like software programmers (many of whom are nocturnal). They do not fall under any formal dress code and often show up in jeans and a t-shirt.

The division of labor improves how each function gets executed. Specialists in operations prepare a superior brand of lemonade, purchasing people can find the best vendors, and sales people at the stands are the best at serving customers. But once the work is divided, it has to be integrated and coordinated. The amount of material being purchased has to match the volume of lemonade that operations needs to make. The volume that operations makes needs to match the amount of lemonade being sold at the stands. In order to manage this divided work, Joey needs some business processes to coordinate the efforts of the specialists.

Joey hired an administration specialist who can design and operate the information and decision processes that integrate the various functions in the business. The specialist, with the advice of the people in the organization, designed a process in which the people operating the stands report what they sold each day. They also forecast what they think they will sell in the next few days. The specialist adds up these forecasts and tells the operations people how much to produce, the purchasing people how much material to buy, and the distribution people how much to deliver to each stand. In large companies this administrative function is called Supply Chain Management. This function coordinates the flow of work between the specialist functions.

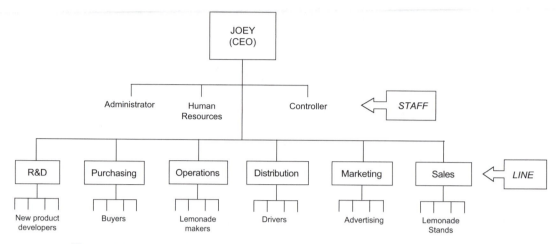

Figure 2.6. Functional organization.

Joey also hired a controller. This specialist manages the flow of money and of information about money. The controller hires other specialists like accountants who are trained in accounting and control systems. So when the stands report what they have sold to the supply chain administrator, they report how much money they earned in the process. The controller matches the supply amounts with the money amounts to keep the business in control and make sure that there is no "shrinkage" (theft) of inventory.

So as Joey's business grows he can afford to add some new types of specialists. The sales, operations, purchasing, and distribution functions are operating functions. They do the work. The controller and supply chain administrator are support functions. They coordinate and control the work. As Joey adds operating functions the business gets more complex. The complexity requires that Joey add support functions to see that the divided work is integrated in order to serve the customer. Further increases in volume allowed Joey to add a New Products (R&D) unit to devise new offerings at the stands. Joey also adds a Marketing function to work on the stand advertising as well as with R&D on new products. Another support function, human resources (HR) was added. HR manages the salary structure and sees that people are paid "at the market rate," devises incentives (like bonuses) to get people to work harder, and sees that everyone gets the training and development that they will need.

Joey's organization looks like the one shown in Figure 2.6. It's a functional structure and shows several layers of managers in the vertical division of work. All companies, like Joey's, start out with this vertical and horizontal division of labor into a functional organizational structure.

How to Read an Organization Chart

Everything on an organization chart starts from the top. The top dog is in the top box. An organization chart can show the whole company, or it can show just one department or function.

The straight lines are important because they show the line of authority or hierarchy within the organization. The CEO (or general manager) is at the top and has the final authority on all decisions. The functions all report to the CEO, as shown by the lines leading up to the CEO box. So, for example, sales does not report to marketing or vice versa. They both report directly to the CEO and therefore are equals in the hierarchy. This is also what is called the first level of the reporting structure. The level below, shown in Figure 2.6 with the fork—shapes, labeled "buyers," "drivers," and so on are known as the second level of the reporting structure.

The CEO's "span of control" is the group of people who report directly to her. For example, in Joey's functional organization shown in Figure 2.6, Joey has a span of control of 9 (all the function managers plus the administrator, human resources, and controller). The higher up in an organization a person is, the lower the span tends to be. At the CEO level, it's rare to find a span of control greater than about 15. At the shop floor level or in a large sales organization, a manager can have a span of 50–100 people. This is because at lower levels, the work is predictable and people can be managed through rules and processes. At higher levels in the organization, the work is highly unpredictable and people have to be managed on an individual, hands-on basis.

All organizations have a further distinction of roles called "line" and "staff" roles. Staff jobs are the ones that support the general manager (or CEO), functions, and business units. Typical staff jobs are in human resources, finance, accounting, legal, and information technology. A line job is one that is "on the firing line" so to speak, because the people are in the part of the organization that produces and/or delivers the product. Typical line jobs are in operations (manufacturing), product development, research and development, sales, marketing, distribution, and after sales service (customer service).

Origin of the terms "line" and "staff"

As with many terms in business, the origins of line and staff come from military applications. The British Naval term "ship of the line" (1704) referred to the battle line. Similarly, "the Line" (1802) meant the regular, numbered troops in the British Army, and these were different from the auxiliary or guard units. The earliest use of the term "line" was in 1557 and denoted a 'sense of things or people arranged in a straight line.'

The term "staff" also has military origins. In 1702 it referred to a group of military officers that assists a commander. The root of the word in ancient Greek and Latin means "support, pillar, tie around, encircle."

Source: www.etymonline.com and www.askoxford.com

Multi-business Unit or Divisional Organization

As Joey's lemonade stands saturate his business area, his growth slows down. Most businesses like Joey's have a growth goal. There are two basic ways to grow. One is to offer similar products or services in the existing business area. This strategy is called diversification. The other growth strategy is for Joey to stay in his existing product line but move into new business areas or geographical markets. This strategy is called expansion. If a business has a skill or expertise that can be leveraged to expand into new products, the business diversifies first and then expands geographically.

In Joey's case, the market had associated his business with the lemon in his lemonade. Joey and his purchasing people had cultivated a unique source of Meyer Lemons, which gave his lemonade a unique taste. So Joey decided to build on his special lemon franchise and offer lemon cakes at his lemonade stands. The diversification was successful and as volume grew he went through the same division of labor process to add specialists in the cake business.

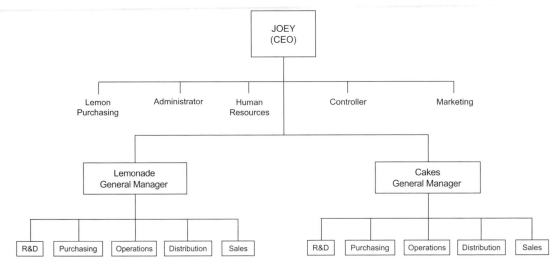

Figure 2.7. Multi-business unit organization structure.

The bakery business was similar in some ways to Joey's core business (lemonade) and in some ways different. He could use the same stands as his sales outlet and use the same delivery system to supply the stands. He could use the lemon source and lemon buyer. And finally he could use his marketing and brand expertise. The main difference was that the cakes needed baking. Setting up his own bakery was too expensive so he outsourced the baking to a local bakery.

Joey's cake business became successful and grew. He added some new sales people as local coffee shops became interested in his lemon cakes. And with growth came the need for a separate business unit to manage the cake business. He now had two businesses. Each of them was a profit center and had its own organization. Each organization was a single business functional organization. The structure is shown in Figure 2.7. There is a general manager for each business showing the increased vertical division of labor. Each business is self-contained except that lemons are purchased centrally and the brand is managed by a central marketing function. Therefore, you'll see a "lemon purchasing" group and a "marketing" group on the staff level. These two groups serve both the cake and lemonade businesses.

MATRIX ORGANIZATION

When growth slows in his original business area, Joey looks for opportunities to expand into new, but usually nearby business areas. If there are already existing lemonade stands in the area, Joey may enter the new area via an acquisition. If there are few stands Joey may enter by starting up his own stands and growing organically like he did in his original neighborhood. In either case he brings his unique Meyer Lemon recipe and access to supply as his competitive advantage. After entering three new business areas, Joey has to create a new organization to manage the new areas. He created a matrix organization of businesses and areas as shown in Figure 2.8.

Figure 2.8 shows a further division of labor. Each area is now run by an area general manager who is responsible for the profit and loss of the businesses in

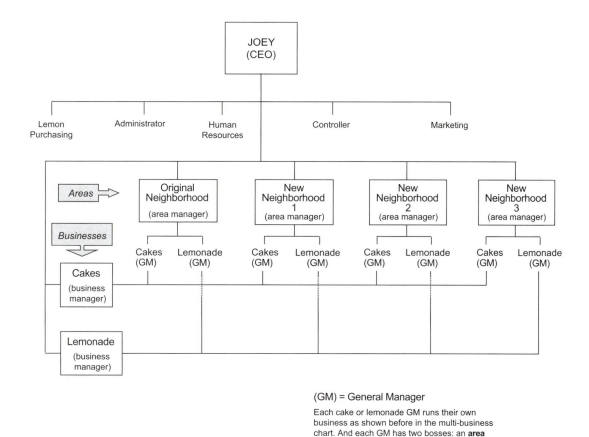

Figure 2.8. Matrix organization.

the area. These managers might come from acquisitions or maybe they were the ones who built the business in the area. They are experts in their area and seek to grow by finding new locations for lemonade stands. They manage the local interactions between businesses like sharing delivery of both cakes and lemonade to the stands. In addition to the area managers, there are business managers who look at the businesses across the regions. Business managers move good ideas from one area to the others. If people want to move from one area to another, the businesses can provide a career path that is companywide. The benefits of the matrix come from managers looking at the situation through area lenses and through business lenses. Each sees what the other can miss.

The matrix requires that Joey be an active manager. The intent is to have a dual focus in the organization. This dual business and area focus can yield benefits but also can generate disputes. A business manager may recommend that an area adopt a new product that is selling well in another area. But the area manager may believe that the product will not sell well in her neighborhood. Joey must see that these differences result in healthy debates and are quickly resolved, even if he has to be the final decision maker. Thus the division of labor brings expertise to bear on the business decisions. But it also results in disputes between area businesses and functional specialists. The leader role needs to evolve with the division of labor. Joey needs to grow from managing a lemonade stand, to managing a group of stands, to running a multifunction business, to managing a portfolio of businesses, to finally leading a team to manage a portfolio of businesses, areas, and functions.

At about this time Joey decides that managing a matrix organization is too much of a headache. So he sells his business to a big international food company and decides to go snowboarding for a winter in Colorado.

SUMMARY

In this chapter we learned about some of the basic concepts in business. There are several different types of businesses, like a sole proprietorship, partnership, corporation, nonprofit, and others. Each type has its benefits and weaknesses, and the choice of which type of business to use often depends on local laws, tax laws, and other considerations. We also covered some basic economics, like supply and demand, the value chain, and fixed versus marginal costs. And finally, we looked at what happens when a company grows. Most businesses start out as functional organizations and then move to product line or business-unit organizations. As a company grows it tends to diversify its products and/or services or it expands its markets. In order to meet the demands of these different areas, a business has to add focus to its organization. This increased focus and specialization can be more complicated to manage. The most complex organization to manage is the matrix, in which the managers have to place equal focus on a separate business unit as well as a geographic region.

3

Business Strategy

In preparing for battle I have always found that plans are useless, but planning is indispensable.

—Dwight D. Eisenhower

Preparation is everything. Noah did not start building the ark when it was raining.

—Warren Buffett

In real life, strategy is actually very straightforward. You pick a general direction and implement like hell.

—Jack Welch

I believe that you have to understand the economics of a business before you have a strategy, and you have to understand your strategy before you have a structure. If you get these in the wrong order, you will probably fail.

—Michael Dell, September 10, 1998.

WHAT IS BUSINESS STRATEGY?

Strategy is the combination of means, methods, and approaches used to achieve objectives and goals. Business strategy is *what*, *where*, and *how*:

- What are you going to do?
- What is your business proposition?
- What goals and objectives do you have (growth strategy, profit goals, market share desired, etc.)?
- What is your competitive position? What are the strengths and weaknesses of your competitors? How good are their products?
- What is the business environment you operate in? Commodity or high value? Long or short cycle time?
- What trends can be expected in your industry?

- Where are you going to compete (not just geographically, but also the range of product lines, markets, distribution channels, and services)?
- Where do the threats and opportunities to your business come from?
- How are you going to compete?
- How will you use your company's particular success factors and competitive advantages?
- How will you erect sufficient barriers to entry against other competitors?
- How will you keep your customers from switching to competing products?
- How will you differentiate your product or service against potential substitutes?

The answers to the questions above normally result in a vision statement, which tells people in a few sentences what the company does. Sometimes the vision statement also tells how the company does its business by stating its core values and overarching goals. In theory, a vision statement is supposed to last for a long time, but in practice, it often changes when a new chief executive officer takes over.

Strategy requires tough choices. A good business strategy allows you to say "No" to a great idea. Strategy is important because it drives the human energy of the business as well as directs where resources (cash, investments, manufacturing production, brainpower) are applied. A well-articulated strategy tells employees, investors, customers, and competitors what business a company is in — as well as what business a company is NOT in.

LEVELS OF STRATEGY

Strategy can be set at three different levels in a company: functional, business unit, and corporate. The lowest level of strategy is normally at the functional or product level. For example, human resources, marketing, manufacturing, and finance all develop strategies to serve the product lines and the business, as well as develop the people within the functions. Functional strategies might include decisions on outsourcing accounts payable (finance), building an organization design consulting group (human resources), implementing a global advertising program (marketing), or adding a third production shift (manufacturing).

The next level up is the business unit level. Often called, "business strategy," it looks at how the business can maximize its profits using the resources it has. This is the level where the company actually competes. It is here that the strategy "rubber" meets the road. Strategic choices at the business unit might include whether to build a new semiconductor plant, whether to license a technology, or whether to reorganize the sales force along product lines rather than geographies. Sometimes a business is also segmented by product lines. In this case there can be product line strategies. Examples include decisions on when to extend a product line by adding new features, or even when to kill a product (usually to introduce a new and improved product in its place).

Large corporations, like General Electric (GE) or Exxon-Mobil, have a corporate strategy that encompasses (1) what businesses the corporation should be in, and (2) how the corporation at the top level will serve the business units best and make them as efficient and profitable as possible. At the least, a good corporate strategy should make the individual business units more valuable together than apart. The strategic choices often involve whether to buy or sell a particular business, whether to invest more money in an existing business unit, how to best transfer a core competence across business units, whether to move a manager from business unit A to business unit B, or whether to enter a new market, such as China, or a new business, such as antiviral technology.

In all cases, it's important to know what level of strategy you're dealing with. In the best companies, the individual strategies of the functions and business units are aligned and support each other as well as the overall corporate level strategy.

DIFFERENT APPROACHES TO STRATEGY

Strategy is a complex subject and one that receives a great deal of focus in universities and most businesses. Many very smart people have spent a lot of brainpower trying to help business people understand the intricacies of strategy. Consequently there are many different and often competing approaches to developing and pursuing corporate and business strategy. Early efforts to analyze strategy came from the military. Battles were likened to industry competitors with "troops" on the "front line" fighting it out in the marketplace. Organizations were structured in a command-and-control hierarchy, with "officers" giving orders similar to an army. Senior managers were encouraged to read ancient Chinese military texts such as Sun Tzu's *The Art of War.* The problem with using a war analogy to come up with business strategy is that there were things like customers who had an increasing say in how they wanted to do business.

Porter's Competitive Strategy

One of the first scholars to come up with a logical and all encompassing approach to strategy was Michael Porter, a professor at Harvard Business School.[1] Porter believed that in order to accurately formulate a competitive strategy for a business, you have to analyze the structure of the industry in which a company is competing. An "industry" means the group of businesses that are competing against each other to offer a product or service to a particular type of customer. Porter's method focuses on studying the five key competitive forces that interact in an industry. The five competitive forces are (1) rivalry among existing industry players, (2) potential new entrants, (3) the threat of substitutes (products or services), (4) the power of buyers, and (5) the power of suppliers. It's rare to find an industry where all of the forces are equally balanced. In most cases, one or more of the competitive forces is dominant and will skew the actions of all the players. In the oil tanker industry the dominant force is the power of the major oil companies—the oil tanker company's customers. The steel industry faces the biggest pressures from foreign competitors (often doing business on the steel company's home turf) and substitute materials. The industry structure will, in large part, determine how big or small an individual firm's profits can be.

Each competitor in an industry will try to maximize their position and market share by erecting and/or exploiting barriers to entry by new competitors as listed below:

- Building economies of scale,
- Differentiating their products or brand building,

- Maintaining large capital requirements to do business,
- Making it difficult for customers to switch to another product,
- Tying up all the distribution channels, or
- Exploiting other advantages (proprietary technology, favorable retail locations, government subsidies, etc.).

The competitors in an industry will also try to gain market share over other rivals by cutting price, offering better service and delivery terms, changing their product or service to better appeal to the customer, or gaining better pricing on raw materials. Until recently, companies faced with an industry that is dominated by buyer power had little choice but to either sell to the demanding customer on their terms or choose different types of customers. Supplier power is similar to buyer power and generally a company had to swallow hard and accept the supplier's terms. Labor, in this case, is also considered a supplier. Lately, however, many companies have taken a different approach to powerful suppliers and attempt to partner with them so that both parties to the transaction benefit.

To a large degree, Porter's industry analysis assumes that there is a fixed pie over which to fight. Competitors within an industry must therefore position themselves and their products to guard the market share they have and, if possible, fight for more share at the expense of someone else. They need to defend against new entrants to the field as well as manage the possibility that buyers will find another product or service that works as a substitute. One of the key assumptions in Porter's model is that companies must choose between providing a low-cost product *or* a high value, differentiated product. This is only a summary of Porter's view of competitive strategy using a structural analysis of industries. For more detail on Porter's methodology, please see his book, *Competitive Strategy*.

Blue Ocean Strategy

Other scholars have tried to describe strategy using different analogies. One recent view is that most companies tend to compete in a "red ocean" where they do battle with each other (again, assuming a fixed pie) until the waters are bloody.[2] The solution is to look for "blue oceans" where competitors are irrelevant because the company is creating a whole new industry and driving demand from customers. In this kind of environment the company assumes that it can grow a whole new pie that has huge opportunities for expansion. The blue ocean strategy fans believe that companies can provide *both* low cost and differentiation in products and services. In this case, both the company and their customers benefit. An example of a recent blue ocean strategy is that pursued by eBay, the online auction company. eBay created an entirely new market. The online auction business is very low cost (transactions take place instantly, over the Internet at very low fees) and high value (potential buyers have an enormous selection at their fingertips, transactions are relatively easy to complete, and sellers have a huge pool of potential customers). Because eBay was the first to invent this business it is the single biggest player and has the most customers. New entrants will find it difficult to compete against eBay, which benefits from the network effects of a large buyer and seller base.

Another example is Cirque de Soleil. This company succeeded in taking the circus experience to entirely new levels. Previously the heart of every circus was a plethora of exotic animals and events taking place in three rings simultaneously. Most circuses were designed to appeal principally to children. Cirque de Soleil got rid of two rings and all the animals, and replaced them with highly skilled acrobats, exotic costumes, sophisticated music, and stage-managed storylines that riveted audiences—particularly adults. In this manner, Cirque de Soleil changed the rules of the game and competed in its own blue ocean.

Core Competencies

Two professors, C.K. Prahalad and Gary Hamel, developed the idea that the key to competitive advantage is a company's core competencies, which they defined as the collective knowledge and coordination skills behind a company's products or services.[3] A core competence spans the entire company and supports several products or business units. The core competencies are not sold as such to any end users, but they are combined into products or services that can be sold, either to consumers or to other companies for use in their products. Honda's core competency is gasoline-powered engines, Sony's is its ability to miniaturize electronics, and Philips has a core competency in optical media and digital imaging. Honda sells cars, motorcycles, lawn mowers, and generators. Sony sells the Walkman, Minidisc, HandyCams, and other portable electronic devices. Philips sells DVD players, plasma TVs, and digital ultrasound, x-ray, and CT scan machines.

A core competence must meet three tests:

1. It has to provide access to a wide variety of markets,
2. It must make a major contribution to the end product, and
3. It has to be difficult for competitors to copy.

A company doesn't gain a core competence by spending lots of money on research and development or controlling the entire supply chain (what's known as vertical integration). It builds a core competence by taking the knowledge in one part of the business and combining it with other products and processes in a way that is unique to the company. Often a core competence arises because someone in one part of the company talks to someone else and they come up with a different idea for a new product. The story of 3M's Post-It Notes is a classic case of invention meeting opportunity. 3M's core competencies are in substrates, coatings, and adhesives. One of 3M's scientists (Spence Silver) invented an adhesive in 1968 that didn't stick very well. Nonetheless, he thought it would be great for some sort of product, so for 5 years he tried to get the 3M product development people to use his anemic glue. No one was interested until Art Fry, a new-product development researcher, got frustrated with trying to keep his scrap paper bookmarks in place in his choir manual. He applied Spence's re-stickable adhesive to his bits of scrap paper, and voila! Post-It was invented.

Hamel and Prahalad think that a company should focus primarily on its core competencies and that these should drive the strategic direction of the company. Under this philosophy, it means that a company should be organized around core competencies instead of business units and that the primary basis for investing should be determined by the opportunity to build up a particular core competence.

Diversification Strategy

Diversification means expanding into another product line or business. Sometimes companies diversify by creating the capability internally (i.e., building it inside the company or business unit). But more often, a company will diversify its products by buying another company that makes those different products.

Why would a company want to diversify? This is a loaded question and it's the subject of numerous scientific research papers, corporate annual reports, and heated debates. CEOs usually justify diversification strategies because they need to improve the company's earnings growth rate (and they hope, the stock price and their own bottom line). In other cases, a company will say they need to buy other companies to "round out" their own product line. The logic here usually comes down to synergy or fit. The idea is that by combining similar businesses, the company can streamline the operations and cut costs, as well as share common customers, technologies, and/or distribution or sales channels. In the 1980s many companies were buying up other companies in the belief that they could provide "one-stop shopping" for their customers. Banks bought mortgage companies. General Motors bought Hughes on the belief that since automobiles were all becoming more electronics laden, they needed a high-tech electronics company.

Diversification Failure

In the 1980s American Express bought IDS (a personal financial planning company now known as Ameriprise), Shearson (a stock brokerage company), Lehman Brothers Kuhn Loeb (the oldest investment banking firm in the United States), First Data Resources (a transaction processing company), E.F. Hutton (a nearly bankrupt stock brokerage house), and several other financial services companies. American Express wanted to become a financial supermarket where their rich charge-card customers could easily and quickly get financial planning advice, buy some stocks, and perhaps invest in an initial public offering at early-bird prices. The company believed that since all of the companies they bought had something to do with money and finance, there was obvious synergy between the various acquisitions. They also believed that they could combine "backroom" activities (accounting and transaction processing) across all of the newly acquired units and cut costs, thus making all of them more efficient. It didn't exactly pan out that way. IDS targeted mostly mid-western customers who owned farms and had modest incomes and conservative investment philosophies. This group of customers was far removed from the average American Express Card "member" and American Express discovered that it really didn't know how to sell other services to these people. Shearson got into trouble after investing in several bad real estate deals followed by the stock market crash in 1987. American Express was forced to write off its entire $1 billion purchase price for Shearson. The sharing of backroom activities was more wishful thinking than reality. Eventually American Express got rid of the CEO who shepherded these acquisitions and installed the head of IDS as its new CEO. Harvey Golub sold all of the "noncore" businesses like the brokerage houses and the investment banks and focused instead on the charge cards and financial planning.

Sometimes diversification makes sense. If a company has a proprietary skill or competitive advantage, such as a sophisticated distribution capability like Wal-Mart, or a particular expertise in marketing consumer packaged goods, like Procter & Gamble, then buying another company that can benefit from that specific expertise is a good use of funds. In general, diversification is good when

1. The activities in both businesses are truly similar and a transfer of skills from one to the other results in a significant competitive advantage.
2. The acquiring company's management actively promotes the skill transfer process (it doesn't happen by itself).
3. There is enough overlap in the value chains of the two companies that they can both benefit from sharing resources.

Pepsi and 3M are examples of companies that got diversification right. Pepsi successfully purchased and integrated Gatorade, Tropicana, and Quaker Oats. 3M has bought several companies (such as Hörnell International and CUNO) that share obscure technologies that 3M applies to a variety of products.

General Electric's Number One or Number Two

Shortly after Jack Welch took over as CEO of GE in 1981, he fired half of the 200 people on the strategic planning staff and instituted direct business reviews with the 14 business managers and himself. In addition, he instituted a very simple strategy. It stipulated that every business unit in GE had to be either number one or number two in its industry against competitors. If the business did not meet that criteria, the choice for the business manager was to "fix, close, or sell" the business. Business managers were further directed by GE's 3-circle vision: a business had to fit into a "core" (power generation or lighting), high technology (aircraft engines, medical), or service (financial services) domain of the company. During the first 9 years of his 2-decade leadership, Mr. Welch sold more than 200 businesses, but he also bought 370 others. As with many initiatives championed by GE, soon many other companies followed GE's lead and adopted the number one or number two benchmark in setting their own strategic goals.

Scenario Planning

Scenario planning is another way of looking at strategy, but from a longer-term point of view. As with many types of strategic planning, scenario planning started in the military following World War II. The U.S. Air Force imagined many possible attack strategies that its opponents might invoke and came up with counter offensives to answer them. Royal Dutch Shell, the big oil company, has used scenario planning for over 3 decades.

Scenario planning involves imagining a series of events that could plausibly happen in the future (generally between 5 and 10 years out). For each event, a story line is developed that can then guide a business in how it chooses to react to the uncertainties that inevitably follow. For example, when Shell started scenario planning in the early 1970s, it did so because it was worried about the price of oil—a critical natural resource that affected Shell's value chain and profitability. Shell imagined two scenarios: (1) that the oil price would remain stable and (2) that there would be a major oil price spike. Scenario number one was generally seen to be unrealistic given the increasing power of the Organization of Petroleum Exporting Countries (OPEC), most of which are Islamic and antagonistic to the United States because of its support of Israel. On top of that, demand for oil was rising due to the increasing American consumption of oil. Both scenarios painted very detailed pictures of what would happen to gas prices, energy costs, interest rates, unemployment, and political uncertainty, to name just a few variables. When the oil price shock of 1973 actually did arrive, only Shell, among the major oil companies, was prepared and its managers knew what decisions they had to make and did so quickly. Shell grew from a relatively small player in 1973 to the number two oil company in size (after Exxon).

Scenario planning does not predict the future, but it allows managers to imagine several very realistic possibilities for the future and plan ahead. It allows them to go on maneuvers before using live ammunition. Scenario planning forces people to question their assumptions about the world and therefore see reality more clearly.

Balanced Scorecard

All too often a company's strategy is defined as a nice batch of words, like "provide intelligent solutions to surpass customer expectations," that do little to tell an employee how to act in her everyday job. The Balanced Scorecard is a performance management system that defines and measures four components of a company's strategy and vision. Each of these areas—financial, business processes, employee learning and growth, and the customer—then gets a series of goals and measurements that show employees how to choose the right action and thus support the strategic mission of the company. For example, some measures in the customer area might include customer satisfaction (as indicated by periodic surveys), share of customer "wallet," percent of customers who are repeat purchasers, and so forth. In the employee learning and growth area, a company might track and measure employee morale, the number of suggestions for process improvement, and absenteeism. In the internal business process area, a company might track the degree to which new computer systems and technology has been implemented and how well those systems have reduced turnaround time for order fulfillment. Financial measures include the typical numbers such as profits, operating costs, return on cash invested, and so forth. When a company ties the various measures together, it often sees a cause-and-effect relationship. High employee morale (resulting rom, say, more streamlined order processing) often translates to higher customer satisfaction, which in turn, shows up in customers paying their bills on time (and therefore, lower accounts receivable and a higher return on the company's cash). The Balanced Scorecard started as a measurement system, but many companies now use it to help drive the strategy down through the organization.

THE STRATEGY SETTING PROCESS

How does a company choose a strategy? In some companies, the chief executive officer (who might be the same as the owner) decides upon a strategy all by herself after looking at the demand for her products, her competitors, and what her company is able to produce. In other companies, strategy is set through a long and very complex process that might involve a large number of employees. However, in many companies, strategic planning is done only after the earth makes a complete revolution around the sun, and the budgets for each business are set at the same time. In other words, very little actual effort is really put into the process.

DSM (Dutch State Mines) is a specialty chemical company that follows an extensive strategy development process. It starts with a vision statement from the CEO. The vision statement usually says where the company wants to be in 5 years. It details targets for sales, market share, growth, market capitalization (i.e., what it hopes shareholders will think the company is worth), what businesses it will be in, which ones it will exit, and so forth. Every 3 years the company holds a Corporate Strategy Dialogue among its top 40–50 executives. The outcome of this dialogue is a list of top strategic priorities. These include things like what products they will produce, what markets they will enter, how much profits should grow, where they will do business, and how to attract the best talent. In addition, each priority gets a deadline specifying what success looks like and when the goals are to be achieved. Once the strategic priorities and goals are defined, the businesses have to figure out how to get there. The Business Strategy Dialogue (DSM) is the next step and it provides a roadmap to help the businesses achieve the goals. In short, this step consists of five excruciatingly detailed phases that force the business managers to really understand the current business environment at the local and more global (big picture) level, as well as look at the various options the business has to grow. The final steps include planning exactly how the business will achieve its targets and how it will know if it has succeeded (performance measurement). The Business Strategy Dialogues happen about every 3 years. (With all that work, who would want it to occur more often?) But once the Business Strategy Dialogues were finished, every DSM business had a set of detailed plans on how they were going to get to their strategic priority goals, and a set of tools to measure if they were achieving their targets on schedule.

A DAY IN THE LIFE OF A CHIEF STRATEGY OFFICER

Jim Schneck
Vice President, Strategy and Corporate Development
Maritz Inc.

My career has almost entirely been in consulting before I came to Maritz. I graduated with a degree in electrical engineering and went to work for Anderson Consulting, now known as Accenture. There I consulted to big company clients in the information technology area, particularly in voice and data networking. Then I went on to work for the big strategy consulting firm, McKinsey & Company. During that time I got an MBA from the Kellogg School of Management at Northwestern University. At McKinsey I focused more on business strategy, but also sometimes got to use my technology background to help clients understand how technology could help them achieve their strategies. After McKinsey I joined another management consulting firm started by a group of ex-McKinsey partners. I stayed there for 7 years, but then left to work with a subgroup that split off to provide pure strategy consulting services to clients. So I've had a pretty varied background with large and really small firms.

One day I was speaking with a buddy of mine from business school and he mentioned that Maritz was looking for a director of corporate strategy. It sounded interesting partly because it was a mix of internal strategy and client work, but also because of the lifestyle change—almost no traveling! I joined Maritz in May 2004.

Maritz is kind of an unusual company in that all of the headquarters of the seven business units are here on the same campus in St. Louis, Missouri. Maritz sells a wide range of services that help our clients (28 of the 50 largest companies worldwide) to understand, develop, and motivate the people in and around their businesses: customers, employees, sales partners. A good example of how our businesses work together is the program we have with the car dealers of a large auto company:

- Our Research business helps the dealers understand how satisfied their customers are with different parts of their experience at the dealerships.
- Our Learning company then comes in and teaches the dealership employees what they learned, how to improve, and builds training programs based in part on the customer feedback.
- Our Incentives business unit then builds an incentive program to entice the employees to act differently (along the lines of the customer feedback and training).
- Finally, our Rewards business and Travel business can provide different kinds of awards (from high definition TVs to trips to Hawaii) to the best performing employees.

So, our businesses can be used by clients, alone or in combination, to help them understand, enable, and motivate their people. To help our clients understand and motivate their customers, we have businesses such as Loyalty Marketing, which builds programs like getting points or airline miles for using a client's credit card. We also have an Interactions business that designs and conducts special events like product launches (for example, a traveling show for a car company that comes into a town and lets customers take a test drive of a new car and win prizes).

One of the common threads among all of our products and services is the extensive use of technology as a platform. Many of our programs use the client company's intranet to deliver the content, whether it's communicating to the sales force, helping the top sellers choose their well-earned rewards, or delivering training modules.

In addition to our seven business units, we have identified four industry sectors where we'll focus: financial services, automotive, pharmaceuticals, and the high tech/telecom arena. This gives us sort of a matrix to manage along with the functional areas.

My job is lead strategist at the corporate level. I was brought in to establish an overarching enterprise strategy that stretches across all of our business units, sectors, and functions. One of the core strategic commonalities among all of our business units is that we manage the customer experience on behalf of our clients. Using our sales and marketing programs, we help our clients grow. Our clients include all the major car companies, Bank of America, Hewlett Packard, Minolta, Penske, AT&T, AstraZeneca, Shell Texaco, American Express Financial Services, Motel 6, and many others.

When I got here, there was no common corporate-level strategy. What we've done since then is roll up all of the business unit strategies and the function strategies and look at them together. We've also incorporated the various sector strategies into our planning process.

Getting to an all-encompassing strategy with such a wide variety of business units—all of which have operated pretty independently and sometimes even in competition with each other—has been an iterative process. We invited all the senior leaders of these business units to a series of meetings. The first time we did this was about a year ago, and it was the first time that this group (all the business and other corporate leaders) had ever gotten together to work on strategy.

For each meeting, my group directs the content and the flow. We use both the big group and small groups. First, we talk as a large group about what we're trying to solve. Then we get the leaders to work together in small groups to come up with creative solutions. We have found that more interesting ideas come out of the smaller groups. Then we come back together as a big team to decide which actions to take. The small groups have 3–4 hours to work on the issues and they can work wherever they want: they go for walks together or play golf or whatever. It sets up the whole dynamic of them talking to each other and understanding the position of people in other business units and functions. It also forces them to brainstorm over some possible solutions.

In addition to an overarching strategy, we've broken down the actions that we need to take into four areas we call planks. They are—growth, customer-focused innovation, productivity, and performance culture. Each business unit shows how it plans to tie into the corporate planks and drive the program deep into its own unit. For example, under the "performance culture" plank we saw a need to establish a culture of personal accountability. So we developed a leadership development program for our high-potential people. Each business unit had to give up some of their top employees for about 5 weeks to attend the program. It involved 2 weeks of preparation and 3 weeks of attendance. We run about 30 people through the program each year and have both internal and external faculty. Participants learn the skills and competencies required to become a leader at Maritz. It's also established a network of people who can work together and help us build the kind of culture we need.

We've been using the "blue ocean" strategy framework to add a bottom-up type of process to the top-down approach we already have. Top-down strategic thinking is what is typically known as "classical strategy" work, like the Porter model, and most of the other models out there. Blue ocean is more bottom-up strategic thinking. In our case, we open up a two-way dialog with our clients. We try to surface from the bottom-up what our clients' customers are trying to accomplish and the interactions they have with the client company to accomplish them. Then we see how our clients might make more innovative use of technology to "open up" the interactions with their customers to make it easier for both the customer and company. One example of this is a major insurance company making the car insurance quote process more transparent by putting it online. This was revolutionary when they did it because now customers can compare prices. When we're done with the process, we have a number of new, innovative ideas. Sometimes Maritz can help the company to develop a solution for those ideas, and sometimes we can't, but we are willing to take that risk to be an innovative partner with our clients and help them in the right way. We would rather have our clients be successful by working on the right things than just try to sell them things that we have.

We've also used this co-creation approach in our internal strategic planning meetings. We put together small mixed groups comprised of a business unit head, a sector leader, and a functional head. Then we facilitate a discussion among them to identify things like our competitive advantage and a whole series of other questions. Each group comes back and reports its conclusions.

Each iteration of these meetings gets us closer. Real strategy isn't created in big all-hands meetings. Real strategy—the kind that's meaningful to the organization and can be acted upon—comes out of ad hoc conversations resulting from the combined insights of each participant. That's where you get the "Aha!"

In order to succeed in a career in strategy you need a few key skills:

- Analytical problem solving capability
- Flexibility: sometimes you are building strategy, sometimes managing projects, and other times working with people to help them understand a needed change and facilitate group activity to help accomplish that change
- Solid business knowledge—an MBA is very useful here
- "EQ"—it's often called "emotional intelligence." It's a personal component—an ability to facilitate consensus, to get people on board

This job is great in so many ways. It really pushes me on all levels. I enjoy establishing a path from the client co-creation meetings to the corporate-level strategy. It stretches me.

A typical day:

8:00 AM	Check e-mails in the office. I've got a full day ahead of me so I get a mental picture of where I can fit small chores in.
8:30 AM	I meet with one of the 4 people in my group. We're in the process of conducting our final performance evaluation meetings for the 12-month period. We review everyone periodically during the year, but there are more progress reports. In these year-end reviews we go over specific plans, goals, and measures from the past year and develop new ones for the year going forward.
10:00 AM	Group meeting with my staff. We discuss current initiatives in each of the business units. Two of us flex across the initiatives that each business unit is pursuing. We make sure that they are aligned with what the rest of the company is doing and with the four corporate planks. The others in my group each have a "dotted line" reporting relationships to the sectors. This means that I'm their main boss, but they also work for the sector leader. My staff in each sector is the first line of strategic review of sector-level strategy. During our meeting, they report back on what's going on in each sector.
11:30 AM	I prepare the agenda for our weekly executive committee meeting tomorrow morning. These are long (and sometimes boring) meetings and I'm responsible for the strategy dialog among the group. These meetings are the worst part of my job. I personally have more of a bias toward action and making decisions. But the meetings are necessary to help develop the dialog among the leaders of the businesses, sectors, and functional units.

12:15 PM	Lunch with the sector head for Automotive. We talk about the next strategy offsite meeting. He's got some ideas on how we can open a dialog among the business unit heads on sharing specific customer data with a view to enhancing product offerings across the units. He thinks that this can be combined with some of the co-creation data we've been surfacing in a couple of the business units.
1:00 PM	I meet with the head of our Interactions business unit. These are the folks who stage special events for companies that want to put out an attention-grabbing message on a new product, a new marketing promotion, or even a new organizational initiative. We're working on a program for one of Interactions' clients. The client is launching a new organization change initiative to move the company to a more customer-centric organization capability.
2:00 PM	I call one of my peers in the Corporate Executive Strategy Board. This is a subgroup of the Corporate Executive Board, a for-profit corporation that provides research, executive education, networking, and decision support tools for their executive members. It's a great group and they host retreats each year where members can share best practices and the status of current corporate initiatives. They're all really smart people. I wanted to find out how my colleague's program on translating strategy into execution is going in his company.
3:00 PM	I meet with a subgroup that is working on a cross-organizational issue of streamlining some of our corporate management processes. We've identified the percentage of everyone's time spent in meetings—it's pretty amazing! Now we're moving on to the next step of looking at which meetings can be eliminated to free up additional time.
4:00 PM	The CEO and CFO [chief financial officer] call me into an ad hoc meeting. They are trying to figure out a process to make the numbers for the next fiscal year even better than planned. I counsel them on building a process and developing a template so that each organizational unit can report out changes to their plans in the same way.
5:30 PM	I pull out my strategy course materials for the leadership development program. I need to prepare my session on strategy for the class I'm teaching tomorrow afternoon. Since I've got the weekly 4-hour marathon meeting with the leadership team, I won't have any time tomorrow to prepare.

A DAY IN THE LIFE OF A STRATEGY MANAGEMENT CONSULTANT

Francis Gouillart
Co-Founder and Partner
ECC Partnership

I grew up in France near Strasbourg. I was always quantitatively driven. I liked math, but I was a bit different in that I also really liked humanities. My first exposure to business was when a group of people came to visit our high school. They were from the business school in Toulouse and they talked about what they were studying. I found it fascinating.

The rest of my education was in preparation for business school. I wanted to build the best business model in finance, but then I discovered the human aspect of business. Business isn't all about the numbers, it's a living, breathing entity with human emotions that impact everything in the business.

I got my undergraduate degree in business in France (ESSEC) and then went to the University of Chicago for my MBA. My first job was with Trane, the air conditioning equipment manufacturer. I signed on to a rotational program, which is basically a management training career track. The first task I was given was to analyze "scrap." No, seriously, the plant manager told me to go and look at the trash in the factory's garbage cans and see what I found. I thought that this was some kind of hazing ritual, until one of the workers pulled me aside and told me that Trane used lots of copper in the manufacturing process. Copper was expensive then. I found that we could separate out the waste copper and resell it. We made between $200,000 and $300,000 on selling recycled copper. This was a great education for me. I learned about the reality and practicality of real world business. I saw how you could impact the bottom line by doing something different or unexpected. I was with Trane for a total of 4 years, including 2 years working as the head of strategy in Europe.

While I was with Trane, several of the big name consulting firms cycled through. I saw how they analyzed everything and then used insightful thinking to come up with some pretty impressive analyses and answers. But the negative side of the consultants I encountered was their arrogance and condescending attitudes. I really wanted to do strategy consulting, but without the bad attitude. I figured that there's got to be a way to formulate strategy and impact change management, but with a more human face.

I moved back to Europe and started a small firm in Paris. It was called Marketing Innovation Development (MID). I partnered with a German guy my age who went to Stanford and three elder consultants. They were eager to get the new American-educated blood into the European consulting scene. Those were heady times since we were a small strategy boutique competing against the big firms like Boston Consulting Group and McKinsey. We built a successful firm and eventually sold it to what is now Mercer Delta consulting.

About that time (1985) I decided to move back to the United States. My wife is American and we had a daughter born in France. But in evaluating the educational systems then, we decided that the U.S. system was superior.

Throughout my professional career I've always maintained one foot in academia and one foot in the "real world" of business. I think part of my success as a consultant has been due to the fact that I like to marry academic thought leadership with actual business problems. I'm good at creating useful tools and models for executives from ideas that come from the universities. I've been lucky to work with a number of well-respected academics on things like the Balanced Scorecard and the Blue Ocean Strategy.

So in 1985 I joined a group of academics from Harvard who had started up a loosely organized firm called MAC, which stood for Management Analysis Center. It was kind of like a business consulting "body shop" that you could call if you needed advice in a specific domain of business. At the time, MAC was undergoing change itself. It was moving more toward pure strategy consulting with an increased focus on international clients. My experience and background were a perfect fit with MAC.

A few years after I joined, Gemini Consulting bought MAC. Gemini was very information technology-focused in its clientele and approach. My field is really much more pure strategy consulting. At Gemini I became a transformation consultant. This merged strategy with process reengineering, technology, and change management. We helped companies migrate their business approach to something different.

Being the partial academic that I am, I was also writing articles for journals like the *Harvard Business Review* and I'd published a couple of books. One was a book with my colleague, James Kelly, from MAC. Our book actually topped the *Business Week* bestseller list. This propelled my life into a whole different realm of book tours, speaking engagements, and other public events. I hated it. I was just a mouthpiece for what we'd written and I wasn't learning anything new. I had many interactions with journalists at the time, and it seemed to me that they kept trying to trip you up and find contradictions between what you wrote and what you were doing.

In the mid-1990s I got back into strategy consulting. I was working with general managers to create tools and approaches that were valuable to them. In 1997, I created another firm, Emergence Consulting, with three other partners. In 2001 two of my partners were on the first plane that crashed into the World Trade Towers. That kind of took the wind out of my sails to continue with that firm. So in 2002 I went solo. Recently I started a strategy firm with Venkat Ramaswamy, a University of Michigan professor. We use the co-creation approach for new product development and innovation. Our firm is called "Experience Co-Creation Partnership." We hired a couple of people and work within a network of other senior consultants.

How do I go about getting new clients? Well, you don't just get out of college and advertise yourself as a consultant. I've been established for many years and have developed experience and expertise in strategy consulting. Many of my clients call me because they heard me give a speech somewhere, or they read a book or article I've written. Others have been my students (I teach in the executive education programs at Insead in France and at Michigan). I also have a network of professional colleagues who consult in other domains. In some cases, my colleagues refer clients to me for assistance in strategy work.

At any given time I have about 4–5 clients, but right now I'm swamped with 9–10 clients. My projects usually last several months or even years. I usually work for the general manager of a business unit or the CEO. I work at the intersection of strategy and innovation. The questions I help managers address are, "How do I grow? How do we invest?" and so forth. We run workshops where we present what the customer experiences when using the company's products. Our technique is a bit different: we actually go to three or four representative customers and film them using the product. Or in other cases we go into a retail store and have film crews asking customers how they use a particular product. We call it "co-creation" because this is how we identify things that customers need. A customer might not even know that she has an unmet need until you ask her a bunch of questions. We look at the discrepancy between the product and what customers do with that product.

For example, a company that sells adhesive-based films hired us to help them sell more of their stuff into the new home construction industry. We took a film crew to one of the big homebuilders' construction sites and started talking to their employees. Construction is a very male, macho world, but the head of sales on this particular job was a woman. She said that a big portion of their market is divorced or widowed women. The first thing that a woman wants to be able to do in her new home is to take a long bath in a nice bathroom (this is true even if the woman is usually too busy to soak in a tub). The problem arises during construction of the new home: the tub invariably gets all banged up and looks awful. Construction workers stand in the tub in their dirty boots, hammering nails into the wall. We took our video of the sales woman telling us about this back to the executives at the company. After some brainstorming sessions they figured out that they could make a protective adhesive liner for the inside of the tub, and brand it with the homebuilder's company name. It was a win-win solution for everyone!

This is a challenging job. It's great in that it provides lots of variety, whether consulting to different industries, countries, or types of businesses. I love the front-end discovery of new businesses. I also like to learn about different countries; I've been working a great deal in India, Brazil, Mexico, and Chile lately. We're constantly creating something new. I also get to work with some really interesting people (including some very eccentric general managers). I enjoy having colleagues to work with; it gives me mental interaction, a sense of partnership as well as thought leadership.

The downside of this job is the travel—it's usually too much. I'm always off to the airport on Sunday night for a week in Europe or Asia. I can't control my schedule because it's at the mercy and desires of my clients. This can make life difficult from a personal standpoint. Some consultants also don't like the fact that their recommendations aren't always followed, but that doesn't particularly bother me. I'm in this business for the long haul.

What kind of skills do you need for this work? I'd say you have to have a balance between left brain and right brain thinking. The left side of the brain drives the typical strategy consultant. It's the analytical, quantitative, and logic-based thinking needed to understand the cost structure of the market and the competitive landscape. Right brain thinking is intuitive, sensitive to comments, analog reasoning, geographic reasoning, a sense of empathy, a humanistic view of life, and inspirational. Both are important because in order to thoroughly understand a business situation, you have to have some degree of ability to analyze and use logic. But in order to convince a senior executive of the wisdom and necessity for change, you have to use empathetic listening and understand where the executive's resistance might be coming from. I love the interaction!

My typical day:

I actually have five different types of days: at-home days, public speaking days, workshop days, company visit days, and filming days.

At-Home Days

My at-home days are the most boring part of my job. I spend it in my home office doing paperwork, follow-up phone calls, some interviews, and preparation for the other types of days. I often start with a call to India at 6 AM to about 8:30 AM. I work with clients over the phone and coach them on the various streams of strategy development we have going on.

Between about 8:30 and 9:30 I have breakfast with my wife and son. He's 14 years old. My daughter is older and is now on her own. After breakfast I go into my European and East Coast calls (I live near Boston), followed by West Coast calls and finally at 7 PM I might have a call to Japan.

Public Speaking/Presentation Days

These are probably my easiest days. I travel the night before to wherever it is that the client wants me to deliver a speech. The speeches usually last about

90 minutes to 2 hours. I've given these speeches so often that I could do it in my sleep. The night before I usually go to the room where I'll be talking and make sure that the microphones work, the stage is set up the way I want, and I test the equipment that I'll use with my laptop.

Workshop Days

The days where I'm conducting client workshops are harder to do. I'm on my feet all day long—often 7–8 hours at a time—and I have to be thinking and paying attention constantly. We set up workshops with the client and their executives and other managers to work through strategy issues and review any data we've collected in the field, from customers and such. I spend a good part of my time coaching them and asking pointed questions about what they have seen in the presentations we've heard. I'm in front of a whiteboard or flip chart and it's very mentally stimulating, but also very exhausting. Then we often go out to dinner with the client after the workshop. These are very long days.

Company Visit Days

These days are a mixture of meeting with new clients, where I'm scoping out the project and asking questions about what the company wants me to help them do. I'm often meeting with senior executives and doing interviews with them. In these interviews I not only try to find out about their business and understand the current strategy, but I'm also trying to build rapport with the people I interview. I start by asking where they came from, their background. Then I ask what problems they see with the company's current strategy: their concerns, the threats they see, what their pain points are. I follow this with questions about their aspirations for the company, where they think it should go, what they want to create, and so on. I ask factual questions about how they perceive their customers. At the same time that I'm asking questions, however, I'm also starting a teaching dialog with them. I try to show them that strategy development comes from listening to their customers, not their competitors (the more typical approach to strategy). All of the successful companies, like Starbucks, Cirque du Soleil, and Southwest, created new emotional bonds with their customers by listening to them and developing a unique product.

Filming Days

The days we're out meeting with actual customers and filming them are the most fun, but they can also be exhausting. It starts long before we actually get to the customer's site. First we identify the customers we'd like to talk to. Then we think about what we want to ask and how we'll go about doing the interview. We also prepare the customer for the interview in advance. The actual interview on film is hit or miss. Sometimes the conversation flows well, other times I have to work hard to sustain a good discussion. And you never really know what you'll get. In the evenings, I spend time going over the films to see what we can edit to present later to our client. These are long and often very rewarding days.

JOBS IN BUSINESS STRATEGY

Strategic planning departments have come in and out of favor over the years. Many companies today prefer to tackle strategy among the top leadership team (these are usually the people who head the major functions and staff units along with the CEO). In some cases, this group will seek outside help from management consulting firms, such as Accenture, McKinsey & Company, Roland Berger, PricewaterhouseCoopers, and others. One of the best ways to start a career in strategy is to pursue jobs in these consulting firms. This is also an excellent way to learn through experience how an actual business functions.

The management consulting firms tend to follow an "up or out" career path, whereby each consultant gradually takes on more responsibility, from participating on a client engagement team, to supervising a team, to eventually becoming a partner in the firm. Part of the requirement for becoming a partner (the "up" part) is that the consultant must demonstrate an ability to bring in new clients and new projects. Many talented consultants, however, do not like to do the marketing (and schmoozing) required and thus move "out" of the organization. Often, these consultants are recruited by client companies to high-level executive positions, which usually require a great deal of strategy expertise.

INTERNET RESOURCES

If you are seriously interested in pursuing a job in a consulting company, the first place to orient yourself is on the following Web site: http://www. soyouwanna.com/site/syws/consulting/consulting.html

It discusses the difference between the various firms and how to get a job at one of them. On this site, you will even learn valuable tips on how to interview at a consulting firm. (It is MUCH more difficult and tricky than a normal interview, as they almost always ask you to solve a case problem in 15 minutes or less.)

The following links are useful for more information on careers in specific strategy consulting firms:

http://www.accenture.com/
http://www.mckinsey.com/aboutus/careers/
http://www.pwc.com/uk/eng/car-inexp/graduate/strategy-group.html
http://www.rolandberger.com/career/en/html/ask_us/ask_us.html
http://www.bain.com/bainweb/Join_Bain/case_interviews.asp

SUMMARY

Business strategy is the combination of management decisions that address the questions of what, where, and how the business intends to win in the marketplace. Strategy can be addressed at three levels: the function, the business unit (or product unit), and the corporation. Ideally the strategies for all three levels are aligned, support each other, and move the corporation as a whole to its end goal.

There are several methods and approaches to determine strategy. Porter's industry competitiveness model is a top-down approach that analyzes what the company's competitors are doing and whether there are switching costs for customers, barriers to entry, and other product or service substitutes. A Blue Ocean Strategy presents a different, and more bottom-up method of finding (or creating) a market where there are few competitors. Several other approaches to determine strategy include diversification, understanding core competencies, implementing the Balanced Scorecard, scenario planning, or requiring a business to be number one or number two in its market.

Finally, the strategy setting process can be very simple or very complex depending on the complexity of the company and the rigor of its planning processes. The key to pursuing a good strategy is that it be logic-driven and address all factors of the what, where, and how questions.

4

Leadership

The task of the leader is to get his people from where they are to where they have not been.

—Henry Kissinger

Consensus is the negation of leadership.

—Margaret Thatcher

I believe in benevolent dictatorship, provided I am the dictator.

—Richard Branson

A leader is a man who has the ability to get other people to do what they don't want to do and like it.

—Harry S. Truman

WHAT IS LEADERSHIP?

In terms of the business anatomy, leadership is the "heart" of the business. All businesses need leaders. Just as a person can function (poorly) with a bad heart, so can a business. Bad leaders exist, but they eventually run a business into the ground and/or get replaced. Good leaders are harder to find, and truly excellent leaders are the exceptions.

Leadership is a process by which a person or group influences other people and gets them to carry out specific goals and objectives. A good leader is a person whose values, character, and integrity foster trust, respect, and motivation for other people to embrace the organization's mission and accomplish its goals.

The domain of leadership is one of the most widely studied in the business arena. This means that for every notion of leadership and what makes a good leader, you can find a variety of views. Margaret Thatcher's definition of consensus seems strange given today's focus on teamwork, emotional intelligence, and empowerment. Hitler got a lot of people to follow him and do things that might have been foreign to them, but most people would agree that the world does not need more of his type of leadership.

FAYOL AND TAYLOR: PRINCIPLES OF MANAGEMENT

Henri Fayol was a Frenchman who developed some of the first theories of management in 1916. He believed that management (leaders) had five main jobs: plan, organize, command, coordinate work, and control (make sure that the work is getting done properly). In today's era of top managers being hauled in to court we see that several of them believe that command or control was not in their job description. (Ken Lay, the former CEO of Enron, claimed that he didn't know what was going on in the company as it was being run into the ground; and Bernie Ebbers, former CEO of WorldCom and now serving time in jail, denies that he ever ordered subordinates to fake the books.) Fayol also said that there are 14 principles of management that are common to all effective organizations:

1. Specialization (division of labor)
2. Authority with responsibility (she who gives the orders better be obeyed)
3. Discipline (no slackers)
4. Unity of command (everyone deserves only one boss)
5. Unity of direction (the Big Cheese is the big brain)
6. Subordination of individual interests (no personal calls/texts/e-mails while at work)
7. Remuneration (a fair day's pay for a fair day's work)
8. Centralization (all decisions are made from the top—no freelancing in the field)
9. Chain of command (orders come from the top and get transmitted down through the organization along lines of authority—like the military)
10. Order (no chaos allowed—everything and everyone has its place)
11. Equity (everyone should be treated fairly, but not necessarily equally)
12. Personnel tenure (lifetime employment is good)
13. Initiative (figuring out a plan and making it happen)
14. Esprit de corps (don't worry, be happy)

Fayol would probably have a heart attack if he saw some of the more successful companies today (Pixar with chaos as the norm, decentralization of decisions, teamwork, and so on).

Around the same time, Frederick Taylor, an American, published his views of "scientific management," which sought to codify how to manage employees. Taylor ran around factories with a clipboard and stopwatch timing each individual task. Unlike Fayol, who focused more on the top managers, Taylor focused on the workers. Taylor developed five principles of management:

1. Break down each task into its component parts ("business process redesign" in today's lingo), study the best way to do the job ("benchmarking"), and do only the necessary parts while eliminating the rest ("work out").
2. Select the right worker for the job (hire for attitude and ability).

3. Train the worker (train for skills).
4. Provide financial incentives for doing the job correctly (skill-based pay, and pay the person—not the job).
5. Divide the work and responsibility (worker bees execute tasks and managers plan them).

Both Taylor and Fayol espoused what became known as "scientific management" which involved breaking down jobs to their component parts and analyzing them, often using time and motion studies. The purpose was to make the work more efficient, thus benefiting both the worker and the company. But later managers misinterpreted those goals and used the time and motion studies as a means to regulate and punish underperforming workers. The union movement arose, in part, because of the often brutal conditions that workers were forced to endure through the actions of unthinking managers.

Although many of the concepts from the scientific management movement now seem archaic, several of today's modern management techniques build on the Taylor and Fayol principles. Some of the current iterations of these principles can be seen in the drive for quality improvement, employee selection and development, and skill-based pay.

LEADERSHIP AND POWER: USES AND ABUSES

Leadership is the exercise of power. But where does that power come from? Leaders get their power from their position in a group or organization (they are the boss and they control key assets) and from their personal influence (they know all the right people, they are personally persuasive, and they know how to get things done). Power in organizations is good. Without someone in charge, you would have anarchy.

A good leader must have a high motivation for institutional power; that is, her or his top desire is the ability to influence other people for the good of the institution's mission.[1] But that desire for power must be tempered by maturity. The good leader is not an autocrat or a dictator. Nor does she try to be best friends with her subordinates. The good leader is fair and applies the rules to everyone on an equal, open, individual, and logical basis. She inspires confidence, trust, loyalty, and the will to work hard to get the job done. And perhaps a bit surprisingly, a good leader empowers others to help them do their jobs. This means sharing power, which paradoxically, increases the leader's own power and control.[2] By giving people the autonomy to do a job and the opportunity to figure out the best way to do that job, the leader builds trust and motivation and increases the desire of people to work for them.

So, what is a bad leader? Someone who has a high motivation for personal power and is immature about how power is used. The classic autocrat will order people around, punish them when they don't do the job precisely as directed, and generally treat them like worker bees (low-level workers who don't deserve respect). How do bad leaders get to be leaders? As Jack Welch has said, "They kiss up and kick down." By treating their bosses like gods but abusing their subordinates, bad leaders step on top of others to get the best for themselves. In addition, power abusers often feel that the "power pie" is one size and unchangeable, so in order for a leader to have the most power, the workers must have the least. It's a win–lose situation. In fact, it works the opposite: the more the leader reduces a subordinate's power, the less power the leader has.

Good leaders are like orchestra conductors: to make beautiful music the conductor has to give each musician the opportunity to play their instrument as they know best, but under the guidance and coordination of the leader. The more musicians in the orchestra there are (who are, hopefully, on the same page of music) the louder and richer the sound. The best conductors, like the best leaders, define the direction for the orchestra and build the lateral networks that foster trust, respect, and camaraderie among the members.[3]

Power is like a virtuous or vicious spiral, depending on how it is used. People who are "low in organizational power" would tend to foster lower group morale, behave in more authoritarian ways, try to retain control, restrict opportunities for subordinates' growth, supervise too closely, use coercive rather than persuasive power, be more insecure, and attempt to control a territory (les "petits chefs" or "little bosses"). In contrast, people "high in organizational power" would foster high group morale, behave in more cooperative and less critical ways, be less rigid or authoritarian and more flexible, delegate more control, and develop and help promote their subordinates.[4]

Women CEOs

1. Patricia Woertz (Archer-Daniels-Midland)
2. Brenda Barnes (Sara Lee)
3. Mary Sammons (Rite Aid)
4. Anne Mulcahy (Xerox)
5. Patricia Russo (Lucent)
6. Susan Ivey (Reynolds American)
7. Andrea Jung (Avon)
8. Marion Sandler (Golden West Financial Corporation)
9. Paula Rosput Reynolds (Safeco)
10. Meg Whitman (eBay)

CAPTAIN OF THE TEAM: WHAT DOES A LEADER DO?

As the leader of a company, the CEO is responsible for setting the direction or vision of the company and deciding how to get there. The CEO is the final arbiter of all decisions within the company and is responsible for all the good and bad things that happen. The CEO is the owner of "The Buck Stops Here" sign. The leader also has a responsibility to see that the company does business in a way that is ethical, legal, and serves all of its stakeholders in the best manner possible.

Managing Stakeholders

What are stakeholders? They are the collective group of people that comprise shareholders (owners), employees, customers, suppliers, and the public. Shareholders or investors expect the leader to manage their investment responsibly and spend it wisely in order to make good and steady profits. Employees expect to be treated fairly and be paid a decent wage for the work that they put in. Customers expect to buy products and/or services that are of a sufficient quality and utility to justify the price the company is asking. And if there is a problem with the product, customers expect the company to stand behind their product and fix or replace it. Suppliers expect to be paid for their goods on the terms the company has agreed to. And the public expects the company to be a "good citizen" by not polluting the environment and giving back to the communities in which it operates. Every one of the stakeholders expects honesty

Women Executives by Mike Keefe
© Mike Keefe. Reprinted with permission.

and lack of deceit in how the company deals with them. It is the leader's job to make sure that everyone inside the company works hard to live up to the various expectations of the stakeholders. As we will see, many company leaders have not behaved in the most exemplary manner.

Balancing Act

The CEO of a company must balance the realities of the external environment with internal decision processes. So if a company faces a tough competitor in a new market or country, the company must balance the actions it takes with the impact on all of the stakeholders that might be affected. For example, a company that does business in a developing country might be tempted to cut costs (by employing cheap labor, looking the other way when factory conditions aren't up to American standards, polluting the local river, and so on) to make higher profits. But in the end, these actions come back to haunt the company (like when Nike was found to employ cheap factory labor in Asia) and often can hurt sales in its home country.

Developing Leaders at All Levels

The CEO's other, perhaps less known, responsibility includes developing future leaders. General Electric's Jack Welch is known for his almost single-minded quest to develop general managers (future leaders) at all levels of the company. Similarly, Andy Grove (Intel) has been accused of being a closet professor because he likes to teach others. In both cases, these CEOs believe strongly that a company does not excel based on the talent in the top office alone. The truly successful companies (and CEOs) develop leadership talent all along the spectrum and at several lower levels of the organization.

Are Great Leaders Born or Made?

The answer is "Yes." This is an age-old and much debated question, and the consensus is that leaders are both born with some necessary qualities and gain others throughout their life. Those who believe that leaders are born argue that true leaders must have the following traits, which, they say cannot be learned:

- A spirit of adventure
- Exceptional intelligence
- Charisma
- Extreme persistence
- Ability to influence
- Strong self-confidence
- Common sense
- High intuition

Nonsense! Say those who believe that leaders can be made—and that includes the entire industry built around leadership training and coaching. The "made" camp cite the following arguments:

- Anyone can be a leader—all it takes is desire and commitment.
- One can learn all the necessary leadership behaviors:
  - Developing people
  - Ability to influence others
  - Building teamwork
  - Ability to think through multiple, complex options
  - Taking calculated risks
  - Developing a clear vision
  - Empowering people to act on their own initiative
  - Developing creativity in oneself and others
- Leadership is a skill and a habit; how it is practiced can be modified as needed.
- There are numerous examples of great leaders throughout history who have very different styles. There is no perfect style for all situations.

LEADERSHIP STYLES: HOW DOES A LEADER DO IT?

There are almost as many styles of leadership as there are leaders. In the old days, when managers were all men (without exception), the prototype of a good leader came from the military, where most of the men had served. A good military commander gave orders for the good of the unit, everyone was treated the same (this was considered fair), and the subordinates obeyed and carried out the orders. This kind of leader is typical in a top-down, command-and-control hierarchy when it is necessary to control a large number of resources and the work is fairly predictable. There is no discussion about the wisdom of a particular decision and employees either carry out the orders or passively resist them for as long as they can get away with it. This type of leadership is called authoritarian or patriarchal (acting like the father for the benefit of his sons). Some extreme forms of this kind of leader are called autocrats, or more cynically, a despot, tyrant, or dictator (which more often applies to the head of a malevolent government). Questioning the authority of an autocrat, especially if you are low on the totem pole, is out of the question.

The top-down leadership style works fine if the company's business is stable, predictable, and tasks don't vary a whole lot. For decades this kind of leadership was normal. But a number of factors made the traditionally authoritarian leader look more like a dinosaur:

1. World War II made the world look considerably smaller, and the collapse of the Berlin Wall opened up huge new markets.
2. The rise of commercial airline travel brought people from different cultures together. This facilitated the exchange of ideas for new products, services, technologies, and partnerships.
3. More women entered the workforce and moved up the hierarchy. They brought a different style of leadership and management, which was often seen to be more effective in certain circumstances.
4. Commercialization of the Internet (early 1990s) meant that customers could get information quicker and from a wide variety of suppliers.
5. The exponential growth of computer power and networks gave people faster and quicker access to data, thus reducing the need for leaders to manage information flow.
6. Free trade agreements sprouted all over the world. These reduced tariffs and the costs of doing business internationally. Goods and people could now travel across borders more easily and at lower relative cost.
7. As more people finished high school and went to college, more of the mundane stuff got programmed into software. This meant that the workforce was better educated and, in general, more "professionalized" and you just can't manage a thinking human being as if she were a stupid monkey. Or if you did, she would leave to go work for your competitor.
8. As more companies and entrepreneurs got into newer and broader markets, the demand for talented workers escalated to a point that there's now a "war for talent." The best companies seek to be the employer of choice to attract the best workers, so leaders have to provide opportunities for people to learn and further develop their skills.

All of these developments made doing business the "usual" way much harder. The business environment became more competitive as many new companies entered different markets and information flowed much faster. Remember when Microsoft was just a little two-person firm that sold a Quick and Dirty Operating System (Q-DOS) to mighty IBM when it was trying to break into the PC market? There was no way that a typical CEO could possibly get his arms or mind around all the complexities of the market.

As businesses became more complex (selling a wider variety of products to a larger and more diverse number of markets and customers) the smart companies realized that they could not govern by edict, and a less authoritarian style started to take effect. The new leadership prototype came from the weekend sports games and the leader was seen more as a coach than a military commander. Consensus building became more necessary as companies found that it was far more effective to work in teams with members from the different functions and departments of the firm. In this way a team represented all of the brains of the company pulling together as one group with a common goal. In addition, a team with functional experts was much better at getting its arms and brains around a thorny issue. New products could be thought through from design

Our Credo

We believe our first responsibility is to the doctors, nurses and patients,
to mothers and fathers and all others who use our products and services.
In meeting their needs everything we do must be of high quality.
We must constantly strive to reduce our costs
in order to maintain reasonable prices.
Customers' orders must be serviced promptly and accurately.
Our suppliers and distributors must have an opportunity
to make a fair profit.

We are responsible to our employees,
the men and women who work with us throughout the world.
Everyone must be considered as an individual.
We must respect their dignity and recognize their merit.
They must have a sense of security in their jobs.
Compensation must be fair and adequate,
and working conditions clean, orderly and safe.
We must be mindful of ways to help our employees fulfill
their family responsibilities.
Employees must feel free to make suggestions and complaints.
There must be equal opportunity for employment, development
and advancement for those qualified.
We must provide competent management,
and their actions must be just and ethical.

We are responsible to the communities in which we live and work
and to the world community as well.
We must be good citizens—support good works and charities
and bear our fair share of taxes.
We must encourage civic improvements and better health and education.
We must maintain in good order
the property we are privileged to use,
protecting the environment and natural resources.

Our final responsibility is to our stockholders.
Business must make a sound profit.
We must experiment with new ideas.
Research must be carried on, innovative programs developed
and mistakes paid for.
New equipment must be purchased, new facilities provided
and new products launched.
Reserves must be created to provide for adverse times.
When we operate according to these principles,
the stockholders should realize a fair return.

4.1. Johnson & Johnson's corporate credo.

concept all the way out to manufacturing, distribution, and after-sales service. Teamwork can take longer, but often the results are much better.

So how does today's leader manage a team of experts from different parts of the company with different views of a problem or process? Some people

Table 4.1. Some sample vision and mission statements

Mission (Values)	Vision (Business model)	Who said it
Quality is Job 1	Our vision is to become the world's leading consumer company for automotive products and services	Ford Motor Company
We will forsake violence and pursue truth in resisting the opponent	Eliminate British rule and establish a democracy in India	Mahatma Gandhi
When it absolutely, positively has to be there on time	We are the world's most recognized and trusted name for air express delivery services	FedEx Express
At IBM, we strive to lead in the creation, development, and manufacture of the industry's most advanced information technologies, including computer systems, software, networking systems, storage devices, and microelectronics. We translate these advanced technologies into value for our customers through our professional solutions and services businesses worldwide	Innovation that matters	IBM
Touching lives, improving life	Be, and be recognized as, the best consumer products and services company in the world	Procter & Gamble
We will ensure a stress-free car rental experience by providing superior services that cater to our customers' individual needs ... always conveying the "We Try Harder"® spirit with knowledge, caring, and a passion for excellence	We will lead our industry by defining service excellence and building unmatched customer loyalty	Avis
We improve the quality of people's lives through the timely introduction of meaningful technological innovations	In a world where technology increasingly touches every aspect of our daily lives, we will be a leading solutions provider in the areas of healthcare, lifestyle, and enabling technology, aspiring to become the most admired company in our industry as seen by our stakeholders	Philips (consumer products, lighting, semiconductors, medical systems)
The mission of Southwest Airlines is dedication to the highest quality of customer service delivered with a sense of warmth, friendliness, individual pride, and company spirit.	We are committed to provide our employees a stable work environment with equal opportunity for learning and personal growth. Creativity and innovation are encouraged for improving the effectiveness of Southwest Airlines. Above all, employees will be provided the same concern, respect, and caring attitude within the organization that they are expected to share externally with every Southwest customer	Southwest Airlines

say it's like herding cats: you do it very carefully. The first thing a leader does is make sure that she's got the right people on the team. Most organizations need functional specialists as well as generalists who can see the bigger picture. A good team will have a combination of both types of people and most importantly, people who are willing and able to put aside their own personal goals for the good of the group. Then the leader needs to make sure that the team knows what its goal, or "charter" is, what it is to deliver, and when it is to be delivered. And finally, most teams have a set of "rules of engagement" or processes by which discussions are carried out and decisions are made. These can include things like not insulting your teammates, listening to one another's opinions, and appointing people to take notes and facilitate the process. Numerous books have been written about creating and managing effective teams in organizations.

The leader's role in most organizations today is to inspire people to work for the good of the organization. That means setting the strategy, the vision for the company, and its mission. And then the leader needs to communicate those sentiments to the employees in a way that people can embrace the company's goals and become inspired to contribute. A mission statement is a declaration of the company's values, its reason for being, and its overarching social and/or corporate goals. A mission statement should reflect the company's culture and help employees decide upon the "right thing to do" in times of stress. A vision statement is more detailed and sets forth where the company sees itself in the future and how it intends to get there. A vision statement should be clear, realistic, achievable, future-oriented, and aligned with the company's values. Some examples of mission and vision statements are listed in Table 4.1.

You'll notice that some companies seem to blend mission and vision and values. Other companies don't publish any of these as separate documents, but instead follow a corporate philosophy, code of behavior, or credo. Figure 4.1 shows Johnson & Johnson's 60-year-old credo, which has guided the company's behavior through the ups and downs of its history.

Leadership Styles

Transactional

Task-oriented: "If you do X for me, then I will reward you with Y salary, Z promotion, or W special benefit. If you fail to do X properly, then you will be punished." Example: Harold Geneen (former CEO of ITT).

Transformational (also called Charismatic)

Interpersonal orientation and motivation of employees to a higher inspirational purpose: "We need to accomplish X because it will bring Y to the community. We all need to pitch in and be part of this higher moral purpose." This type of leadership usually depends on a very charismatic leader with the following characteristics: idealized influence, inspirational motivation, intellectual stimulation, and individualized consideration. Example: Katherine Graham (former CEO Washington Post).

Pseudo-transformational

Similar to transformational leadership except that this leader uses his influence with more sinister motives. He also usually lacks one of the four components of a true transformational leader: individualized consideration (care for the well-being of others). Example: Ayatollah Khomeini and Adolf Hitler.

Coaching

The boss helps subordinates change and grow on a personal level by giving them challenging, but doable assignments. It won't work if the subordinate doesn't want to change.

Democratic

Workers get a voice in decisions. This brings increased organizational flexibility and responsibility and generates fresh ideas. The downside is that the organization gets too bogged down in the process (meetings, consensus-building) and people feel leaderless.

Open Book Management

Applies more to privately held companies where the practice of sharing financial information with all employees fosters a greater sense of trust and commitment between employees and management. Proponents also believe it encourages an entrepreneurial, we're-all-in-this-together culture. Example: SRC Holdings, a manufacturing company.

Management by Walking Around

Popularized by David Packard of Hewlett-Packard, this style involves getting out of the office and learning about what the employees are doing, the challenges they're facing, and how they go about solving the issues.

Level 5 Leadership

Jim Collins, author of "Good to Great," determined that only those leaders with qualities of extreme personal humility and a fierce drive to succeed—what he called "Level 5 Leaders"—could transform a company to "sustained excellence" over a long period of time. Example: Darwin Smith (former CEO of Kimberly-Clark).

Finally, leaders use their position, personal expertise, talent, and charisma to influence others to follow them in a quest to achieve a goal or purpose. Leaders act as role models for others and often don't believe that something just "can't be done." Good leaders also know their own limitations and surround themselves with people who are better than they are in one or several dimensions. Some leaders have personal "rules" or codes of conduct, and others fly by the seat of their pants and follow their gut. Jack Welch, the widely admired former CEO of General Electric had eight rules of how to lead:[5]

1. Leaders relentlessly upgrade their team, using every encounter as an opportunity to evaluate, coach, and build self-confidence.
2. Leaders make sure people not only see the vision, they live and breathe it.
3. Leaders get into everyone's skin, exuding positive energy and optimism.
4. Leaders establish trust with candor, transparency, and credit.
5. Leaders have the courage to make unpopular decisions and gut calls.
6. Leaders probe and push with a curiosity that borders on skepticism, making sure their questions are answered with action.

7. Leaders inspire risk taking and learning by setting the example.
8. Leaders celebrate.

SOME EXAMPLES

So who are the good, the bad, and the truly ugly leaders? Here's a rogue's gallery of some notable CEOs.

Andy "Mad Hungarian" Grove—Paranoid CEO

Blunt spoken and intensely curious, Andy Grove was the legendary CEO of Intel for 11 years. During that time, Intel grew at annual rate of nearly 30 percent. Grove, a Hungarian Jew and survivor of Naziism and Communism, came to the United States in 1957 with nothing and put himself through college, ultimately earning a Ph.D. from UC Berkeley. Grove's personal history taught him that failure was always an option and could arrive in blindingly fast speed. His view of management was that change is inevitable and a leader must embrace change and guide the employees to change at a rate that is just below their maximum comfort threshold. Grove's paranoia led him to believe that one often didn't see a cliff until he'd walked off of it. Thus he encouraged "helpful Cassandras" to challenge him and his views on company policies and direction. This attitude allowed Andy Grove to metaphorically step out of his own skin to view the business landscape as an unbiased strategist. One such event was when Intel's profits dove from almost $200 million in 1984 to less than $2 million a year later. He and Intel cofounder, Gordon Moore, symbolically fired and rehired themselves when they decided to get out of the company's star product line, memories, and build a new business around microprocessors. Grove reinvented the company a second time in 1990 when he branded the Pentium microprocessor with the slogan, "Intel Inside." This was nothing short of revolutionary: an engineering company staffed by computer geeks turning into a smooth marketing machine that developed the world's fifth best known brand.

Today Andy Grove is the benevolent "Senior Advisor" of Intel and has actively encouraged the new CEO, Paul Otellini (also a UC Berkeley graduate), to follow the next revolution in microprocessors. Intel is now eliminating the Pentium processor and the new strategy is to design microchips that will go into virtually everything, not just personal computers.

"Neutron" Jack Welch—America's Toughest (and Most Admired) Boss

Jack Welch shepherded General Electric through 2 decades of constant change. When he became CEO in 1981, GE was a huge organization (404,000 employees) with $27 billion in revenues. GE had developed a huge bureaucracy to match. Welch famously decreed that all GE businesses must either become number one or two in their industry or else fix, close, or sell the business. In the process of delayering and streamlining the company, Welch eliminated a quarter of GE's jobs while more than doubling its profits by 1985. This earned him the nickname "Neutron Jack" after the bomb that leaves buildings but vaporizes the people inside. But Jack Welch also changed the mindset of the corporation by requiring honesty, trust, and openness of all employees. Instead of detailed strategic planning sessions with reams of paper and endless presentations, Welch held strategy sessions with the business manager and his top-level executives. (And yes, they were all men. . . . GE under Welch did not do a good job of promoting women or minorities.) These meetings were problem-solving events that looked as much at the business as at their competitors. Welch also instituted the famous "work-out" process whereby employees in a business gather in a town hall meeting with their bosses to discuss ways to get rid of unnecessary work and processes. The bosses have to make decisions on the spot to address employee suggestions.

Perhaps the biggest compliment to a CEO is that other companies copy his tactics. GE popularized "benchmarking"—a means of systematically learning best practices from other, noncompeting companies. Jack Welch is one of the most widely imitated and admired CEOs in recent years. *Fortune* magazine named him Manager of the Century in 1999 because Welch essentially changed the way that business was done. He blew up Taylorism with the then revolutionary idea that man is not a machine. He took an axe to corporate bloat and eliminated layers of useless bureaucracy.

Welch has said that his top strategic priority while at GE was developing the talent necessary to bring the best out of each GE business and the best out of the people who run those businesses. In that regard he has succeeded since GE is now regarded as the gold standard of management training. You'll find many ex-GE managers running companies such as 3M, Boeing, Home Depot, Honeywell, Albertsons, Rubbermaid, Goodyear, and AlliedSignal.

Meg Whitman—Open-minded Influencer

As CEO for the world's biggest auction site, eBay, Meg Whitman doesn't exactly look the part of the boss of a huge company that has changed the way people do business on the Internet. She is old fashioned and very low key. And in an era when many Internet companies (Yahoo, Amazon.com) struggle to become profitable, Meg Whitman has delivered solidly increasing profits for 8 years. In 2005, eBay delivered $4.3 billion in revenue and shepherded the sale of more than $40 billion worth of stuff (including $1,200 for a used brussel sprout). Not bad for a company that doesn't actually own anything. How does she do this? Her style is very collaborative but decisive. She works hard to enable other people to get things done that benefit the customer, whether it is the buyer or the seller community on eBay.

> I think CEOs are terribly overrated. The whole concept of the superstar CEO is nuts. When you look at successful companies, there are a whole lot of folks doing a whole lot of things to make them successful. Being a "superstar" has an awful lot to do with timing.
>
> —Jim Kelly, CEO of UPS from 1997 to 2002

In 1999, eBay had a severe technical glitch that shut the site down for 24 hours. Meg personally reached out to customers to update them on site changes and solicited honest feedback. She is the antithesis of the top-down command and control leader. She seeks opinions from others and remains open and flexible to all ideas, regardless of their source.

Lee Iacocca—Superstar CEO

The superstar CEO is usually not the best leader for an organization in the long run. This type of CEO tends to be consumed by gaining personal attention and grabbing the credit for a job well done, while putting the blame on the subordinates. Lee Iacocca was a superstar CEO of Chrysler in the 1980s when the automobile manufacturer was in bankruptcy and on the verge of collapse. Mr. Iacocca successfully rallied the general public around his plan to get the U.S. government to guarantee a loan to bail out the company. He appeared personally in several television commercials, telling the public how it was their patriotic duty to support Chrysler and buy the company's cars. Iacocca symbolically took a salary of $1.00 per year in order to show that he was not personally benefiting. (What was less known at the time were all the stock options he negotiated, which would later make him very rich.) Mr. Iacocca did a good job leading Chrysler through a difficult time, but he did not solve the long-term problems of the company (poor quality cars compared to the Japanese and Europeans and severe industry overcapacity).

Harold "Mean" Geneen—Micromanager Extraordinaire

Harold Geneen came to ITT, a stodgy telecommunications company, in 1959 as its president. In 10 years, Geneen turned ITT into a huge conglomerate of 150 individual companies that operated worldwide. There was no apparent rhyme or reason to why a company was picked to join the ITT stable other than it had the potential to earn money. One of the companies even maintained the White House hotline to Moscow. Other companies included Avis Rent-A-Car, Continental Baking (Hostess Twinkies), Hartford Insurance, Grinnell (fire equipment), and Sheraton Hotels. Geneen was an autocratic leader and his method of keeping track of such a widespread empire was strict operational control. He believed in checks and balances and enforced draconian discipline from his managers. He would hold marathon 4-day meetings every month (14-hour days) where each manager was called up to the front of the room among his 120 or so peers and grilled on the status of his operation. If the hapless manager got a fact wrong, Geneen would pounce and turn that manager into mincemeat by publicly humiliating him. Geneen reveled in making his managers squirm and sweat. He made *Fortune* Magazine's list of the "world's meanest bosses" and *Fast Company*'s tally of "Bosses from Hell."

"Chainsaw" Al Dunlap—Rambo in Pinstripes

Albert J. Dunlap came to Sunbeam, a small appliance company that made things like electric blankets, blenders, and barbeques, with a well-earned reputation for turning companies around. As CEO of Scott Paper Company he radically cut costs and the value of company stock rose by 225 percent during his watch. The corporate directors of Sunbeam were hoping for similar results. What they got was a psychopathic leader with the personality of a pit bull on amphetamines. Dunlap knew only one way to restructure companies: massively reduce the number of employees, products, and manufacturing facilities under the guise of eliminating waste and inefficiency. Within weeks after Dunlap's arrival, he fired half of Sunbeam's 6,000 employees and eliminated 87 percent of the company's products. The human resources department was cut from 75 people to 17, and the information technology department was eliminated entirely. The rapid cuts turned the company into chaos and left the remaining managers struggling to even operate. Some costs actually rose as the company had to hire consultants—often the same people it had just fired—at double or triple the rates they were paid as employees. Dead computers made it impossible to keep track of shipments; some customers got three orders rather than one, or were shipped the wrong products. At one point, managers had to manually prepare invoices for customers like Wal-Mart and Sears. Dunlap screamed at his managers and belittled them for being inept. He would throw papers or even furniture and shout so violently, just inches away from a manager's face that his hair would be blown back. "Hair spray day" was code for a possible Dunlap tirade.

In the end, Dunlap's actions caused some strange accounting tricks, such as counting products sold if they received the order in December, but delivery wasn't until June. The company was forced to use its line of credit to fund daily operations and ultimately it collapsed under the weight of huge debt and not enough income. Dunlap was fired 23 months after he arrived.

THE BOARD OF DIRECTORS

The board of directors is the boss' boss. All publicly traded corporations (and most private corporations) in the United States are required to have a board of directors. This is a group of between 7 and 20 people who are picked to supervise the chief executive officer. Often, though, the CEO is also the chairman of the board of directors so he or she is the top dog among the group paid to supervise him. Isn't this a strange thing? It's sort of like supervising yourself. And what's more strange, the CEO often gets to pick the people he wants to have serve on his board of directors. Naturally most CEOs would say that they pick people who have specific talents and expertise, and often they do. But at the same time, the CEO tends to pick his buddies who are also CEOs of other firms. After all, what better way to have someone help you run a company than to ask someone else who is running their own company? But the cozy relationship doesn't end there. A subset of the board of directors, usually a group of three to five board members, serves on a "compensation committee" that decides how much to pay the CEO. Since no company wants to be known for paying their leader in the bottom-third of the CEO pay range (what would that say? That this CEO is not as good as the average?), the compensation committee usually recommends a hefty salary and benefits package. Add to this mix the fact that our underpaid CEO probably serves on the board of directors (and maybe even the compensation committee) of some other companies and therefore can continue to ratchet up the CEO pay scale by recommending a higher salary for his other CEO buddies. And in case anyone has questions, the compensation consulting firms (sometimes derided as the "compensation mafia") like Towers-Perrin and Hay legitimize the high rates of CEO pay with their studies and reams of statistics showing how CEOs really deserve such rich pay packages.

So what? You might ask. Why does this matter? CEOs have big jobs running big companies. The problem with this is that CEO pay in the United States has spiraled out of control over the past 2 decades. It has led to some enormous inequalities in pay between the CEO and the average worker (see Figure 4.2).

As of 2004, CEOs in America took home 431 times as much salary as the average U.S. worker.[6] The next highest pay disparity wasn't even remotely close to that of the United States. In Venezuela, the CEO takes home a mere 50 times what the average worker does.[7] But even more amazing, in Japan, a very small country with the third largest economy in the world (after the United States and China), the average CEO earns only 11 times that of the average worker. Back

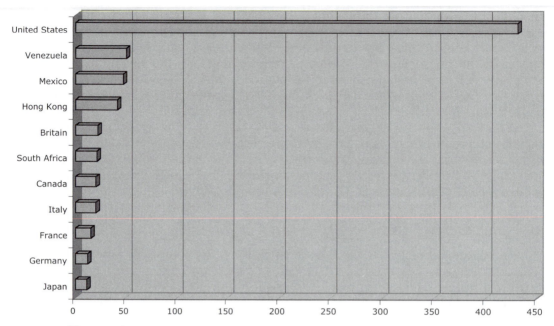

Figure 4.2. Ratio of CEO to worker pay worldwide.

in 1980, the average CEO in the United States earned 46 times more than the average worker. If wages had grown equally for workers and CEOs, the average worker today would be earning $110,126 per year, instead of the $27,460 that he currently earns (see Figure 4.3).

This kind of wage inequality would be somewhat more palatable if everyone shared equally in the downturns. But when big companies like United

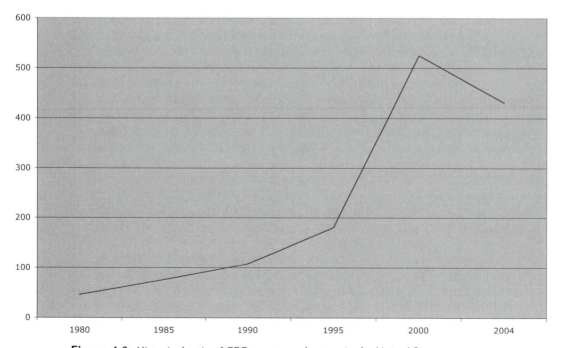

Figure 4.3. Historical ratio of CEO pay to worker pay in the United States.

Airlines and General Motors cut worker pensions, health care benefits, and wages, while at the same time giving their executives big bonuses, it starts to look mighty unfair. And managers these days wonder why they're getting such a bad reputation.

Corporate Governance

Corporate governance means "how the company is managed" or governed. It encompasses the authority structure and relationships of the people at the top of the corporation that decide the company's direction and set the tone of the company's culture. Corporate governance can be something as simple as how many signatures are required on company checks, or whether people get paid time off for participating in charity events. Corporate governance at the top level refers to the structure and composition of the board of directors, what kinds of things they can decide, how they decide them, and what kinds of things they delegate to the CEO and senior management. Corporate governance includes questions such as

- How many directors will make up the board of directors?
- How many of these directors will be from outside the company?
- How are the directors chosen and are they truly "independent" of senior management?
- How do we hold the board of directors and senior executives accountable for bad business decisions?
- How will the company decide to get more capital (issue debt, issue stocks, sell assets)?
- What kinds of limitations do we put on the senior executives regarding big money decisions?
- Who is protecting the interests of the shareholders?

During the 1980s and 1990s, many boards of directors faced increasing scrutiny from shareholders (the company owners) about executive pay. The new mantra became "pay for performance." That is, if a CEO is doing a really good job and increasing the value of the company (and thus, the value of the stock), then she should be paid well. However, the converse—if the value of the stock dropped the CEO should be punished—was not always implemented. In fact, in far too many instances the CEO received her bonus even if the company didn't meet performance targets. In 2005, the median CEO pay (where half of all CEOs were paid more and half were paid less) was $8.4 million, and they got an average 10.3 percent pay raise over their 2004 salary.[8] Michael Eisner, Walt Disney's CEO for 20 years, did a fine job in his early tenure, but during a 13-year period, he was paid $800 million. Disney shareholders would have earned more during that time had they invested in boring old U.S. Treasury bills instead.[9]

So has governance gone bad? The board of directors' primary responsibility is theoretically to the shareholders, or owners of the company. But, as mentioned before, the directors are most often chosen and appointed by the CEO, so their loyalties can often get confused. The U.S. Congress in 2002 attempted to help boards of directors and CEOs realign their priorities with those of the shareholders. The Sarbanes-Oxley Act, also known as SarbOx or SOX, signif-icantly tightened up the audit and reporting requirements of publicly traded corporations. CEOs and CFOs (chief financial officers) now have to personally certify that the annual reports and other required financial statements are correct. In addition, corporations may not make personal loans to its officers or directors, and auditors must now be fully independent and may not provide any other types of consulting services (like tax accounting and advice). Penalties for misbehavior are much tougher and include high fines and jail time.

Good governance is a balancing act. A company's leaders need to be attentive to the shareholders, the unions, the customers, the suppliers, the employees, and the communities in which the company does business. Those different groups very often have different and conflicting agendas. What's good for the employees might not always look so good for the shareholders at first glance. A good leader is able to balance the demands of the conflicting groups. A truly great leader is able to get the various groups to embrace and support his or her vision.

Failure is an Option

Starting in 2000 it seemed that the executive suite had a revolving door on it. The list of CEOs and presidents who were fired or otherwise "stepped down" is long. Some of the most flagrant offenders include:

- Jeffrey Skilling (Enron)
- Kenneth Lay (Enron)
- Andrew Fastow (Enron)
- Richard Scrushy (Healthsouth)
- John and Timothy Rigas (Adelphia)
- Dennis Koslowski (Tyco)
- Bernie Ebbers (Worldcom/MCI)

Everyone listed above left after various accounting improprieties came to light—also known as "cooking the books." Some of these tricks were obvious, like overstating earnings and understating expenses, or treating a long-term capital cost as a current operating expense (Healthsouth and Worldcom). Other tricks were extremely complicated and used specially designed financial entities to hide debt and shift risk away from the main corporation (Enron). And some CEOs treated the company as their own personal piggy bank that financed a lavish lifestyle (Koslowski and Rigas). All the executives listed above are either on trial or in prison for their crimes.

Aside from outright fraud, many CEOs are fired for lesser, noncriminal offenses. The main reason, according to a survey of board members,* is that the board of directors lost confidence in the CEO's ability to deliver the kind of financial performance expected of them. The same survey found that the top reasons for firing a CEO were: mismanaging change, ignoring customers, tolerating slackers, and being in denial of reality. Carly Fiorina, former CEO of Hewlett-Packard, was fired after a contentious acquisition of Compaq Computer. The actual integration of the two companies went well, but the business logic of the acquisition was not clear, and Ms. Fiorina's personal style clashed significantly with the internal culture of Hewlett-Packard.

*Leadership IQ study of 1,087 interviews with members of boards of directors. Summary is available on www.leadershipiq.com/news_mismangement.html.

A DAY IN THE LIFE OF A COO

Roger McCarthy
Copresident, Vail Resorts, Inc.
and Chief Operating Officer, Breckenridge and Keystone Ski Resorts

I grew up in New Zealand. My mother was a schoolteacher, but she didn't start until she was in her forties, after she went back for her master's degree. I had a diploma in industrial management from a technical institute in New Zealand. Education was important in my family, but I didn't want to just go and get a degree in something and not know what I would do with it. So I went to work at Whistler ski resort (north of Vancouver, Canada) in 1971. I worked in a hotel for 6 months and then I went to work for the ski area—mostly because I ran out of money. My first job there was loading the T-bar. Whistler was pretty lean in those days and there were only four ski patrollers on duty on the weekends. They used me to carry explosives for them—I guess because they knew I could ski without dropping anything. It was a lot of fun.

I went back to New Zealand, and after 4 days, I realized that my goal in life was to run a ski resort. I went back to Whistler and joined the ski patrol. I needed some avalanche and first aid qualifications, so I got those. It turned out that in my first year as a ski patroller, I was the most qualified guy on the patrol, but I had no experience. One of the senior patrollers was hurt and out for the season and I was quickly put on the team that did helicopter "bombing" for avalanches. We threw explosives out the window to trigger avalanches. It was a blast! Two years later I was appointed assistant patrol director and 2 years after that I was the patrol director.

In those days risk management was just coming to the top of ski resorts' agendas. There was a big lawsuit where an injured skier sued Stratton resort in Vermont. This was a wake-up call to ski resorts to really look at the risks inherent in skiing and figure out ways to reduce those risks. So I was asked to work with Whistler's lawyers on some of these risk management issues. In October 1978, Whistler got a new president. He asked me to go into lift operations and see if I could "fix" the system. We had 100 employees in lift operations and that whole group had a very different focus than what I was used to in the ski patrol. Key issues were training, maintaining a high level of service, and whether we were hiring the right people (these are the front line of the ski area and interface with customers regularly as they load the lifts). By contrast, in the ski patrol you're responsible for rapid decision-making and your actions have high visibility especially in times of crises. As director of the ski patrol I created flow charts to show exactly how everyone had to respond in predictable (but rare) crises, like a lift breakdown when we had to evacuate hundreds of people stranded on the lift. Well, the person who replaced me as ski patrol director just couldn't handle the stress and he quit. The new president asked me if I could do both jobs: overseeing lift operations and the ski patrol. I thought it was a huge responsibility. But in a short time I had it under control and then they gave me the grooming and on-mountain risk management too.

By this time I had over 160 people under me. I got involved in training, employee service motivation and I loved it! I also joined the local Chamber of Commerce. The "Spirit of Whistler" program was in its infancy. It's similar to Breckenridge's Friends Welcome program. It aimed to get everyone in

Whistler—whether or not they worked directly for the ski area—to think like and act as a host to our many out of town visitors. As part of this program I would often ski the mountain trying to catch people doing the right stuff. A few years later, *Ski Magazine* rated Whistler Resort number one in service in North America.

In 1990 I left to work at Blackcomb. I was hired as director of human resources. (I had really applied for the job of vice president of operations, but they gave that job to an internal candidate.) I was freaking out. I didn't know anything about human resources, but the fashion at the time was to hire someone who knew the business and then let them hire a technical expert in the function. So I hired a very talented woman who knew the technical part of HR. The reason I moved to HR was that as director of HR you can impact every part of the organization. I could see my fingerprints everywhere. I told my boss that my goal was to stay in this position for 2 years and then I would go and run a resort. He rolled his eyes at that statement.

As luck would have it, the company (Intrawest) was looking to purchase Mont Tremblant in Quebec. I was part of the due diligence team assigned to figure out the value of the resort and how much money we'd have to spend to bring it up to world class standards. You can size up a ski resort just based on a tour of the vehicle maintenance shop. You can see the spending pattern (or lack of it), how they maintain their fleet, if they retire older vehicles and thus assess the company's approach to capital costs. But underlying these hard data, you can also discern the employees' work ethic, their pride, the values espoused by the company, and whether it encourages innovation and creativity. A badly maintained vehicle fleet will foster negative attitudes on the part of the employee who consistently gets stuck on the mountain at 2 AM when he's grooming a ski run. That just spirals downward like a domino effect. It also speaks to the way the company treats its employees.

Mont Tremblant was a totally different culture. The whole company was French–Canadian and unionized. Our biggest challenge was to try to merge the cultures of the two companies. On top of that, Tremblant was technically bankrupt and the resort suffered a huge amount of deferred maintenance.

I came back to my boss and nominated myself to run Mont Tremblant. I persuaded him that you can't transfer our company culture simply by hiring a French–Canadian to run the resort. And because I'm a New Zealander, not an English-speaking Canadian, it was an added advantage. The first 2 months, we spent over a million dollars in paint alone. I spent a lot of my time crawling under cats [snow grooming machines] asking the driver questions in my broken French. I didn't need to ask him because I had all the numbers back in my office, but it was a great way to connect with them on their level. I made a point to open a dialog with the workers, and I broke down a lot of hierarchy and barriers. In the end we succeeded in turning Tremblant into a world-class destination resort, something that didn't even exist in the East.

When you're running a ski resort you really have to be innovative and creative. At Whistler we built a restaurant at the top of the mountain. In Tremblant we created excitement by building a ski trail down a cliff. It was literally a 40°+ slope! We called the ski run "Dynamite" and organized an extreme skiing event around it. Here in Breckenridge, we built North America's highest lift, the Imperial Express high-speed chairlift. Our ski patrollers have kept it running all except a handful of days since it opened. That's nothing short of miraculous since it sits at 12,840 feet above sea level and the winds in the bowl can hit over 80 miles per hour! We've gotten huge press from the new lift. At Keystone we created a buzz over how we "own the night" because we offer the only night skiing in Summit County. It's great for attracting a different demographic of skiers and riders (snowboarders).

I ski about 70 days per season. Most of the time I'm out on the mountain watching how people use the resort. I spend a majority of my time working the people issues. It's rare for us to have lift breakdowns, but I have jumped on a snowmobile to deliver pizzas to the guys changing a gearbox on a broken lift. It just shows them that I know what they're going through, they do important work and I appreciate their extra efforts.

We're a lean operation here. I have 16 direct reports between the two resorts and there are only five layers between me and the lowest lift operator. I've been COO of Breckenridge for 6 years and we've had zero turnover in the senior management team. Keystone is a different story. I changed a lot of the management staff and reduced the layers from nine to five. My philosophy is that I can help you with the issues but in an operation this big, I don't have time to teach you how to do your job. If you're smart you'll figure it out, but if you can't then you just won't make the cut. That said, we hire for attitude figuring it's hard to train someone to be nice to guests and coworkers. We almost never fire someone for lack of technical skills, it's always for lack of interpersonal skills.

We have an extraordinary team of leaders who make it happen—some are relatively new, others have been in the business for over 30 years. Like any team, there are highly skilled specialists and others who are generalists. In the end we manage people, regardless of their specialization and in turn provide great vacation experiences. It is very complicated but at the same time very simple.

We're open 22 weeks of the year and on the day before we open and the day after we close, you could fire a canon down Main Street in Breckenridge and hit no one. But then we suddenly ramp up and it's a 7-day–per-week job. The best part of my job is the creative design. Right now I'm trying to get the Town Council to embrace our ideas on how to reduce traffic up to and through Breckenridge. We've got a gondola plan that would run parallel to the river and bring people from Main Street up to their condos on Peaks 7 and 8. It's an ongoing discussion.

In the meantime, we're turning Breckenridge into one of the top destination resorts in North America. We had just under 1.5 million skier visits last year, and we will beat that handily this year.

A not-so-typical day:

8:00 AM	Meeting with the financial analysts from Breckenridge and Keystone. We go over last week's numbers (skier days, revenues, etc.).
10:30 AM	Met with our graphic arts group to discuss a presentation I'll be giving next week to the Breckenridge Resort Chamber. I'm to update the BRC on the gondola plan and the Peak 7 development. It's an ongoing process of educating the local politicians and business owners on where the resort stands competitively, why we need to build the new retail/residential area and why it's good for the Town of Breckenridge.

11:00 AM	Drive over Vail Pass to attend weekly Executive Committee meeting in Vail. This day was not typical as our CEO, Adam Aron, announced that he is resigning. Geez, what a day this will be!
2:00 PM	Head back to Breckenridge and fielded a number of calls on the way (in between all the cell phone dead zones).
2:10 PM	Call from Lift Operations. The Independence Chair is down again. They expect to have it up again within 5 minutes.
2:15 PM	Call from Keystone's director of human resources. We're going over some performance appraisals. One employee, a woman, is turning into a real star. She came up with a very creative solution to a guest complaint. We need to find a way to help her grow into a bigger position over there. Another employee is a bit of a problem. He just can't seem to take the initiative to get his job done properly. I think we'll have to tell him to find greener pastures elsewhere.
2:30 PM	Lucy, our VP of Marketing, called. She is getting numerous inquiries from the press about Adam's resignation [former CEO]. Also, she wants to set up a time to go over the new marketing campaign.
3:00 PM	Unscheduled meeting to brief all of my staff on Adam's resignation. We discussed Vail Resorts' plan for appointing a successor. I assured them that I did not want the job even if it was offered. (I would hate dealing with Wall Street.) Meanwhile we went over some other ongoing issues, like lift operations and the purchase of new "core strengthening" office chairs (they actually look like a medicine ball on wheels). You gotta be a bit of a ski fanatic to work here.
3:45 PM	Quick phone call to our head of vehicle maintenance. I checked some numbers with him on his budget for March—our biggest snow month. We have to make sure that the scheduled retirement of some of the older vehicles isn't done prematurely, and that they're maintained up to the end.
3:50 PM	I put in a call to Ernie Blake, mayor of the town of Breckenridge. I couldn't reach him, but I want to update him on Adam's resignation and set up a time to discuss our gondola plan.
3:55 PM	Eric Mamula, one of the town council members, called to ask a question about the Peak 7 residential development complex.
4:00 PM	Met with a new hire. He was brought on to research and assess some of the newer snow-making technologies. The resort spends too much money and energy in pushing air through pipes to make snow. There are groundbreaking new technologies and we need to be on the forefront of adopting them.
4:30 PM	Mountain operations called. They want to set up the snowmaking for the annual snow sculpting competition in a different place this year. We make the snow that creates the 12-foot-high blocks that the competing teams carve up. We'll try the new location. Last year the noise annoyed the neighbors over at Peak 8, so we'll move it to Peak 9.
4:35 PM	Read the recent batch of letters from guests. Many are highly complimentary especially over the new Imperial Bowl lift. A

couple of guests complained about the type of music that we play at the base of Beaver Run chair—too rude and not fit for children, they said. I get our communications director to look into it.

4:55 PM   Prepare for a meeting with our corporate attorneys to go over our risk management issues. The Colorado Skier Safety Act protects the resort from most lawsuits since it puts the burden of risk of injury squarely on the skier. Still, we review our risks and management plan.

5:00 PM   A journalist from the *Summit Daily News* calls about Adam's resignation. I told her to call Adam.

5:10 PM   Met with our director of mountain operations for Keystone and Lucy, VP marketing. We're planning something truly outrageous for President's weekend to really energize the guests there.

5:30 PM   A sales rep from one of the big ski manufacturers drops off a pair of new skis that they'll be marketing next season. One of the nice benefits of this job is to test drive skis from your office.

6:00 PM   I get a call from one of my neighbors who's writing some sort of business reference book. She wants to interview me to be part of the book.

6:10 PM   I spend the next 40 minutes going through e-mails. Most are asking about Adam's resignation.

7:00 PM   My wife and I head over to Keystone to have dinner with one of Vail Resorts' major shareholders. I think I know what the topic of discussion will be.

A DAY IN THE LIFE OF A CEO

Gail Plummer
Chief Executive Officer
Altair Global Relocation

I grew up in Austin, Texas. My dad was a heating and air conditioning mechanical contractor and he had his own business. It was a bit different back then because he had all unionized employees. I worked at his company during the summers and saw all the stress and risk that my dad took on as a result of owning his own company. I quickly decided that I never wanted to own my own company. So I went to the University of Texas at Austin and double majored in Spanish and history. I thought I wanted to teach Spanish, but after 2 years of doing it I was bored to death. After my first son was born, I went into real estate and discovered that I really liked the management side of the business. In 1981 I became the relocation director for a local real estate firm and shortly thereafter got a divorce. Three years later I married Bill, who worked for a relocation company. In 1989, Bill and I joined forces and started our own relocation company, now named Altair Global Relocation. Ironically, I think that the experience of working at my dad's company really helped me understand management and prepared me for entrepreneurship.

So what does a relocation company do? We move transferring employees and their families for our corporate clients. We do everything to make the experience as painless as possible. Imagine that you're an employee at a big multinational company. You've been offered a fantastic promotion into a really exciting new position with the company, but it means that you have to move to Indonesia. Your spouse has a high-powered job at another company and this poses a big problem. Will your spouse move too? And what about your kids? What kind of schools are available in Indonesia? And what do you do with Ollie, the dog? Can you take him too? Who will take care of your mother who has the early stages of Alzheimer's disease? Do you sell your house or rent it out? All of these questions and more can cause huge stress to an employee and the family. We come in to help answer these questions and ease the stress. We'll get appraisals on your house, help you sell or rent it, we'll organize the moving company on both ends of the move, we'll help find a new house, schools, language lessons, the best place to shop, and even counselors to help the family deal with the cultural and family issues. We also give you information on tax laws, immigration issues, visas, and cost of living calculations. We can even provide an analysis of the best headquarters or expansion cities for the company and its workforce.

In the old days a company used to just give the employee a check and say, "Here, this should cover your move. See you in Singapore next week." But that money was taxable to the employee! So unless the company "grossed up" the check (by including the amount of income taxes that the employee would have to pay) it was unfair to the employee, in many ways. On the other hand, if the company pays a third party like us to do all the logistics and detail work of the move, then it's a business expense that the company can legitimately write off on its tax returns. In addition, we have economies of scale and get low negotiated rates with many third party vendors (banks, moving companies, real estate agents, and so on) so we can provide the services for much less than an employee could buy on her or his own.

Ours is a people-oriented business. Moving is the number two stress factor in a person's life (after the death of a loved one and just ahead of divorce). Moving means uprooting yourself from all that's familiar—friends, family, favorite places, favorite restaurants, sports events, and so forth—and adapting to many new things in an unfamiliar location. When we help employees we have to be part efficiency engineer and part trusted advisor. We assign a person to each employee that we're relocating and make sure that we understand his or her needs and address them in a timely and sensitive fashion. That said, we adapt our methods to whatever the culture of the client organization is. Some clients (and their employees) like to be very hands-on and search for information on the Internet. Others want to be guided and have their hand held during the whole process.

As for our own employees, we look for people who can fill a number of roles. They have to be able to switch their train of thought in an instant from one client to the next. They have to be detail-oriented, but not detail-possessed. They have to be compassionate as well as good negotiators. And there's a lot of stress and time pressure to get things done right the first time. Over half, about two-thirds, of our own employees are women. We hire people for skills, experience, and attitude. In our business it's incredibly important to make sure that those employees who interact with clients—even the receptionist—have very good people skills. We hire from our competitors and from related service-oriented industries. We're usually able to get the cream of the crop because we offer a career path and training for employees who want to advance themselves. Some key skills are necessary in this business and experience counts for a lot. Sure, we'd love to be able to hire the most congenial employees who have years of good experience in what we do, but that's the rare find. If we have to choose between an individual with great skills who is extremely arrogant, or someone who will fit our culture but has no skills, we'll always hire for cultural fit. We pride ourselves on hiring really good people and letting them run with the ball. I guess it's working because our employee turnover is exceptionally low.

One of the reasons our company is so successful is our positive, team-oriented, "can-do" attitude. There's no negativity here. Our employees are loyal to each other and to the company. I think that's why clients hire us. I believe very strongly in positive reinforcement and rewarding people for a job well done. I recognize people through pay, private thanks, and public thanks. Every quarter we host a breakfast buffet at the country club. It's kind of the "state of the company" meeting for all employees. I always end the meeting with an opportunity for people to publicly say thank-you and recognize their coworkers. It's really touching to hear some of the things people say. On one occasion, one of our employees had everyone in tears when he thanked them for backing him up during the 3 months he was hospitalized. I let it go for as long as it takes. The thank-you session usually runs about 15–20 minutes, but I think the record was 45 minutes long! It's always an uplifting way to close before everyone heads back to work.

My primary job as CEO is to lead the strategy of the company and the execution of the strategy. We're currently working with a couple of partners, one in London and the other in Hong Kong, who will enable us to have a truly seamless and global reach. In this manner, we can be the single point of contact for our clients who have employees moving anywhere in the world. We're also investing heavily in technology. We have an Internet-based system that allows our clients to track, in real time, what is happening with any of their employee's relocation process. We've already won some big awards for this system.

My secondary job is to be the steward of the culture and values. Most of my day is spent communicating—by phone, e-mail, voicemail, in person, and in "spirit." Everything I do has an underlying message to further our motto: "Aim High, Play it Straight and Make it Fun." I spend a lot of time on the staffing side of our business. I believe that you send a message to everyone with the kind of people we hire. So I review every open position with the human resources manager. I interview every senior manager that we hire. I also approve every advertising program that we do because, again, it sends a message about the kind of company we are. I talk to clients to find out how we're doing. I travel often to our other two offices in Connecticut and California. I make sure that I'm in touch with the pulse of the company.

But even with all of those efforts, I still find that I have to spend time getting to know our employees. When the company was only 20 people, it was easy. You knew everyone, their spouses, kids, and outside hobbies. But now with 150 employees, you can't know everyone. So I started a luncheon series called "Twelve at twelve." I take 12 people, somewhat at random, and invite them to a catered lunch in our conference room. We make sure that we get a cross-section of people from different departments and tenure in the company (veterans and new hires). I usually make a couple of key points about the company and then I open the discussion up to questions. I encourage people to ask anything they want. It's a great way to get to know people, and they even learn about each other too.

My third job as CEO is to develop and grow people. I try to build their self-confidence, skills, and give them a sense of where they fit in the company.

All of our managers have to stack rank everyone in their department. But we don't force them to fire the bottom 10 percent. Sometimes you just need to give people some additional training and the tools to improve themselves. On the other hand, if it's clear that someone won't make it here, we tell him or her early on that they don't fit. In the long run you're doing them a favor by letting them go. It costs a lot to have someone fail. We try to avoid it by being very careful about who we hire in the first place.

It's funny, I never thought I'd be a CEO, let alone own a company! We're a privately held corporation and I own 56 percent of the stock. Bill and our kids own the rest, so I don't have a boss. The buck really does stop here. We're the largest woman-owned relocation company in the world. Now that I'm in this position, I can see some key skills that have served me well. I'm very competitive, but I also think the following attributes are necessary to be successful:

- The drive and ambition to want to win.
- An ability to lead people. You have to inspire loyalty and trust; people ultimately have to want to work for you. But you have to be deserving of that loyalty.
- You have to be visible.
- A desire to build people—thank them, grow them, nurture them, and reward them.
- An ability to make the tough decisions. You have to look out for what is best for the company as a whole without sacrificing something for one person.

What's the downside of this job? The demands on my time are the toughest. It can be difficult to stay focused with all the interruptions. And I think women by their nature, try to be all things to all people. But I love leading people! I lead through inspiration and motivation. I try to bring out the best in people and inspire them to do the best they can. I love this business because you can really think outside the box. And this is a great job because I can really make a difference in so many peoples' lives.

A typical day:

8:00 AM	I spend the first hour of my day going over e-mail with my office door shut. I pride myself on having an open door policy, but it can be a trap. Sometimes you just never get anything done! So now I schedule myself for an hour of private time with no interruptions. I find that I'm actually more productive throughout the day.
9:00 AM	Senior management meeting with my two direct reports, the chief operating officer (responsible for HR, IT, domestic and international operations) and the chief development officer (responsible for new business, new products, and client communications). We discuss the status of our discussions with our new Hong Kong partner. We also talk about whether we want to expand our California office now that we won a major contract with a big movie production studio.
10:00 AM	On the way back to my office from the meeting, I stop by Shirley's desk. She's been swamped with a particularly tough

	move assignment for a big food retailer. I tell her to take tomorrow off. She protests, but I tell her that we'll cover for her. She's courting burnout if she doesn't take some time off.
10:15 AM	One of our top sales people, Mitch, stops in with the head of our IT department. A customer told Mitch about some additional features they'd like to see on our web-based reporting system. Mitch has checked it out with IT, but it will cost more than this quarter's IT budget can handle, so they need my approval to pursue it. Seems like a no-brainer to go ahead with it.
10:45 AM	I put in a call to a colleague on the Alzheimer's Association of Dallas. I'm on the board and we're organizing a big fundraiser to take place a month from now. He and I discuss some of the details of the event.
11:10 AM	My cell phone rings. It's my daughter. She's graduating from medical school at the end of the month and wanted to find out about Bill and my dinner plans for that evening.
11:15 AM	Mitch stops by again, this time with our controller. We have a young woman in the accounting department who hasn't been happy and her work has suffered for it. But apparently she mentioned to Mitch that she has always wanted to try sales. Mitch thinks she'd be a great fit and besides, she has too much of a sense of humor to be an accountant.
11:30 AM	The head of HR stops by with a candidate for a job in our sales organization. I chat with him for a while. He seems like a bright and outgoing fellow, but I'll have to check with others to get their "read" on whether they think he'll fit here.
12:00 PM	Lunch with Bill, our "Chairman Emeritus." He's semi-retired now, but he stops in occasionally to meet with our finance and legal folks.
12:40 PM	I meet with our legal folks. They've done an analysis of some new laws pertaining to real estate in several states.
1:00 PM	Our marketing director stops in. She's got the storyboard for a new advertisement that our agency proposed. She wants to run it by me before they proceed into production.
1:00 PM	I compose an "e-mail blast" to everyone in the company. It's about our joint partnership agreement with the London relocation company. I tell them to stay tuned for details on some of the new products and services they're offering and how we can leverage those in our shop.
1:30 PM	The head of sales calls me. He wants to know if I would have time next week to meet with a client they've been courting. Every once in a while they trot me out to help make the sale. I think I can stop at the company's New York headquarters on my way to a business conference in Orlando.
1:45 PM	One of our senior project managers calls me. She's got a particularly sticky situation with one of our client's employees. The employee is being transferred to Dubai, but his wife all of a sudden refuses to go. It's put a real strain on their marriage, and of course, we get dragged into it. Our project manager has several ideas on how to handle the situation and wants to validate them with me.

2:00 PM	On the way to get a cup of coffee, I stop by our travel department. I wanted to find out what kind of arrangements they've made for my trip to Orlando next week. I tell them to route me through New York.
2:15 PM	Craig, our contractor on our mountain house, calls. They've discovered a water leak that has damaged the flooring. Luckily the repairs are all under warranty, but what a major inconvenience this is.
2:30 PM	I attend a meeting with some of our senior project managers. We're strategizing how to staff the new movie studio account. The studio needs to move 40 animation artists (cartoonists) from several parts of Asia into Singapore. We don't yet know if this is to be a permanent move or just temporary. This particular account will be different in many ways. We'll be helping the studio relocate crews for temporary assignments while they film movies on location. It's like building an entire temporary city wherever they go. Funny how we have a lot of people volunteering to work on this project.... I think they're hoping to meet Harrison Ford.
3:30 PM	A friend of mine calls. She just got hired by a major international oil company and is in charge of all of their employee relocations. She and I strategize on when I can get to Houston to try to get the company's business.
4:00 PM	I wander around the halls and stick my head in people's offices. It's part of my checking in to see how things are going. It's also a great way to find out what people are working on.
5:15 PM	I put in a call to the manager of our "Client Solution Center." She had left me a message about a company who wants to have us consult with them on a proposed move from San Francisco to Colorado Springs. We discuss the approach we'll take and the fee scale.
5:30 PM	I'm off to a planning meeting for another charity I support. I'm on the executive committee for the Dallas Summer Musicals. These are great ways to be involved in the community and it's also helped us win some business.
7:00 PM	I meet Bill to host a dinner for a client who's here in town. We're taking the senior management team to The French Room—one of the best restaurants in Dallas. We want to show our appreciation to them and thank them for their business.
9:30 PM	Back at home I unload my briefcase. As usual, I've brought home more work than I can possibly finish tonight. No matter, I've got an hour of useful and uninterrupted reading time. It's a good way to catch up on industry information, memos, and other internal happenings in the company.
10:30 PM	Time to call it a day. I'm definitely not a workaholic and I really value my sleep. It's how I keep myself charged up all day.

Jobs in Leadership

Unless you are starting your own company, like Joey and his lemonade stand, leadership is not a job that you really apply for. The good news is that leadership jobs are available in every industry in the world and at many levels. The best way to become a leader is to study other leaders and learn what has made them successful. Why do other people want to follow them? Most leaders are very intelligent, so it's also a good idea to become smart and very talented at something (engineering, chemistry, accounting, finance, marketing, and so forth). And because a big component of leadership is managing people, it helps if you're a good communicator (and listener) and like to motivate and work with people.

SUMMARY

Good leadership is a key factor in any successful business. There are many types of leadership styles, and the best leaders will use a combination of styles depending on the particular situation. Leaders have five main jobs:

- Set the strategy, monitor its execution, and promote the organization's culture and values.
- Inspire their followers to be the best they can be for the good of the organization.
- Manage the often conflicting demands of stakeholders (employees, owners, customers, vendors, and the community).
- Balance the realities of the external environment with what is best for the organization and its future.
- Develop other leaders inside the organization.

History has shown that a variety of good, bad, and truly atrocious leaders can get to the top of an organization. Thankfully, boards of directors today have much less tolerance for the absolutely horrid leaders.

5

Finance and Accounting

Capital is the world's most cowardly commodity. It cuts and runs at the barest jiggle.

—a vice president at the bank, Continental Illinois

CEOs don't like to hear a lot of laughter coming from their accounting departments.

—Bob Newhart, comedian and actor

[Creative accounting practices] gave rise to the quip, "A balance sheet is very much like a bikini bathing suit. What it reveals is interesting, what it conceals is vital."

—Abraham J. Briloff, author of *Unaccountable Accounting*

WHAT IS FINANCE?

Finance is the provision of capital (money) when and where it's needed. It is also the act of managing tangible assets (machinery, equipment, factories, offices), intangible assets (trademarks, patents, technical expertise, brands), debt, and capital budgets. The finance department in a big company usually keeps track of the company's money and makes sure that the CEO has enough to pay salaries, fund operating budgets, and invest new capital in large, long-term investment projects. That's the internally-focused part of the job. The externally-focused part of the finance department's job is to interact with the capital markets. These markets include Wall Street (the New York Stock Exchange and NASDAQ) and other international financial exchanges, such as the Chicago Board of Trade and the London Stock Exchange, where the company raises money by selling pieces of paper called stocks, bonds, and fancy derivatives.

WHY IS FINANCE IMPORTANT?

Without someone minding the money, the money might easily walk out the door. The finance manager will often speak with external analysts to answer their questions about the details of a company's financial statement, forecasts for future growth (called "guidance"), and plans for additional funding. If a company is considering buying another company (called a merger or acquisition) the finance department usually has the job of calculating the value of each company and determining the combination of stock, debt, and cash that will go toward the final purchase terms. If a company has a pension fund (fewer companies do these days), the finance department along with the treasury function must decide the best place to invest the pension assets as well as the annual contribution requirements to the fund.

The finance department has an additional task on its plate as a result of the Sarbanes-Oxley Act of 2002. The act specifies an enormous number of new rules that every publicly-traded company in the United States must follow, or else the officers of the company risk jail time. Many of the rules have to do with financial reporting requirements and regulatory compliance issues. The finance department is usually responsible for making sure the rules are followed.

And finally, since the U.S. government likes to tweak the tax code every couple of years, the finance department, along with the accounting function, has to fully understand the implications of any new rules, and make sure that the company complies with them, and take advantage of any opportunities for tax savings.

Money has a cost—it's called the interest rate. Whether a company is actually borrowing money from a bank or it uses its own cash flow to finance its operations, the cost of the money is always important. The finance department minds the money and tries to ensure that the company is making the best possible use of the money to which it has access.

A "Zero Interest" Islamic Loan

Say you want to buy a house. The house costs $200,000. So you go to your friendly neighborhood Islamic bank and ask for help in buying the house. The bank agrees to help you. So it buys the house in its own name and agrees to sell it to you at the price of $300,000 after you have paid monthly installments of $2,500 over the next 10 years.

Although the bank didn't charge any "interest" on the loan, it found a way to gain income for the time value of the money it has loaned. Do you think that this is interest or not?

The Concept of Interest

A dollar today is worth more than a dollar tomorrow. Unless you are operating in a strict Islamic society under Shariah Law, which bans the collection of interest, most people, businesses, and governments must pay interest in order to use cash. Interest is the cost of rent to use money over time. The amount of that rent varies with the relative scarcity of capital, current interest rate, and credit worthiness of the borrower. If you go to a bank and borrow $100 with a promise to pay it back in exactly 1 year, the bank will charge an interest rate, usually stated as an annual number. Let's say that the bank will charge you 8 percent per year. This means that you will have to pay $108 to the bank 1 year from now. (You'll pay the $100 principal that you borrowed plus an additional

8% or $8.) This is an example of a simple interest rate calculation and the mathematical formula looks like this:

$$P_n = P_0 (1 + nr)$$

Therefore, a simple interest loan schedule over 5 years would look like this:

	Starting balance	Interest calculation	Ending balance
Year 1:	$100.00	$100.00 (1 + (1 × 0.08)	$108.00
Year 2:	$108.00	$100.00 (1 + (2 × 0.08)	$116.00
Year 3:	$116.00	$100.00 (1 + (3 × 0.08)	$124.00
Year 4:	$124.00	$100.00 (1 + (4 × 0.08)	$132.00
Year 5:	$132.00	$100.00 (1 + (5 × 0.08)	$140.00

Notice that the interest is always the same each year; namely $8.00, because the interest is only charged on the original principal amount of $100.

But a simple interest rate loan is hard to find these days. More often you will pay compound interest, where the interest is charged on the principal and on the accrued interest (that is, interest that is charged, but not yet paid). The mathematical formula for calculating compound interest looks like this:

$$P_n = P_0 (1 + r)^n$$

A compound interest loan schedule over 5 years would look like this:

	Starting balance	Interest calculation	Ending balance
Year 1:	$100.00	$100.00 (1 + 0.08)^1	108.00
Year 2:	$108.00	$100.00 (1 + 0.08)^2	$116.64
Year 3:	$116.64	$100.00 (1 + 0.08)^3	$125.97
Year 4:	$125.97	$100.00 (1 + 0.08)^4	$136.05
Year 5:	$136.05	$100.00 (1 + 0.08)^5	$146.93

Now if you were a banker, which type of interest would you rather receive? If you're a borrower, which type of interest would you rather pay? In the compound interest scenario the banker earns $6.93 more than in the simple interest scenario. One other point about the formula and compounding that is worth noting: take a look at the effect of the "n" or time periods. Bankers realized early on that if they calculate the compound interest over shorter and more frequent periods of time, they get even more money! So a typical mortgage loan on a house uses monthly calculations rather than the annual time periods in the examples above. In the monthly scenario, you have to adjust the interest rate to reflect a monthly rather than an annual rate. Therefore, the "i" in our equation would be 0.0067, which is 0.08 divided by 12, and the final interest, compounded monthly over 5 years (60 months) would be $49.38. Here's the equation:

$$\$100.00(1 + 0.0067)^{60} = \$149.38$$

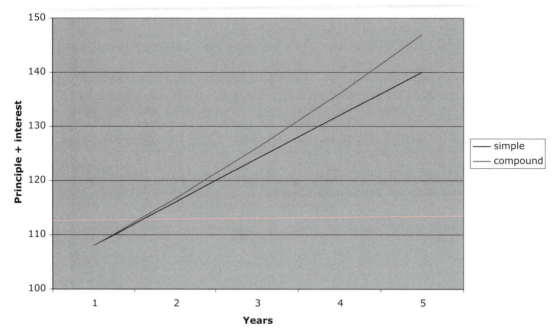

Figure 5.1. Simple versus compound interest.

Compound interest has one other difference to simple interest. It grows at an exponential rate over time (this is what the interest raised to the power of "n" accomplishes). If we plot the growth of principle over time and compare the effects of simple versus compound interest the graphs would look as shown in Figure 5.1.

Notice that the simple interest scale is linear (a straight line) while the compound interest is curved and grows at a faster rate (that is, the slope of the line increases) as time increases. Now you know why banks like longer term loans (to good borrowers) and why savings accounts get bigger over time (when left undisturbed).

Present Value and Future Value

The loan interest schedules shown in the section above are in fact, the same interest schedules you would earn if you put $100 into a savings account that paid 8 percent interest each year. What we have just shown is the concept of future value. That is, the future value of $100 today *after* 5 years of earning 8 percent interest is $146.93. Or, stated another way, the present value of $146.93 5 years *from now* at 8 percent interest is $100.00. Present value is the reciprocal of the compound interest equation. A present value equation looks like this:

$$P_0 = P_n \div (1 + r)^n$$

Present value and future value are very important concepts in finance. Present value gives you a way to compare apples to apples when looking at different types of investments that might have different interest rates and pay-out periods. A typical finance department decision is how to invest capital. For example, say a company needs $150,000 at the end of 2 years to buy out a partner's interest in a particular technology. How much would the CFO have to deposit in an account that pays 7 percent interest in order to have that money when she needs it? Stated another way: what is the present value of $150,000 invested at 7 percent 2 years from now?

Pn = Principle value at the end of n time periods.
P₀ = Principle at the begining.
n = number of time periods.
t = interest rate (expressed as a decimal)

$$\$150,000 \div (1 + 0.07)^2 = \$131,015.81$$

The answer, $131,015.81, is the amount that the CFO has to put aside today in order to have $150,000 2 years from now.

Things get a little more complex when we're looking at multiple cash flows over time. Let's say that Joey is looking to expand his snowboard shop to give him more production capacity. He's got two options. The first is to build an addition to his existing shop, which would entail $75,000 in building costs, renegotiating his lease to expand the space, and would give him 150 square feet of additional space, or roughly two workstations. He figures that he can increase his net income by $10,000 in year 2 and $30,000 in year 5. The second option is to build an entirely new facility three blocks away on a vacant lot that's for sale. The cost of land and building would be $475,000 and would net him about 1,875 square feet of space, which could be set up more efficiently than his current manufacturing operation. He figures that production would increase slowly in the first couple of years and as they gain more orders and experienced machining people, but later he could use expansion space to generate about $300,000 in additional income by year 5. The formula to calculate the present value of the future cash flows for both of these scenarios is shown in the following mathematical equation:

$$PV = \frac{C_1}{1 + r_1} + \frac{C_2}{(1 + r_2)^2} + \frac{C_3}{(1 + r_3)^3} + \frac{C_4}{(1 + r_4)^4} + \frac{C_5}{(1 + r_5)^5}$$

You'll see this written in shorthand like this:

$$PV = \sum \frac{C_t}{(1 + r_t)}$$

It means that the present value is the sum of each cash flow discounted by 1 plus the cash flow's associated interest rate. This formula for present value is also called a discounted cash flow formula and it's used extensively in valuing assets.

The present value formula looks complicated, and in the old days it meant crunching a lot of numbers to get at the answer. Then people realized that many of these equations repeated themselves in different scenarios so they published present value rate tables. (See http://www.exinfm.com/excel%20files/pv_fv.rtf to download a table.) In these tables, you look up the number of years on one axis and the interest rate on the other to get a multiplier for your cash flow. Nowadays you can put the numbers into a spreadsheet and program the

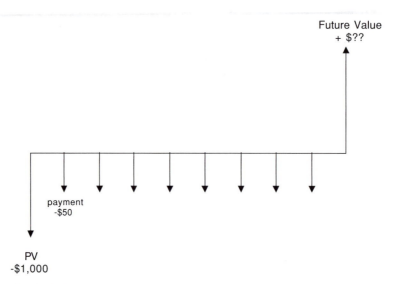

Figure 5.2. Schematic diagram of positive and negative cash flows.

appropriate formula to calculate the numbers for you. Or you can buy a financial calculator that will also figure out the answer.

There are two important points to make regarding present value calculations. The first is to fully understand the cash flows and the interest rates and make sure that the interest rate time period matches that of the cash flow. That is, if you are using monthly cash flows, make sure that the interest rate in your formula is expressed as a monthly figure. The second point is to make sure that the sign (positive or negative) is consistent for each type of cash flow. Cash coming in is positive and cash going out is negative as shown schematically in Figure 5.2.

Let's go back to Joey's snowboard facility expansion options. Figure 5.3 shows what the two options look like from a cash flow perspective:

Option A

	capital cost	additional rent	increase in net income
Year 1	(75,000)	(12,000)	(12,000)
Year 2		(12,000)	10,000
Year 3		(12,000)	20,000
Year 4		(12,000)	25,000
Year 5		(12,000)	30,000
		Net Present Value:	($24,940)

Option B

	capital cost	rent	increase in net income
Year 1	(475,000)	-	-
Year 2			50,000
Year 3			125,000
Year 4			225,000
Year 5			300,000
		Net Present Value:	$17,982

Figure 5.3. Joey's Snowboard Shop expansion options.

In each scenario we've shown the net present value, which is the present value of all the cash flows minus the initial investment. As you can see, Option B (building a new facility) has a positive net present value, meaning that this is a better investment than Option A (expanding the existing facility). The incremental increase in cash flow from building a bigger building is a sounder choice, if the assumptions that went into these cash flow projections are correct. Joey has assumed that business would continue at the same pace it has in the past. In each calculation he used the same discount rate of 9 percent per year. One could argue that using the same discount rate for each scenario is not right, since building a new facility is a larger investment of capital up front and poses more risk. Thus a higher discount factor makes more sense. Assessing risk is one of the primary domains of finance, and it's the topic of much debate on exactly how to evaluate risk.

Risk

One of the key factors in finance is the concept of risk. Oddly enough, very few scholars have attempted to actually define risk. One definition is "Risk is exposure to a proposition of which one is uncertain. Suppose a man leaps from an airplane without a parachute. If he is certain to die, he faces no risk. Risk requires both exposure *and* uncertainty."[1]

In the world of finance, risk is often used to describe unexpected variability (both positive and negative) of financial returns on assets. In other words, say that you invest $100 in the stock of Joey's Snowboard Shop and he has a particularly bad year, so the value of your investment drops to $80. The next year there is a record amount of snow, Joey sells twice as many snowboards as the year before, and your stock is now worth $140. If the stock had traditionally risen by 7 percent each year, you would *expect* to average a 7 percent annual increase in your investment. However, as all investment advertisements say, "past performance is no predictor of future performance." The volatility of your investment in Joey's Snowboard Shop would be called highly risky, since it dropped 20 percent in year one and increased 75 percent in year 2.

There are a number of other types of risk that finance professionals must deal with. The following table outlines them briefly.

Market risk	A normal and increasing stock market suddenly takes a turn for the worse dragging all stocks with it. This is called a bear market (20–35 % drop in values)
Interest-rate risk	An investor who is counting on a certain predictable interest rate (such as when investing in bonds) faces interest rate risk if the rates change radically
Currency risk	Large companies often face currency risk if they do business in foreign countries and their investments in those countries are in the local currency (such as a capital asset like a factory). If that country devalues their currency by half, the company has just lost half of the value of its investment. Many oil-rich countries faced a severe decline in revenue when the U.S. dollar fell relative to other foreign currencies, thus causing the value of exported oil (always sold in dollars) to drop

Asset-class risk	Investors (and CFOs) have three main asset types to choose from: stocks, bonds, and cash. If an investor has too much money allocated to one type and has not diversified adequately into the others, the risk is that a market correction (drop) can wipe out a large percentage of the investor's net worth
Management risk	This is the case of putting your money into a mutual fund that is run by an idiot
Sector risk	Sector risk is similar to asset class risk but it involves putting all of your nest egg into one basket, such as stocks in gold or utility companies. A sector refers to a particular industry type (utilities, consumer goods, gold, technology, health care, etc.)
Country risk	Your brother comes to you with the "investment of the century" in Indonesian telecom stocks. This is a country risk in addition to a sector risk
Credit risk	Your cousin Vinny, who has landed in jail several times for check forgery, asks you for a loan. You perceive him to be a credit risk
Tax-rate risk	Several companies base many of their investment decisions on tax benefits they can gain. The risk is that the government could change the tax code, making the investments worth less

Saving, Spending, Borrowing, and Investing

The finance department's job is to mind the money. That means making sure that the company has enough money to fund its daily operations (salaries, raw materials, rent, electricity, etc.) as well as additional expenses that the company has committed to fund (plant or geographical expansions, bonuses, the annual sales conference, etc.). Another part of the finance department's job includes investing money that the company earns on selling products and services. Since money is more valuable when it's working (earning interest) the finance department's job is to look for the highest paying place to put the firm's money to work. Many banks offer savings accounts and certificates of deposit that allow you to "park" your money with the bank for, say 3 months, while the bank uses your money. At the end of 3 months, you'll get your original money back plus some additional money called interest. The other side of investing is that it can be risky. That is, in putting your money to work, you expect to receive all of your money back at the end of the term. But what if the bank you put your money into is now bankrupt? There is a risk that you won't get all of your original money back. Generally speaking, the higher the interest rate, the higher the investment risk. Today the Federal Deposit Insurance Corporation insures most bank depositors (up to $100,000) so the risk of losing your money in a bank is low—and so are the interest rates that banks pay. But a chief financial officer or treasurer of a corporation has many other options when deciding where to put the company's money to work. Here are some possibilities:

- Invest the money in stocks, bonds, derivatives, hedge funds,
- Lend the money to another company and earn interest on it, or
- Buy capital assets and put the money back into the company's operations.

And finally, if the company doesn't have the cash flow to meet its immediate needs, the finance department has to find more money. It can do this in three ways: issue stock to sell to outside investors, issue bonds, or borrow money from a bank or other institution.

The "Quants"

Quantitative analysts, "Quants," are people who use computers to analyze historical and current data about stocks, bonds, currencies, and anything else that has a number value in order to spot trends, predict future values, and devise sophisticated arbitrage opportunities for their firm. The practice is often called financial engineering, quantitative finance, or technical analysis. Generally quants work for the big Wall Street investment banking houses like Goldman Sachs, Merrill Lynch, and ChaseMorgan and are paid heaps of money for their work. Quants usually have Ph.D.s in mathematics, engineering, or computer science. They must thoroughly understand complex financial concepts (Black-Scholes, risk-assessment formulas, options, futures, bonds, derivatives, etc.). They also have to be very skilled in statistics, stochastics, calculus, algebra, as well as computer programming (C++).

> Quants tend to be bachelors (few are women) who live in apartments as messy as the room they left in grade school. Many of them drink hard after hours, mostly with fellow workers. They mate, if that's the word, mostly on one-night stands.
>
> —Steve Barnett, Ph.D. in anthropology, quoted in *Time*, April 11, 1994.

So what do these quants actually do? They dream up all kinds of derivatives, which are securities whose underlying value comes—or derives—from a bet on the future value of something else (stocks, bonds, interest rates, Mexican copper, Congolese diamonds, etc.). Derivatives help companies manage risk. If, for example, an airline, like Southwest, believes that the price of jet fuel will be higher 6 months from now, Southwest can purchase an oil futures contract. In this case, Southwest buys oil for the next 6 months at today's prices. This sounds great, right? But what if the price of jet fuel actually drops in 6 months? Southwest has now paid more money for jet fuel than it needed to. All derivative contracts are bets on something, and zero-sum games; there is a winner and a loser. In the mid-1990s many people lost money on a certain type of derivative called an interest-only strip. These pay interest that comes from a basket of government-backed mortgages. Essentially, a fund manager can buy just the interest part of a mortgage and someone else can buy the underlying value of the mortgage principal (the principal that's been "stripped" of its interest payments). The bet in this case is that the interest being paid by homeowners on the pool of mortgages will continue to be higher than the actual market interest rate. As long as interest rates don't rise, the interest-only strips will be good performers. The trouble is, that some derivatives can get amazingly complex and some mutual funds either didn't fully comprehend what they were selling or chose to keep their customers in the dark. Piper Jaffray's Institutional Government fund lost nearly 25 percent of its value in 1994 as half of the assets were in "government-backed securities," namely interest-only strips when market interest rates rose.

WHAT IS ACCOUNTING?

Accounting is the function of gathering, measuring, reporting, and analyzing quantitative and financial information about a particular economic activity,

Table 5.1. Financial versus managerial accounting

	Financial accounting	Managerial accounting
Who gets the information?	External stakeholders (investors, creditors, regulators, government entities)	Internal employees (managers, workers, executives)
Why is it provided?	To summarize current status of the business based on past performance (and to allow comparisons with other companies where necessary)	To give managers useful and current information about the operating performance of the business; to help individual operating units/departments execute the business strategy
What's the timeline?	Historical	Current and future
Is it regulated?	Yes, by FASB, GAAP, other government authorities	No. No rules other than basic mathematics
What kind of information is it?	Financial statements (Income statement, balance sheet, statement of working capital, etc.)	Whatever you want... (Just-in-time system cost/benefit analysis, productivity of a particular machine, customer profitability, department profitability, etc.)
What is the focus/unit of discussion?	The whole company	Whatever piece you want to analyze

Source: Adapted from "Management Accounting," 2nd ed., 1997.

usually a business. Some practitioners also distinguish between two types of accounting: managerial and financial. Financial accounting is the traditional accounting information that a business needs to present to its bankers, investors, the government, and other people *outside* the company. Management accounting, in contrast, is quantitative information that is useful to people *inside* the company to help them make better decisions. Financial accounting is regulated by the FASB (Financial Accounting Standards Board) in the United States and all accountants must follow generally accepted accounting principles (GAAP). In contrast, there is no official body or rules on how managerial accounting must be practiced. Financial accounting reports information about traditional financial measures (income, expenses, debt, assets, etc.) and usually on the entire corporation or business. Managerial accounting reports information that managers want to know, like how much is this particular department costing me and does it make any money? Or how profitable is a particular customer to the company? These questions look at both financial and nonfinancial data like how many hours do our employees spend on a particular task (hand-holding that customer when the order doesn't arrive on time). Table 5.1 summarizes the differences between financial and managerial accounting.

In addition, a distinction is often made between public accounting and private accounting. A public accountant is someone who works for anyone (the public) and offers her services for a fee. H&R Block, the tax return specialists, are public accountants. So are the "Big Four" accounting firms: PricewaterhouseCoopers, KPMG, Deloitte Touche Tohmatsu, and Ernst & Young. In contrast, a private accountant works for an individual firm. Big companies, like General Electric and Wal-Mart, have lots of accountants working for them, but all of them are private accountants. Many of the services provided by public and private accountants overlap. They are listed and described in Table 5.2.

FINANCIAL STATEMENTS

Financial statements are the end product of the financial accounting function. Most businesses need some sort of financial statements in order to obtain credit, contract with suppliers, attract investors, and develop partnerships with key customers. Financial statements answer questions like: How much money does the company owe? What kind of assets does the company own? Is the company profitable? Does it have too much inventory on hand? What is the annual turnover (revenue) of the company?

Why Are Financial Statements Important?

Some people think that numbers are boring. But numbers, especially on financial statements, can tell some very interesting stories if you take the time to read them. Even if a business isn't required by someone else to produce a financial statement (Joey's Lemonade Stand, for example) financial statements are extremely important because they paint a picture of how the business is doing. It's crucial to be able to understand all the components that go into a financial statement and their effect on "the bottom line" or net profit. If you understand how, for example, excess inventory or high costs of materials reduce the resources that the business has to use for other things then you are a step ahead.

The following sections will describe the financial statements that are most often used in business.

The Balance Sheet

The balance sheet, also called a position statement, is a snapshot of a company at the close of business on a particular date. The balance sheet has three main sections, the *assets* of the business, its *liabilities*, and the *owner's (or owners') equity*. Assets are things (cash, property, stuff, the warm fuzzy feeling that comes from a good brand, etc.) that the *company owns* and can use in the course of doing business. Liabilities are things that the *company owes* to someone else (a bank loan, a promise to pay a supplier for goods delivered, taxes due but not yet paid, etc.). Liabilities are also seen as a claim on the assets of the company. Owner's equity is a claim on the assets of the company by the people who own shares. Owner's equity is the difference between assets and liabilities, or what's left over when the company pays off all its debt.

$$\text{Assets} = \text{Liabilities} + \text{Owners' Equity}$$

In a balance sheet, assets must equal the total of liabilities plus owner's equity. That's why it's called a "balance sheet." Generally speaking, a business hopes to have more assets than liabilities. If the opposite is true (more liabilities than assets) the company is in a precarious situation and is probably facing bankruptcy.

Table 5.2. Public versus private accounting services

	Public accounting		Private accounting
Common names	Certified public accountant—CPA (United States) Chartered accountant (the United Kingdom and Commonwealth countries) Certified practicing accountant (Australia) Certified general accountant (Canada)	Common names	Certified internal auditor (United States)
Auditing	An audit is an outside, objective, and unbiased evaluation of an organization, company, system, or process. Usually the public auditor will produce a report or letter stating that whatever was examined conforms to generally accepted accounting principles or other certifying bodies.	Internal auditing	Internal auditors usually perform some of the same tasks as external auditors. The idea is to make sure that the company is following established procedures and following management's policies.
Tax services	Public accountants will help a person or corporation prepare and file their quarterly and annual tax returns. This service can often include advice on how to reduce your tax liability in the future	General accounting Budgeting	Private accountants will record transactions and prepare reports for internal management, creditors, or government agencies. Budgeting involves tracking forecasted revenues and expenses against actual numbers
Management advisory	Before the days of the accounting scandals (2002), which led to the demise of Arthur Anderson, many of the Big Five accounting firms offered management consulting services. Now most of those firms have clearly separated (or eliminated) the advisory services.	Cost accounting Project accounting Management accounting	These services are generally internal to the organization and involve tracking and analyzing costs and other factors to provide reports that are useful to managers and executives inside the company.

Joey's Snowboard Shop
Balance Sheet – June 30, 2006

ASSETS			LIABILITIES		
Current Assets			Current liabilities		
Cash			Accounts payable		1,500
Checking	2,500		Payroll		2,977
Savings	3,500		Credit card – VISA		220
Total Cash	6,000		State sales tax		1,370
			Total current liabilities		6,067
Accounts receivable	7,500				
			Long term liabilities		
Tools & equipment	12,000		Loan on truck		12,500
Inventory – work in progress	13,500		Bank of Breckenridge (laminating machine)		6,423
Inventory – parts	5,000		Total long term liabilities		18,923
Total current assets	30,500				
			TOTAL LIABILITIES		24,990
Fixed assets					
Truck	23,000		EQUITY		
Computer & office equipment	6,500				
Laminating machine	22,400		Joey – capital		10,000
Total fixed assets	51,900		Joey's parents – capital		20,000
Other assets			Retained earnings		42,410
Pre-paid insurance	1,500				
			TOTAL EQUITY		72,410
TOTAL ASSETS	97,400		TOTAL LIABILITIES & EQUITY		97,400

Figure 5.4. Balance sheet.

Let's take Joey's snowboard manufacturing business. Figure 5.4 shows the balance sheet at the end of his fiscal year. A fiscal year, or financial year, is the 12-month period that a business uses to keep its accounting records. Many businesses use the calendar year (January 1–December 31) as their fiscal year. But some businesses, especially those that have distinct seasons, choose a different fiscal year. Since Joey's busiest months are September through March, he uses a fiscal year of July 1 to June 30.

The assets section of the balance sheet is separated into two types of assets: current assets (those that will be "consumed" within a year or less) and other assets, which often include long-term investments, fixed assets, plant, property and equipment, and intangible assets (goodwill such as a killer brand name, trademarks, or patents). And within those two categories, the assets are listed in order of liquidity; that is, how fast they can be sold for cold hard cash (that's why cash is listed at the top of the statement).

Similarly the liabilities section of the balance sheet is also split into current liabilities and long-term liabilities. Current liabilities are debts that will be paid off within a year or less. Long-term liabilities are loans that stretch for more than a year.

A useful indicator of financial health of a company is to divide the current assets by the current liabilities. If the result, called the current ratio, is more than one, it means that the company has enough liquid assets to cover its short-term debts. In Joey's case, the current ratio is $30,500 divided by $6,067 or 5.03, which means that his company has plenty of short-term debt coverage.

The equity section of the balance sheet shows how much of the company is actually owned by the owner(s) and/or shareholders. Since Joey's business

	Acronym	Other names		
		Sales	Income	Turnover
Revenue				
− Cost of sales (cost of goods sold)	CoGS			
= **Gross Margin or gross profit**	EBITDA	Earnings Before Interest, Taxes, Depreciation and Amortization	Operating Margin	
− Selling expenses				
− General and administrative expenses (includes depreciation)				
= **Operating profit**	EBIT	Earnings Before Interest and Taxes	Operating income	
− Interest expense				
+ Other revenues				
− Other losses				
= **Earnings before taxes**	EBT	Earnings Before Taxes	Pretax net income	
− Income taxes				
= **Net Income**	E	Earnings	Net earnings	
Earnings per share (net income Ö total shares outstanding)	EPS			

Figure 5.5. Basic layout of an income statement.

is a very small corporation, the net income is included as equity because Joey puts it right back into the business (that is, he doesn't pay dividends to shareholders; namely himself or his mom and dad). Sometimes you'll see an entry for retained earnings in the equity section. Retained earnings are the increase in the owner's (stockholders') equity after taking into account any operating losses and any dividends paid to stockholders. If a business loses money through its operations—that is, it didn't sell enough products and services to cover its operating expenses—then this shortfall will come out of the owner's (and/or shareholders') pockets. In this case, you'll see a reduction in owner's equity. But in Joey's case, it looks like he is doing well at selling his handmade snowboards.

The Income Statement

The income statement tells you whether a business is succeeding at its primary goal: making money. An income statement lists the revenues and expenses of a business over a period of time, usually 1 year (although shorter and longer periods are also possible). The difference between revenues and expenses is called net profit—or net loss if a business spent more than it earned during the period of time in question. For this reason, income statements are often called "profit and loss" statements (or the "P&L").

The very first or top line shows revenues earned from gross sales. Gross sales are the revenues that come from selling the company's products or services. So when managers talk of "top line growth" they're talking about selling more stuff. Similarly, when a manager talks about "the bottom line" she means net income, the last line of the income statement. In order to improve the bottom line, a company has to increase revenues, cut expenses, or both. And as they say, "the devil's in the details."

Income is always listed first followed by expenses. Within these categories, accountants often list the operating numbers separately and before the nonoperating numbers. Expenses are usually listed in order of biggest to smallest. So a basic financial statement will flow as shown in Figure 5.5.

Revenues are anything that the company earns from sales or services. If you hear someone referring to "top line growth" it means that the business is trying to increase sales and/or revenues—the top line of an income statement. Sometimes discounts and returns are shown as separate line items and sometimes they aren't. Expenses are any outflows, or "use of assets" in accountant-speak, related to the company's efforts to sell stuff. Cost of goods sold is whatever expenses a company incurred in order to produce the product or service it sells. Selling expenses are any outflows directly related to getting people to buy the product (commissions, sales salaries, advertising). General and administrative expenses are the squishy stuff that a company has to have in order to do business, but these costs don't contribute directly to selling or making a product (officer salaries, legal and accounting fees, telephone, utilities, office equipment and stationary, depreciation, insurance, coffee, sodas, the Friday Beer Bash, and so forth). Other revenues and losses are items that don't have anything to do with the primary business purpose, like royalty income, patents, gains (or losses) on stock investments, a personal loan to an employee, and so forth. If a company has what are called "extraordinary items" like onetime costs from buying another company or uninsured losses from a tornado or earthquake, these expenses would go at the bottom underneath net income.

As with the balance sheet, the income statement tells a story. We can use ratios to get a snapshot of financial health and point us toward areas that warrant further research. Listed below are some of the key profitability indicators:

$$\text{Gross margin percentage (or "gross margin")} = \frac{(\text{Revenue} - \text{Cost of goods sold}) \times 100}{100 \text{ Revenue}}$$

$$\text{Operating profit margin (operating margin)} = \frac{\text{Operating income (EBIT)}}{\text{Sales revenue}}$$

$$\text{Profit margin} = \frac{\text{Net income}}{\text{Sales revenue}}$$

$$\text{Return on assets} = \frac{\text{Net income}}{\text{Total assets}}$$

The gross profit margin percentage tells you how well the company is pricing its goods relative to the cost to make those goods. The larger and more stable (constant) this ratio is over time, the higher the expected profitability. Operating margin reflects how well management is controlling costs. A high number is good. The profit margin is the bottom line margin that is usually quoted when discussing profitability. It shows how well management has been able to turn sales into profit available for shareholders. In all of the margin calculations, you have to make sure that you use industry comparisons, because a profit margin of 5 percent in the grocery business would be excellent, but that kind of margin in a high-tech company would be grounds for dismissal.

Return on assets, often abbreviated ROA, is a good way to find out how well management is using the assets a company owns (like plant, property, and equipment). A higher number is better, and again, comparisons are more useful when made within an industry.

Now let's look at Joey's Snowboard Shop. Joey's income statement is shown in Figure 5.6.

Joey's Snowboard Shop
Income Statement for Year Ended June 30, 2006

Revenue from Sales		
Gross sales		306,000
Less: returns (snowboards, bindings)	5,300	
Less: discounts	2,400	7,700
Net Sales		298,300
Cost of goods sold		
Inventory on July 1, 2005	12,500	
Purchases	87,000	
Plus: Freight	1,580	
Manufacturing expenses		
Shop rent	26,800	
Manufacturing salaries	45,200	
Insurance	10,200	
Electricity	14,520	
Total manufacturing expense	96,720	
Less: Inventory on June 30, 2006	(14,500)	
Total cost of goods sold		183,300
Gross proft from sales		115,000
Operating expenses		
Selling expenses		
Sales salaries & commissions	38,600	
Free snowboards given out	12,500	
Advertising	5,600	
Total selling expenses	56,700	
General and administrative expenses		
Bookkeeper salary	9,000	
Office supplies	800	
Telephone	4,800	
Total general and administrative expenses	14,600	
Depreciation	2,800	
Loan payments on truck	3,077	
Loan payments on laminating machine	6,669	
Total operating expenses		83,846
Income from operations		31,154
Less income taxes		11,256
NET INCOME		42,410
Earnings per share (300 shares outstanding)		141.37

Figure 5.6. Joey's Snowboard Shop income statement.

Here are some of the ratios we can identify for Joey's business:

$$\text{Gross margin percentage} = \frac{115,000}{298,300} = 38.55\%$$

$$\text{Operating margin} = \frac{31,154}{298,300} = 10.44\%$$

$$\text{Profit margin} = \frac{42,410}{298,300} = 14.22\%$$

$$\text{Return on assets} = \frac{42,410}{97,400} = 43.54\%$$

His business is looking good. If anything, he could probably afford to take on some more debt to expand his operation.

Other Financial Statements

The balance sheet and income statement are two of the most important financial statements that a company generates. But there are others that can shed additional light on how well a company is managing its money. The statement of cash flows shows how much money moved in and out of the company during a particular period of time. This statement deals with cold, hard cash, not "income" which can include noncash items like depreciation.

Another statement that's particularly useful for corporations is the statement of changes in shareowners' equity. It shows how equity has either increased or decreased during the year as a result of dividend payments, new stock issues, and stock repurchase activities.

The statement of changes in financial position shows how a company has used its working capital, which is the excess of current assets over current liabilities. That is, the money that's left over after a company has serviced its immediate debts. Most businesses need a decent buffer of cash in order to buy supplies to make products—this is often done on short-term credit and shows up as "accounts payable." The products are sold, often on short-term credit and show up as "accounts receivable," which are collected and turned into cash, which then goes to pay the accounts payable and the cycle starts over again.

WHERE ACCOUNTING AND FINANCE MEET

In most companies, accounting and finance are under one executive, the chief financial officer (CFO). This person is usually a member of the executive or management committee and often also sits on the board of directors. The reporting relationships below the CFO look like the chart shown in Figure 5.7. The CFO reports to the CEO of the company. Underneath the CFO is usually a treasurer, who handles the company's dealings with the external regulators and markets. The treasurer is the keeper of the piggy bank and is responsible for managing the company's money (getting the highest rate of interest possible for savings and the lowest rate of interest for loans). The finance department reports to the treasurer. On the accounting side, there is usually a Controller who runs the accounting department. This person usually has an advanced degree in accounting and her job is to be fully versed in current accounting and reporting rules and regulations. The Controller's job is to mak sure that the company's money is being used at optimum efficiency, this includes managing the budget process, the accounting, and the audit functions. The Controller is also responsible for the financial statements and ensuring that they are accurate and comply with all accounting rules and standards.

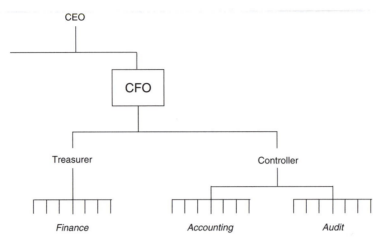

Figure 5.7. Organizational structure of the finance and accounting functions.

The CFO's job is to manage both functions as well as participate in setting financial policies and corporate planning, such as decisions on whether to buy or lease a new manufacturing facility.

Both the accounting and finance groups get together to work out the audit and control systems that the company needs. Sometimes because of the heavy requirement for data the information technology function also reports to the CFO. However, as IT has become more complex as well as strategic to the competitiveness of the firm, IT often has its own executive (chief technology officer) who reports to the CEO.

The Audit Function

Auditors, as those who staff the audit function are called, are the in-house verification team. They count the inventory, check the records, and make sure that the financial statements conform to generally accepted accounting principles and that they accurately reflect what is going on in the business.

> Brakes on a car don't slow you down. They're what allow you to go fast.
>
> —Robert Simons, Professor at Harvard Business School (speaking about financial control processes)

Control Systems

As companies grow they expand the markets they sell products and services into, hire more people, and increase the complexity of their operations. At some point a large company needs to install control systems to ensure that people are doing the right thing and basic procedures and ethics are followed. Control systems span the company and are designed to do three things:

- Verify the effectiveness and efficiency of operations
- Verify financial reports
- Ensure that everyone is complying with all local and home country laws

A control system can be as basic as requiring two signatures on a company check. Or it can be mind-numbingly complex. All good control systems share the following five components:

1. Control culture	Management sets forth the tone, philosophy, values, culture, and ethics of the organization. This is done through verbal and nonverbal means, such as promoting the right people and "doing the right thing"
2. Risk assessment	The company analyzes the internal and external risks it faces and sets forth goals and objectives to manage those risks. This has to be balanced by a realistic view of what the organization can handle without taking focus away from the core purpose (selling products)
3. Procedures	Once the risks are identified, the company puts policies and procedures in place that tell people how a certain activity is to be carried out. These can include ID badges, pass protected areas, reporting relationships, surveillance systems, signature authority, spending limits, policies on vacations, and so on
4. Communication	This entails both collecting internal and external data about possible threats and opportunities, compliance, internal reports, and anything that allows management to make better decisions. It is also about communicating the importance of complying with control systems and signaling upstream if someone observes a breach of ethics
5. Monitoring	Monitoring means checking that the systems a company has in place are actually working and doing what they're supposed to do. It also means evaluating the adequacy of the control systems against the cost (money, time, loss of focus, etc.) of implementing them

Some Control Failures

The 1990s were rife with control failures, like Enron, WorldCom, and Adelphia. Citibank, the bad boy of the control world because it continually gets itself into trouble, was censured for misbehaviors in its private banking group in Japan.

What causes control failures? Most people say it comes down to an ethics problem. Ethics failures are driven by personal, organizational, or systemic causes. Personal ethics reflect a person's propensity to engage in the seven deadly sins: pride, envy, gluttony, lust, anger, greed, and sloth. Organizational ethical problems are usually caused by a desire to conform to the prevailing "group think" and be a member of a group with a shared belief system. An immoral group culture can contribute to huge ethical transgressions. (The Abu Ghraib prisoner abuse scandal is an example of group culture gone bad.) Systemic ethical problems are usually traced to the external environment, such as the economic and social institutions that establish the rules by which organizations have to play.

> Honesty is the best policy—when there is money in it.
>
> —Mark Twain

In the Enron case, one of the biggest and most spectacular examples of a control failure, we saw all of the above. Certainly there was no shortage of personal sins on the part of the top executives at Enron. The organizationally-inspired ethical lapses came out in the culture that Jeffrey Skilling, the former CEO, encouraged. He hired really smart college graduates and pitted them against each other in a tough-guy, sink-or-swim culture. It fostered cutthroat competition and little personal cooperation. The systemic problems became obvious in how the U.S. government requires companies to hire and pay their own auditors. It's kind of like asking the prisoners to guard the inmates. Enron's auditor, Arthur Anderson, was hired and paid by Enron's board to verify and attest to the fact that Enron was following the rules. How could the auditor object to what Enron was doing if by doing so it would be out of a job?

INVESTORS: SHAREHOLDERS AND BONDHOLDERS

Investors are people who buy assets of a company—either stocks or bonds—with the expectation that the value of those financial assets will return a higher amount of money to them over time. An increase in the value of a financial asset is called a "capital gain." Of course, investors can also lose money, in which case it's called a "capital loss." (These terms have nothing to do with "capital punishment" although the many investors and employees who suffered huge losses in the Enron downfall probably wouldn't mind capital punishment for Enron's former managers.)

Shareholders are people or institutions that own the stock of a company. In theory, they have a say in how the company is run and can vote during the annual meeting. In reality, there is not much that a disgruntled shareholder can do other than to vote with their money and sell the stock.

Bondholders are people or institutions that own debt that the company has issued. Debt is a promise to pay back the initial principal loaned plus interest. Bondholders are also called creditors and they will be discussed in a later section.

Stocks

Every corporation, publicly or privately held, has stock. In a private corporation, the stock might be held by one person or a few people. A small company will probably issue 100 shares of stock. So if someone owns one share of stock in a company that has issued 100 shares, that person owns 1 percent of the company. A large company usually issues many hundreds or thousands of shares. General Electric, for example, has 10.5 billion shares outstanding! So even if you buy 1,000 shares of General Electric stock, you only own a miniscule fraction of the company. A stock is a claim of ownership on a company's assets *after* all its debts have been paid. This means that if a company goes bankrupt and is forced to liquidate (sell everything and cease doing business) the stockholder is the last person to be paid from anything leftover. That's why owning stocks is usually considered riskier than owning bonds.

Common versus Preferred Stock

There are two basic types of stock, common and preferred. Common stock is the most common and is easily bought and sold. Preferred stocks carry several rights above and beyond common stock. If a company is to be liquidated, preferred stocks are senior to common stocks, which are at or near the bottom. Preferred stock usually has a par value (or base value) and it pays dividends earlier and often at a higher rate than common stock. Preferred stock can have special voting rights associated with it, such as two votes per share, where common stock usually only carries one vote per share. Some companies use preferred stocks as a defensive mechanism against unwanted takeovers by others. So why wouldn't everyone want to own preferred stocks? In many cases preferred stocks are not available to just anyone (like in a privately held company). In other cases, preferred stocks are more expensive, and the per-share and/or dividend value is capped, whereas common stocks have greater upside (and downside) potential (because their value is not capped).

Stock Exchanges

Publicly held companies issue stock that is traded on open and public exchanges, like the New York Stock Exchange, the NASDAQ, and the London Stock Exchange. These exchanges are little changed since the days when people would gather at the center of town and shout offers to sell a stock to buyers standing around bidding for the stocks. Buyer and seller would agree on a price, trade money for shares, and the transaction would be completed. Today we have stockbrokers, who arrange the purchase and sale of stocks and traders, who stand on the floor of the exchange, and carry out the actual transaction. The aggregation of individual trades is called "the market" and it generally reflects a consensus of opinions about a particular stock or industry. Some people affectionately call this "Mr. Market" attributing a personality to the consensus opinion and implying that Mr. Market has a mind of his own.

Stock Split

Every once in a while a company that has issued stock, decides to call back its stock and issue more than one share for every share it has called back. This is called a stock split. In reality what happens is that the company decides to revalue the price of a share of stock, so that more shares are issued but the total value of the company (number of shares multiplied by the price per share) stays the same. For example, a company that has 100 shares of stock that sell for $50 per share, decides to split its shares on a "two-for-one" basis. Before the split, the company's market capitalization (value) was $5,000 (100 shares × $50 per share). Now the company has 200 shares of stock outstanding but the price per share has dropped to $25 and the company's market capitalization remains the same (200 shares × $25 per share). Stock splits of two-for-one, three-for-one, and three-for-two are most common, but other ratios also occur.

Very often, after a company splits its stock, the price (post-split) jumps. Many people think that a stock splitting company is conveying a positive forecast for the future. Others think that by making the per-share price lower, it opens the ownership of shares to a wider group of people and therefore, the price will trend upward. One company, Berkshire Hathaway, has never allowed its shares to split, and as a result, one share of its original "A" stock was worth about $90,000 on April 6, 2006. (That's up significantly from the average $15 per share that Warren Buffet, CEO of Berkshire Hathaway, paid when he started accumulating shares in 1962.)

The Annual Meeting

Every publicly held corporation in the United States is required to hold an annual meeting. It's an official gathering of the company's owners where the CEO discusses the status of the business and brings important items up for a vote among shareholders. It's also an opportunity for shareholders to ask questions of the company's management.

Proxies

A proxy in a corporation is a piece of paper that authorizes someone to vote at a shareholder's meeting on behalf of a shareholder. The company sends out proxy statements notifying each shareholder of an upcoming meeting. Along with the proxy statement are documents that describe what will be discussed at the meeting and usually a ballot form to cast a vote for or against the particular agenda items.

As mentioned before, it is very difficult for individual shareholders—even those who own a lot of shares—to effect change in a company's management. Many companies have rules specifying, for example, that more than 70 per-cent of shareholders must vote "against" a particular ballot question before management even has to listen to them. Thus, even though the shareholders theoretically own the company, they are quite powerless to make meaningful changes in management (like removing an overpaid and ineffective CEO).

In some cases, groups of shareholders band together to start proxy fights against the corporate managers. A recent example was the long and acrimonious proxy battle between Hewlett-Packard's management, led by then CEO Carly Fiorina, and a large group of shareholders who objected to HP's takeover of Compaq Computer. Hewlett-Packard's shareholders were subject to letter and telephone campaigns from both sides that attempted to sway the shareholder to vote in a particular way. Hewlett-Packard's managers won the fight.

CREDITORS

A creditor, also known as a lender, is a person or institution (bank, company, government, foundation, etc.) that lends money to another person or entity like a corporation. In return for lending money, the creditor receives interest payments (rent) on the principal amount of money it lent. In some cases the creditor receives payments of interest and principal and in others the creditor gets interest only until the final loan balance is due.

Loans and Leverage

Why would a company want to get itself into debt? Wouldn't it be safer to avoid debt entirely? Yes, if a company's cash flow (that is, money coming in minus money going out) is highly unpredictable, it's probably best to avoid debt if possible. But debt, also known as leverage, can be a very good thing. If a com-pany thinks that it can generate a higher return on an investment than it would have to pay out in interest costs, then it can use the "leverage" to its advantage.

Let's take for example Joey's snowboard manufacturing operation. Joey purchased a laminating machine for $28,000 2 years ago. If he'd had the cash, would it have made sense to purchase the machine for cash, or do what he did, which was take out a loan for $18,000? The laminating machine allows him to make snowboards much faster. He can turn out three snowboards in a day, compared to one without the machine. Joey's snowboards sell for between $300 and $500 each and he sells an average of 765 boards a year. The average net income on each board is about $55. So Joey can make $110 more (2 × $55) each day by using the laminating machine. The interest on the loan is less than $3 per day. This is a no-brainer!! Joey has used leverage to make more money for himself and his shareholders.

Bonds

A bond is a debt security, which is a fancy way of saying a loan. The issuer of a bond (the debtor or borrower) owes money to the purchaser of a bond (the creditor) and promises to repay the principal value (the money borrowed, also known in bond-speak as the "par" or "face amount") and interest (the coupon) on a specific date (the maturity), which is usually more than a year hence. Debt securities (also called debt instruments) that are issued for a term of less than a year are called bills, certificates of deposit, or commercial paper. They are treated as money market instruments, which is cash that earns more interest than a savings account. The world's biggest beggar, the U.S. Treasury, has issued some 8.4 TRILLION dollars of bonds, notes, and bills. (This is as of July 28, 2006. For the up-to-the-minute number, go to http://www.publicdebt.treas.gov/opd/opdpenny.htm.) China and Japan are the biggest buyers of U.S. debt. Most companies call debt that matures in a year or more a "bond," but the U.S. Treasury uses the word "bond" for any debt that, upon issue, matures in 10 years or more. A "note" is a U.S. Treasury debt security maturing in 1–10 years, and a "bill" is a promise by the U.S. government to pay back the loan in less than a year.

Bonds are issued by a wide variety of entities, but not usually by people. One exception is the rock star David Bowie, who in 1997 issued $55 million worth of bonds that were secured by the future royalties on his songs. These are known as "Bowie Bonds" and several other rock stars including Rod Stewart, James Brown, Iron Maiden, and Marvin Gaye have followed Bowie's lead by issuing their own bonds. The usual bond issuers tend to be supranational agencies like the European Union or the Asian Development Bank, national governments, state and local authorities, government-chartered agencies like Freddie Mac and Fannie Mae, and corporations like General Electric.

There is a whole alphabet soup of the different types of bonds available. The following listing shows are some of the varieties available.

Fixed rate bonds	Fixed rate bonds have a steady coupon (interest payment) throughout the life of the bond.
Floating rate bonds	The coupon on these bonds are linked to some sort of index, like LIBOR (London Inter-Bank Offered Rate) and the interest payment (and rate) changes, usually every 3 months.
High-yield bonds	Otherwise known as "junk bonds" they pay higher rates because the underlying credit rating of the borrower is poor, and thus the payback potential is risky. Michael Milken made a small fortune for himself and his investors in the 1980s by trading junk bonds because he saw that the *actual* default rate on this type of bond was far lower than the market had priced it. (That is, the market overestimated the risk involved in these bonds, thus making them a relatively safer investment than predicted.)
Zero coupon bonds	These bonds don't pay any interest. Series E savings bonds issued by the U.S. government sell at a big discount from par depending on the prevailing market interest rate (and where investors think

	that rate is going in the future). Creative investment houses can create zero coupon bonds by "stripping" the coupon part of a fixed rate bond from its principal value and selling the two income streams separately.
Inflation-linked bonds	This is a relatively newer creation since the 1980s. The principal value of the bond increases with the rate of inflation so as the bond matures, the interest payment increases. This type of bond generally has a lower coupon rate than fixed rate bonds. The U.S. government sells these as Treasury Inflation-Protected Securities (TIPS).
Municipal bonds	These bonds are issued by a state or city. They are usually fixed rate bonds but the interest payments on them are tax free to the bondholder, making them an attractive investment for high-income individuals. The coupon on these bonds tends to be quite a bit lower than a regular (taxable) fixed rate bond.
Asset-backed securities	This type of bond is secured by cash flows from other assets like a house or plant and equipment. Fannie Mae and Freddy Mac, two quasi-government agencies in the United States sell mortgage-backed securities on the open market.
Subordinated bonds	These bonds are subordinate to other bonds that an issuer has sold. So if the borrower goes bankrupt, the higher priority bondholders are paid before the holders of "subordinated bonds" because they are higher in the pecking order. Subordinated bonds are therefore riskier than regular bonds and carry a higher coupon rate.
Perpetual bonds	"Perpetuities" don't have a maturity date. They pay and pay and pay. Some of the early ones, called UK Consols date back to 1888 and still trade today.

Bonds and Interest Rates

Bonds are inversely correlated to interest rates. That means that as the interest rate rises, the value of a bond falls, and conversely, if the interest rates fall, the value of a bond rises. Why is that? Say that you buy a 30-year bond for $1,000 that has a 7 percent annual coupon. If you hold this bond to its maturity you'll receive $70 each year in interest. This is true no matter what the prevailing interest rate in the market is. A year after you bought the bond, the market rate of interest drops to 5 percent. Now, all of a sudden people are knocking down your door with offers to buy your $1,000 bond for $1,400. New 30-year bonds that are issued are only paying $50 per year, so the $70 you are earning is 40 percent higher than what everyone else is getting. Therefore they are willing to pay 40 percent more to buy your higher yielding bond. But notice that the yield on a $1400 bond paying $70 per year is 5 percent ($70 ÷ $1400 = 5 %). Coincidence? Not exactly ... that's the market interest rate. Now say that the next year the market interest rates are up to 9 percent. New 30-year bonds now have to pay $90 per year to keep up with the market rates. Your $70 annual interest payment doesn't look so hot anymore. So if you wanted to sell it and buy a higher yielding bond, you'd only get $778 (that's $70 ÷ 9 % = $778). In actuality your bond in year 3 would be compared with other 28-year bonds and priced accordingly. The graphic in Figure 5.8 shows the inverse relationship of bond values to market interest rates. As the bond matures (say, in year 28 or 29) the value of the bond will be close to its par value of $1,000 because there are few or no interest payments remaining.

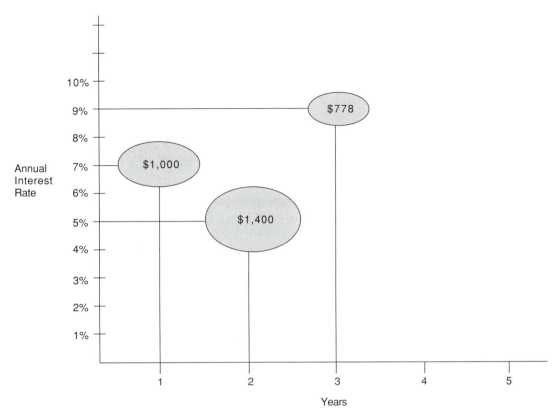

Figure 5.8. Value of a bond at different market interest rates.

It's probably becoming apparent that bonds are subject to interest rate risk. That is, if a bondholder locks herself into a fixed income and interest rates change, she will either gain or lose value in her initial investment—at least on paper. Most bond mutual funds hold huge quantities of different types of bonds with varying maturity dates. The fund revalues the aggregate price of a share in the mutual fund each day at the close of business depending on the various prices of the bonds in its portfolio.

What Is a Credit Rating?

In addition to interest rate risk, bonds also carry a credit risk. That is, most borrowers (issuers of bonds) have a credit profile or even a score from one of the internationally recognized bond rating agencies like Moody's Investor Services, Fitch IBCA, or Standard and Poor's. The rating agencies analyze each bond issuer's financial statements and their business prospects and give the issuer a letter grade. The grade indicates the likelihood that a bond issuer is able to repay the debt when it's due. The rating also affects the interest rate that the issuer must offer in order to entice people to buy their bonds. Generally speaking, the higher the rating, the lower the coupon rate of the bond. The basic rating system is as shown in Table 5.3.

The Yield Curve

A yield curve is a graphical representation of what happens to the yield of otherwise identical bonds as the maturity changes. In quant-speak a yield curve

Table 5.3. Bond ratings

Rating	Risk assessment	Example (as of April 2006)	Investment category
AAA	Highest quality, the "gold standard" with little risk of default	Wells Fargo Bank Pfizer	
AA	Very high quality, high likelihood of repayment	Abbott Labs Bank of America	
A	Very safe "mid-grade" bond, but some risk if business conditions become tough	Archer-Daniels-Midland Nordstrom	"Investment grade"
BAA or BBB	Middle of the road safety, not a huge risk but not risk free	Black & Decker Westinghouse	
BA or BB	The issuer's long-term future is somewhat doubtful	American Airlines Dillards	
B	Significant risk of default if the business conditions become tough or the economy falters	Echostar (Dish Network) Eastman Kodak	"Speculative"
CAA or CCC	These are high risk (regardless of business conditions)	America West Airlines SIRIUS	
CA or CC	Significant risk in any case	Bally Total Fitness U.S. Air	
C	This issuer is probably in the tank already and not paying interest on the bonds	Fedders Tekni-Plex	"Junk"
D	These bonds are in default	Enron Dana Corporation	
N	Not rated—either because the issuer didn't want to be rated or the company is too new		

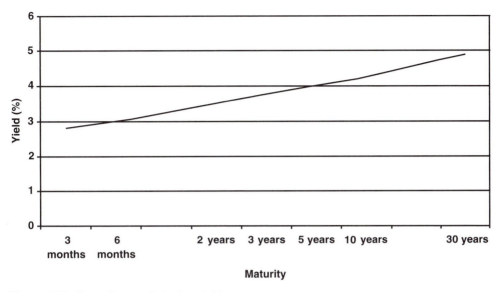

Figure 5.9. Normal upward-sloping yield curve.

is "the term structure of interest rates." A normal yield curve will slope upward, meaning that the longer the term of the bond is the higher the interest rate. Figure 5.9 shows a normal yield curve. An upsloping yield curve means that Mr. Market thinks that the near future is stable and longer term bonds have inherently more risk associated with them, since no one knows with precision what will happen to the economy 10 or 20 years from now.

Sometimes, however, the yield curve shows the opposite relationship, so that shorter and middle-term bonds have a higher yield than long-term bonds, as in Figure 5.10. This is called an inverted, inverse or reverse yield curve. Inverted yield curves don't occur very often, but when they do, the financial markets take notice. Many people think an inverted yield curve signals a recession around

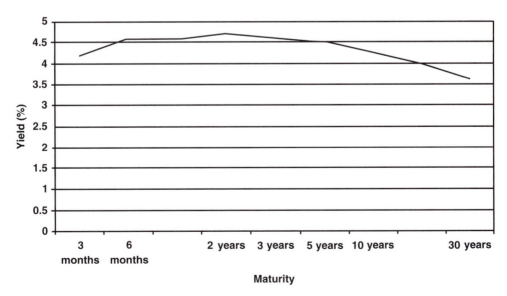

Figure 5.10. Inverted yield curve.

the corner. It can also mean that Mr. Market thinks that the current high rate of inflation will fall. From 1978 to 2006, 2-year treasury bonds have paid more than 10-year bonds only eight times. Essentially the picture painted in Figure 5.10 means that Mr. Market thinks the future is gloomy and you'd better take your money out of stocks and bonds and put it into cash.

A DAY IN THE LIFE OF A CHIEF FINANCIAL OFFICER

Paul Brooks
Chief Financial Officer
Experian

I was born in South London and grew up all over the United Kingdom. My father's job took him to different places in the U.K. so I switched schools several times. I finished the American equivalent of high school in Surrey and went to Cambridge to study economics. When I graduated, employment was plentiful and I rather drifted into accounting. I figured that it would be good training and give me flexibility for a career in business. But to get the best accountancy qualification—the equivalent of a CPA (certified public accountant) in the United States—I had to do a minimum 3 years as an auditor. So I joined KPMG and soon found that the work was mind-numbingly dull, especially as an audit junior, and the salary was low. On top of that, I was studying at night to get through my accountancy exams. There were two benefits to that boring job: the camaraderie among my cohort was great, and as an auditor, you get to see a wide variety of businesses. After 3 years I qualified as a chartered accountant. I wasn't sure whether I would stay with KPMG and work my way up to partner, or go out and get a job in industry. At about that time an opportunity came up to go to Dubai with KPMG for 18 months. I had just got married and it seemed like a nice diversion. We had a great time, as Dubai was booming on the back of its new oil wealth and the job carried more responsibility than I would have had at the same stage in London. But I was now set on developing a finance career in industry, so I came back and took a month off to look for a new job.

I ended up joining ICI, the biggest chemical company in the U.K. At that time, ICI was a huge, global company. I joined in the plastics division, one of the largest, as a "financial analyst." The routine work involved preparing the financial plan, budget, and monthly financial report. But aside from reviewing financial performance, my job involved providing overall "business support." This meant helping the sales VP on things like pricing decisions, the production guys on which products were most profitable, the planning VP on whether planned investments made financial sense, and so on. It was a very challenging and interesting job. The problem was that the business was losing money in those days. So it put more pressure on finance to come up with creative ways to cut costs and increase revenues. At the time, ICI was undergoing a number of strategic challenges. So they decided to downsize the divisional leadership and move it to Brussels, Belgium. I was one of the lucky handful of people chosen to move. Brussels is a great city! The food is terrific, people are cosmopolitan, and you've got easy access to many European countries. I spent 2 years there working with the CEO and heads of marketing, sales, production, and planning/development. The industry had some severe overcapacity issues, and one of the things I was closely involved with was buying a competitor's business. We then consolidated all of our combined production in our most efficient plants, shutting the others. So a lot of my work in this role involved business strategy.

That was a great job, but I'm a very impatient person. I wondered, "Where do I go from here?" I envisaged building a career at ICI. But in order to do this, ICI's management career track meant that you had to spend time in three places in the company: (1) in a business, which I'd been doing, (2) in the corporate head office—London, and (3) in a factory. So my next logical move was back to the head office. I did that and took on a job with the corporate financial reporting group. My responsibility was the group balance sheet and cash-flow. This beat audit for the dullest job I'd ever had! However I have to admit it was good experience. The work was very repetitive, each quarter going through the same process, and it often required long days and weekends, especially at the fiscal year end. I survived that for 2 years. Career-wise, my next job should have been in an ICI factory, but I felt it was time to move on, and in particular to get closer to a business again. So in 1985 I looked outside for a job.

I took a job as a project director in the industrial services division of a large British company called GKN. I was tasked with reviewing a large number of possible new ventures. One of them developed into negotiating a joint venture with the leading emergency plumbing and drain cleaning company in the United Kingdom to tackle the U.S. market. Pretty glamorous business, eh? So GKN sent me over to California as the CFO of this fledgling enterprise, while our partner company provided the CEO. It was an enormous challenge. We were given $20 million in start-up capital and had to find offices, hire employees, set up all the financial accounts and business processes. Basically, we were starting a business from scratch. After the first 3 years, we'd bought five companies in Northern and Southern California and had established a profitable company. However, by then GKN's strategic focus was changing and it didn't want to invest any more money in the joint venture. So it sold its share to the partner company. I spent much of the next year unraveling GKN's side of the business, and then went back to the United Kingdom.

I then took a job with a long-established British trading company, Inchcape, which had its origin back in the nineteenth century. Inchcape had interests mainly in the Middle East and Far East, mostly in a distribution role. I worked in the Marketing Services Division as the finance director. Marketing Services acted as a middleman for a broad range of large companies, like Procter & Gamble, Ford, and Timberland. Products ranged from potato chips to tractors to silk scarves! With our long tradition of operating in Asia we would market, sell, and distribute their products in what were the more difficult-to-penetrate markets for Western companies, like Japan, China, and Thailand. I spent a lot of time overseas. Marketing Services was a huge division with 30,000 employees and profits of about $150m on sales of about $5bn—quite thin margins! But our division had some pretty challenging strategic issues: the brand owners were increasingly looking to take over the distribution and sales themselves as these markets became more important. So over time, our profits came under increasing pressure. This was a familiar challenge for me! I always remember the Inchcape chairman's comment "You can put good management into a bad business, but you've still got a bad business."

Inchcape was a conglomerate and as such, it came under pressure to break itself up. The company decided to try to separately list or sell each of its divisions. I was sent to Singapore for 2 years to oversee the process of separating the Marketing Services Division. In the end, we ended up selling the business to a Hong Kong company. They offered me a good job there, and I loved working in Asia, but it was time to get back to the United Kingdom.

I came back in 1999 and joined Experian, which is a subsidiary of GUS plc, a British company, which owned several retailers including Burberry and Argos. Experian is one of the world's largest providers of credit information on consumers and businesses. I joined the company as the finance director for the non-U.S. side of the business that was headquartered in Nottingham, England (best known for Robin Hood). I was attracted to Experian because, unlike a couple of my previous employers whose business model was under challenge, Experian had clear long-term growth prospects in a dynamic and expanding industry. I was specifically looking for a company with these kind of characteristics this time. I also knew that Experian had a big presence in California and a possible move back there appealed to me. After 18 months in Nottingham, I got the opportunity to take on the Global CFO role for Experian in Costa Mesa, California. Up until then (2001) Experian's U.S. business was underperforming. So GUS management decided that management changes were necessary. Our current CEO, Don Robert, was recruited as COO and I was asked to come over to the U.S. as CFO. Don then hired a new team, which is still in place today.

In the past 4 years, we've done over 80 acquisitions! I've reviewed all of them. We've worked hard to integrate the new companies into our operation and business model. We've also succeeded in growing our business organically, that is, from the inside out. The vast majority of our purchases have done really well for us. Our function, finance, developed a process for monitoring acquisition performance after their purchase. It's a rigorous model that gives us a great way to benchmark how we've done, what we've learned and how we can improve the acquisition and integration process next time.

Finance is a numbers and analysis function. I guess I'm always trying to analyze things to see how we can make them better. Our initiatives have included an annual analysis of client and product profitability. We analyzed our pricing schemes and looked at the trendlines for products and how well they sold. We took this on for the businesses in Experian and they've since really come to appreciate this service. We also monitor the performance and business developments of all our competitors to help ensure we stay ahead of them.

In order to succeed in finance you definitely need a head for numbers. But there are some other key skills necessary to move up the ranks in finance in order to reach CFO level:

- Ability to prioritize and delegate work. This is the essence of any top job. I keep a long list of things that need to be done. Some are things that must be done—like getting financial statements produced, or attending an acquisition meeting with the CEO. Many are things that you think need to be done—like analyzing and recommending improvements on an under-performing part of the business. You've only got a limited number of hours in the day. So it's then all down to delegation. I absolutely love doing spreadsheets, but very early in my career, I realized that I shouldn't be spending my time doing that so I learnt to let it go and delegate the work to others. Since delegation is so important the key is to have a great team in place that you can rely on. And you can't ever predict your day. Priorities constantly get shifted around. So you have to be very careful about managing your time.

- Relationship-building and influencing skills. You have to be good technically, but it's crucial to be able to interact well with other people. I have to use my skills of persuasion in order to try to influence the CEO and other business heads to give full weight to the financial elements of any business decision.
- Analytic skills. Particularly when dealing with business people. On any proposal, however passionately advocated, it's the finance guy who needs to be the cool voice of reason assessing whether it stacks up.
- Technical competence. You have to know the basic financial and accounting principles. At my level, you can't keep up with all the technical detail, but I know where to go to get the answers I need.
- A hell of a work ethic. You won't find many people who get anywhere near the top of an organization that don't have this. You just can't cut corners. The work has to be done right the first time.

This job is full of challenges. As I said, time management is a big challenge. I try to be one step ahead of where I think the next problem might be lurking. I pick up on conversations and try to look for things that could impact our performance. Another challenge is choosing the right approach, or tactic, to persuade people to do the right thing. It's best to avoid confrontation if you can. I don't want to see Experian commit to a project that could be too risky or otherwise harm our track record of stellar growth. (In each of the past 4 years, we've achieved double-digit growth in sales and profits.)

Thankfully, I don't have to deal with Sarbox (the 2002 Sarbanes-Oxley Act). As a British company, we don't have to comply with it. I know that many of my counterparts in American companies have been pulling their hair out trying to set up all the financial and control processes that are required. We do have to comply with information security regulations, but that's part of doing business. Since a big part of our business deals with information security and risk management, we have an entirely separate operational function that handles it.

The best part of my job is the intellectual challenge and variety of issues that I get to deal with. I like to address new and different problems and make decisions about them. Everything that comes to me is difficult—otherwise, it wouldn't get to my level in the organization. I love that!

A typical day:

6:45 AM   I usually get to the office early so that I still have a few hours of the day that overlap with our UK operation. E-mails come in overnight (during their day) that often need immediate attention. Today I do a quick scan of e-mails, one of which requires a phone call before I head off to the first meeting of the day.

7:00 AM   Meeting of our Global Operating Board. This is a meeting of the top nine managers in the business that takes place at least monthly to make key business decisions. It's a teleconference with three of us, including the CEO, in California, our marketing services president in Chicago, two more in Nottingham, one in London, and one who's visiting our Rome office.

Today we start with my making a financial presentation on last month's performance and the latest outlook for the year. The first half forecast is looking a little softer than we'd like, so we agree that some cost-cutting is necessary in a couple of parts of the business. We go on to discuss some proposed changes to the management organization, the progress that is being made with our top global customers (these are mainly banks), and then we go on to review an acquisition in Canada, which we approve, and the sale of part of our South African business which is necessary as part of the government's new Black Economic Empowerment legislation.

8:00 AM   Scheduled weekly "catch-up" call with our UK CFO. I brief him on relevant aspects of the Global Board call and then we go on to talk about one of our UK businesses which is under-performing, what's causing it and what actions should be taken. He tells me about one of the acquisitions they're looking at, and I give him some initial feedback and we discuss one of his staff members who may need to be replaced.

8:30 AM   Phone call with our French CEO in Paris. I've got a trip scheduled there next week. We discuss some of the meetings he's setting up for me while I'm there.

8:50 AM   Phone call from the CFO at GUS, our parent company to discuss some details of the upcoming "demerger." A few months ago, GUS management announced that it will spin off its two remaining businesses (Experian and Argos Retail Group) and list them on the London Stock Exchange, hopefully in October 2006. So my job is even more complex than usual and it will get bigger when I'm CFO of an independent public company. Something to look forward to!

9:30 AM   On the way to getting a coffee and I bump into the president of our U.S. Credit Services business and we talk about how one of our new credit products is performing. He tells me that they may be looking to invest more in it as it's proving a great way of winning business from our biggest competitor, Equifax. I suggest he get some time on the agenda for us to discuss it.

9:45 AM   Back to my office to check on e-mails. I see one of them is a report I had asked for when I was in the United Kingdom last week. This is a rare week where I'm in the office all week. I've made six round trips to Europe alone (mainly the United Kingdom) in the past 10 weeks! Next week I'll be in Paris for a French Board Meeting and in Holland for a meeting with our treasury head there—these are the guys who look after our banking relationships, ensure all our cash around the world is properly handled, and manage our borrowings and foreign currency issues.

10:00 AM   I meet with our controller, Mark, and credit services finance SVP, Tony, to discuss how we organize our accounts receivable and collections function. A recent internal audit report indicated that there might be an internal control risk, so we agree on the changes that need to be made to address that. Although I don't spend much time myself on the basic accounting of our sales, purchases, accounts payable and receivables, the payroll, and so forth, I have to be absolutely confident that these functions are on track and well run. You can do all the great business support things you want, but if this area screws up, you're a failure as a CFO.

10:35 AM	Don, our CEO, puts his head round the door and has a couple of issues he wants to raise with me. He's been approached by an investment bank with a proposal to acquire one of our competitors. We discuss whether there might be anything in it, and agree that we'll get one of our M&A (mergers and acquisitions) directors to do some analysis to see whether we want to follow up on the proposal. He then tells me about some of the employee incentive plans he wants to put in place when we spin off, and how much he thinks we can afford to budget for this. He also briefs me on a conversation he's just had with our parent company CEO in London.
11:00 AM	Short drive up to First American Corp, where I meet with the CEO and CFO of the joint venture we have with them, which provides real estate information to mortgage lenders, like whether a particular house requires flood insurance or whether its property tax has been paid. We own 20 percent, so our partner runs it, but we get regular briefings from them on performance and today they also bring up an acquisition they'd like to make. They want my initial feedback on whether we would be prepared to put up our share of the investment, which would be about $15m.
12:10 PM	Back to the office. Quite a busy day today. So I ask Amy, my assistant, to grab me a sandwich and I work through lunch, with just a quick check of the Internet to see how Crystal Palace, my English soccer team, is getting on (it's now 8:00 PM in the United Kingdom). They're losing 1–0!
12:20 PM	Quick check of e-mail and respond to a couple of quick ones.
12:30 PM	Urgently arranged meeting by Doug, our technology finance SVP to discuss a capital expenditure proposal for some IT equipment. We don't need this equipment until September, but if we buy now the vendor is offering an attractive discount. We discuss some of the issues: will we definitely want it in September? Might the same discount be available then? Are we sure we can't get an even better deal from another vendor? We decide to pass on it.
1:00 PM	Amy has forced her way into my diary—she always complains I don't give her enough time, and she's right of course! She needs to discuss flight options for next week's trip, where I'll be staying, and what additional meetings I want her to arrange. We also discuss my diary and travel plans for the following 3 weeks. A big part of her job is screening phone calls from everyone from software vendors to irate consumers who think there's an error on their credit report. Some of these may be people I may want to talk to (but not the irate consumers!). So she checks whether this is the case. Finally I hand her my expense receipts from my last trip. She then prepares my expense report and makes sure it's paid.
1:30 PM	Our external audit partner from PricewaterhouseCoopers has asked to meet with me to give me some feedback from our recently completed year-end audit. They provide a formal letter of issues that they want to point out to us, but this is more informal and "off the record." He tells me their view of how efficiently the audit process went, and what they thought of our systems, controls, and staff. He is fairly positive and I tell him I thought

that the audit went quite well, especially given the post-Enron world where the auditors feel they have to be far more confrontational than they used to be.

2:10 PM   Quick check of e-mail, and just time to read an acquisition proposal that is going to be discussed at review committee meeting tomorrow.

2:30 PM   Interview for a new head of internal audit. The current head, Allen, is being promoted into a new role, and we're using an executive search firm to find a replacement. I've given them a very clear brief as to exactly what the job entails and the sort of person we're looking for. They've discussed a number of possible candidates with me, and I'm now meeting a shortlist of three. This is the first of those interviews.

3:40 PM   Another quick check of e-mail to see if anything needs urgent action/response—I probably get about 40 to 50 per day. I return a couple of phone calls before my next teleconference.

4:00 PM   I have a scheduled call to Hong Kong with our preferred candidate for a new role of CFO Asia-Pacific, our biggest potential growth market, who has asked to talk to me. He wants to know more about Experian, what our plans are for the region, and what the job will involve. Because we're currently small there, he's nervous about leaving his current job with a big U.S. multinational. A call that I thought would take about 15 minutes goes on for over an hour, but you can't invest too much time in people issues. I try to use my best persuasive skills on him. He finally says he'll discuss it with his wife and get back to us in a couple of days.

5:10 PM   I meet with Mark to review the latest version of a major presentation (120 pages of PowerPoint) about the business the Global Board will be making to Investment Analysts in London in July. We agree on quite a lot of changes. Jobs like this often come the way of finance, because we have a strong network across the business, and know the business well.

5:45 PM   Another presentation to prepare—this is one that I'll be making to a management conference in Rome in 2 weeks time. It's on our financial performance and the challenges of becoming a public company. I ask one of our financial analysts, James, to come up to my office and I explain to him the way I want the presentation to flow and sketch out the rough content of the slides. He's a whiz with PowerPoint, and once he's drafted a "straw-man" presentation it will be easy for me to give him the edits to make it into the finished article.

6:15 PM   I quickly check e-mail again before I leave for the day. There's one paper I still need to read for a meeting tomorrow, but I figure I can do that at home over a glass of wine. The days are quite long and very busy, but they're always different, and very exhilarating!

INTERNET RESOURCES

Educational Sites

University of Arizona finance course: www.studyfinance.com

This is an excellent self-paced study course sponsored by the University of Arizona. It features a basic finance and accounting module that allows you to "click through" increasingly complex concepts. Peppered throughout are short quiz questions to test your understanding of the concepts.

Contingency Analysis: http://www.contingencyanalysis.com/
This is a site established by Glyn Holton, a noted expert in risk analysis. You'll find several of his papers there along with a group of links to Web sites and blogs focused on risk.

Quantnotes.com: http://www.quantnotes.com/
Their stated goal is "We aim to provide premium publications and research quality information. Every month we provide introductory articles where you will learn about various financial instruments and how mathematics you may be familiar with is applied daily by banks to fairly price these instruments." Their explanations require no fear of mathematics.

CNN Money: http://money.cnn.com
As one of the few synergistic results of the AOL–TimeWarner merger, CNN was combined with Fortune and Money magazines to produce a very useful Web site full of current and historical information on business, companies, and industries. You can get back issues of articles, and there is a "Money 101" section that provides some investment basics.

Financial Statement Analysis

MSN Money: http://moneycentral.msn.com/home.asp
This is one of the top-rated free Web sites for free investment and personal finance information.

Investopedia: http://www.investopedia.com/university/financialstatements/
An extensive site with heaps of information about financial analysis. It will help you prepare for several certification exams in the financial arena. It's a bit heavy on the advertising but that's the price for good and free resources.

Ameritrade: http://www.ameritrade.com/educationv2/fhtml/learning/readannrpts.fhtml
Ameritrade's site helps investors understand and analyze financial statements. It's a little rudimentary, but it will help the beginner.

American Association of Individual Investor's web site: http://www.aaii.com
The AAII is an organization dedicated to helping individual investors become self-sufficient and knowledgeable buyers of financial assets and products. To get the most benefit, and access the resources online, you have to join the organization ($29 per year in 2006).

Morningstar: http://www.morningstar.com
Morningstar is a top-rated stock and mutual fund analysis company. Their site offers a lot of free content and educational articles. With a subscription to premium service ($13.95 per month in 2006) you can access some very sophisticated portfolio analysis, research, and screening tools.

Job Assistance Sites

Quant jobs (interview tips): www.quantfinancejob.com

Go to this site if you're masochistic enough to actually want a job crunching numbers. It will help you learn what kind of education and experience you need, and even how to tackle the job interview.

SUMMARY

Finance and accounting are two extremely important functions in a business. Together they mind and count the money. Finance is concerned with getting capital when and where it's needed and for the lowest possible cost to the company. Interest is the biggest cost associated with getting money. Interest on money is like rent on an apartment. Money is more valuable today than it will be tomorrow, and we saw how to calculate the present and future values of money. The price of money (interest rate) depends on a number of factors like the market interest rate and the risk that the borrower won't pay.

Accounting is the function that gathers, measures, reports, and analyzes financial information about a business's assets, liabilities, and net worth. Managerial accounting is a branch of the accounting function that collects and analyzes data specifically requested by managers. Financial accountants can be either public (available for hire by anyone) or private (employed directly by a company) and they are the people who put together the financial statements that go to external stakeholders. Two of the most important financial statements are the balance sheet and the income statement. Both tell a story about how well a company is managing its assets and producing revenues and profit.

Finance and accounting are both concerned with controlling how assets in a company are deployed. Both functions help senior management to make decisions about issuing new stock, new debt, and how the company's capital is managed. Bonds are a form of debt that carry both interest rate risk and credit risk. Senior managers of a company have to understand how the structure of the business impacts future decisions they might make. The finance and accounting functions are important in helping managers evaluate the business.

6

Marketing

Marketing Blunders

Colgate introduced a toothpaste in France called Cue, the name of a notorious porno magazine.

In Italy, a campaign for Schweppes Tonic Water translated the name into "Schweppes Toilet Water."

When Coors translated its slogan, "Turn it Loose" into Spanish, it read as "Suffer from Diarrhea."

The Chevrolet Nova never sold well in Spanish-speaking countries because "*no va*" means "no go" in Spanish.

Swedish vacuum manufacturer Electrolux used the following in an American ad campaign: "Nothing sucks like an Electrolux."

Ford's Pinto flopped in Brazil because Pinto is Brazilian slang for "tiny male genitals."

The California Milk Processor's campaign "Got Milk?" failed in the Hispanic market because it roughly translates to "Are You Lactating?"

Kinki Nippon Tourist Company couldn't understand why it kept getting requests for unusual sex tours from customers in the English-speaking markets it just entered.

WHAT IS MARKETING?

Marketing is one of the core functions in any business, but its definition often sounds nebulous and squishy. For example:

- Marketing is an organizational function and a set of processes for creating, communicating, and delivering value to customers and for managing customer relationships in ways that benefit the organization and its stakeholders.[1]
- Marketing is human activity directed at satisfying needs and wants through exchange processes.[2]
- The marketing concept describes a management function and business philosophy, which emphasizes exchange, markets, consumers, and competencies, all underpinned by formal and informal sources of information.[3]
- The aim of marketing is to make selling superfluous. The aim is to know and understand the customer so well that the product or service fits him and sells itself.[4]
- The management process of anticipating, identifying, and satisfying customer requirements profitably.[5]

Now that this is as clear as mud, let's try to explain what marketing is and what marketing people actually do. At its base level, marketing tries to satisfy human needs, wants, and demands by identifying and announcing a product or service at a price and place that is valuable to the person with the ability and desire to purchase that product or service. Marketing involves research, strategic planning, product design, product development, product lifecycle management, brand management, advertising, media purchasing, sales promotion, supply chain management, distribution, channel management, international trade, and customer relations to name but a few activities. Where marketing used to be all about developing products and then coercing and/or cajoling people to buy them, today's marketers are increasingly more sophisticated in using research, data analysis, and logic to find solutions to problems people have. In the past, marketing was little more than the marketing mix of 4Ps: product, price, place, and promotion. Today the 4Ps are derided as being too unidimensional and limiting. Companies now look at market share (automobiles), share of wallet (Citibank), share of stomach (Coca-Cola), share of eyeballs (Internet usage), and so

Job Rotation to Marketing by Dilbert
Dilbert: © Scott Adams/Dist. by United Feature Syndicate, Inc. Reprinted with permission.

on. Moreover, as companies move from selling individual products to selling "solutions," or bundles of products, software, and services, the marketing function has moved more toward relationship marketing that embodies a long-term view of satisfying customer needs as the customer goes through different growth and life stages. This is also called customer-focused, or customer-centric marketing.

Finally, marketing has been called a philosophy of business that embodies psychology, sociology, and economics rather than a simple business function or process.

WHY IS MARKETING IMPORTANT?

What if you developed the perfect combination of products and services to solve world hunger, but you had no way to tell the world about it? The discipline of marketing offers not only a mode for communicating your message, but also a strategy for getting the message out to the key people who need to hear about it and in such a way that they will actually listen. Good marketing is important because it can alert people with a problem that they didn't know they had (say, foot fungus) to an available solution (the dermatitis drug being advertised). Critics say that marketing is evil because it propagates frivolous consumption (that is, it makes people spend money that they don't have on products they don't need).

STRATEGIC MARKETING PLANS

Most companies engage in some form of strategic planning at the top or corporate level (see Chapter 3). The marketing function, if it exists in a business, is normally tightly connected to the strategic planning function. This is because a business that makes stuff or provides a service needs to get the word out about what it does. As a business grows, its product range often increases and diversifies into a number of different areas. Strategic marketing plans provide a process by which managers can look systematically at the company's strengths and match those with opportunities in the marketplace to better define and pursue the kind of business the company is good at. A good marketing plan describes the optimal product mix that the company should pursue, the target markets (i.e., desired customers), how much money the company will spend to make it all happen, and controls (budgets, timelines, expected results) to help measure whether the company is succeeding in its plan. This section will describe some of the methods used to help companies plan their marketing strategies.

The SWOT Analysis

SWOT is an acronym for a widely used technique to assess market and business strategy: strengths, weaknesses, opportunities, and threats. The SWOT analysis provides a framework to study the environment in which a firm operates. Strengths and weaknesses usually refer to characteristics of the business itself, while opportunities and threats tend to be external to the firm. Some examples under each category are listed as follows:

Strengths	Weaknesses	Opportunities	Threats
Superior product technology	Few new products in the research and development pipeline	A weak competitor is exiting the market	Interest rates are likely to rise
Market dominance (leader)	Critical employee relations problems	Chinese middle class is growing (more customers)	Critical shortage of skilled engineers
Low production cost	Production is dependent on world price of platinum	A breakthrough in nanotechnology shows promise for new product features	New government has protectionist tendencies
	CEO is in bad health and we have no succession plan		Increasing oil prices will impact transportation and production costs

A SWOT analysis is most useful when a company is considering a particular project or proposition that requires a decision. Some examples are:

- Should we double our production capacity?
- Should we open an office in Vietnam?
- Can we diversify our product and service portfolio?
- Can we triple our revenues in the next 5 years?

You'll notice that a SWOT analysis has many similarities to what is done in the strategic planning function. Marketing and strategic planning are often tightly connected, especially where a particular product is core to the company's brand and image (like Coca-Cola).

BCG Growth–Share Matrix

The Boston Consulting Group (BCG), a leading management consulting firm, developed a method to help managers analyze their business portfolio, that is, the group of products and services a company offers. BCG plots products and services against two axes: market growth rate on the vertical (y) axis and market share on the horizontal (x) axis. Generally speaking, a high market growth rate means that your product or service is attractive and you're finding many new customers who want to buy your product. A high market share is usually good too. It means that your product is preferred over those of your competitors, or if you don't have competitors yet (you will) you can enjoy monopoly profits for a while. BCG further classifies products into four boxes as shown in Figure 6.1. The idea is that products tend to go through predictable phases (a product lifecycle) as they are introduced into the market. Ideally, you want a mixture of the products in the matrix to provide you with a balanced portfolio of products.

"Cash cows" are products that hold high market share but don't have a future of rapid growth in the market. These products usually are high-volume, high-margin, dependable products for the company's bottom line. Cash cows

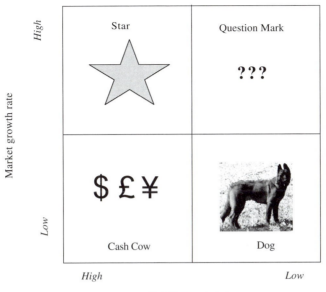

Figure 6.1. BCG Growth–Share Matrix.

generate lots of cash that can be used to fund other products. "Stars" are those products and services with high market share and a high growth rate. They are usually at the start of their lifecycle and need heavy upfront investment to get them launched and into the market. The hope is that they will eventually become cash cows. New products that require a lot of cash to launch, but their success in the marketplace is still unclear, are called "question marks." They could either go on to become stars and eventually cash cows, or they could get to the last category, "dogs" (now renamed "pets" by BCG). Dogs are in low-growth markets and have low market share. They only generate enough cash to support themselves. There is no reason why a company should keep a "dog" product unless it can either turn it into a cash cow somehow, or sell it for cash.

IDENTIFYING YOUR CUSTOMERS

For decades the big automobile manufacturers and their dealers thought that they were selling cars primarily to men. Auto dealerships were stark, sterile, and smelled of tires and oil. The salespeople were geared up to talk RPMs, horsepower, and engine torque. The whole concept was that it's the man of the house who does the car buying. But a funny thing happened on the way to the dealership: it turns out that women make the purchase decision in over 70 percent of the cases! Where car salesmen thought that women just pick the color, it turns out women are choosing the type of car, its features and options, and how to finance it too. Thus, marketers have learned that there are several points—or "moments of truth" as Procter & Gamble calls them—in the process of buying and using a product.

All marketing professionals segment the market for their products, whether it is by age, income, gender, education level, lifestyle, hobby preferences, or any number of other characteristics. The idea is to identify a group of people who are similar in some way so that the company can tailor its products more effectively to this target group, and thus sell more products. The big question for marketers is what is the best way to identify and target the particular customer group for a particular product. This section will describe some of the recent efforts used to answer "Who is my customer?"

Customer, Shopper, User

Procter & Gamble (P&G), a consumer packaged goods manufacturer, has one of the world's premier marketing organizations. P&G makes products like Tide, Pringles, Secret deodorant, Pampers diapers, Charmin toilet paper, Oil of Olay, Wella hair products, the high-end SK-II skin care line, Cover Girl cosmetics, Gillette razors, Crest toothpaste, Bounty paper towels, Bounce fabric softener, and many others. P&G segments their customers into three groups: customer, shopper, and user. The customer, for P&G, is the retail store (Wal-Mart, Kroger, Safeway, Walgreen, etc.) that carries its products. The shopper is the woman (and most times it is a woman) who picks the product off the shelf and purchases it. The user is the person who will be using the product—and that may or may not be the same as the shopper.

The distinction between shopper and user is important. Anheuser-Busch, the makers of Budweiser, discovered early on that it was primarily the woman of the household who does the grocery shopping. When the shopping list says "beer" Anheuser-Busch hopes that she chooses Budweiser. So how does the company get her to remember which beer to buy? They use advertising that's designed to humor women (often featuring young men making fools of themselves) and at the same time differentiate their product from the competition. Recent Budweiser ads featured talking frogs and lizards, a donkey dreaming of becoming a Budweiser Clydesdale, friends yelling "Whassup" to each other, and a bunch of guys praying to a "magic fridge." These were productive ads since every dollar spent on advertising generated over $6 in sales. In contrast, Miller Lite introduced a series of "Catfight" advertisements featuring mudwrestling supermodels. Although the ads entertained their male viewers, Miller Lite's sales did not increase.

Customer Profiles

Forty years ago Daniel Yankelovich suggested that companies look at different ways to segment their markets. He stated that nondemographic traits, like values and preferences, actually influence customer buying habits more than the traditional categorizations based on income, gender, age, etc. That led companies to parse their customer population into categories like Joe Sixpack, High-tech Harry, Nascar Dads, Soccer Moms, Yuppies, Dinks (dual income no kids), Finks (fixed income no kids), and so on. This activity is known as customer segmentation, market segmentation, or psychographic segmentation (because it's based on psychological and demographic traits). Today Yankelovich says that companies forgot something along the way: to connect the nature of their products with why any customer would want to buy them. Companies need to look at where their products and services fit into the scheme of a customer's life and values. Is the purchase a potential life-changing event (choice of cancer treatment center), a medium-level choice (an automobile), or a relatively minor decision (a new razor)?

Many retailers combine past purchase data with customer profiles to describe specific customer groups. For example, Tesco, the UK grocery chain, offers a loyalty program where customers present their grocery card each time they visit the store in exchange for discounts on certain items. Using this data, Tesco segments their customers into "convenience," "finer foods," and "cost conscious" by the kinds of grocery purchases each customer has made. Since Tesco has each customer's address, it also sends out promotional coupons tailored to the specific type of customer. The company claims that these coupons have increased sales by £100 million (about $170 million dollars) annually. Furthermore, Tesco also knows which items in the store must be priced at or below the competition's prices and which products (caviar) have less price-sensitive consumers. The grocer can even set store-specific prices for certain products in certain neighborhoods.

Other scholars have urged companies to look at customer profitability and spend more resources on those customers who are most lucrative to the firm (and much less on the "demon" customers who are money losers). Best Buy not only segments its customers into groups such as *Jill* (busy moms who just want a product to do a certain task), *Barry* (high-end, big spenders who buy only the best), and *Buzz* (tech geek who buys the latest equipment), but it also designs entire retail stores around a particular customer type. In a Jill store, for example, the sales associates place all the small appliances at knee-level in wide central aisles, and offer a kids' play area inside the store. Sales increased dramatically.

One of the first marketing professors, Theodore Levitt, used to say, "People don't want to buy a quarter-inch drill. They want a quarter-inch hole!"[6] Levitt derided companies for their myopia and missing what the customer really wanted: a solution to a problem they were having. Many companies today segment their markets based on the wrong criteria and miss the boat on where their customers' true needs are. Royal Bank of Canada uses what has become known as lifestyle profiling. Using more than 80 different criteria, the bank has developed a demographic grouping of people in various stages of life, such as:

- Youth—18 years and younger,
- Getting Started—18–35 years old and going through early life experiences such as graduation, buying a car, buying a house, getting the first mortgage, getting married, etc.
- Builders—35–50 years old in their peak earning years while having families and building careers. They tend to borrow more than they invest.
- Accumulators—50–60 years old who suddenly realize that they need to save for retirement. They tend to be interested in financial planning and investment services.
- Preservers—"seniors" over 60 who are interested in maximizing their retirement income and preserving their lifestyle. They are candidates for estate planning services.

But within each of these groupings, Royal Bank of Canada has also identified subgroups that are candidates for specialized banking services. One such subgroup is the young, debt-laden medical professionals who have just graduated with a degree in medicine or dentistry and want to build their own private practice. The bank offers loans for medical equipment and mortgages for their first office, in addition to help with reducing the burden of student loans. Since

Royal Bank of Canada identified this subgroup in 2004, the bank's market share of this segment has increased from 2 to 18 percent, and revenues are 3.7 times more per client than the average customer.[7]

MARKETING APPROACHES

Marketers can choose from a number of different methods to get customers. Once a company has identified who its potential customers are, it must then decide the best approach to use to turn them into actual customers.

Mass Marketing

The original mass marketer was Ford Motor company selling one type of automobile in one color (black) to everyone in the country who could afford it. There was no effort at differentiating either the product or the type of customer who might purchase the product. Today's mass marketing takes the form of advertisements that are designed to appeal (or at least attract the attention) of the widest range of people possible. They are the annoying ads hawking low-interest equity loans, the cheapest used cars, and the widest selection of furniture, and they saturate your favorite television program. The strategy with mass marketing is to produce a fairly uniform product that will satisfy the most possible people.

Mass Customization

Mass customization is a way of bringing personalized and customized products to the mass market but at an affordable price. The products, however, are not usually exactly tailored to each person, but they are fairly easily modifiable so that the customer has the sense that the product is customized. For example, you can go to www.toyota.com and order a Prius. The first screen asks for your zip code and then presents you with six option packages to choose from. The packages are various configurations of airbags, leather seats, choice of stereo systems, antitheft devices, a vehicle stability control system, Bluetooth wireless capability, a backup camera, special fog lights, and a navigation system. Then you get to choose the interior and exterior colors and add on any accessories (CD changer, cargo nets, glass breakage sensor, floor mats, ski racks, etc.). At the end, you get a price for the vehicle, including the estimated monthly payments and a date and dealer where you can pick up your made-to-order car.

Relationship Marketing

Grocery stores pioneered relationship marketing in the early 1980s by issuing loyalty cards to anyone who wanted them. The key benefit to the customer from these cards was a discount on selected items in the store. In some cases, a customer got a free tank of gas after a certain dollar level of purchases. Other businesses followed, like restaurants and flower shops, and often kept track of past purchases and rewarded the customer on her tenth visit with something free (dinner entrée or free bouquet). Relationship marketing's primary goal is to retain all of its current customers, without attempting to differentiate between high- or low-value customers. Relationship marketing is most useful under the following conditions:

- When there are several alternatives for the customer to choose from,
- When the customer makes the selection decision, and
- When there is a regular need or desire for the product or service.

Relationship marketing does not include a feedback loop. So the vendor does not necessarily know if the customer comes back because its product or service is pleasing the customer, or if the customer returns only because there's no suitable competing product or service.

Internet Marketing

Often called online marketing and e-marketing, Internet marketing uses specific technology available on the Internet that allows marketers to more precisely identify potential customers. Some technologies include cookies, permission marketing or "opt-in" policies, and RSS (really simple search). For example, when you type in a search term such as "aircraft carriers" on Google, the results page will show a number of advertisements offering you the option to (1) buy aircraft carrier hobby models via shopping.com, (2) find a job on an aircraft carrier via monster.com, or (3) buy aircraft carrier memorabilia (baseball caps, photos, zippo lighters) on e-bay.com. These search engines use algorithms to identify people with similar interests and point them (for a fee, of course) to the companies that sell products or services that might interest the search engine user.

One-to-One Marketing

One-to-one marketing is a method of identifying customers by their individual needs and designing customized products and services to that particular customer. This is followed by a feedback loop that tells the company how well that specific product or solution satisfied the customer and how it can be improved in the next go round for that customer. One-to-one marketing was popularized by Don Peppers and Martha Rogers in the mid-1990s. It's a marketing approach that relies heavily on computers to track individual customer preferences. The philosophy of one-to-one marketing is that it's a lot cheaper in the long run to continuously please a group of loyal and high-value customers than to try to dig up new and more fickle customers all the time. It's also a philosophy that is built on trust: the customer trusts the marketer to use the information he gains about the customer wisely, and in return, the customer will get a better product or service. In order for this transaction to succeed, however, the marketer must actually be listening to the customer and hearing what he says. One-to-one marketing is almost the opposite of mass marketing. It can be expensive for a company to carry out, but it can also be a very valuable relationship if done properly.

Amazon.com is a company that has used many one-to-one principles in acquiring and keeping high-value customers. It has built a "learning relationship" with customers who buy books, music, and any of the other products Amazon sells. Every time a past customer visits Amazon's Web site, she is presented with a customized screen that welcomes her and suggests a number of items that she might want to purchase. These suggestions are driven by Amazon's database of her past purchases as well as comparisons with other customers who bought some of the same types of items. So for a customer who recently bought several books about dog shows, the next time she logs onto Amazon, she will be presented with dog nutrition books, dog health books, a DVD to play for your dog while you're out, and designer dog collars and leashes. Furthermore, Amazon has a feedback loop built into each product shown on screen. Anyone can rate and discuss product features of any item purchased on the site.

CUSTOMER RELATIONSHIP MANAGEMENT

Customer Relationship Management (CRM) is a business process for aligning the interactions between a company's customers and all of the interfaces in the company with the end goal of enhancing customer loyalty and profitability. CRM is enabled by technology—not driven by it. The one-to-one marketing gurus, Peppers and Rogers, define CRM as follows:

- Identify customers individually.
- Differentiate customers or customer groups based on their needs and value (to the company).
- Interact with customers in a way that benefits them and the company.
- Customize the relationship over time based on the company's understanding of the customer's needs and values.

Peppers and Rogers further state, "Companies with a winning CRM strategy examine customer interactions through the "eyes of the customer," and build customer-focused strategies and processes to establish and maintain long-term profitable customer relationships."[8] Implementing a CRM strategy is a cross-functional effort that requires support from the top executive team, a coherent customer strategy, and significant budgets for (1) reengineering key processes (particularly those that relate directly to how the customer interacts with the organization, (2) installing the proper information technology infrastructure to support the CRM initiative, and (3) training people in how to function under the new CRM program. CRM is cross-functional because a successful implementation requires input from marketing, sales, supply chain, new product development, finance, the MIS department, and human resources, to name a few.

If implemented properly, CRM can bring immense profits and value to a company and enhance the customer's interactions and loyalties. If implemented improperly (as in 55% of cases)[9] CRM can cost many millions of dollars, annoy customers, and demoralize employees. Most of the failures can be attributed to management's notion that CRM is just software that will manage the company's customers for it.

When Brands Become Part of the Language

Entirely new products that were developed to serve a particular purpose often become so established in the public's mind that they are often turned into commonly used nouns and verbs. Some examples:

"Please pass me a Kleenex."

"Can you FedEx the package to me?"

"Let me Xerox that report."

"I googled our professor."

"Can you text (or SMS) me your plans for tonight?"

The "Big Mac Index"—*The Economist* magazine's worldwide cost of living rankings.

"Volvo liberals"

"Do you need a band-aid for that cut?"

BRANDS AND BRANDING

David Ogilvy, founder of the giant advertising agency, Ogilvy and Mather Worldwide, defined a brand as "the intangible sum of a product's attributes: its name, packaging, and price, its history, its reputation, and the way it's advertised." Bernard Arnault, chairman of LVMH, the world's largest seller of luxury brands including Louis Vuitton, Dior, and Dom Pérignon, says that a "star brand" must be "timeless and modern, fast growing and highly profitable." In concrete terms, a brand is the name, look, logo, symbol, design, slogan, character, and/or packaging that uniquely identifies a particular product or service and differentiates it from its competitors. But brands can also be services, like FedEx, the overnight courier company, e-Bay, the online auction company, or Google, the Internet search engine. All successful long-term brands share some essential characteristics:

- High quality
- Simple, cohesive identity
- Consistency and predictability
- Great design
- Symbolism of a particular value
- Innovation

Brands are usually expensive to establish and maintain, but the benefit to a company supporting a brand is that it can charge a premium price over the nearest substitute. This is, in part, why a bottle of Coca-Cola costs more than a bottle of RC Cola. The opposite of a brand is a commodity, something that has no additional value other than its inherent properties. But some companies have cleverly managed to brand even commodities. DeBeers, the diamond cartel that controls about 70 percent of the world's diamond sales, has managed over the past century to create and maintain an aura of rarity, luxury, and high value for a commodity that is in actual fact, not rare, luxurious, or particularly valuable—after all, a diamond is just a bunch of tightly packed carbon atoms. If not restricted by DeBeers, the average rock would sell somewhere in the range of $2–30 depending on quality.[10]

The World's First Brands

Misty Mountain Tea

Cloudy Mountain Tea

Garden in the Sky Tea

Merchants in China during the Song Dynasty (960–1127 CE) used brands to inflate the perceived quality of low-grade teas and increase sales. This was probably the wrong strategy, otherwise the brands might still be around today.

Source: Evans, John C., 1992, "Tea in China: The History of China's National Drink," Greenwood Press, New York.

Top 20 Global Brands

1. Coca-Cola
2. Microsoft
3. IBM
4. General Electric
5. Intel
6. Nokia
7. Disney
8. McDonald's
9. Toyota
10. Marlboro
11. Mercedes
12. Citi
13. Hewlett-Packard
14. American Express
15. Gillette
16. BMW
17. Cisco
18. Louis Vuitton
19. Honda
20. Samsung

Source: Interbrand and *Business Week* 2005 rankings

Brand Equity

Brand equity is the value of the brand. While the term is often thought of in a financial sense, as in the annual global rankings of the most valuable brands (see box) or an entry on the company's balance sheet, brand equity can also be an intangible feature of a product or service as seen from the customer's perspective. Brand equity can manifest itself as loyalty to Crest versus Colgate, name awareness, a perception of higher quality and superior design (iPod). Often brand equity comes from the fact that a particular product just does the job better than any other product.

Brand equity is easy to destroy, particularly if marketers don't connect the main reason customers buy the product to the aura of the brand itself. Swissair is an example of diminished brand equity. For many decades Swissair was the defacto leader in safe, efficient, and reliable air travel with a taste of luxury. Because Swissair was from Switzerland, a neutral country, travelers would pay a little extra because they believed that the chance of a Swissair flight being hijacked was low, and the chance of getting to their destination on time was high. In the mid-1990s Swissair's management feared that the European Union (of which Switzerland is not a member) would shut the airline out of lucrative routes and impose high taxes on it. In response, the management purchased a 49.5 percent share in Sabena, the national airline of Belgium. Sabena had chronic financial problems and a reputation for particularly bad service. If that wasn't enough, Swissair went on to buy minority shares in several other small European airlines, many of which also had shaky finances and dubious quality ratings. These airlines included TAP (Portugal), Austrian Airlines, Turkish Airlines, LOT (Poland), and Air Littoral and Air Liberté (two financially troubled French airlines that served the lower end of the market). Swissair's management failed to understand the connection that customers made between Swissair and high-quality service. On October 2, 2001, Swissair was grounded, unable to pay for jet fuel to get its fleet back into the air. Shortly thereafter, the company ceased to exist.

Brand Extensions

Once a brand is established, companies often try to get more bang for their invested bucks by "extending" a brand across other products or services. A brand extension is a method of using leverage (the power of a particular brand name) to transfer the positive associations of an established (and branded) product or service to other products or services. Sometimes this works and sometimes it doesn't. Brand extensions work well in two types of cases:

1. The original product is modified to allow for several other products to do the same (or similar) job but with a slightly different twist. This is called a line extension. An example is the Sony Walkman tape player expanding into a Sony CD player.
2. The original brand is used to endorse a conceptually similar type of product or service to indicate shared characteristics with the main brand. This is called an endorser brand. An example is Marriot expanding into Courtyard by Marriott, Residence Inn, and so forth.

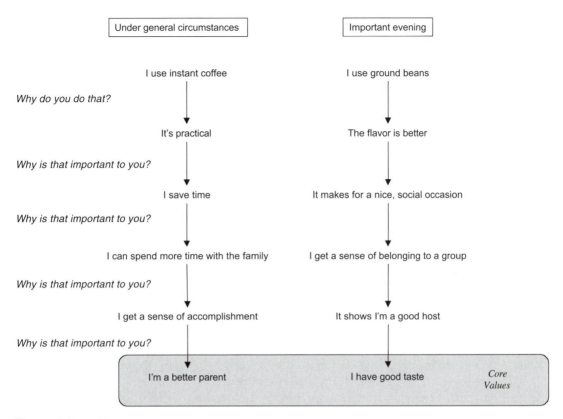

Figure 6.2. Laddering process.

Numerous fashion companies have tried extending their brands into any number of other products (Ralph Lauren bed sheets, Tommy Hilfiger purses, Calvin Klein underwear, the Swatch automobile).

Laddering Process or How to Get at Core Values

So how does a manufacturer get a customer to buy their product over a competing brand? There are only so many ways to advertise the benefits of a particular soap: rich lather, great scent, superior deodorizer, extraordinary moisturizer, powerful aphrodisiac, or beauty secret of the stars. Probably hundreds of soaps on the market can make the same claims. A relatively recent technique called laddering theory (also called benefit laddering, means-end chain, argument mapping, and cognitive linking) attempts to connect product attributes with certain core values held by consumers and which the attributes reinforce. Under laddering, an interviewer asks a consumer several questions about a particular product and why she or he likes the product. As the consumer answers each question, the interviewer probes deeper in an effort to get at the consequences from using a product and from those consequences to a core value, like self-esteem, independence, happiness, wisdom, a sense of belonging (to a particular group), or being a good wife/mother/father. Figure 6.2 shows an example of a cognitive chain leading down to the core values. In this example, we've taken a consumer who uses both instant coffee and ground beans. The circumstances for using one or the other can change depending on the situation. In this case, the product attributes are different, but so are the consumer's values and reasons for choosing one product over the other.

There are a couple of caveats to this methodology. First, it depends completely on the consumer's perceptions, which might change given a different circumstance as we saw with the coffee example. And second, this type of analysis only works for high-involvement goods, where there are several nuanced choices and the usage is quite personal. (It's doubtful that any value could come from analyzing the brand of cement that you might choose to pour over your driveway.)

One of the main benefits to the laddering approach is that it helps a company produce highly effective advertisements. These have sometimes been called lifestyle ads because they evoke a feeling or cultural value rather than dwelling on the product's characteristics. Infinity, Nissan's high-end automobile brand, attempted a lifestyle ad by depicting photos of rocks, tranquil streams, and forests—but no cars! Pepsi produced a very successful advertising campaign in the early 1960s called the "Pepsi Generation" that targeted the baby boomer generation's lifestyles and attitudes.

Unique Selling Proposition

Another way that companies seek to differentiate themselves from their competitors is by identifying and marketing their "unique selling proposition" or USP. The USP defines what *exactly* the product will do for you, and why it is very different from competing products or services. For example, Head and Shoulders' USP is that you will get rid of dandruff by using their shampoo. FedEx urges you to use their service when "your package absolutely, positively has to get there overnight," Dominos promised pizza delivery in 30 minutes or less, and M&Ms candies "melt in your mouth not your hand."

Service businesses attempt to define a unique selling proposition based on their particular competitive advantage (a better technology than others, cheaper price, faster turnaround time, and so on.)

ADVERTISING

Once a company has figured out who its customers are and how it will market to them, it needs to get the word out. Some of the first ads were sales messages found on papyrus in ancient Egypt. The first advertising agency, started in 1843 in Philadelphia, was a broker for ad space in newspapers. Today Madison Avenue (the New York street where most big ad agencies are headquartered) provides all the services associated with getting the product name and brand image out in the public psyche.

> Half my advertising is wasted, and the trouble is I don't know which half.
>
> —Lord Leverhulme, founder of Unilever

Generally speaking a company will choose one advertising agency in a specific geography (United States, Europe, Asia) to produce the creative message that entices a consumer to buy Tide detergent instead of Wisk. The agency is also then responsible for buying up media time on television and radio programs, and purchasing print ads in newspapers, magazines, the Internet, and on billboards. Some agencies have offices worldwide and can adapt or create new ads for many different cultures. Other services can include shepherding product promotions and targeted events to get consumers to try the product. Pepsi launched a campaign in Dallas called the "Pepsi Challenge" that offers consumers in shopping malls a taste test between Pepsi and Coke. Other campaigns include giving away free automobiles on Oprah's popular daytime show and product tie-ins with major league sports teams. Some of the biggest advertising firms offer direct marketing (junk mail), polling, and public relations services.

As consumers have gotten more advertisement weary and products like TIVO help them skip past TV ads, the agencies have had to become more creative in getting the message out. Some television ads are specifically designed to spell out a message when people use their TIVO machines to fast forward past the ads. Other campaigns include "guerilla marketing" tactics such as planting good-looking women in bars, who demonstrate the use of their new cell phone's features. And coming to a mobile phone near you: everything you didn't really want to know about underarm deodorant. One British ad agency, Mother, even got consumers to volunteer to be telemarketing victims when it offered a choice of wake-up calls (Heidi Klum, Rapper Ice-T, and Darth Vader) on the morning of Target's post-Thanksgiving Day sale. FedEx featured prominently in the story line of the movie, *Cast Away*, about a FedEx executive lost on a South Sea island (FedEx claims it did not pay any money to the filmmakers).

Advertising effectiveness is measured by rating points (RP) and target rating points (TRP). A rating point refers to the population of the universe that is impacted (i.e., has seen) an advertisement. One rating point equals 1 percent. Target rating points refer to the percent of the target market (say, men between 18 and 34 years old) that is impacted. So a television show that has 5.8 TRPs is only seen by 5.8 percent of the target market.

Advertising is a necessary evil if you're a consumer trying to enjoy your favorite TV program. But it's an indispensable part of marketing, and some would argue that the world is better as a result of advertising. How else would we find out about all the cool products we can buy?

A DAY IN THE LIFE OF A MARKETING MANAGER

Eric McCarthey
Senior Vice President
Managing Director, Global 7-Eleven Business Unit
The Coca-Cola Company

I came into Coca-Cola in a sort of serendipitous way 25 years ago. I was a region manager for the Charthouse restaurant chain in Portland, and I was working the floor one night at the restaurant. A bunch of guys from Coca-Cola were there. They were enjoying their evening quite a bit and had drunk too much. I wouldn't let them drive home. One of the guys was a senior executive and he was so impressed with the way I treated them that he said, you need to come and work for our company. I told him that I wasn't interested and had a good job where I was, but he was persistent.

I eventually joined as a territory sales manager in Portland, Oregon, and Vancouver, Washington. I was working all of the different parts of the market that used our products. Then had a sequence of pretty quick promotions that took me to Denver (chain sales and some business development), to Coca-Cola's headquarters in Atlanta (business development for the entire United States), and to Irvine, California (first as a Senior National Account Executive to set up a West Coast office, then as a director for several customer groups, and finally as senior director responsible for all the customers based on the West Coast).

After Coca-Cola won the Burger King account back from Pepsi in 1990, I was asked to come back to Atlanta to head up that new team. It was a huge job because Burger King is our second largest customer in the United States and Coca-Cola's sixth or seventh largest worldwide. Five-and-a-half years later I was promoted to vice president and ran the worldwide Burger King business. At that time, we were starting to put business teams around some of our largest customers.

Then in late 1995, I took a general management development assignment. I moved to Oslo, Norway, where I was deputy division president responsible for all the marketing in the North Sea countries (Norway, Finland, Sweden, Denmark, Iceland, Lithuania, Estonia, Latvia) plus Russia and Kazakhstan. It was the most thrilling 2 years of my career, but it felt like a lifetime. It was intense, very intense. We were building our infrastructure, literally from scratch, in Russia, and we were transforming the business in Scandinavia for a number of reasons. One of which was our bottling partner went south on us so we had to step in and assume the bottler role until we could pull in a new partner, Carlsberg. I was traveling half the time in Scandinavia and half in Russia. I'd go to the big cities like Moscow, St. Petersburg, and then I'd go out to the hinterlands in Siberia, Vladivostok, and other remote places. We were establishing relationships with stores and restaurants to carry our products. Before 1994 you couldn't get a Coke in Russia (Pepsi was there before we were).

I was just enjoying the living daylights in what I was doing, and I had to come back to Atlanta in 1997 to present our business plan to senior management. It was kind of a serendipitous event. We had finished the presentation and after the meeting was over the chairman of the company and the president of the North America business pulled me aside and said they wanted to talk to me. I didn't know what they were going to do: fire me, kill me, or whatever. They said, "Look, we're going into the last 2 years of our Burger King contract. We do not feel comfortable with the relationships that are in place." There were new people at the top in Burger King, and Pepsi was rattling their sabers threatening to get the business back again. So they asked me to come back and head up the Burger King team to ensure that we keep the account. It was a tough call for me because I'd purposely sought out this career development assignment in Scandinavia and Russia. In the past, no one ever got to the top of Coca-Cola without having been a general manager of a country or geography. But, when the chairman said, "we need you," my loyalty genes kicked in, so I moved back. We successfully retained the Burger King business worldwide for another 10 years.

In 2000 I was asked to head up all the sales and marketing for all of North America. That meant all of the restaurant business—it's about a $3.8 billion business for the company. I did that into 2003. Then in 2004, I was asked to take over the global 7-Eleven business. With about 30,000 stores worldwide, 7-Eleven is Coca-Cola's third largest customer. We had gotten into a pretty bad situation with them and the account was at risk. I guess I have a reputation for being a problem solver/change agent and so senior management wanted me to come in and repair and realign some key relationships on the team and with the customer.

Running customer teams involves four basic things:

1. You're responsible for the overall strategic plans globally for the business against the customer. That means identifying all the product categories and beverages we sell and how that portfolio is applied in the 7-Eleven business from country to country, as well as the growth plans for new categories we want to get into for identifying new opportunities and new revenue streams for that customer business.
2. Lead and coordinate all the alignment related to supply chain, finance, production, sales and marketing, business building initiatives, etc. The Coca-Cola company makes concentrate, we sell it to bottlers, the bottlers turn around and produce finished goods, and they sell it to the retailers. Big global customers, like 7-Eleven, expect us to work across a very diverse bottler system to coordinate all of that work on their behalf.
3. Manage a team of 22 business development, operations, and marketing executives in North America, Hong Kong, and Bangkok who understand how we go to market in each different country. The team members are local coordinators who drive the planning process and steward the relationship between our business system and the customer's business system. They also spend time problem solving (across supply chain, marketing programs that have issues, customer service issues, and other areas).
4. Build relationships at a number of levels: inside Coca-Cola with other functional groups, geographic managers, and business managers; outside Coca-Cola with the 7-Eleven managers; and with our bottlers in various countries.

A big part of my job is building relationships at multiple levels both within and outside of my company. Building trustful relationships is not easy. It requires really learning how to listen. But it also requires general communication skills, where you learn how to problem solve, form a business case, and present it clearly to a customer.

The most successful marketing people have a natural set of instincts around the whole supply chain. By this I mean:

- Understanding the customer's business model, how you fit up against it, and what value you bring to it.
- Consumer acumen—Who are the consumers who use the product or services? How often do they use it?
- Business system knowledge—How does the company make money? And understanding that from beginning to end. How does your customer make money? How do those two relationships fit with each other?

Good marketing people also need the following skills:

- Planning and organizing skills
- Interpersonal skills
- The ability to use disparate pieces of data to be able to analyze and reframe back to the customer new solutions, new concepts—we call it influencing through analytics

- Systematic and logical thinking
- Creativity to come up with new ideas

Marketing defines what you sell based on competitive portfolio, consumer insights, basis of competition, capabilities, and the core competencies of your business system. Sales brings it to the market, makes the connections to what the customers need, and differentiates it in terms of execution. But neither can be successful without the other being successful, so there's an interdependence between them. The best companies in any industry have built a culture where the two learn to work collaboratively with each other. There's a constant stream of information going back and forth. We have a culture where listening is appreciated and integrating new information is appreciated. Speed and response and adaptability to the fast changing nature of the market are best done when you've got the marketing side of your organization and the sales side working together. You don't have functional silos. It's constant work: you've got to nurture it, you've got to reinforce it, and you've got to lead it correctly. Our company purposely gets marketing people out into the commercial side of the business so they can see the whole picture. We also cross-rotate marketing and sales people.

Some of the frustrations that I have on the customer side, changes in direction, changes in their priorities (which are fairly frequent) cause us to go through multiple changes on our side, so you're having to adapt and be very flexible. And the same thing is true on our side. Our team sits between two very complex business systems: 7-Eleven's got their business system and we've got ours. And we're the bridge between those two systems. There's traffic jams all the time, and miscommunication all the time. There are misaligned priorities sometimes and misinterpretation of things. The frustration typically occurs at multiple levels especially when you've got that degree of complexity. So I find myself sometimes putting out fires at my counterpart at 7-Eleven because somebody got the wrong information.

On the other hand, I really get charged up when I can make a contribution that I can see that will have a sustainable impact. We're making the business system that I'm a part owner of stronger and better. I also have an intense curiosity to learn new stuff about the consumer, about leadership, about our own business system and the customer's business system. It's like a giant university of stuff that's always undergoing change metamorphosis. There's not one boring day.

I really like to help people develop, grow new skills. I'm at a mode in my career where I've reached many of my own goals and have proven that I'm successful, so now I can turn to others and help them become successful. It's really rewarding and it's a growing part of how I see my work going forward.

A typical day:

6:00 AM	Before starting the commute in to work, I spend some time reviewing e-mails and responding to the messages from Asia. They're at the end of their day, so I can probably still catch a few of them on the phone when I get to the office.
7:30 AM	Arrive at the office and run into a colleague in the elevator. She's working on our new TabEnergy promotion and wants to meet

	with me later today to talk about the launch and product display strategy for 7-Eleven stores across the United States.
7:45 AM	Check e-mail and voicemail messages. I return several voicemail calls from Europe. We schedule a conference call for tomorrow at 8:30 to discuss a couple of supply chain issues we're having with our 7-Elevens in Hungary.
8:15 AM	Quick phone call with Harry Yeung. He's our point man in Shenzen for the 7-Eleven account in China. He's got some ideas on tying in a promotion for us with the Visit China 2006 tourism board this year. We schedule a conference call for Friday with the entire Hong Kong and China team.
8:30 AM	I review the latest sales reports that came in overnight from our Southeast Asia stores. The past 2 days have been unseasonably cold in the region, so our sales are down. But even so, it looks like our new Black Cherry Vanilla Coke is doing better than Pepsi's cherry cola there. I'll have to have our folks in Bangkok work up a comparative presentation for 7-Eleven's central office there to argue for more shelf space, and particularly at the lower shelf height, because it looks like younger girls are the most frequent buyers.
9:00 AM	Conference call with our European team. We strategize over the roll-out of several new product launches over there. Coca-Cola Light Lime is a big one. There's been a change in 7-Eleven's strategic priorities in Eastern Europe. They are looking at focusing their existing retail stores more on fresh and pre-made foods, thus reducing the available shelf and display space for soft drinks. This change will require numerous adjustments on our side: the merchandising strategy inside the stores and our distribution frequency (stock-outs are a bigger risk).
10:30 AM	Meeting with the Logistics Executive Committee. We talk about a new RFID tag system that is cheaper (Wal-Mart and Kroger both require this) and also lets Coca-Cola Enterprises, our bottler, imprint even more details about when and where the product was bottled and allows faster tracking. This could be useful in an upcoming product tie-in with the new movie, *Cars*.
11:00 AM	I attend the monthly North America Executive Committee meeting. This is the operating group for all of North America. I sit on it because 7-Eleven is such a huge customer. We talk about upcoming product launches and marketing strategies across our different customer groups. During the year we have between 17 to 20 promotional initiatives in North America alone (350–400 worldwide). We also get a presentation from a member of the McDonald's team who tells us about a particularly innovative theater tie-in they did in Toronto.
1:00 PM	I get a call from the treasurer of a company for which I'm an external director and on the audit committee. She and I discuss some of the financing options that the company is considering.
1:40 PM	Review some of the RACI charts and prework material in preparation for the meeting on the initiative I'm heading. It's called "Working as a Global Team" and it's an effort to streamline all of the corporate functions in Atlanta and

coordinate their work more effectively with the local geographies around the world as well as the business units that cut across those geographies. It's a big project and we're working to shape the culture toward more accountability and transparency. We're clarifying roles and responsibilities, and trying to understand decision rights and decision inputs. It's all part of our ongoing refinement of processes to help us manage the matrix we all live in.

2:30 PM   Discussion with one of our flavor R&D scientists in the hallway. She's discovered a way to imitate an oddball fruit, Durian, that's highly popular in Asia. Since we produce all the concentrate syrups for 7-Eleven's proprietary ice drink, "Slurpie," we might be able to turn this into additional sales at not much cost to us.

2:45 PM   I pass by one of our team member's office and stop by to chat. He's been offered a position in our Denmark office and is mulling over the pros and cons. I offered him my impressions of when I was working in our Oslo office. He's got a wife and kids and is hesitant to uproot the family. Part of my job is mentoring other people and helping them to grow professionally.

3:00 PM   Product launch meeting with the Coca-Cola Blak new product team. They are introducing a new coffee-flavored carbonated cola product. We're working with them to roll it out simultaneously in all 7-Elevens across the country with special in-store displays and product tasting events. We're also planning a breakfast food tie-in promotion with Kraft and the new Coca-Cola Blak.

4:20 PM   I get a call from our 7-Eleven team member in Queensland, Australia. He's responding to some questions that came up during my visit there last week. We were in a corner grocery store chain that competes with 7-Eleven in Sydney and noticed some different ways that Pepsi had positioned its products. I had asked him to get more information about how that approach was working in the Australian market. We spend some time going over numbers that he's put together.

5:00 PM   I work with my assistant and the graphics department to put together a presentation I'm giving next week at our annual meeting in Miami. It's the top 150 managers of the company and we're working on a project called "Manifesto for Growth," which is sort of a blueprint for how we want to take the company into the future. We've got some really terrific ideas and I'm really jazzed about where this company is going.

INTERNET RESOURCES

General Marketing Information Sites

American Marketing Association: www.marketingpower.com
This is a very rich site sponsored by one of the largest associations for professional marketers. It has a career section including a job posting board, many best practice areas, a comprehensive academic resource center, webcasts, and numerous other benefits for practitioners.

The Chartered Institute of Marketing: www.cim.co.uk/cim/index.cfm
A site similar to the American Marketing Association, it is the world's largest professional body of marketers.

Peppers and Rogers Group: www.peppersandrogers.com
This is the consulting arm of Carlson Marketing group and features white papers from the "1-to-1 marketing" gurus, Don Peppers and Martha Rogers.

CRM Software Vendors

Siebel Systems: www.seibel.com
With over 3.7 million users of its software, Seibel is ranked the number one provider of CRM software products. Siebel Systems was purchased by Oracle in January 2006.

SAP www.sap.com
SAP's claim to fame is their enterprise resource planning (ERP) software that helps companies run their supply chains, customer service operations, and other functions. The company also offers CRM software and is ranked by Gartner as the number two market share holder.

Oracle: www.oracle.com
Oracle, a Redwood City-based provider of database software, was on an acquisitions spree in 2005, having purchased PeopleSoft, a major provider of human resources and CRM software, JD Edwards (financial management and supply chain management) and Siebel Systems. Oracle is now the number one market share leader in CRM software applications.

Salesforce.com: www.salesforce.com
This company provides software that resides on its own central computers. Companies can purchase a usage contract that is priced on the number of salespeople it has. Salesforce.com's software is targeted to support the sales department.

SUMMARY

Marketing is a key function in any business. Even if you're running a corner bakery, you hope to have marketing by word-of-mouth to let people know what great bread you sell. Most companies need a marketing function for a variety of reasons. Marketing helps companies analyze the reason their products and services sell well (or not so well) and can propose new ways to position the product and/or improvements to the product based on customer feedback. Marketing also plays a key role in determining the company's strategic direction. Many

Coca-Cola's Diet Vanilla Coke
Photo courtesy of Coca-Cola (downloaded from http://www2.coca-cola.com/presscenter/imagebrands.html on March 14, 2005. Reprinted with permission.)

of the market analysis tools are useful for assessing a company's overall strategy.

Once a company has identified who its customers are, it can choose a variety of ways to communicate with them and build their loyalty. A brand can foster a sense of loyalty and trust. Using tools such as the laddering process can help companies understand which attributes of the products or services appeal most to consumers and why. And finally, we saw how advertising works with marketing to get the message out to the consumer.

7

Sales

The consumer isn't a moron; she is your wife.
—David Ogilvy, author of *Confessions of an Advertising Man*

There is only one boss. The customer. And he can fire everybody in the company from the chairman on down, simply by spending his money somewhere else.
—Sam Walton, founder of Wal-Mart

Don't sell the steak; sell the sizzle. It is the sizzle that sells the steak and not the cow, although the cow is, of course, mighty important.
—Elmer Wheeler, author of *Principles of Salesmanship*

When an employee wants a raise, only the customer can grant it. It is up to the employees to figure out how to add enough additional value to get the customer to pay for it. Customers will pay if there is value. Stockholders won't.
—Fred Smith, Founder, Federal Express

WHAT IS SALES?

The sales function and sales people are probably the most familiar to us of all the business functions. We've all experienced a helpful sales person at our favorite retailer as well as an irritating call at dinnertime from a direct marketer. We've all probably heard a joke about a used-car salesman, seen a movie like *Music Man* that's based on a salesperson, or even been a salesperson at a local store. What's not well known is that sales is probably the most transformed of the business functions. For example, economists like to pose a trick question: "What concept or idea has resulted in the greatest source of increased productivity in the United States since the end of World War II?" Most people answer "the computer," but the right answer is self-service and the consequent elimination of sales people. We all engage in self-service at our local gas station or when buying a book on

Amazon.com. This self-service transformation continues today at many retailers and Web sites.

WHY IS THE SALES FUNCTION IMPORTANT?

Every business has a sales function of some kind. This is because every business has seen that it gets more revenue when some people specialize in selling. These people inform and persuade customers to buy. That is, they inform customers about products and services—especially new ones. Salespeople describe the products, what they can do, their features, as well as how the products can help the customer. Then they try to persuade and encourage the customer to buy their product and not a competitor's product. The amount of effort that goes into selling a product depends on how complex it is and how essential it is. Some products are bought—toothpaste. Others have to be sold—life insurance. Selling also varies if you are selling to a consumer or to another business.

DISTRIBUTION CHANNELS

A channel is a way to get goods and services to a customer. Coca-Cola has several distribution channels: fountain sales through restaurants and gas stations, can and bottle sales through convenience stores, grocery stores, entertainment venues (sporting events, theaters, amusement parks), and vending machines. Today, many companies use the Internet to supplement their traditional distribution channels, and some companies, like Amazon.com, use only the Internet because they don't even have physical stores.

In this section we'll look at the various channels used by the "B-to-C" (business to consumer) and "B-to-B" (business to business) manufacturers and service providers.

Selling to the Consumer

Traditionally, sales to consumers went through three primary channels, or methods of distribution. The retail store was and still is the channel through which the largest volume of merchandise and services reach the consumer. However, the formats of these retail outlets changes constantly. The second channel is selling through catalogues that are sent to the customer's home. Sears and Roebuck started the mail order catalogue business during the late 1800s in the United States. During that era most people still lived on farms and didn't get into town often. So Sears brought the store to them. The last channel was the door-to-door sales person. Today with fewer people at home this one is a shrinking channel. We'll review these channels and then discuss the new ones like the Internet.

Let's start with the door-to-door channel. There was a time, long ago, when everyone knew their Fuller Brush Man and their Avon Lady. These people routinely called at our homes. But today, there are few people at home. Everyone has a job outside the home. Some door-to-door companies like Amway and Mary Kay continue to thrive. They use a different sales model. These are recruiting businesses. That is, the successful people are ones who recruit a lot of people to sell door-to-door (or office-to-office) and get a percentage of their sales. The people who are recruited sell initially to all their friends and family. A few continue and succeed but most quit when they encounter the difficulty of cold calls and selling to strangers. But if you recruit enough people you sell a lot to friends and family. A variation is the party model. In this model the salesperson recruits someone to host a party of friends and family. The salesperson then brings products from Tupperware or Fredericks of Hollywood. The host gets a percentage of the product sales. So some forms of sales at home still exist.

Retailing was the original family business. Sales took place through mom-and-pop stores. Like the Fuller Brush Man, mom-and-pop stores are disappearing. Store formats from department stores, super markets, discount stores, club stores, big box retailers, category killers, to franchises have all replaced the mom-and-pops as well as each other. The mom-and-pop stores just couldn't match the lower prices that the big retailers achieved through buying in ever-larger quantities. Main street shops disappeared as the big retailers gathered into shopping centers, malls, mini malls, and strip malls. Today many malls, like the Mall of America, are entertainment centers. They are a kind of Disneyland with stores.

The one constant feature of retailing is that it changes. Malls are now struggling. People can do almost all of their shopping at Wal-Mart or Target, which are usually not in malls. Hence, the move to attract people to malls with entertainment. The Wal-Marts are now under attack by the likes of Best Buy. Rather than appeal to the mass market, Best Buy designs stores for customer segments. They have designed stores specifically for suburban mothers, small businesses, young men who are gadget freaks, and so on. These stores not only sell products but they also provide the customer with a shopping experience. Banks that sell to consumers are following the trend. These so-called retail banks are converting branches into financial services retail stores. By the time you read this chapter there will be a new type of retail store to sell something to you.

Catalogue sales, the third channel, made life convenient because the store came to you at home through the mail. You could order products by mail or telephone and the merchandise would be delivered by your mail carrier. This mail order channel was at its peak when most Americans lived and worked on farms. Their local retailer could only afford to stock a limited number of items. The catalogue could offer a broad range of merchandise and store it and mail it from a central warehouse. When people left the farm for the city, the department stores replaced the mom-and-pop general store as well as several catalogues. Sears then opened department stores in the cities.

The catalogue, however, continued for rural consumers and for some city customers who could order from a catalogue and pick up their merchandise at their local Sears store. The catalogue came back after women entered the workforce. It became more convenient to shop from home, call in your order, and charge it on a credit card. The catalogue made a comeback as a channel for selling to consumers. But once again the catalogue is being replaced, this time by the Internet.

In the mid-1990s, retailers like Amazon began to appear on the Internet. For those people with Internet connections, Internet shopping is more convenient and offers an even broader array of merchandise. Jeff Bezos, founder of Amazon.com, adopted the name Amazon because it's the largest river in the world. Amazon.com offers the largest assortment of books in the world. Even the largest stores at competitors like Borders and Barnes and Noble could not afford to stock all the books that Amazon could offer and store in central warehouses. And now with the rise of Federal Express and UPS overnight delivery, you don't have to wait to receive your order. As a result, sales over the Internet are increasing constantly.

Top 20 reasons you know you're traveling too much

1. You have a clear preference in airline magazines.
2. You have a year's supply of shampoo and conditioner—all in 1-ounce containers.
3. The family dog growls at you as you approach the house.
4. You have a reserved space at Park-n-Fly.
5. Samsonite asks you to "beta test" a new carry-on bag.
6. You know the 3-letter airport designations of all the major cities worldwide.
7. You've memorized (without trying) all the international and major domestic flight schedules (arrivals and departures) at your local airport.
8. You know your frequent flyer numbers by heart.
9. Your spouse buys new towels with "Mine" and "Welcome Home" printed on them.
10. You wake up and can't remember what city you're in—and you're home!
11. You have a favorite airport—*and terminal*—to get your shoes shined.
12. You do your Christmas shopping in airline gift catalogues and duty free shops.
13. You can pack for a business trip in the time it takes to toast a frozen waffle.
14. You have more flight miles than all of the flight attendants—combined!
15. You look forward to the first of the month because you'll get new meal selections, new magazines, and new airline movies.
16. You could write a guide to airport snack bars (rated by the number of Rolaids®)
17. You turn down dinner at the Four Seasons for a sandwich at home.
18. The agents at the airline clubs greet you by name.
19. You know the shortcuts in several airports to the shortest security lines.
20. You have special security line shoes that you can whip on and off in seconds.

Another twist on Internet retailing is the many auction sites like eBay. eBay was started so that people trading obscure items, like Pez candy dispensers, could find other people who were also interested in these same items. Selling obscure items instead of trading them soon became the norm. A manufacturer of very large shoes for men could find only a few customers in a city. It could find more through a catalogue. But over the Internet, the manufacturer can find a few customers in thousands of cities. Today the Internet and sites like eBay are facilitating the resurgence of the mom-and-pop store but in a different guise. In 2005 there were 150,000 people or mom-and-pops that made their living by selling merchandise on eBay. There were an additional 70,000 in Germany and 60,000 in the United Kingdom. So on the Internet the moms-and-pops coexist with the billion dollar retailers.

In retail today, the customer wants a choice. Retailers find that a customer is better informed when shopping with a catalogue or Web site. They compare prices, and then go to the retail store to observe and try on the merchandise before buying. Or they may buy over the Internet and if not pleased, return the merchandise to the nearest store. A retailer today uses all the channels to sell to the consumer.

Selling to Institutions

The sales function that sells to businesses, hospitals, or governments has gone through and will continue to go through the same kinds of transformations. As firms have gotten larger, their sales forces have specialized. There are sales specialists today for every type of product, customer, channel, and region. And like the retailers, firms sell through all channels for different purposes. In this section, we'll walk through the various channels available to a business to market its products and services to other businesses.

The direct sales force, which calls on the customer, is reserved for face-to-face discussions that are needed to sell a new product or convert a company into a new customer.

The direct sales force has five main jobs: (1) get new customers, (2) get an existing customer to buy more products, (3) buy different products, (4) get them to try new products, and (5) make sure that every customer—new and existing—is happy. In many companies today there is no sales organization on the organization chart. It's still there, but it's called "customer development" instead.

Within the direct sales force there are two more divisions: inside sales and outside sales. Inside sales people generally don't travel outside the company's home office. They are hired to receive phone calls or visits from customers to their showroom or operation. The inside sales force also answers Internet queries and is available to help customers choose the best product or service for their needs and answer any questions. Outside sales people, in contrast, go out and find new customers as well as service the existing ones. Outside sales people often travel a great deal. They too must be very knowledgeable about their company's products and services and be able to advise customers on the proper application and use for their products. Furthermore, since the outside sales person is often the only representative from the company that the customer sees, this sales individual has an important role as the company's "face to the customer."

In addition to direct sales, many business-to-business companies will use distributors and value-added resellers (VARs). Distributors are usually supply houses that stock products from a number of related companies, many of which offer competing products. Distributors can often provide unbiased product and service advice, special financing and purchase terms, but they are usually not as knowledgeable about the products as a direct sales person would be.

A VAR is a company that adds an additional component to a product it buys and then sells it to the end user. The product of a VAR can be as simple as embroidering or embellishing a plain t-shirt to resell to teenage girls, or as complex as packaging sophisticated software with a bundle of hardware (like a trading floor in a bank, or a paint station in an auto manufacturing plant) and selling it to the company that will use the system. The retailer, Best Buy, will put together an entire office or home theater for you. They'll charge you more for the end product than you would pay had you put the system together by yourself. In this way Best Buy acts as a value-added reseller.

The Internet, and particularly companies like eBay, is another channel for the business-to-business sales. The Internet can be a double-edged sword for the business channel. Most manufacturers have a Web site that they use to offer product sales. The issue they often face is whether the Internet site will compete and take business away from any of the other channels. Each manufacturer approaches this differently. Some only provide product and service information on their Web site. Others argue that the purpose is to make doing business with them as easy for their customer as possible, so why not offer products over the Internet? The flip side of the Internet sales comes up when a company sees its products sold by someone else (not directly authorized to sell its products) on a Web site like eBay. After the dot.com bust in 2000–2001, many computer hardware manufacturers saw their lightly-used equipment up for sale on eBay. So the question such companies face is "Do we offer our products new on eBay as an additional channel?"

Call Centers

One channel that's common to both B-to-C and B-to-B sales is the call center—or "care center" as they're known in companies that are trying to be truly customer-centric. The more forward thinking companies are actually using their call centers to sell products to customers. (The backward companies still see call centers as cost centers that have to be aggressively managed to reduce price—and thus outsource them to places like India.) Companies have discovered that it's far easier to sell a customer a new product when they call you to ask a question about a product they already have. Banks are trying to use call centers in this way, but the jury is still out on whether they can master the technique. The idea is that if you call to find out your checking account balance, the telephone banker will give you that information, but also ask if you'd be interested in a mortgage or a low-interest credit card today. As mentioned in the MIS chapter, information technology is key to making such a call center sale work. If the telephone banker offers you a mortgage not knowing that you're already a mortgage customer, then it reduces the banker's credibility (and wastes your time).

Other companies use call centers as an opportunity to turn around an angry customer. "Service recovery" as the lingo is known is an important way to retain customers, and in some cases, even turns them into strong advocates for the company. If a customer calls in and complains that something with their purchase is not right, the person answering the phone has an opportunity to not only fix the problem but also give that customer something more (extra supplies, a discount on future purchases, or some other benefit). Good service recovery can prompt a satisfied customer to broadcast his or her positive experience to other people. One of the most well-known stories is that of the department store, Nordstrom. The company will usually refund or exchange any product in an effort to provide excellent customer service. One urban legend (rumor) has it that Nordstrom even refunded the purchase price of snow tires—even though the company has never sold snow tires or any other automotive products.

WHO IS THE CUSTOMER?

Is the customer the guy trolling the new car lot? Or is the customer the wife back home? In the chapter on marketing we saw how Procter & Gamble (P&G) has identified three different constituents for its products. P&G says that their *customer* is Wal-Mart, Safeway, Target, and all the other retailers who sell P&G products. The *shopper* is the person who buys those products at the retail store and the *user* is the person who actually puts on the underarm deodorant or shaves with the Gillette razor. So to whom does P&G sell? All of them. As you can imagine, the different groups: customer, shopper, and user will respond to different types of sales efforts because their interests are not always the same. Similarly in a hospital, the purchasing department has a good deal of say in what products get bought for use in the operating room. A medical supply sales person might call on the purchasing director at a hospital. That discussion will probably focus on cost savings of whatever batch of products the sales person is offering. But the doctor who uses these products will also have a voice in those decisions. She is interested in the efficacy of the product, its ease of use, and any contingent side effects or aftereffects. How does a company know which customer to target and how does it satisfy all of those customer groups?

Many businesses are starting to wake up to the fact that the primary customer is not just the individual standing in front of the sales person. Car dealers find that women are responsible for influencing the choice of 81 percent of new vehicles in 2005.[1] In contrast, women influenced only 40 percent of new car purchases in 1985. So what's a dealership to do? Many of them are hiring women from apparel stores in shopping malls and training them to be car sales people. An added benefit to this strategy is that more men prefer to buy a car from a woman than from a man.

Moreover, women are responsible for the purchase decisions in a number of arenas that might surprise you:[2]

- 80 percent of all household purchases
- 92 percent of vacations
- 75 percent of all travel arrangements (business and vacation)
- 91 percent of houses
- 51 percent of consumer electronics
- 89 percent of new bank accounts
- 80 percent of healthcare decisions

In 2019, two out of every three richest people in the United States will be women.

What these statistics mean is that if you are trying to sell a vacation product, like a scuba or ski trip, you will have to make sure that the product appeals to women as well as men. Ski resorts have discovered this fact and they now offer ski packages that feature women-only ski clinics followed by a day at the spa.

Similar statistics can be seen in the rising power of Hispanic and Asian populations in the United States. The cable news broadcaster, CNN, developed a separate channel with its own distinct programming for the Spanish-speaking market. Asians account for a full 5 percent of the U.S. population and they have tremendous buying power with many unmet needs. The bottom line for a sales person is—know your customer ... she might be the one wearing the pants in the family and speak a native tongue other than English.

Segmentation of the Sales Force

Most large companies are able to employ specialized sales people to address the various different customer types. The first level is a local sales person who handles customer accounts in a particular region. As a customer grows and opens offices and operations across a larger region or even nationally, it usually wants to place one big order for all of its regional or national offices. In this way the customer exercises its bargaining power to get a better price and/or better service. The supplier's answer is to establish key account teams with a sales person (or group of sales peo-

Sales at Hewlett-Packard

A long-standing joke at Hewlett-Packard is that if HP had to sell sushi, the typical sales call would be, "Want to buy some cold, dead fish?"

ple) who focuses on those bigger accounts. The process continues as a customer expands internationally. For large global accounts, most companies establish global account managers who run a team of product and service specialists. Each of the company's largest global customers then get a global account manager and account team assigned to them. This allows the company to sell specific products and services to the customer and at the same time have specialists talking to their specialist counterparts inside the customer's organization. IBM, for example, has groups of hardware, software, services, and outsourcing specialists on a global account team. In this manner, if a customer is thinking about out-sourcing a particular activity (like the backroom data entry in accounts payable) then that customer wants their outsourcing specialist talking to IBM's outsourc-ing specialist discussing all the nitty-gritty details of how such an arrangement would work.

So now the sales function doesn't look as simple as it used to. You've got multiple channels, multiple regions, and even nations and multiple products and services that no one sales person can get his or her arms around. The best sales people know their customers exceedingly well and know how to make the customer want what they're selling. It means that the sales person has to know how to improve the customer's business and convince the customer that the product or service they're offering is the solution to the customer's problem. So how do you motivate a sales person to go from good to truly great?

REWARD STRUCTURE (OR INCENTIVES)

No sales person worth his or her salt will do this work for free. It usually involves turning up your courage to ask a stranger to listen to you and then face the possibility that the stranger will tell you to take a hike. Cold calling is tough, but the rewards for excellent salesmanship can be astounding.

Salary or Commission?

The old fashioned way of compensating sales people is to put them on a fixed salary like everyone else in the company. The benefit to this is that the company can direct the sales person's efforts to push certain products over others and it can move sales people to new regions more easily. In addition, as the amount of sales increase, the cost to the company of paying the salespeople decreases in proportion. The drawback is that fixed salary doesn't reward a really talented sales person—it's not a true pay for performance plan.

On the other side of the pay strategy is a straight commission plan. A commission is a percentage of the value of the sale that's paid to the salesperson who did the work to produce that sale. For example, if a salesperson sells 100 widgets worth $100 and her commission schedule is 10 percent then she would pocket $10. The benefit for a really good sales person is that they can make a ton of money on straight commission (but it can be very expensive for the company). The downside is that the company doesn't have a whole lot of control over how, where, and what a sales person sells. He'll sell the easy stuff to his best customers. He also might not spend enough time doing after-sale service for a customer, preferring instead to chase the next commission.

In actuality, most companies use a combination of salary and commission to compensate and motivate sales people. The trick is getting the right mix of salary level and commission schedule so that both the company and the sales person benefit. These hybrid compensation plans can be incredibly complicated and can include considerations such as paying commission on the gross value of the product sold, the gross margin (so that the sales person sells more of the profitable stuff), or some other metric.

Furthermore, a company can also make a decision on what kind of expense reimbursement policy it will follow. In order to generate sales, a sales person usually has to incur expenses that other people in the company don't have. This includes taking clients out to lunch or dinner, travel costs, phone calls while on the road, and so on. Companies that offer an unlimited expense reimbursement plan encourage a sales person to pull out all the stops in entertaining a client to get the sale. These are often used in high value, long selling cycle products like airplanes and expensive medical equipment. Per diem expense plans mean that a sales person gets a fixed expense budget for each day. It's simple for the company to administer, but often the perdiem rate doesn't always keep up with the actual cost of gas, food, lodging, and other expenses. A limited expense reimbursement plan is an administrative nightmare for everyone. The company has to monitor the expenses and make sure that it's only paying 32 cents per mile, an approved range of hotel bills, discount coach airfare, and legitimate cell phone bills. The sales person has to worry about how much of some expense a company will or won't pay, rather than worrying about how to satisfy the customer.

Quotas

Quotas are widely used in business. They are quantitative targets given to a sales person to induce them to sell a certain number or value of a particular product during a particular period of time. Quotas achieve three objectives:

1. Establish a benchmark for sales people to aim at (and thus provide motivation).
2. Encourage sales people to sell some things more than others.
3. Set a standard against which a sales person's performance can be evaluated.

An example of a quota is a sales person must sell $150,000 worth of product A, 60 units of product B, and generate 3 new proposals during the month of October. If she achieves all of those targets, then she has met her quota. If she exceeds her quota then she often qualifies for additional rewards, like public recognition or special awards.

> I don't care if he reports to me or not . . . just let me set his quota.
>
> —a sales manager

Public Recognition and Award Programs

Both public recognition, like becoming a member of the "President's Club" and an award program are designed to motivate and inspire sales people to a higher than normal level of performance. Many additional perks come as a result of achieving President's Club level (often the top 5 or 10 % of all sales people and/or those who achieve 150% of quota or more). Members of the President's Club often get treated to a first class ticket for themselves and their spouse to a nice resorthotel. They also get public recognition from the company, its top officers, and their peers as a truly exceptional sales person.

Award or incentive programs are short-term events that are designed to feature or promote a particular product or service, or target a new region or group of customers. But the programs also fire up the sales force to put out extraordinary efforts. Incentive programs are often structured as a contest where a sales person gets a particular award for bringing in 10 new accounts over the 2-month period of the event. Some companies, like Maritz (see the "Day in the Life" section of Chapter 3) specialize in designing and administering award programs. Prizes can include expensive watches and jewelry, the salesperson's weight in gold, two servants for a day (who, of course, can only perform jobs that are legal), or an all-expense-paid weekend for two in Las Vegas.

A DAY IN THE LIFE OF A SALES EXECUTIVE

Vincent Roche
Vice President
Global Sales
Analog Devices, Inc.

Analog Devices (ADI) is a 40-year-old business-to-business company. We sell silicon chips—we call them "hardware"—that go into other companies' products. Our products translate the real world to the digital world by sensing, converting, processing, and presenting electronic information. In essence our chips process signals—audio, radio, electronic—into something that the computer can understand. Many of our customers use a combination of our software with their own or a third party's software to give the computing element the instructions as to what to do with that data stream. Our chips go into a huge array of products, like computers, Internet switches, cell phones, medical diagnostics, automobiles, digital cameras, and televisions. Imagine processing light streams containing information from the world wide web at the rate of 10 billion cycles per second—well that's one of the applications that our devices perform! Even my BlackBerry is powered by our chips.

I was born and raised in Ireland, and graduated from high school in the late 1970s. At that time, Ireland had several of the characteristics of a third-world country. Unemployment was staggering (over 20%) and most people lived modestly and many were relatively poor. I'm from a lower middle class family, but I went to school with kids who couldn't afford to eat. Like many Irish, I imagined my way out of my hometown into electronics and engineering. I attended University of Limerick, which became one of the top engineering schools in Ireland. At around the time I was a senior in college, Ireland was courting the electronics industry and many companies, such as Apple and Hewlett-Packard were opening up plants in Ireland. I had three to four job offers before I even graduated.

My first job was with Texas Instruments (TI) in the United Kingdom. It was a graduate rotation (training program) in sales and marketing. We developed ideas in emerging segments and worked on selling and marketing them. I moved up through TI's sales department and then joined one of their distributors.

I really wanted to go to California. Like for most young Irish, California had a mystical allure to me and of course everyone imagined that becoming a millionaire was guaranteed on arrival! Of course, the real world is somewhat different. When I made it to the Golden State in the mid-eighties I joined Fairchild Semiconductor, considered to be the forefather of famous companies such as Intel. I joined as an applications engineer. From there I moved into international marketing. This gave me my first exposure to doing business in markets outside of the United States and particularly Asia. At that time we referred to the region as the Pacific Rim as business was not yet possible in mainland China which was just beginning to awaken from communism and to modernize its economy.

In the late 1980s I'd been in California 3 years and was taking a vacation back in Ireland. By chance I was contacted by my current company, ADI, who really wanted to bring someone on board with international marketing experience, but particularly someone who could speak the language of Silicon Valley. Funny how random life can be sometimes. So I moved back to Ireland and joined ADI's marketing department where I learned how to define new product areas, introduce the products to market, and develop the advertising and public relations activities for them. I spent 5 years in marketing and then took a promotion to a product line management job for one of our product lines. I was given P&L responsibility, which was a new experience for me. It forced me to learn how to run the R&D function along with managing the product investment plans — and ultimately make the returns expected by the company.

Then 5 years ago, the CEO tapped me to run the sales force, based at our headquarters in Boston, Massachusetts. I had always had ideas on how to deepen our customer engagements and accelerate revenue growth from my prior vantage points as an individual contributor sales engineer and product line manager. Now the time had arrived to put the ideas into action. As the leader of the sales organization I also wanted to balance the voice of the customer with the voice of the product line by putting a stronger sales management team in place. As in all industries competition increases over time and it's no longer sufficient to deliver only technology to customers. Today we have to deliver a complete experience, such as product customization and an excellent technical and product delivery service, to our ever-more demanding customers.

ADI has a very diverse business. We have 50,000 customers worldwide and 10,000 products. We have a large global footprint, which means that we do business practically everywhere on the planet. Half of our business is in Asia and half is in the Americas and Europe. Half of our business goes into capital equipment, such as a factory automation and medical diagnostics applications, and half goes into personal electronics, such as cell phones, MP3 players, and high-definition digital TVs.

We have three primary channels for selling our products. First, we have a captive sales force that calls on about 1 percent of our customers, but these are our biggest and most technologically advanced customers and, of course, the ones with the largest available opportunity. This sales force, currently about 500 people strong, is the group that I oversee. This group gets involved in helping our customers to select and utilize our silicon chips in product research and design phases, and they help procure these products in volumes to support the customers' manufacturing needs.

Roughly 50 percent of our sales go through a second channel: our distributor network. These are independent companies that carry our products along with other suppliers' components. They provide a broad range of products and services, and can offer attractive risk management, credit terms, and personalized help typically to our smaller customers. The third, and emerging channel, is our Internet site. You can actually buy our products over the Internet from any part of the globe. We offer this service but as yet it's in its infancy. The more technology-competent younger generation is likely to figure out how best to leverage this service.

This is the best job I've ever had! I can provide the eyes and ears for the company at the customer level — to the real world so to speak — and keep an eye on our competition. I'm like a "canary in the coal mine" that provides the voice-of-the-customer. I look at factors underlying business trends in the marketplace.

While my product line colleagues develop the new and exciting technologies and products, I am responsible for leading the company into exciting new geographical markets in regions such as China, India, Russia, and Brazil.

With the increasing complexity of managing customers comes the need for continuous adaptation and skill building within the sales force. One such area of skill creation is in the area of customer conversation management. There are various languages of selling,[3] which is a metaphor based on different cultures:

- Spanish—the sales engineers speak continuously with the customer's product design engineers and discuss features, functions, and costs.
- Russian—middle managers at the seller and buyer talk to each other about entire product platforms, risk/reward factors, etc.
- Greek—the so-called C-level executives of each company discuss market share, growth, profitability, and creation of mutually valuable opportunities.

I get involved most of the time at the "Russian" level of sales and sometimes at the "Greek" level.

I'm responsible for creating the top-line growth in revenues through collaboration with my business unit peers on the CEO's staff. My job is to focus the organization on the creation of the highest return opportunities and to solve problems that have the most impact. I also handle issues that bubble up to my level because my subordinates have exhausted all of their means to solve a problem—by this time the problem is toxic. On rare occasions, we have to get the CEO involved.

In addition to running our sales force, I also wear a corporate marketing hat. This involves getting the corporate message out to the public, public relations, marketing communication, advertising, and web activities. All of those activities are handled by a group of about 80 people, which I also supervise. The product marketing function resides in the product line organizations and they provide the product-specific content.

My management philosophy is (1) hire great people to lead the organization, (2) be abundantly clear on expectations, (3) create a culture that craves success, and (4) focus them on the things that will make the maximum impact. Through the years the company has successfully developed some of our most capable contributors in the engineering and sales areas from the pool of college talent.

A good sales person is an opportunity creator and a problem solver. I can typically tell within a few minutes of meeting someone if they'll be a good or great sales person. You can get a sense for how they think about things, their drive, energy, interpersonal style, and so on. We tend to look for the following skills and traits when hiring:

- A sense of adventure and a vision
- Business acumen
- A love of the "hunt and chase"
- Reward-driven personality—most top sales people love money
- Orientation toward deal closure
- Good communication and influencing skills, ability to orchestrate collaboration

- Ability to speak the technical language (for our business that usually means a technical degree)
- Results-oriented, persistent, and some level of ability to accept rejection!
- Time management skills—you have to manage your energy on productive tasks

Sales is a great job here at ADI. A sales person 2 years out of college can earn more than an engineer with similar tenure here. We put new sales people through a 1-year training program, which could start with manning the customer support telephone lines. We affectionately call them "telephone fodder." We get about 50,000 calls per year into this group in the United States alone. It's a great way to learn the products, learn how to talk to customers, and help them solve basic problems. It's a bit like drinking from a fire hose. After that program and other training courses, a sales person will be assigned a territory and he or she will be "flying solo" under the guidance of an experienced sales manager. Our highest performing sales people will ultimately be among the highest earners in the corporation.

As with any job, this one comes with a few frustrations. I don't like to manage reactive things at the expense of proactive things. This happens both inside and outside of ADI. Inside ADI we have some alignment issues, like all complex companies, across the product and customer domains that occasionally produce obstacles to working smoothly across the organization. This is particularly challenging when offering solutions (packages of products, services, and software) to customers. But I'm an optimist with a high level of stamina, and I don't give up until we figure things out. Outside of ADI we have to deal with reactive situations in making sure the customer gets the service they deserve and products they ordered when and where they expect them.

The extensive travel can be stressful. I can spend about two-thirds of my time on the road, and a lot of it is in Asia. The jet lag and lack of sleep is constant so it's necessary to keep physically fit and keep life as close to normal as possible. Boston's Logan airport is always a challenge at the end of a long trip—the baggage handlers seem to ensure that my bag is last to appear on the "belt!" On balance I'm not complaining though, as I get to do some personal travel to great vacation spots with my family in Europe, North and South America, and Asia.

On the other hand, my job is a continuous adventure. I'm at heart a technology buff. I feel like a kid in a candy store because I get to see the really cool whiz-bang stuff that our customers are developing. ADI is always involved in the early stages of innovation. This job is great for adventurous people who like change and ambiguity. I thrive on interactions with people and developing new ideas and insights. The hunt and chase of getting the sale is invigorating. Fundamentally I love dealing with people and creating win-win scenarios with our customers.

I really have two completely different types of days. My in-office days are almost entirely tied up with meetings and phone calls. We've got the typical office-type meetings like the weekly business operations reviews, annual planning and budgeting cycle discussions, management meetings with my peers and the executive committee in investment decisions, strategy and operations reviews, top-level talent assessments, product line status reports, and various communication meetings with my employees and the PR/marketing groups. What I'll describe here is a typical day out of the office.

A day on the road in the life of a sales executive:

5:00 AM	*Ohayou Gozaimasu* (good morning)! Welcome to the land of the rising sun! Thank goodness my BlackBerry phone works around the world. I've already had two phone calls with folks back at headquarters regarding Intel's new Pentium chip. We're supplying the power source that accurately and reliably delivers power and monitors operating temperature.
5:20 AM	I go to the hotel's fitness center to squeeze in a 1-hour workout before my breakfast meeting. It's the only thing that keeps me sane. I'm a bit of a fitness buff, and with all the mealtime meetings I have while on the road, it's the only way to balance the calorie load and keep my stamina and alertness for the wall-to-wall meetings. A great motivator that forces me out of bed at 5AM is the need to perform with a bit of dignity in my hobby of Olympic distance triathlons (running, cycling, and swimming).
6:45 AM	I call an executive at one of our Silicon Valley-based key customers, a leader in the Internet equipment market. They are set to revolutionize the way companies can produce high-quality video images and sound from anywhere around the globe in real time direct to the desktop PC. The system is relatively cheap because we collaborated early in their product development cycle to optimize the system design around the best available silicon chip and software technologies. Maybe I won't have to spend so much of my life in airports anymore.
7:30 AM	Breakfast meeting with my Tokyo-based staff and my product line colleagues to understand the agenda and plan for the day ahead. First on the agenda will be a meeting with a product line executive from Sony to trade ideas and comments on the state of the markets we serve and to discuss the quality of our collaboration and explore further opportunities. We supply the digital signal processor (DSP) chips that "read" images from a digital camera and turn them into the zeros and ones that the camera's computer can understand. Our DSP chips can also adjust the image data before it gets to the camera's brain.
9:00 AM	Our CEO is traveling with me on this trip. He's here to meet with the head of Toshiba Medical, a leader in the development and supply of leading edge medical diagnostics technology, among other things. Toshiba Medical is developing a new CT scan machine that requires a very sophisticated chip. This chip converts magnetic resonance signals into computer language that Toshiba then programs to generate colorful (and informative) displays that can simply save lives when interpreted by skilled medical staff. ADI is the only company that that can provide this chip with the accuracy and computing speed needed to produce a reliable image. However, Toshiba has some concerns about supply and the risk they face if we can't deliver. This is where we bring out the big guns (our CEO) to convince them that we will supply what they order without fail.

12:00 PM	Sushi lunch meeting with Sharp Corporation executives at their design center. I brought some of our design engineers to meet their counterparts in Sharp. Sharp is talking about a new type of video signal chain that will allow the user to receive a much clearer picture in a flat panel television screen, but it requires a different type of integrated circuit architecture. The engineers on both sides are talking about the possibilities in what appears to be a form of secret code! This is how many key projects come to pass.
2:00 PM	Called on a customer we're trying to do business with. They provide factory automation equipment and with Toyota's expansion in the United States, we hope to get some of the business from Toyota's supplier.
4:00 PM	Met with the Japan sales force. We discussed some new products coming out and how we will position them in the market. We talked about the status of current accounts (revenue growth, product line expansion opportunities, sales trends, etc.). We also talked about some new technologies that our designers have been working on.
6:00 PM	Phoned an executive at Nokia, in Finland. We discussed the request for proposal (RFP) Nokia has issued for a component that will go into one of their new mobile phones. We're trying to beat out an entrenched arch competitor for this contract.
7:00 PM	I rejoin our CEO as we head out to a dinner we're hosting for several of NTT Corporation's senior executives. It's a relationship building effort. NTT (Nippon Telephone and Telegraph) is one of Japan's largest companies. We do business with them indirectly but want to make sure that they know how much we value their relationship. It starts with a traditional tea ceremony in one of the country's best Kaiseki restaurants (these are Japanese gourmet meals that entail about 20 courses of elaborately decorated plates of mostly vegetarian foods). Then we go straight into beer, plum wine, sake (rice wine) ... Gee, the Japanese sure like to party and always do it in moderation! But this is one surefire way to get them to relax a bit. All in all they have figured out the formula for living long lives!
11:00 PM	Time to catch up on my "day time job!" The e-mail stream has no sympathy for time or place. It'll be an hour or so before I can say *Oyasuminasai* (good night).

INTERNET RESOURCES

How to sell: www.justsell.com

There is no shortage of Web sites that promise to tell you the secret to sales success. This is one of them.

Marketing to women: www.trendsight.com

This is the Web site of author and consultant Marti Barletta. She is an expert in how to sell products to women and writes frequently for other publications like *Advertising Age*.

Marketing Profs: www.marketingprofs.com
This site offers many articles on selling (notwithstanding its name). To get access to much of the content, however, you need to sign in as a member (which is free).

SUMMARY

Sales is one of the most transformed functions in business. The self-service trend has made many salespeople redundant. At the same time, a proliferation of new channels and the rise of women's buying power has placed more demands on sales people to work harder and smarter and truly understand what they are selling and to whom.

The old channels of door-to-door selling and the mom-and-pop retail stores have faded as new channels inspired by big box retailers like Target and Wal-Mart have taken their place. The Internet is also transforming how sales are transacted and forcing many businesses to rethink their entire sales model.

As customers become more multinational and more diverse, sales people are forced to reorganize themselves—often into teams of product and service specialists—that cater specifically to the more demanding customers. In addition, previously underserved groups, like women, Hispanics, and Asians, are gaining influence over the majority of sales in virtually every product and service category. Companies ignore these groups at their peril.

Finally, we looked at the different ways that companies motivate and inspire their sales people to produce extraordinary returns. Most companies use a combination of fixed salary plus commissions. Several also supplement that compensation with personal recognition and special motivational events.

Sales can be an exciting career with rich monetary rewards. Like any career, those who work hard will excel.

8

Management of Information Systems

Software is the competitive weapon of the new millennium.
—Ann Winblad (venture capitalist)

It used to be, if you wanted information, you had to go up, over, and down through the organization. Now you just tap in. Everybody can know as much about the company as the chairman of the board. That's what broke down the hierarchy. It's not why we bought computers, but that's what they did.
—Frederick Kovac, Goodyear

To err is human, but to really foul things up requires a computer.
—Anonymous

WHAT IS THE MANAGEMENT OF INFORMATION SYSTEMS?

The information system (IS), also called information technology (IT), represents the arterial supply (veins, arteries, lymphatic system) of our business anatomy. IS and IT are everywhere in a business and most businesses can't run without them. Information technology consists of four parts:

1. Hardware (computers, servers, routers, switches, etc.),
2. Software (Microsoft office, Quickbooks, Adobe Photoshop, and so on),
3. Networks (the telecommunications infrastructure that glues it all together), and
4. The people who design, program, maintain, and run it all.

MIS is the management of information systems. What information do users want? How do users want to interact with that data? MIS involves programmers (who tell the computers how to handle the data), technology architects (who plan how that data comes in, gets distributed, stored, and deleted), systems analysts (who are the diplomats negotiating between what the businesses want and what the IT group can deliver), and MIS managers (who have to make it all happen).

The Automation of Information and Communication

Back in the Stone Ages before computers (c. 1970), most of life was manual. That meant that to pay for a bag of groceries you could either pay cash or write a check. Your check would be stamped by the grocery store, they'd write down your driver's license number and make sure that your telephone number was on the check and send it off to the store's bank. A month or two later, you would get your cancelled check back in the mail with your statement. Isn't this a quaint way of doing business? Aside from spending way too much time writing checks in order to purchase something, it was an expensive way to do business. People at the grocery store, the store's bank, the clearinghouse, and your bank all had to handle the check you wrote to buy a twelve-pack of Coke. Not only that, it took several days before the grocery store actually saw the money land in its bank account. (This was a useful feature, called "float," if you were a college student on a tight budget.)

Today most of life is digital. The few Neanderthals who still write checks will soon be extinct. You pay for your groceries with a credit or debit card, or flash a small microchipped "smart card" past a card reader to get a soft drink from a vending machine. In Finland, one of the more technologically advanced countries, you can even use your cell phone (preferably a Nokia) to purchase everything from bus tickets to theater tickets. Credit card, water, and electric bills are easy to pay via Internet or automatic debit from your checking account. But how does all this electronic money change hands? And who keeps track of all these transactions?

In the 1970s the United States shepherded a system known as the automated clearing house (ACH) that processes payments electronically. It's an association of companies (banks, credit card companies, and so forth) that track the movement of money and enable quicker settlement of money owed and paid. In 2000 the ACH processed more than $12 trillion in payments.[1]

Since the actual technology portion of IT (hardware, software, and networks) changes so rapidly, this chapter will not spend any time describing the specific technologies available. Instead, we'll discuss the concepts and the people in MIS and what they do.

Most Computerized Countries

1. Switzerland 70.9
2. United States 66.0
3. Singapore 62.2
4. Sweden 62.1
5. Luxembourg 62.0
6. Australia 60.2
7. Denmark 57.7
8. South Korea 55.8
9. Norway 52.8
10. Canada 48.7

(Ranked as number of computers per 100 people)

Source: *The Economist* Pocket World in Figures 2006.

WHY IS MIS/IT IMPORTANT?

Information technology and information systems make life easier for companies by organizing data in a way that is useful (that is, easy to find, easy to understand, can be manipulated to give answers to questions, and automates a tedious but important process). Information systems generally fall into two categories: those that handle a particular type of transaction or activity, and those that handle entire processes that usually span functions and/or business units within an organization and specify various process parameters during their execution.[2] Transaction processing technologies include:

- e-mail—this certainly spans functions, business units, and even companies, but it does not specify any process parameters (roles, tasks, rules, etc.).
- Computer-aided design (CAD)—this is used for one particular task and does not span functions or business units.
- Electronic data interchange (EDI)—transmits information between two entities, often a buyer and a seller.

Some examples of process-enabling information systems are

- ERP (Enterprise Resource Planning) Systems—Software and hardware that together generates invoices, monitors payment and credit terms, follows customer orders and product deliveries.
- SCM (Supply Chain Management)—This technology helps manufacturing operations keep track of their inventory, production schedules, and work flow.
- e-Procurement and e-Marketplace—These are business-to-business applications that match buyers and sellers, organize bids, arrange delivery, credit terms, route purchase requests to suppliers, and monitor payment and delivery of items bought and sold.
- CRM (Customer Relationship Management)—These types of applications track end-to-end customer related activities from marketing and sales functions to customer support.
- Web Services—this is a relatively new arena comprising an Internet- or Intranet-based (and yet to be developed) "service grid" much like an electric grid that serves as a common foundation for various types of application software. Software vendors offer the most up-to-date versions, with maintenance and support, and they will even program their software to work with the databases of their customers.

These process-enabling information technologies are often huge undertakings and can take years to design and implement across a large organization. Many business leaders complain that these big IT projects do not live up to all they are touted to be. And the statistics seem to support this view. Ninety-eight percent of IT projects with budgets over $10 million are either over budget, late, or do not deliver the promised results.[3]

Business Process Engineering

Process-enabling information technologies can significantly enhance a company's ability to respond better and faster to customer and/or supplier demands. These technologies can also provide managers in the company with better and faster information that help them make crucial decisions about where to spend critical and supply-limited resources. But what is sometimes overlooked is that process-enabling technologies often force managers to analyze and even change the way a particular process is being handled. It can even surface questions about the company's strategy and organization.

For example, in January 2000 Federal Express restructured its entire company under a new corporate brand, "FedEx." While the reorganization could be seen as a "same monkeys, different branches" type of corporate initiative, the change actually had huge implications for how business was done in FedEx. First, several of the independent companies that FedEx had bought in the years prior (Caliber, RPS, Roberts Express, and others) were now combined and re-branded as FedEx Logistics, FedEx Ground, and FedEx Custom Critical. On top of that, the previously independent and separate sales forces, accounting systems, IT systems, tracking systems, and so on were now merged into one big FedEx system. The strategic goal was to make it so that any FedEx customer— whether a large multinational customer, or the small home-based business— would have one toll-free phone number to call, one Web site, one invoice, one account number, one sales team, one customer service representative, and so on for all of its needs. FedEx would from then on become a single face to every customer it had. This initiative required enormous changes in all areas of the company. FedEx spent over $100 million on the reorganization over 3 years, and roughly 10 percent of its annual revenues on upgrading its IT infrastructure.

The IT group was combined with sales, marketing, and supply chain solutions into a single group, FedEx Services, that served all of the other FedEx businesses. (For more on FedEx's supply chain solutions group, see the "Day in the Life of a Supply Chain Executive" in Chapter 10.) Prior to the reorganization, FedEx had already moved to leverage its technology and expertise in managing information by providing logistics and warehousing services for business customers. This meant that a person could order a Dell computer on the Internet and the order would simultaneously go to Dell's manufacturing queue and to FedEx, which considered itself part of Dell's assembly line. FedEx would bring parts in to Dell's plants from all over the world on an as-needed (just-in-time) basis. This saved Dell a heap of money (they don't have to build and maintain extra warehouses) and time (faster assembly of computers). The FedEx system prior to 2000 worked fine if all you used was FedEx's express shipping service. But if you were a large global customer that needed express shipping, freight forwarding, and ground transportation services, you had to deal with several sales forces and several invoices from several different FedEx businesses. This was a pain in the neck for most customers, and UPS (FedEx's biggest competitor) took full advantage of the situation. The new strategy meant aligning all of the FedEx operations under one roof so that service in every domain was seamless to the customer. From an IT standpoint, it was a huge undertaking (imagine getting five separate companies' IT systems to talk to each other, let alone work well together) and one that impacted every part of how FedEx did business as well as its strategic direction.

So 6 years after the fact, how did that big FedEx reorganization work out? The company's stock has grown an average of 25.2 percent every year for the past 5 years. It's number 2 on *Fortune*'s "America's Most Admired Companies" list, number 40 on the *BusinessWeek* 50 list of best performers, and number 20 on *Fortune*'s "Best Companies to Work For." Within the IT world, FedEx is seen as an innovator and one of the most sophisticated users of ERP technology.

All too often, general business managers see the IT department as a "black box" filled with nano-geeks who are nocturnal and speak in 3-letter acronyms.

What the managers don't always realize is that information technology and how it is implemented in the organization can have profound effects on how the business is actually conducted.

THE PEOPLE IN MIS

Information technology is often thought of as the combination of computers and software that make a business run and allow people to talk to each other. But without the masses of people who fill specific roles in MIS, all you would have left would be the boxes. The MIS people are what make those boxes talk to each other and perform meaningful work. Table 8.1 lists a rogue's gallery of the types of roles that MIS people fill.

Most Wired Countries

1. **United States**
2. **Iceland**
3. **Netherlands**
4. **Finland**
5. **Denmark**
6. **Sweden**
7. **Norway**
8. **Switzerland**
9. **Australia**
10. **Austria**

(Ranked as number of hosting services per 1,000 people)

Source: *The Economist* Pocket World in Figures 2006.

Eunuch Programmers by Dilbert
Dilbert: © Scott Adams/Dist. by United Feature Syndicate, Inc. Reprinted with permission.

INFORMATION PROCESSING

One of the primary jobs of the IS/IT function is to process information in a way that is useful for business leaders. What does that mean? Say you keep track of all the football and baseball scores for each season, and perhaps you even run a betting pool for your friends. You've got this on a spreadsheet showing the games, teams, scores in each quarter/inning, and perhaps even a list of which player produced which score. All of those numbers are just data. It doesn't become information until you start to ask questions like "How many field goals did the Flaming Falcons score in the first quarter of every game they played?" In order to figure out the answer to that question, you could scan your columns of data for first quarter field goals for that team and add them up. That's pretty mindless work. Or you could tell a computer to do it for you. That's called programming a computer. To program a computer, you write out, in very exact terms and in a language the computer can understand, what each individual step requires and what the computer needs to look at in order to count the proper scores so it can provide the answer. It may sound tedious at

Table 8.1. The people in MIS and what they do

Role	Common titles	Job description	Salary range
Big Kahuna	CIO (chief information officer) CTO (chief technology officer)	This is the highest-ranking position in MIS. She or he usually reports to the CEO, is responsible for all IT infrastructure, strategy, and operations in the company	$160,000–300,000
Little Kahuna	IS manager IS director Account executive	Manages all the IS systems in a particular business unit or a part of the company, and/or responsible for significant parts of the IT infrastructure	$90,000–175,000
Diplomats	Business application delivery director Senior business systems analyst Client technologies manager	Works as a liaison between business users to understand their requirements, budgets, and timeframes, and then directs IT development and implementation of business applications. Also explains to business people what IT can do (or can't) given business constraints (budgets, schedules, etc.) and strategic needs	$80,000–155,000
Information architects	Systems analyst IS planning manager Systems programming manager Consulting technical solutions architect Business application delivery manager	Develops the networking architecture, the strategy for enterprise-wide hardware and software, and plans for systems growth and future development. Evaluates existing systems and technology for current and future needs. Writes documentation that details a program's development, logic, coding, and any changes made	$42,000–140,000
Interpreters	Project manager Senior client/server programmer Lead software engineer Developer Senior engineer	Takes information and user requirements transmitted from analysts and turns it into language that computers can understand. Develops and maintains process-enabling information technology systems such as ERP, CRM, and supply chain programs	$50,000–118,000
Security guards	Computer security manager Audit manager Network security systems manager	Protects corporate systems from hackers and phishers; protects customer data; assures corporate compliance with regulatory requirements such as the Sarbanes-Oxley Act	$62,000–105,000
Grease monkeys	Database administrator Maintenance manager Client technologies manager Client/server programmer Database librarian Engineer	Troubleshoots, maintains, and repairs all systems (servers, desktop systems, network, hardware, software, etc.) and ensures data integrity. Reviews, analyzes, tests, and debugs operational systems that support client/server software applications	$48,000–105,000

Role	Common titles	Job description	Salary range
Road pavers	Telecommunications manager Network manager Software engineer Data modeling analyst Programmer	Coordinates, maintains and manages the network infrastructure. Develops data models to meet the requirements of the internal IT organization. Maintains integrity of data by reducing redundancies	$46,000–98,000
Garbage collectors	Technician Computer operator Data control clerk	Purges unnecessary data, keeps systems free of junk. Performs routine maintenance tasks. Loads and observes peripheral equipment, reports error messages, runs backup tape drives	$20,000–50,000

first—you can probably get the number faster than you can tell the computer to do it. But if you have many teams over many quarters, and you might want to ask the same question again in a year, then it's probably easier to get the computer to do the drudgework. This is called programming a computer to respond to queries (questions). Did you ever wonder how the sports announcers, particularly during a televised football game, come up with the endless supply of statistics they recite? They have people running computer queries on a particular team or player to tell you that, for instance, there are only 10 teams in the NFL that have won more than 30 games over a 2-year period (Pittsburg is ranked twice on that list) or that John Elway (former quarterback of the Denver Broncos) had the second worst passing record in Superbowl history (second only to Ben Roethlisberger, quarterback of Pittsburg).[4]

Data Warehousing

Data warehouses are large repositories of multiple, large, and integrated databases from several parts of an organization. Many companies have developed data warehouses to allow them to query, process, analyze, and report data that comes from a variety of sources or view the history of transactions for trend analysis. For example, Wal-Mart uses data that it gathers from the scanners at its checkout counters to spot trends in what kinds of products people buy together (a disposable camera to go with the infant-sized diapers). Savon Drugs uses similar scanner data to fuel an automated inventory analysis and order system. Banks use data warehouses to help them analyze customer risk and credit profiles, to manage their relationship banking programs, to analyze mergers and acquisitions, and even to monitor how the individual branches are performing.

Here we need to make a distinction between data warehousing and transaction processing. Processing a transaction—whether it's scanning an item at a checkout counter for the purpose of ringing it up on a cash register and collecting money for it, or whether it's generating an order to pay a bill electronically via your Internet banking software—needs to happen relatively fast. A customer will not wait all day for a scanner to tell a cash register what item it is she wants to buy. She just wants to pay for the item and get going. In fact, she probably doesn't even care if a scanner or a computer is involved. Similarly, the reason people sign up for Internet banking is speed and ease of use. Therefore, transaction processing systems (the computers and software that enable these events to happen) must be designed with simplicity and speed in mind. You don't want some company executive gumming up the works by telling the computer to "drop everything" so he can find out how many customers bought umbrellas on a stormy day in New York. This is where data warehouses come into use. A company might decide to store all of the information from transactions in a data warehouse (usually in a separate computer system that is compatible with the transaction processing system). In this manner, a company can do both simple and sophisticated queries on the information that it has collected without causing the primary transaction computers to slow down.

Data Mining

Data mining (also known as KDD—knowledge discovery in databases) is what companies do when they are looking for patterns in various bits of information that either they or other companies have collected. Then they use that information to gain competitive advantage, such as offering customers new products, targeting advertising dollars more effectively, predicting future events, or even making a profit from selling to others the information they have gathered. One example of data mining is the grocery store "saver" card that grocery store chains will offer to their customers for free. Each time you go to the checkout counter, you have the cashier scan your card so that all of the cat litter, diapers, and beer you just purchased is now identified with you personally. The store, using your history of purchases, can paint a picture of the type of person you are (this is called market basket analysis). If you shop consistently at one store, they probably can guess what your income level is by where you live (presumably near the store).

SAS, one of the leading data mining software providers, claims to help its customers build closer relationships with their customers (1-800-flowers.com), identify a company's most profitable customers (Morgan Stanley), reduce costs (Saint John's Health System), or even predict and prevent armed robberies (Absa Bank in South Africa).

Legacy Systems

The term "legacy," whether applied to systems or applications, means "old." It's a legacy of the past, and often connotes a system that has outlived its useful life and is more problem than solution. Legacy systems are combinations of hardware, software, and databases that were designed and installed many years (or decades) ago. They are still used today, however, because the cost of upgrading the systems is usually enormous and would require an immense amount of change to the organization and how it handles data, and, in some cases, how it transacts business processes. Many new software solutions attempt to leave the old systems in place and install "middleware" on top of the legacy systems to make them more user-friendly in today's environment. But the legacy system is always there ... just like the crazy aunt in the basement.

Decision Support Systems

Decision support systems are a combination of a computer and software that enables business users to manipulate and analyze data on their own. It's one of the tools that managers use to help them make a decision (that's why it's called decision "support"). A spreadsheet on a desktop or laptop computer is a simple decision support system. More complex decision support systems can involve huge computer networks spanning several business units and even agglomerations of companies. Decision support systems can exist alongside or completely separately from data warehouse operations.

Data Silos

These are typically collections of data or individual databases that are kept and maintained by individual departments or functions. The term "silo" comes from the ubiquitous silos of grain in the Midwest, where the only way things could move was up or down—not across. In many cases the data stored in each silo is quite similar, but because each department wants to own and control its own data, they do not share across the organization.

Data silos may start out innocuously when one department wants to keep track of something that's highly important for its own use, but is less relevant for the rest of the company. Over time, as these data silos become larger and sometimes more valuable, they can grow to monstrous proportions.

Data Marts

Data marts are small collections of data and usually focus on a certain subject or department. They are often (but not always) subsets of larger data warehouses. Furthermore, data marts tend to carry a less sophisticated form of data with less "granularity" (i.e., it cannot be broken down into smaller parts as easily). Data marts, when they exist in each department, can turn into data silos as the data in each is often redundant, or worse, slightly different, thus making any kind of reconciliation between the types of data nearly impossible.

Swivel-Chair Networks

Imagine the harried computer network administrator in a windowless room monitoring a bunch of computer screens that aren't tied together electronically. This poor soul roams around the room in his beat-up chair on wheels checking to make sure that all systems are go. This is what's known as a "swivel-chair network."

Who Owns the Data?

This is where MIS and IT get interesting. The big question of who owns the data and who gets access to certain data is a strategic question that is often not addressed where it should be; namely, at the top of the organization. For example, many companies have turned to centralized call centers to handle inquiries from customers. Most banks now have a toll-free telephone number that you can call to find out your account balance, if a certain check has cleared, and/or the status of a loan application you submitted. In many companies these call centers are seen as a way to manage costs (locate all the customer questions, complaints, etc. in one place so that your employees can be more "productive" in doing their regular work). In other companies, the call centers are seen as another marketing channel (see Chapter 7 for more information on channels) through which they can sell the customer another product or service.

But this type of cross-selling (the sale of a product or service from one part of an organization to a customer of another part of the organization) often backfires if the salesperson doesn't have enough or the right type of information. Imagine a call center service agent trying to induce a customer with a high-checking account balance to open a brokerage account that would allow that customer to buy and sell stocks and bonds. If the customer already has a brokerage account with the bank, the call center agent is wasting the customer's time. If the customer is a college student who just received by wire transfer from her parents, her semester's allotment of cash for living expenses, she clearly is the wrong person to have a brokerage account.

Now imagine the discussion that takes place inside the bank that's trying to turn their call centers into mini-sales forces. The Private Banking group patterns itself after Swiss Banks who are known for their extreme secrecy. The Private Banking group says that all of its information on customers should stay private—that is, only within the Private Banking group. The credit card issuing group, meanwhile, would like to get its hands on the names of the bank's richest customers and sell them a credit card with the customer's favorite pet printed on it. Ditto for the lending department.... How big a mortgage can we sell this high net-worth client? Or how about an unsecured line of credit? Similar discussions take place inside most companies when it concerns which group (function, business unit, geographic region, etc.) "owns" the data that they control. Does the whole enterprise own that data, or do the individual groups get to parcel it out on a "need to know" basis?

In fact, these are very strategic questions. The answers to these questions and how those decisions are implemented help to determine the company's business strategy—whether senior management intended it or not. In an ideal situation, senior managers from the information systems department sit with senior managers from the top of the organization and they jointly decide on the answers to the following six questions[5]—all of which impact the corporate strategy:

1. How much should the company spend on IT?
2. Which business processes should get the bulk of our IT budget?
3. Which IT capabilities need to be standardized across the entire company?
4. How good is good enough for our IT services?
5. How much security and privacy risk will we accept?
6. Who's in charge of a big IT initiative? [Hint: it's not the IT department.]

Now back to the bank trying to cross-sell or up-sell (selling a higher margin product or service) to a customer on the phone. If the bank has decided that it will turn its call centers into profit centers by first making sure that it retains its existing customers, and second selectively expanding the products and services it offers to its customers, then it probably will turn to a more sophisticated customer relationship management system and/or predictive modeling software. This way if a customer calls to ask a question, the call center agent will know when the last time the customer called, what it was about, how the call was resolved, and if any other products or services were discussed. Predictive modeling software can help a call center agent "guess" why a customer is calling and offer practical solutions to a problem. Nykredit, a Danish mortgage bank, broadened its business into multichannel retail, commercial, and agricultural banking offering products in asset management, insurance as well as credit. Nykredit's chief technology officer claims that since they have changed how the bank views customer data (it's owned by the corporation, not the individual groups) they have been very successful at cross-selling products and now more than half of Nykredit's customers buy from multiple product lines.[6]

SYSTEMS DESIGN

Systems design is an integral part of what the IT function does. Specifically it means designing, building, and maintaining a computerized system that satisfies the needs and desires of a particular organizational group (function, business process owner, business unit, etc.) and for a cost that is reasonable and affordable. It means putting together the package of hardware (PCs, mainframe computers, routers, switches, etc.) and software and programming it all so that it satisfies the customer's demands. This process is often easier said than done. There are two groups— often with different priorities—that must come together and agree on what the system should do and at what cost. On the one side you have the technology people (computer programmers, information systems managers, systems analysts, information architects, and hardware and software specialists) who want to build the best and fastest systems possible with cutting-edge technology. On the other side, you have the business managers who want a system that will deliver the world to them but for the lowest cost and without making them change the way they do business.

Designing an information system, whether it's to send a shuttle into space or a home monitoring and alarm system, has to take several key issues into account. Here we'll summarize some of the main factors that a systems designer must think about.

End Product Utility

Will the system do what it's supposed to do? The end user doesn't really care what bundle of components (hardware, software, switches, routers, network design, etc.) the system is made of. The end user just wants to make sure that the system works reliably, and preferably at a price that's affordable. In practice, this means that the system designer has to sit down with the user and find out exactly what the user wants the system to do. The designer also needs to know what's not so important so that any tradeoffs can be managed.

System Reliability

A computer system that only works when it feels like it is pretty much useless. Any system that's worth designing is worth ensuring

System Requirements by Dilbert
Dilbert: © Scott Adams/Dist. by United Feature Syndicate, Inc., Reprinted with permission.

that it will operate most if not all the time. Some critical systems, like operating a 777 airplane in flight or running a nuclear power plant, are so important that they've been designed with multiple levels of redundancy (that is, extra computers and backup systems). So if the main system fails, another backup system or module can pick up in a heartbeat.

The main "breakage" points in a computer system are the software (it's got to be reliable under many different circumstances), the hardware (ditto—and you often get what you pay for here), the operating environment (heat, humidity), and the reliability of the power source. The system has to be designed to cope with all of the potential causes for failure.

Repair and Upgrades

If a system goes "down" then the operators need to be able to identify and diagnose the problem quickly—often within seconds—and then repair the problem. So most well-designed systems have a self-monitoring feature that can probe its component parts to find out in advance how well things are working. Hewlett-Packard's high-end printers can tell you from any authorized computer on the Internet how much useful life is left in a print cartridge and when certain parts need to be replaced or serviced. In addition, if a system has to be repaired quickly, then it also must be designed to be easily repaired— either from a remote location, or on site with minimal disruption to nearby equipment.

The same is true for upgrades to software or hardware. It has to be relatively easy to do and in such a way that won't cripple the end user's operation.

SECURITY

Back when *Leave it to Beaver* was popular, security was a nearly nonexistent business that concerned only a few industries, like banking and personal protection. Today we have national and international terrorists, hackers, phishers, identity thieves, and any number of people who will try to separate people from their money in some of the most creative ways. Add to that the congressional mandates brought on by the Sarbanes-Oxley Act of 2002, and you have an entire industry that serves large and small businesses. In all cases, information technology is at the heart of the security industry.

Hacker and Phisher Patrol

Hackers and phishers broadly encompass the realm of computer-literate people who attempt to gain access to systems and/or data that is otherwise unauthorized to them. The word "hacker" is thought to come from someone who cuts irregularly, with no specific skill. In the case of computer programmers, it implies a person who doesn't have much skill or technical elegance in devising a clever and ingenious software program. In fact, the opposite might be true. A good hacker is someone who can get past formidable firewalls and other security protections by exploiting network weaknesses and illicitly gain access to highly secure data or a forbidden Web site. While some hackers are hired by companies to find their computer security holes, other criminal hackers (called crackers or black hackers) exploit security failures for personal financial gain, enhanced reputation in the hacker community, criminal intent, or to cause trouble (such as creating and propagating viruses, worms, denial of service attacks, or completely shutting down an important network). Examples abound of young and brazen computer geeks who successfully hacked into the private networks of MIT, the FBI, or the U.S. government. One such hacker, Kevin Mitnick, became the poster boy and most notorious American hacker after breaking into Pentagon computers through unauthorized access to the ARPAnet (precursor of the Internet). He even managed to "erase" a warrant for his own arrest. He served 5 years in jail and now runs his own computer security company (www.kevinmitnick.com). Mitnick claims that his methods relied more on his social engineering talents (using manipulation, deception, and influence to gain information from a trusted insider) than any specific knowledge about computer and network operations.

Phishers are criminals who use social engineering methods to defraud people out of personal information for the purpose of financial gain. Phishers usually pose as a trusted source (the person's bank, an account executive from their e-mail service, etc.) in order to get them to reveal their passwords, bank account, and/or credit card numbers or other personal and private information. The word "phishing" is a hacker modification of the word fishing (hackers frequently replace "f" with "ph" from an early type of hacking called "phone phreaking"). Some popular methods are to send a person an e-mail message posing as their own bank and requesting confirmation of a password or social security number. The pop celebrity Paris Hilton was hacked when thieves got to her T-Mobile cell phone service. They reset her password and sent a text message to her. Then they posed as T-Mobile customer service and got her to reveal other personal data so they could listen to her calls, read her e-mails, and so on.

In most of the criminal cases, it's the old problem of a confidence man talking someone into doing something for them that they would not normally do. No amount of high-tech security software and equipment can stop a system break-in if an insider metaphorically leaves the keys in the lock.

Internet Banking—Swiss Style

Swiss banks are known worldwide for their secrecy. Many African dictators have long held secret bank accounts holding their ill-gotten wealth. But Swiss banks are also on the cutting edge of using technology in banking. Unlike most U.S. banks, Swiss banks do not rely on a person's social security number to identify their customer. UBS, the largest Swiss bank and number 7 worldwide, has a 3-part interactive login system to ensure the safety of its customer data. UBS provides each online banking customer with a small calculator-like device. It has a slot for a card that is mailed separately. When a customer enters the UBS Web site, she is asked for her Internet banking contract number. After inputing that number, the Web site produces a 6-digit number. The customer then turns on her little calculator device with the card inserted, and punches her PIN (that she had previously chosen) into the calculator. Next the calculator asks her to put in the 6-digit number from the Web site. After she does this, the calculator displays an 8-digit array of letters and numbers, which she must then plug into the UBS Web site. Only after all of the sequence of numbers are verified, does the UBS customer get access to her online banking data.

Keeping Business and Customer Data Safe

Sarbanes-Oxley is the name of a sweeping U.S. federal regulation that took effect in 2002. It was the result of congressional ire over the massive frauds taking place at some of America's largest companies. The bill, variously nicknamed "SOX" or "SarbOx," requires company managers to certify that their internal documents and data management processes are up to snuff and cannot be compromised by keyboard-wandering fingers. As a result, an entire industry has emerged that will help companies to comply with all the rules and regulations in SOX. One such company, ClusterSeven, will automatically track commands that are input by a user into a spreadsheet and take a "snapshot" of the spreadsheet nanoseconds before each modification is made. Another company, Njini, offers a service that will track and manage "unstructured data," that is, documents that sit on employees' desktop computers. For example, a management policy could stipulate that anything produced by the legal department can only be printed on a certain printer, or that only employees within the human resources department can open particular files, or that any files that are in JPG (picture) format cannot leave the graphics department.

A DAY IN THE LIFE OF AN MIS MANAGER

Monica Herbold
Vice President, Information Systems
A West Coast Bank

I grew up in a blue-collar family in Ohio. My goal in life was to become a secretary. I got a journalism scholarship but I thought it would be too competitive. So I switched into accounting at Kent State University, but after a summer internship in tax accounting I figured it just was not exciting enough for me. I finally got my degree in 1982 from Cleveland State University in computer science with a minor in finance. I'd interned while at CSU, which helped me land my first job after college with TRW Automotive. It was a great job with a lot of other young people and we learned a great deal of IT by sharing each of our experiences.

Since my husband was going to school in California, we moved and I got a job with Nissan Automotive. I was part of one the largest technical system rewrites on the West Coast at the time. I came in as a technical analyst and was there 11 years. I was really good at the technical stuff, but management kept using me for my analytical and leadership skills. At Nissan, as in many companies, there was a tendency to develop projects and ideas and "throw it over the wall" to the business units without much assistance in how best to use it. I wanted to improve things so that we could see our solutions better solve their business problems. We formed a "Bases Covered" team to improve the acceptance of technology though improved communications and support. Turned out I was pretty good at communicating between the technology groups and the business units.

Nissan downsized and I took the incentive package to leave. I spent a year at IBM and was hired by IBM's client—the bank I now work for. That was 7 years ago. It was still a "mom-and-pop" shop using older technology. I went into the e-business group and put together an intranet. It was an incredibly political project and involved negotiating between all the different groups who wanted things done their way.

Now I'm responsible for the primary call center systems. So if you call in to find out if a check has cleared, or what your balance is, you can either "talk" to our computer system or you can request a live person. In either case, the information that pops up on the agent's computer screen or is read to you by a computer over the phone, all comes from our databases. I also support the sales and marketing systems for our commercial clients (big companies the likes of Kmart, Wendy's, and so on).

Our bank is actually the product of a merger between two smaller banks. For years after the merger, the two banks had operated somewhat independently. Now we have a new COO and CIO and they both want to integrate the organizations. The CIO—my boss' boss—was hired to improve our division's processes. It's a good thing, but it's causing significant change and stress in the organization.

I have three main responsibilities:

1. I have to implement the technology to support any large projects that my clients decide to undertake. For example, the call centers have to be able to see in real time what is happening to any and all of our retail customers' accounts and answer any questions at a moment's notice if someone calls in.
2. If the Web side of our business decides to change the way something is shown or how a customer interacts with our Internet site, I have to adapt my systems to support it.
3. I have to "keep the lights on" for all the call center technology. That means watching for data errors and making sure that the servers are up and running all the time. This is tough because we live in a 24/7 world and you have to be able to take some servers off line to do maintenance before they crash.

Here at the bank we have "mom-and-pop" tools to track projects. We estimate the time it takes to do a project but we don't even have minimal information to know if we're on track. Can you believe it? We have no Virtual Private Network here, so telecommuting is nearly impossible. Besides, I really have to meet with people face-to-face. In my job, you've got to maintain a good relationship with everyone because you never know when you're going to need their help in the future. You can't burn any bridges. We just have too many projects going on at any one time.

I love working with the super smart technical and business people. I like dealing with the new, cutting edge, strategic business problems.

I sleep with a pager next to me. We have an alert system and if an emergency occurs I get notified. At the end of October our system failed. We had to take it from our primary site, which went down, and move it to our contingent site in another city. It took the assistance of nearly 60 people and a core team working for 36 hours straight.

Nobody in their right mind would want to get into this business. I'm paid really well but life sucks. I'm kind of a sick puppy. I thrive on the adrenaline rush and love to put out fires. But it takes a toll on your health and home life. I don't have any kids (other than my two dogs)—most women in this job don't—and there are a lot of divorces. I think the women managers (55 % of the total here) have a tougher time at this because we are really bad at drawing boundaries. But the pay is great.

To decompress I throw myself into pseudo construction projects like remodeling my kitchen, building a deck, or terracing my backyard. I like seeing physical results after delivering systems with nonphysical delivery.

No day is typical, but here's a snapshot of a day that's not unusual:

6:00 AM	Review of on-call person's overnight report plus current work orders (these are small projects—less than 1,100 hours to complete).
7:00 AM	Try to put a dent into some of the 200 plus e-mails I receive each day (too many of them are "noise" as in FYIs). My staff knows to come and tell me about the important things in person.
8:00 AM	Issues list meeting. These are data-related problems with the integration of data we get from other groups. For example, with customer data, some data elements are very important, others are less so. We have 2 million customers and 4 million accounts. If you are among the 1/2 percent of customers whose data didn't make it through batch processing the night before, you'd be disappointed that the agent wasn't aware of your most recent activities. But what are the chances of you calling in on that particular day?
10:00 AM	Challenger meeting—I sent a team member to attend in my place. (It's a project to replace the existing system with a new system in another part of the business.)
12:00 PM	Meeting on a project dealing with the technical architecture of a solution. We're trying to change how we work together. We're doing "model diagramming" to explore better options. There are hard camps on both sides so it's been tough to get agreement.
12:30 PM	Orthodontist appointment.

1:15 PM	Met with HR department to deal with an employee who got inordinately upset with how his vacation time was mistakenly recorded. He wanted to know how I was going to fix the problem and threatened to go over my head and complain. He wouldn't have known who to go to, so I dealt with it.
1:30 PM	Data-Combo status meeting. This is an internal project in our group. We're restructuring how data comes into our group so that we have fewer errors.
2:30 PM	Dashboard meeting. This is a project to develop a reporting mechanism for the retail call centers. We need to think strategically through the architecture so that we can accommodate future needs as demands grow.
3:00 PM	Met with a reluctant employee who doesn't like to work with people. Gotta try to coax her to be more tolerant.
3:15 PM	I blocked out time to prepare for a client status meeting, but that got eaten up by another emergency (server failure) so I had to cancel tomorrow's meeting.
3:30 PM	Weekly department meeting with my manager and his direct reports to keep current with the new directives from the CIO.
4:30 PM	CTI Roadmap (it's a project to deal with call routing strategies).
6:30 PM	Quick update on the fly from our team who is working on an entirely new hardware infrastructure for the call center. The consulting firm that the business hired defined a new strategy, which we have to implement. It routes calls differently between the automated system and pulls together data from other systems so that it appears on the agent's desktop. It's a monster project.
7:00 PM	Dinner with an ex-employee. I tried to convince him to come back to the bank. He was key to our group because he's got some really rare skills that are very hard to replace. I'm still working on him.
11:00 PM	Pager goes off. We have a problem with a data site, but one of my on-call programmers will handle it.

INTERNET RESOURCES

Business Intelligence Software Companies

SAS www.sas.com

SAS, based in Cary, North Carolina, offers a wide-ranging set of software packages that can be tailored to each customer's unique situation. The company offers software to handle CRM, activity-based management, anti-money laundering, drug development, IT management, performance management, risk management, regulatory compliance, and many others.

IT Research Companies

Gartner Group: www.gartner.com
Forrester Research: www.forrester.com

SUMMARY

Information technology permeates every part of a company. Without IT we wouldn't be able to send or receive e-mail, surf the Internet, process orders, or collect payments. Today's IT function has a tall order. It must make sure that all systems are "go" and downtime is minimized or nonexistent. IT is often seen as a cure-all for whatever ails a company. The truly excellent managers, however, know that a hot new CRM system or other business process enabling technology is only as good as the business logic that precedes it.

9

Human Resources

Talent wins games, but teamwork wins championships.
—Michael Jordan, basketball player

By working faithfully eight hours a day, you may eventually get to be a boss and work twelve hours a day.
—Robert Frost, poet

WHAT IS HUMAN RESOURCES?

Human resources (HR), also known as the "people department," is a staff function that focuses primarily on the people and the "human capital" or talent of a business. Along with the line and other functional managers, HR helps to define the kind of skills the organization requires. HR manages how people enter the organization, how they grow and develop their skills, how they are evaluated, how they develop additional skills, how they transition into other jobs and get promoted, and how they exit the organization. Back in the old days human resources was called "personnel" but that changed as companies realized that a huge part of their assets (or "capital" in accountant-speak) walked out the door every night. People became strategic resources just like a proprietary technology or manufacturing process.

WHY IS HUMAN RESOURCES IMPORTANT?

"All I need is good people!" Many managers believe that smart and talented people can make up for all the other problems in an organization. The jury is still out on whether that notion is true, but the fact remains that people are an important part of running a business—any business. The world's most admired companies like General Electric, FedEx, and Procter & Gamble all place an enormous value on managing people. In these companies, the human resources department is very powerful, well respected, and staffed with exceptionally talented HR managers. Today, the human resources group is a strategic partner in the business, and as such, is responsible for identifying the kind of talent and skills lacking in the organization, going out to "buy" that talent and then nurturing it so that it grows and blossoms throughout the organization. Just as a chief financial officer manages the financial capital in a company, the human resources director manages the human capital of a business. According to Dave Ulrich, one of the gurus of the HR function, HR professionals have four main jobs:[1]

- Champion the employees by fostering competence and commitment
- Partner with senior and line managers to help them execute strategy
- Provide expert advice in how administrative work is organized and executed at the lowest cost and highest efficiency
- Be a change agent to help the organization transform and adapt to environmental and competitive pressures

The tasks listed above are complicated by the fact that HR managers have to maintain both a short-term and long-term perspective. Partnering with line managers and helping organizations transform themselves is often a very long process that can take years. In contrast, providing administrative services, such as payroll, benefits, and health insurance is a task that often gets mired in details and year-to-year cost concerns. So the perfect HR professional must apparently be somewhat schizophrenic: focused on low cost, details of administrivia (the bureaucratic paperwork involved in keeping track of employees, their benefits, pay, and performance records), and they must be long-term strategic thinkers who can help line managers get the most out of their employees. These factors have given rise to two types of HR people as described in the next section.

Who is the biggest employer in the world? Wal-Mart with 1.7 million employees.

STRATEGIC VERSUS TRANSACTIONAL HUMAN RESOURCES

Transactional HR is the day-to-day task of managing the employee benefit programs, the hiring and firing process, administering salary and bonus decisions made by others, running the payroll system, keeping track of vacations, and making sure that labor relations laws are followed. Transactional HR is the traditional role for most HR departments in most companies. Transactional HR is also one of the most important, if often overlooked, jobs of an HR department. A poorly functioning payroll or benefit system wastes everyone's time and causes huge amounts of pain and discomfort in the organization. Therefore, it's imperative that the transactional HR systems operate at peak efficiency, and the people running them are able to properly service their customers; namely, the employees.

Today much of the transactional HR work is being outsourced (like so many other back office types of work) to specialist companies that can do the work faster, more efficiently, and cheaper. Automatic Data Processing Company (ADP) started by offering payroll-processing services to other companies. ADP would handle the paychecks, keep track of the state and federal employment taxes owed, and keep records of employee payroll data. Now ADP has branched into benefits administration, tax management, hiring/firing paperwork, online job postings, and even training programs. ADP sees itself as an external HR department available for hire.

Strategic HR, in contrast, is a relatively newer concept. Starting in the mid-1980s as companies faced increasing global competition, faster cycle times brought on by technology, and stratospheric growth requirements, line managers realized that they desperately needed highly talented individuals to help them execute the company's strategy. HR staffers got a bit of a bad reputation for being detail freaks who were more concerned with policing how a company deals with employees and telling managers what they can't do, rather than thinking and acting strategically to attract and grow the good employees.

The more forward-thinking companies now have HR professionals "partnering" with the line managers to ensure that the organization operates at peak efficiency. This means that HR professionals must understand everything about the line manager's business including the business strategy, the business logic (how it makes money, who its customers are and how it can grow), as well as the external threats and opportunities. Gone are the days when an HR professional was seen and not heard—except to explain in a syrupy voice the details of your new benefits package. Today's strategic HR partner must know how to do an organizational audit and develop state-of-the-art programs that achieve transformational change. Thus, we've seen the emergence of a variety of HR professionals entering the business arena with vastly different talents than even 20 years ago.

HR's Bad Rap

Only 40 percent of employees think their company retains high-quality workers.
41 percent think performance appraisals are fair.
One-third of executives rated HR performance as "good" (24 percent said it was "poor").

Sources: Hay Group survey 2005 cited in *Fast Company* "Why We Hate HR," August 2005, and Watson Wyatt Worldwide survey, cited in *Human Resource Executive*, November 4, 2003.

Administrators, Specialists, and Generalists

As a result of the dichotomy of HR roles—transactional versus strategic—the function of HR has split into three distinct groupings. They are the administrators, the specialists, and the generalists. The administrators do the traditional transactional HR jobs like payroll processing and all the bureaucratic paperwork that's necessary to run not only HR but also the "employee servicing" side of a company. This includes all the new hire documentation, putting in place processes to police who has access to what data, and making sure that managers and employees follow workplace rules. Some executives cynically claim that this group seeks to protect the company from its own employees. (Perhaps those executives should examine their own attitudes to employees. Many of the people policies come straight from the top.) The "back office" administrative chores, while crucial, are repetitive and comparatively mundane. Administrative HR tasks can benefit from batch processing and automation. Therefore, many companies have outsourced these jobs to computer programs (such as PeopleSoft—now part of Oracle), to data processing centers in low-wage countries like India, or to HR consulting firms (Towers Perrin) with

Table 9.1. Three divergent roles of human resources

Transactional roles (cost-centric)	Specialist roles (product-centric)	Generalist roles (customer-centric)
New employee processing Screen résumés, direct promising candidate info to proper manager, set up interviews, issue employment offer letter and contract Set up payroll data, cell phone, pager, desk, telephone extension, business cards, orientation meetings, keys and ID badge, computer network access	**Strategic succession planning** Conduct with senior management a detailed review of the top two-thirds of the employee population. Devise specific career growth goals, job rotations, foreign postings, timelines, and what-if scenarios Work with the board of directors to develop CEO and top officer succession plans Identify best practices in the industry for succession planning	**Business strategy partner** Detailed knowledge of business, its goals, operating environment, how it makes money, its competitors, the market opportunities and challenges Identify and measure gaps between the strategy-in-action (what's really happening) and the strategy-on-paper (what was supposed to happen – the plan). Devise processes to reduce the gap between the two.
Fired employee processing Document cause of firing, disable network access, collect keys and ID badge, produce final paycheck Hand out "pink slips"	**Labor relations** Union negotiations, workman's compensation, unemployment commission regulations, design compliance process policies Develop with the legal department policies for hiring, firing, contracting, etc.	**Envision future talent needs** Identify existing talent gaps and forecast what gaps will arise in the future, both in local markets/offices and in international arena Work with top management to determine top talent needs, coordinate job search with headhunters
HR Infrastructure Supervise payroll administration, state and local tax payments and compliance, record keeping Specify information technology systems that support all other HR transactions	**Benefits administration** Specialized cost–benefit analysis of insurance programs (health, life, and disability) Expert knowledge of pension plans (ERISA regulations), 401K plans, stock option purchases	**Coordinate targeted educational programs** Bring state-of-the-art executive education on current topics such as organization design principles and practices, innovative reward systems, cross-functional innovations in shared processes, legal issues that impact talent acquisition
Benefits administration Administer the sign up process, claim forms for health insurance, life insurance, disability insurance, answer coverage questions Track vacation time Pension and 401K plan administration	**Compensation consultant** Work with top management to identify gaps in compensation policies. Develop expert knowledge in state-of-the-art practices in compensation	**Transformational change agent** Steer the conversation and debate with management on shaping a vision for change, mobilizing commitment, creating the impetus for change, monitoring progress and measuring success

Know how to put together a change management team and guide the change process (or at least know who to call to get it done)

Employee champion

Engage employees in the business, engender a sense of value, champion employees to management, offer resources for personal and skill-based growth, alleviate morale problems (eliminate useless or unclear performance appraisal processes/forms, hire more support staff, reengineer confusing or frustrating processes), give people more control over work schedules

Organizational audit

Conduct audit of effectiveness of business organization (strategy, structure, processes, reward systems, and people practices). Identify "fit" and core competencies. Suggest improvements and/or know which experts to call

Corporate University

Work with top management to identify long-term strategic goals in talent development and current initiatives.

Programs include specific skill development, organization design, "train the trainer" courses.

Work with leading academic theorists on current topics of interest

Labor relations

Adjudicate complaints (harassment, boss–subordinate disputes, peer disputes)

Organize administrative details of plant closings or layoffs, set up post-employment training programs

Compliance with antidiscrimination laws, ensure job posting policies are followed

Performance appraisal system

Administer appraisal review software and/or forms, remind managers of review due dates

Assist business people in completing forms thoroughly and on time

Employee morale

Organize annual picnic, Christmas party, United Way fund drive

Job descriptions

Write and publish detailed job descriptions when required to satisfy ISO 9000 and other certification and ranking systems the infrastructure to drive costs down and service levels up. The key to an effective outsourcing strategy is to move all the "low touch" transactional portion of the work to offsite locations, but retain the work that depends on personal relationships inside the company.

While it might be easy to dismiss the administrative HR tasks as nothing important, if it's your paycheck that didn't get printed properly—or worse, was miscalculated to your detriment—your own productivity on the job will suffer until you get the situation resolved. A smooth and efficient transactional HR is absolutely key to making sure that employees feel valued and taken care of so that they can get on with their regular jobs.

The second HR grouping is the opposite of the administrators: the specialists. These are people who are experts in a given area of the HR function, like pension benefits, organization development, or compensation. These experts know the intricate details of their chosen area and can recite page and verse, for example, of the various ERISA (Employee Retirement Income Security Act of 1974) regulations. They are product specialists who are called upon when a question arises on a particular issue, or to help design new programs. Large corporations generally have a few of these walking encyclopedias on hand, hiding out in the HR department. They are indispensable to the smooth functioning of HR systems that often require frequent updates due to changes in various state and federal regulations. These specialists are product-driven and work with the next category of HR professionals to find the best product that will answer the business "customer's" needs.

The third grouping is the newer cadre of "customer-centric" business partners. They are often moved into a business unit and are part of the business line manager's organization. They are paid by the business and report to the business manager, but retain a "dotted line" reporting relationship back to their functional boss in HR. These "strategic business partners" as they are sometimes called, are HR generalists and owe their primary allegiance to their customer, the business line manager. The generalist is a jack-of-all-trades—at least in the HR field—and must be an excellent listener and communicator. The generalist's main purpose is to help the line manager execute the business strategy. Of course, in order to do that, they must fully understand the intricacies of the business strategy and the impact that good HR practices have on that strategy. They must also be able to call in specialists when needed to provide expert advice on a particular issue. The strategic HR business partner can identify the gap between a business objective and what it will take to achieve that objective. They act as organizational project managers who can call in the right experts to manage the process of organizational change. Table 9.1 lists some of the differences between the tasks of the three types of HR specialists.

According to Jack Welch, one of the most respected CEOs of the twentieth century, "the best HR people are a kind of hybrid: one part pastor, who hears all the sins and complaints without recrimination, and one part parent, who loves and nurtures, but gives it to you fast and straight when you're off track." But furthermore, Welch goes on to stress that they are also very savvy business people: "They *know* the business—its every detail. They understand the tensions between marketing and manufacturing, or between two executives who once went after the same job. They see the hidden hierarchies in people's minds—the invisible org chart of political connections that exists in every company. They know the players and the history."[2]

THE HIRING PROCESS

Hiring is one of the most important jobs of a manager. The job of HR is to make sure that managers get to see the most promising candidates, and don't have to see the losers. Ideally, HR and management will agree on core traits—nonnegotiable personal competencies—that any person coming into the organization must possess. Usually, these are not traits that can be trained. A person, for example, either has integrity, maturity, and intellectual curiosity or she doesn't. Following this established line in the sand, HR and management will then have to decide upon what kind of recruiting and interview process to follow. Do we advertise for applicants? If so, where and in what media (print, radio, trade shows, etc.)? Do we only hire by word-of-mouth so that we get "prescreened" applicants? Each choice has upsides and downsides. By advertising you get a wider pool of applicants, which you then have to sift through. By choosing only personally referred applicants, you might limit the pool of candidates for a position, but you've already benefited from some type of screening.

The interview process is incredibly important. It provides the candidate an early glimpse into the company's culture. It shows how seriously the company takes the decision of adding someone to the team. A cursory interview followed by a yes or no hiring decision should be a red flag to anyone looking for a job. The best companies will have an applicant come back three or more times and talk to several people inside the company.

Interviews should be structured in a way to allow the applicant get to know the company, the job, its challenges, its rewards, and longer term career prospects. The interviews should also enable the company to probe the applicant for several of the key indicators it has identified as crucial to success. General Electric, for example, looks for what they call the 4-E, 1-P framework. The four Es are—positive Energy (a positive and upbeat outlook on life), ability to Energize others, Edge (the courage to make tough decisions) and Execution (make the numbers). The one P is Passion, meaning that a person has a "fire in the belly" for something (and often many things) in life, not just the job, but also a hobby that possesses them.

Whether a company is looking for specific skills, personality attributes, or something more nebulous, such as "clarity of thought" or "executive intelligence," the hiring process usually involves several interviews and often aptitude and personality tests.

The First Psychometric Test—1915

Walter Dill Scott, a psychology professor at Northwestern University, tested 15 engineering graduates at Western Electric in Chicago for "creative potential." One of the high-scoring men later became president of the company.

Dill Scott, whose test debuted just after Ford started up his moving assembly line said, "Men who know how to get maximum results out of machines are common, but the power to get the maximum of work out of subordinates, or out of yourself, is a much rarer possession."*

*Dill Scott, W. *Increasing Human Efficiency in Business*, New York: Macmillan, 1911.

Personality and Skills Tests

The use of personality and skills tests varies across the board. Tests are available to measure typing skills, cognitive skills, IQ (academic intelligence or potential to learn), emotional intelligence, interests, attitudes, personality traits and preferences, motivation, integrity, and many other traits. Some companies refuse to do such testing arguing that the tests do not give them the right information and that job applicants can learn to "game" the system by answering questions the way a company would want them answered. Other companies do extensive testing. Procter & Gamble believes so fervently in testing that they have devised their own that accurately and reliably predicts the performance of a brand manager. Hundreds of published tests are available and some are better than others. The key is that a company using a test must know very specifically what it is looking to screen for and be able to correlate those screening criteria to the job in question. In all cases, the test must have what psychologists call "predictive ability" meaning that the test accurately measures the traits or skills it seeks to measure, and those traits and/or skills actually predict success in the job.

Some companies, like BAA, the British airport operator, use "assessment centers." These are set up to test and evaluate not only new applicants to the company but also existing employees who are bidding for a different job within the company. BAA uses a combination of written and oral tests as well as role-play simulation exercises. The specific tests and exercises vary with the type of job a person is applying for.

Hire for Skills or Attitude?

Why not both? In an ideal world, the perfect employee has a great attitude that matches the corporate culture and is super-talented at precisely the skills the company needs. But the world is not ideal. There are many incredibly talented and smart people with specialist skills in quantum physics, pharmacodynamics, and C++ programming but who have the personality of a ceiling tile. For many companies who value teamwork and have worked hard to create a cohesive culture, the question of hiring a person for skills or attitude is hugely important. The issue comes into play when a company is looking for a technical expert. In most cases, a company will prefer to hire someone because they have the right personality traits (integrity, maturity, collegial attitude) and figure that they can train the person on the technical or skill-based aspects of the job. But in other cases, particularly for highly technical jobs in the biochemical, computer, technical engineering, and pharmaceutical industries, a company doesn't always have a choice and must hire the appropriately skilled person.

Many of the most admired companies say that this choice (to go for skills alone) is a mistake. Microsoft's founder, Bill Gates, has said that he hires only the smartest of the smart. Extraordinarily high IQ combined with pragmatism and "verbal acuity" (the ability to fire intelligent comments back when challenged) are critical traits at Microsoft. In contrast, computer programming experience is less important than superior intelligence. Gates has said that he will not hire the second best or a near fit, even if it means the job vacancy causes hardship for the organization.[3]

Similarly, Herb Kelleher, cofounder of Southwest Airlines, says the overriding feature the company looks for in employees is a sense of humor: "We look for attitudes; people with a sense of humor who don't take themselves too seriously. We'll train you on whatever it is you have to do, but the one thing Southwest cannot change in people is inherent attitudes."[4] Southwest also has some rather unorthodox interview protocols. Applicants get quizzed on how they have recently used their sense of humor at work to diffuse a difficult situation. Pilot candidates who show up in dark suits and ties are often asked to change into the company's "uniform" of Bermuda shorts to complete the day's interviews. (Those who refuse aren't hired.) New job applicants are encouraged to fill in the questionnaires with crayon. All of these tactics help Southwest identify potential employees who have the outgoing spirit and sense of humor that the company sees as critical to its success.

THE APPRAISAL PROCESS

Also called the "performance evaluation" process, the employee appraisal process is akin to getting your test scores as determined by your boss. Most companies strive to review each employee's performance on an annual basis, some do it more often, some less often. The goal is to stage a formal and frank discussion between boss and subordinate about the employee's goals from last year, progress made on those goals, successes, "opportunities" for improvement, goals for next year, and so on. Appraisal reviews can take on many forms. Some companies purchase a computer-based system that prompts the employee and the boss to fill out a questionnaire, which they then discuss together. Other bosses hold a casual, one-to-one discussion over lunch. All reviews tend to share one of three methodologies: a rating scale, an essay statement, or a performance-based contract. The three main methods of reviewing performance are listed in Table 9.2 along with advantages and disadvantages of each one.

The primary purpose of holding a review is to establish how an employee has performed against expectations over the prior period and to set future direction. It's also used to formally document past performance, to set forth the employee's individual development plan, promotion goals, and to determine compensation decisions. A performance review should not be the first time an employee hears that he is messing up. That is, it should be a "review" based on objective, quantifiable, and accurate measures that were established in the prior appraisal meeting.

One very widely used and popular appraisal review methodology is called a "360-degree review." (It's also called a multi-rater, full-circle appraisal or multisource feedback review.) This type of review is more involved (and costly in time and money) since it requires a boss to solicit the anonymous opinions of an employee's peers, subordinates, and sometimes even customer contacts and outside suppliers, in addition to the boss' own view of the employee's performance. Many people feel that a 360-degree review is the most accurate because it paints a broad picture of the employee's relations with a wide group of people. But critics cite the following problems:

- Peer evaluations can't be trusted (What are your peers saying about you? And what are you saying about your peers?)
- Anonymous opinions foster a "secretive" work culture that isn't healthy, and there's no way for a boss to confront the source of any reported problems.
- It's too expensive in time and money, especially for the benefit received.
- Just because "everybody's doing it" doesn't make it right.
- If you can't gauge the value and performance of an employee by talking directly with her peers, customers, and others who work with her, then you're not doing your own job properly.

Table 9.2. The three main appraisal methods

Appraisal method	Description	Advantages	Disadvantages
Rating scale	Employees are scored from "poor" to "excellent" or some similar scale on a variety of traits and skills necessary to do his or her particular job	Structured and standardized Allows for direct and easy comparison with other workers Easily measurable	The traits/skills might be irrelevant to the job Too rigid and narrow. Rating only on specific traits ignores other factors important to employee's effectiveness Meanings can be perceived differently by different raters Tendency for raters to choose the "safe" route and score people in the middle
Essay	The appraiser (sometimes with the employee) crafts a written statement about the employee's performance	Allows a richer set of data to be surfaced Rater can choose to emphasize any aspect of employee's performance Open-ended and flexible	Time consuming Can't compare workers easily to each other Depends very much on writing skills of rater
Management by Objectives (MBO)	The appraiser and employee agree upon a set of specific objectives to be accomplished by a certain date (for example, increase monthly sales volume by $100,000 no later than July 1)	Focus is on results, not the traits required to get those results Job performance is judged on actual outcomes, rather than potential for success or someone's arbitrary perception of performance Dissection of employee traits, skills, and personality is not necessary It's a very black-and-white issue—either the employee succeeded or she didn't Employee gets a sense of autonomy to do her job however she sees fit as long as the results are delivered	Can lead to unrealistic expectations, and does not factor in environmental or other business glitches along the way If the goals are not crystal clear (such as interpersonal skills improvement, or better communication) it can result in poor "reality checking" on the part of employee and a subjective assessment by the rater Some goals must be done in concert with other people or groups. MBO can actually lead to employees acting too autonomously and not being a team player Risk of Machiavellian methods in achieving performance goals. If the employee uses tactics that are outside of the cultural norm but succeeds at goal, she has met the performance appraisal criteria (and ostensibly cannot be disciplined)

Performance evaluation comments	What they really mean[5]
A keen analyst	Thoroughly confused
Active socially	Drinks heavily
Alert to company developments	An office gossip
Average	Not too bright
Bridge builder	Likes to compromise
Charismatic	Not interested in any opinion but her own
Competent	Is still able to get work done if supervisor helps
Consults with supervisors often	Pain in the ass
Delegates responsibility effectively	Passes the buck well
Demonstrates leadership qualities	Has a loud voice
Happy	Is paid too much
Is unusually loyal	No one else will hire him
Judgment is usually sound	Lucky
Spends extra hours on the job	Miserable home life
Uses time effectively	Clock watcher
Will go far	Relative of management

Some Appraisal Comments from Actual Performance Reviews

1. "Since my last report, this employee has reached rock-bottom and has started to dig."
2. "I would not allow this employee to breed."
3. "This employee is really not so much of a has-been, but more of a definite won't be."
4. "Works well when under constant supervision and cornered like a rat in a trap."
5. "When she opens her mouth, it seems that it is only to change feet."
6. "This young lady has delusions of adequacy."
7. "He sets low personal standards and then consistently fails to achieve them."
8. "This employee is depriving a village somewhere of an idiot."
9. "This employee should go far, and the sooner he starts, the better."
10. "Got a full 6-pack, but lacks the plastic thingy to hold it all together."
11. "A gross ignoramus—144 times worse than an ordinary ignoramus."
12. "He doesn't have ulcers, but he's a carrier."
13. "I would like to go hunting with him sometime."
14. "He's been working with glue too much."
15. "He would argue with a signpost."
16. "He brings a lot of joy whenever he leaves the room."
17. "When his IQ reaches 50, he should sell."
18. "If you see two people talking and one looks bored, he's the other one."
19. "A photographic memory but with the lens cover glued on."
20. "A prime candidate for natural de-selection."
21. "Donated his brain to science before he was done using it."
22. "Gates are down, the lights are flashing, but the train isn't coming."

23. "He's got two brains cells, one is lost and the other is out looking for it."
24. "If he were any more stupid, he'd have to be watered twice a week."
25. "If you give him a penny for his thoughts, you'd get change."
26. "If you stand close enough to him, you can hear the ocean."
27. "It's hard to believe he beat out 1,000,000 other sperm."
28. "One neuron short of a synapse."
29. "Some drink from the fountain of knowledge; he only gargled."
30. "Takes him 2 hours to watch '60-minutes'."
31. "The wheel is turning, but the hamster is dead."

To Rank or Not to Rank?

Once an employee's performance has been measured and quantified, some companies, like General Electric, insist on ranking every employee. This is a highly controversial practice with valid arguments in favor and against it. Force ranking is a method by which every employee within a group (business unit, department, function, or some other definition) is ranked from best to worst. At General Electric, where they call it "differentiation," managers are required to segment their employees into three categories of performance: top 20 percent, middle 70 percent, and bottom 10 percent. Then they have to act on those decisions. The top 20 percent gets big bonuses, stock options, praise, training, and lots of other kudos. The middle 70 percent get lots of opportunity to improve with training, motivation, and encouragement. The bottom 10 percent gets fired if they don't leave on their own initiative—plain and simple. GE claims that it took them 10 years to build up the trust, candor, and consistent appraisal system necessary to do ranking right. GE maintains that in the end, differentiation benefits everyone. The employees ranked lowest usually go on to find good jobs doing something that they are truly good at, and in the meantime, GE has gotten rid of underperforming workers and raised the performance standard of the whole team.

There are many critics of ranking and some of their concerns are listed in Table 9.3 along with rebuttals from proponents.

TALENT MANAGEMENT AND PEOPLE DEVELOPMENT

One of the cornerstones and most important jobs of the HR function is to ensure that the company has the right combination of talent on its team. This means more than just pushing resumés from one department to another. It means working with the business managers to identify the key skills and traits required today, as well as 5 years from now. Companies that have "bench strength" have a talented pool of managers and, behind them, talented employees who can develop into managers. The idea is to develop a critical mass of people who can take over an operation (or function, project, business) relatively easily and seamlessly. Succession planning is part of this arena, but so is training and providing an array of challenging assignments to high-potential employees.

Table 9.3. Ranking pros and cons

Criticism of ranking	Rebuttal
▪ Ranking is political, and corrupted by cronyism and favoritism. The people who get ahead kiss the boss' rear end	▪ This is true at some companies. If cronyism is present, the company will eventually collapse under its own weight. You need to establish a healthy environment in order to even start a ranking program
▪ Ranking is Darwinian and forces a dog-eat-dog competition when people are really supposed to work as a team	▪ Ranking in an open and transparent way can build an even better and stronger team. How many truly top performers really want to play with laggards?
▪ Ranking demotivates the middle group because they don't know whether they'll get to the top 20 percent or be shunted into the bottom 10	▪ The middle group is hard to manage, but it provides a great opportunity for training and career-stretching assignments that will sort the high-performers from the also-rans
▪ Ranking benefits people who are energetic and extroverted, while shy and introverted people are pushed aside	▪ True in the United States, where extroversion is highly valued in business. Introverts need to find other professions
▪ It's a fundamentally "male" practice. Women don't need to rank people, nor do they feel comfortable ranking others. So ranking undermines a company's efforts to attract competent women employees	▪ No comment. GE is not known for its track record of promoting women into senior positions

The Diversity Debate

Although there is little outright debate over the benefits of hiring people from minority groups (including women, Hispanics, Asians, African-Americans, disabled, Native Americans, and many others), the fact remains that the upper management ranks in the United States and Europe are staffed predominantly with white men. CEOs and senior managers at virtually all companies agree that they will be more competitive if they are able to bring more diversity to their workforce. Proponents of diversity point to numerous studies showing that a variety of viewpoints on a work team result in better outcomes (efficiency, quality of decisions, innovation, and job satisfaction). Many industries, such as automobile sales, athletic equipment manufacturers, and the ski industry have found that women are the primary decision makers in a number of areas, such as which new car a family buys and where they will spend their vacations. And in fact, many companies make valiant efforts at hiring as many women and minority employees at all levels of the organization. But why, 25 years after this debate started, are there not more women and minorities in senior management? There's no single answer even though truckloads of books have been written on this topic. The reasons given fall into three broad categories:

- Bias (white men still prefer working with people like themselves, and minorities aren't given line or international management experience),
- Personal deficiencies for the job requirements (lack of training or skills, low tolerance for risk, perceived lack of commitment), and
- Structural problems (most organizations are designed by men for men).

I do not believe women have a chance in hell of achieving their deserved status and power in business within the foreseeable future. My daughters might see it, but I won't. The reason is that corporations are largely created by men, for men, often influenced by military or public school models. Hierarchical structures built on authority remain unchanged, and many men find it difficult to accept the rise of women to top management positions—perhaps because they have never learned to deal with women other than as secretaries, wives, girlfriends, mothers or adjuncts to themselves.

Anita Roddick, Founder of The Body Shop

Women, as a group, are making the most progress in gaining senior management jobs and seats on corporate boards, but business still has a long way to go before women and minorities are treated the same as white males in the corporate arena.

Training

Training and organizing training programs is one of HR's primary roles in large companies. In small companies, training is usually in the form of sending an employee off to a computer software class or some other targeted skill development program. In larger companies, such as General Electric, IBM, and Motorola, the HR department helps to staff "corporate universities," which are in-house learning centers that teach leadership, strategic thinking, organization, and process skills. Many of these corporate universities are instrumental in helping management to push forward a range of strategic initiatives. General Electric used its university, Crotonville, to enact many corporate change programs, such as Work Out! and boundarylessness. Both programs were aimed at bringing more candor and trust to the organization as well as getting work done faster.

Ongoing training is one of the main ways that employees grow and develop new talents, as well as polish existing skills. Often training precedes new job assignments that together with the skills training help insure that the employee succeeds under the new challenges.

Job Rotation and Strategic Assignments

Another way to develop people is by moving them into new jobs so that they can experience first hand the work from another point of view. For example, in many companies, engineering often derides marketing people as brainless fools. Until, that is, an engineer is asked to go and spend a few months working in the marketing department. Then she learns how tough it is to be a really good brand manager.

Other companies have norms about what kind of jobs a person needs to have performed in order to move up the managerial ranks. Some of these "stretch" or "challenge" assignments can include turning around a failing or weak business, or successfully managing an operation that is core to the company's major line of business. Fluor Daniel, the giant international engineering and construction company, requires anyone aspiring to a senior management role to have held three different types of jobs: hydrocarbon engineer, construction site manager, and run an operation outside of the United States.

Job rotations and strategic assignments are meant to test an executive and to show upper management (as well as the HR people who are tracking the executive's path) how well he or she performs under stressful situations. The theory is that everybody has a weak spot. The better a person knows their weaknesses, the better she's able to compensate for it and turn a weakness into a strength. In addition, most people learn best from their own experiences. Therefore, the more varied the experience, the more the person will learn.

Transfer to Field Sales by Dilbert
Dilbert: © Scott Adams/Dist. by United Feature Syndicate, Inc. Reprinted with permission.

Of course, the smart companies don't just toss a high potential employee into an assignment for which he clearly is not prepared. The best companies will build upon the employee's past successes and put him into new and challenging roles that senior management thinks he can handle. There are also some temporary job assignments that are low risk to both the employee and the company. Some options are

- Assign an employee to fill in for another worker while he is on vacation.
- Have peers train each other in their jobs.
- Invite someone from another department to come and speak about what they do.
- Have employees "shadow" someone from senior management or another function for a day.
- Give an employee customer service experience for a week.

Building the Generalist

As several managers rotate through different job assignments and attend career building training programs, what emerges is a generalist. This is a general manager who has seen the business from all sides and has successfully weathered a number of challenging experiences.

So why does a business need a generalist? Generalists are what are more commonly known as general managers, who can manage almost anything because they've seen and experienced almost everything. Businesses actually need both specialists and generalists. Specialists are crucial to an organization's ability to get a product or service out the door because they have detailed knowledge about how to program software, build a specialized part, develop an important chemical, engineer a crucial financial transaction, and so on. But the generalist is someone who can see a situation from all sides, can understand the various viewpoints presented by the specialists, can analyze how these components come together to support the company's strategy, and can rally the troops behind them to share the vision and get the job done. Generalists are the future leaders.

MOTIVATION

Since most jobs have some element of annoyance factor, organizations have to find ways to motivate their employees to show up for work each day and do their jobs well. So how does a company motivate a person to do the right thing? There are a number of solutions:

1. Make the job interesting.
2. Pay the employee a heap of money for behaviors that the company values.
3. Give the person control over how and when the work gets done.
4. Hand out significant bonuses that are directly related to the employee's performance.
5. Promote the person to work on a team with other people she respects.
6. Create a work environment that the employee likes (fun, mentally stimulating, fair, information is openly shared, major wins are celebrated).
7. Actually listen to the employee and value his contributions and expertise.
8. Embrace a vision in which the employee passionately believes.

There are two main kinds of rewards: extrinsic and intrinsic, and several of each are listed above. Intrinsic rewards are intangible feelings that an individual experiences through a job or belonging to a certain group. You can't go to the shopping mall and spend intrinsic rewards. Intrinsic rewards include feeling competent to do a job well, being perceived as an expert in a particular field, achieving a personal goal, contributing to a worthy cause, and gaining respect from a group or a person that is important. An individual is the only one who can give herself intrinsic rewards. All an organization can do is create the environment (job design, work conditions, etc.) that makes it possible for the employee to experience intrinsic rewards.

Extrinsic rewards are tangible rewards that an organization can give to a person. These include pay, promotion, stock options, bonuses, perquisites (a company car, a club membership, dinner for two, and so on), a nice title, the employee-of-the-month parking space, a bigger cubicle, or a corner office. You can physically touch and consume extrinsic rewards. You can also leverage extrinsic rewards to buy things. Banks will loan you more money at better interest rates if they see that you've got a good title with a promising career track at a growing company.

Generally speaking, a company needs to offer both intrinsic and extrinsic rewards if it is to fully engage and motivate the kind of behavior that it wants.

Reward Systems

Reward systems span the gamut and are a very controversial topic. Many companies do not even think about a reward "system," and in those cases, they often get behaviors that they don't want. A reward system is a policy that a company sets in place (either by design or by default) to compensate people for coming to work each day and doing a job—hopefully the one they were hired to do. A reward system usually involves measuring something (the number of parts made in a day, the number of chocolate boxes stuffed, the size of the calf to be sold at the market, the amount of sales over a period of time, the number of new clients and their value to the firm, etc.) and then paying the person for what's been measured. Measurement is an important feature in most reward systems because it's often said that you get what you measure. Take the example of Sears' auto service centers, which decided to reward the people who wrote up service orders based on the average size of the repair bills. The bigger the repair orders the more money they'd earn. Well what do you think happened? Not surprisingly, Sears saw a huge increase in the number and value of service orders in its repair shops. However, many of these extra "repairs" weren't actually needed. So when investigators in several states fined Sears millions of dollars, this particular reward system didn't look like such a good idea after all.

$10 per Bug by Dilbert
Dilbert: © Scott Adams/Dist. by United Feature Syndicate, Inc. Reprinted with permission.

Job-based Pay

Most companies pay a person for the job. That is, the job title and its requirements are what determine the salary of the person who holds that job. It doesn't matter if the person has a Ph.D. in astrophysics or a high school diploma as long as he can perform the requirements of the particular job he would get the pay that is specified for that particular job. The U.S. government and most big corporations have pay grade scales or pay bands that set forth what the minimum and maximum amount of pay can be given to a person doing a specific job. One company, the Hay Group, determined most of these pay scales back in the 1950s and 1960s. These pay scales made life easier for managers to slot a person into a specific job and pay grade, but it also limited how much a person could expect to make as they got better at that job. Most pay bands limit the top pay to just 50 percent higher than the bottom pay. As a result, it took a great deal of incentive away from people to learn, improve how the job is done, and excel at the work.

Skill-based Pay

The newer way to pay people is to pay for the skills and knowledge that they have and continue to acquire. This is called "skill-based pay." The practice started in several factories in the late 1960s and early 1970s, particularly in new factories that were designed from scratch. Workers were allowed and encouraged to design the way they want to work. They adopted many of the Japanese techniques for working as a team in an effort to improve quality, reduce waste, and streamline production. One technique was to organize people into smaller, more self-sufficient production cells that made an entire component or piece of the finished product. Workers found that the most efficient way to organize themselves in these cells was to make sure that each of them could do one another's job so that they had maximum flexibility. If Tom was out on a break, then Sarah could pitch in and cover Tom's particular part of the work. The work was more interesting, and as a production cell worker gained more skills, he or she got a raise in salary. Some of the members in the cell acquired additional training in how to repair and maintain a particular piece of equipment. These people were very valuable when the machine broke down and they could fix it in no time. So they got paid more. In the skill-based pay system, pay bands become less relevant because the top pay can be double the bottom pay. In addition, if an employee learns a new skill, like repairing a complex machine, they can also earn a one-time lump sum payment as a bonus. This has the added benefit of being an immediate reward, which most people find more gratifying than having to wait until the end of the year.

Skill-based pay systems are harder to design and implement than the typical job-based system, but the benefits are greater. Generally the workers end up being paid more in a skill-based pay system than they would in a job-based system, but because they are more efficient and flexible, the company doesn't have to hire as many people so the total labor cost is lower. Some of the challenges of setting up skill-based pay are:

- Properly identifying the specific skills for which a company will pay
- Determining the exact skills needed for a particular type of work
- Testing how well a person has learned a skill
- Pricing the skills and individuals accurately against the external market
- Aligning a skill-based pay system with other features of the organization such that it supports the strategy and processes of a leaner, less bureaucratic organization (putting skill-based pay into a top-down bureaucracy will not work)

Pay for Performance

Another controversial reward system is the pay-for-performance type of reward. These often mean setting some sort of quota or minimum requirement of production, such as selling 40 T-shirts in a week, $100,000 sales in a month, or producing 10 widgets per hour. If a person exceeds the minimum requirement, then they get some sort of additional bonus or commission payment. The problem with most of these incentive plans is management greed. Managers figure that if the workers are regularly exceeding their quota then the quota number was set too low, so they raise it, thus depriving workers of the extra money. Workers quickly figure this out and don't perform over their quota. Nobody wins this way.

One company, Lincoln Electric, a Cleveland, Ohio manufacturing company, has a pay for performance system that works. Lincoln Electric pays its factory workers for each piece that they produce and at the end of the year each worker gets a bonus based on his or her individual contribution to the company's performance. Hundreds of Lincoln Electric workers earn $80,000–$100,000 per year under this scheme and the company has made enormous profits over the decades. There are several crucial components to this system:

- Hire people who really value cash (more than time off).
- Make sure that the bonus payout criteria are simple and easy to understand.
- Create and maintain open and honest communication particularly with regard to financial information.
- Management must enjoy making their employees rich.

ORGANIZATION DEVELOPMENT

Organization development is the domain of both the generalist and specialist

You Do What?

Mr. "Wind at his Back"* sported the title, "Corporate Shaman" of Intel Corporation. He's now Corporate Shaman at another company.

"In indigenous tribes, the Shaman is the facilitator of the culture. I studied Native American medicine for 10 years and discovered similarities in how "magick" works in different domains. Magick comes from the Celtic and Wiccan traditions and is used to denote beliefs in "shapeshifting" and the "unexplainable." It's totally separate from magic and magicians.

"My teacher taught me, 'You have to find your own system'—that is, something that generates a presence in your life, rules of the road, values, and a sense of purpose. Corporate culture is all about values, people, norms, behavior, and power.

"I try to surface truth. I know that sometimes I'm going to take an arrow while doing it. If you don't surface truth regularly in business, you don't learn. You have to fail in order to learn. In complex matrix and lateral organizations people tend to fight the truth. They don't realize that they're part of an overarching system, and that their goals depend on someone else's goals too.

"When a system is good and based on truth, you get exponential speed, flexibility, agility, and leadership that honors truth. In a system with a failure of truth, you get power struggles, political games, and no common purpose—all of which slow the organization down.

"How do I surface truth? I pick my moments. Some people are so low on the maturity scale that you just can't go there. When people are ready to learn, the teacher appears."

*Wind at his Back is the Native American name given to a real executive by his Shamanistic teacher, Owl Woman. He is not himself a Native American but he's an avid student of the culture.

HR manager. This involves helping the company change itself when needed to adapt to outside forces. Most healthy organizations, like Procter & Gamble, go through an organizational realignment or change every 5 years or so. The world changes: competitors adopt new tactics, customers demand different types of service, the organization pursues a different business strategy, and the company grows and usually expands into different markets. All of these factors and more are what induce companies to reorient their organizations to better respond to such outside forces. The human resources group usually plays an important role in these organizational change projects and focuses on organization behavior and organization design, both of which fall under the broader category of organization development.

Organization Behavior

Organization behavior is a field of study that combines industrial psychology, organization theory, and in-the-field (empirical) observations of behavior in organizations. It's a wide-ranging domain that includes things like job design, socialization and orientation of new employees, management/worker relations, communication, effects of different reward and motivation systems, self-managing teams, and work group interactions. Much of the union movement in the mid-twentieth century can be traced back to organizational behavior issues. When a job is designed under the philosophies of "scientific management" where tasks are dissected and simplified into component parts so mundane that a trained chimpanzee could perform them, it takes all of the interest away for any human doing the job. Assembly line work in the automobile industry was so boring for the workers that they actually devised ways to make their lives more interesting (like literally "throwing a monkey wrench" into the line). In contrast, breaking jobs down into boring and repetitive tasks made management's life easier since all that was required was to supervise the workers and make sure that they were doing their small part correctly. It was easy to see if a worker was performing properly or not. Workers unionized partly to gain some self-respect and more control over their work life.

Today unions have lost a great deal of power, in part because many of those jobs are moving overseas, but also because management has realized that one can't expect human beings (no matter how unskilled) to perform the same, boring jobs every day for the rest of their working life. The field of organization behavior was instrumental in allowing workers to design their own jobs and create self-managed teams and manufacturing cells where team members learned to do a variety of tasks.

HR professionals must have some grounding in organizational behavior if they are to be effective in helping line managers cope with the multiple demands from employees, bosses, customers, suppliers, other business unit managers, and so forth. Knowledge about how people might react in different situations is important particularly if a line manager is about to implement an organizational change initiative. People are human and most react negatively to change. But if change can be orchestrated in such a way that involves the people who's jobs will be impacted (like including them in the discussions about the reasons for the change and some of the proposed solutions), a change initiative will have a better chance of success.

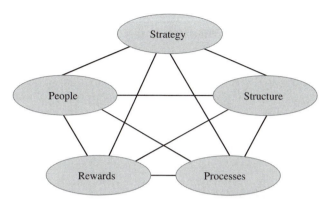

Figure 9.1. The Star Model of organization design. © Jay R. Galbraith. Reprinted with permission.

Organization Design

One task of the of the new, more engaged, and strategically-minded HR executive is to help the line managers develop critical thinking about their organizations, how they are designed, and whether they support the strategy. Organization design is the process of defining and shaping how an organization works in order to effectively implement the strategic goals. By aligning the required tasks, structure, management processes, reward systems, and people practices to support the strategy, one can impact the behaviors that will deliver high performance. An enlightened HR manager should be able to identify a framework to analyze an organization efficiently. There are several such frameworks, like Jay Galbraith's Star Model, the McKinsey 7-S model, Mintzberg's structural pentagon, Ouchi's Theory Z, and many others. All of the models allow an organization designer to move various "levers" in one area of the design to see how they affect another area.

Today's HR professional, who is a partner to line managers, must be familiar with organization design practices so that they can advise and assist the line manager in making the appropriate organizational choices. For example, let's take the Star Model, one of the earliest and most widely used frameworks in business. The Star Model is shown in Figure 9.1.

The Star Model shows the interrelationship between strategy, structure, processes, reward systems, and people. Strategy is at the top because all good organization designs follow the strategy. Structure refers to the organization charts and the locus of power: who reports to whom. Processes are the grease that makes the organization actually work properly. Processes include how new products are developed, how information is distributed through the organization, how tasks are delegated, and how new business is generated. Reward systems are important because they motivate people and define the kind of behaviors a company wants from its employees. And finally, the people area reflects the policies and practices a company installs in order to attract, retain, and promote the right kind of talent it needs in order to get ahead. One of the key factors in the Star Model—and in fact, in any good organization design framework—is that all of the areas must fit together and support each other. So, for example, you can't have an organization strategy that requires people to work together as a team in order to get a product out the door, but then pay each person an annual bonus based on how well that person worked as an individual during the year (that would send mixed messages). Instead, you would need to pay each person a bonus based on how well the group worked together and how many products the company sold.

The HR professional's task in the organization design process is to help the line manager think through the implications of what a new strategy, for example, will do to the other areas of the organization. And where changes are required in processes or people staffing and so on, the HR manager is there to help the line manager implement those changes.

A DAY IN THE LIFE OF AN HR MANAGER

Keith Lawrence
Director-Human Resources
The Procter & Gamble Company

Who would ever have imagined, after growing up in upper state New York, that today I would be part of the world's most admired companies helping champion a transformation of the human resources function? It has been an incredible journey—one of many blessings and a few challenges along the way.

I graduated as an industrial engineer from Rensselaer Polytechnic Institute, the oldest engineering school in the United States. After interviewing several companies I decided to join P&G's largest manufacturing operation, which was in Northeast Pennsylvania. I started as an on-shift team manager. I was fortunate to have several of the experienced employees coach this young, "wet behind the ears" college graduate and keep him from causing too much trouble.

Very early on I discovered an emerging interest in the organization development aspects of the business. This plant was one of the country's first experiments in developing a "high performance work system." As such, it operated radically different than most production facilities of its day. The operating technicians were empowered to run the daily operation, and managers were there to coach them and focus on improving the system. It was a period of steep learning, which led me into changing my career path into human resources. I assumed roles that involved recruiting, employee relations, and work system redesign. With a change in the site leadership I also got the opportunity to begin what has turned out to be a life long passion of learning from others. We visited several other companies to learn about their ways of doing business, and that fascinated me.

In 1987 we had the opportunity to move to Cincinnati. It was a good move for my career, and we felt it would be a better place for our three young daughters to grow up. It has turned out to be a wonderful city to raise a family. I've been very fortunate to work with a number of great leaders and organizations, and have learned so much—both personally and professionally. These experiences have helped me discover that my love for HR work is really change management; that is, improving the effectiveness of our systems and structures so that more people can perform at their peak and enjoy coming to work.

During the last 15 years my HR experiences have taken me across several different businesses and functions at P&G. In the early 1990s I was chartered with Ron Taff to lead a renewal of our definition of high-performing work systems. It was one of the highlights of my time at P&G. We spent 18 months traveling several hundred thousand miles to all the corners of the earth. We visited numerous P&G locations as well as the best organizations in several other industries, like Toyota, IBM, Apple, and HP to name a few. We were able to interview several of the world's thought leaders and consult with many universities and consulting firms. The outcome of this work led to a radically new definition of leadership and how our product supply operations were managed. I also have been able to work on several of P&G's company-wide restructurings, which have led to the company achieving one of its longest periods of sustained profits and growth.

In the late '90s I assumed HR responsibilities for our North America Paper business, which was a "full service" HR role. We provided support for 10,000 employees across multiple locations. Our services included training, compensation, employee relations, benefits, talent recruiting, and development, etc. Our diaper business was going through a major revamping at that time, which required us to be innovative in HR policies and practices. In the past we had always sent managers to start up new machinery. But now we send the operating technicians from one plant to work with their counterparts at the new site to shakedown and startup the equipment. We also worked on simplifying the decision making process to get our new product initiatives to the marketplace faster.

Today (like many others at P&G) I wear multiple hats. I have responsibility for providing HR support for the Global Beauty Care business. My team handles the HR systems that managers and their employees count on for their compensation, benefits, training, etc. I'm also intimately involved in several company-wide projects, such as the integration of the Gillette business. This is my fifth acquisition experience and has been by far the best. Everyone working on this has been incredibly collaborative and committed to doing what it takes to achieve success. In particular, I've been responsible for leading a team handling the onboarding of Gillette employees and the integration of the two cultures. In keeping with "tradition" we have tapped into our broad network of resources (both within and outside of P&G) to develop some new innovative approaches to doing this work. In particular we are striving to "Field the Best of Both" in all that we do. Part of this is to get the new Gillette folks to think about their own unique talents and experiences and how these skills can benefit P&G. We developed new guides that help new employees better understand the unique aspects of the P&G culture—like how decisions are made or what factors are important to advancing one's career. On the P&G side, we're working with long-time employees to encourage them to be more receptive to new people and their ideas. It's still early to tell, but the results look quite promising.

So what keeps me going in this job? I really like making the lives of our employees better every day. I get a kick out of seeing a talented employee who's energized because the work she's doing is challenging and personally rewarding to her.

These responsibilities (as well as a very active family and personal life) make for long but very fulfilling days. Since I'm an early-morning person, my days begin about the same time (4 AM). I find this to be a great time to exercise and get caught up on the news—particularly before the family gets up. I read five newspapers a day, and countless periodicals, books, Web sites, etc. all in the interest of keeping in touch with the world and my field.

A typical day

4:00 AM	Get up, jog in the neighborhood for 30–40 minutes, read the *Wall Street Journal*, *Financial Times*, etc.; spend time with the family before we all rush off for the day.
6:30 AM	I'm in the office catching up on e-mails received overnight and connecting with our partners in Asia (before it gets too late in their day) and talking with Western Europe on key projects or issues.
7:30 AM	The weekly conference call of HR and External Relations professionals to discuss the state of the Gillette acquisition. Folks from all around the world tie in. It's a very routine way of how we conduct business in this "global world."
10:00 AM	A project team meeting to discuss a new reporting tool being developed to proactively track and manage the number of expatriates we have working at P&G.
11:30 AM	A quick "stop by" discussion with a member of my HR team who is developing some new innovative ways to use information technology to communicate with and engage employees. It's very exciting stuff, and it again reminds me of how far we have come from the days when there were no computers anywhere in the workplace. We've made a lot of progress recently in developing new products and services to "win at the employee moments of truth." These are key events in an employee's lifecycle here at P&G. Some examples are when a potential employee meets an on-campus recruiter, when the new hire starts on the first day, how they are welcomed into the organization, when they transition to a new role, how they are treated as they relocate to a new country, and even how they interact after they leave P&G. We're trying to enable more personal touch and "just in time" information using new technologies such as podcasting and blogs.
12:15 PM	Lunch with a P&G retiree who is now out doing volunteer work with the local United Way agencies. I enjoy connecting with folks like Al, plus he asks for copies of P&G practices that he knows I have (like how to set direction or develop a team).
1:30 PM	Tied into a webcast hosted by another company on the "Sins of Traditional Performance Management" approaches. There are over 400 others on this virtual meeting—again from all over the world and countless companies. It is a great (and efficient way) to learn from masters in the field and hear what others are doing. We are looking to revamp this process at P&G and seeking to learn of any other best practices.
2:45 PM	A quick conversation with the vendor who is helping us host a learning forum this fall (which we will again tap into) that includes several of the world's prominent leaders (such as Rudy Guiliani, Richard Branson, and Jack Welch). At P&G we are one of the few "build from within" companies and as such invest a lot in the development of each employee. This session will enable over 400 of our leaders to learn from the experiences of these individuals and strengthen their own effectiveness. This is

an important part of what we do in HR: "Connect P&G with the best" anywhere in the world.

3:30 PM   Quarterly meeting with one of the several people in HR who I coach and mentor. Today we talk about what she is doing to join up to a new organization. I share a copy of our "FastStart" New Assignment Transition Guide and share some experiences (both good and bad) I've had during my career. You can learn as much (if not more) from your mistakes than when everything went perfectly. I learned, for example, that at P&G it's not enough to just be skilled at your job and get the work done. It's critical to build productive relationships with people across the entire organization.

5:00 PM   Wrapped up the workday: checked e-mails and returned some phone calls.

6:30 PM   Met a good friend at the local Bally's Health Club for an hour of aerobic and weight training. We have been doing this together for the last year as "accountability" partners to help each other stay in shape. We are even doing Pilates class on Saturdays!!

7:30 PM   Home to enjoy a relaxing evening with the family. The girls are usually in and out with friends, jobs, or "going out." Tonight we get the chance to watch *American Idol* together and debate whether the "boys or the girls" will win this competition. Only time will tell!!

INTERNET RESOURCES

Educational Sites

HRM Guide: http://www.hrmguide.com/

HRM Guide is a site with many links to articles and other free resources for the HR professional. It's got a number of good introductory articles on everything that the HR function does, as well as several current hot topics in HR.

National HR Association: http://www.humanresources.org/

This is a nonprofit association designed to further the field of HR. Most of the resources are available only to members, but a student membership costs between $25 and $75 depending on location.

HR Guide: http://www.hr-guide.com/

This site has virtually everything you ever wanted to know about HR. It's designed for the HR professional, but can aid the student looking for information and hints (go to the "tough questions" section [http://www.hr-guide.com/data/G353.htm] for a preview of some questions that will really make you squirm). Most of the content is for transactional HR issues (employee behavior problems, what kinds of interview questions to ask, and so forth) or for specialist HR issues (benefits, policies, handbooks, surveys, legal cases, etc.).

Society for HR Management: http://www.shrm.org/

This site is main professional society for the HR professional. It boasts over 200,000 members in 120 countries. It has a number of free resources and lists current events (legislation) as well as many articles on a wide range of topics available to members and nonmembers.

Performance appraisals: http://www.performance-appraisal.com/home.htm

This is a very good resource for learning about performance appraisals. The sponsors (Archer North) also offer consulting on the topic.

Montana State University career center: http://www.montana.edu/~wwwcp/tips.html

This site offers an enormous amount of free tips and resources for job searches, interview tips, etiquette, and so forth. Some of the links direct you to company Web sites where they hope to entice you to pay them to help you out.

Career Information

Career Key: http://www.careerkey.org/

This site offers a comprehensive, professional quality test that helps people decide what careers to investigate.

Bureau of Labor Statistics: http://www.bls.gov/oco/

On this site you'll find the occupational outlook handbook. It has a wealth of information about different types of jobs in virtually all areas of business. It describes what qualifications are best for a particular job, what the job entails, how much growth and demand is predicted for the field, what the average salaries are, and even the kind of working conditions you should expect to find.

Résumé writing:

http://hotjobs.yahoo.com/careertools
http://content.monster.com/basics/
http://channels.netscape.com/careers/resume.jsp
http://www.jobweb.com/Resumes_Interviews/default.htm
http://owl.english.purdue.edu/workshops/hypertext/ResumeW/
http://www.bc.edu/offices/careers/skills/resumes/

Interview skills:

http://interview.monster.com/
http://jobsearch.about.com/od/interviewsnetworking/a/wininterview.htm
http://www.western.edu/career/interview/Interview_skills.htm
http://www.bc.edu/offices/careers/skills/interview/

Organization Development

University of San Francisco: http://www.cps.usfca.edu/ob/resources/

This site has a number of links to articles on various dimensions of organization behavior. It's very much oriented toward theory particularly with a psychology bent.

Organization Behavior Network: http://www.obmnetwork.com

This site is for people who are practitioners in organization behavior (or who want to become practitioners). It offers a number of free resources, job posts, and articles on a wide variety of organization behavior issues.

Organization Design Forum: http://www.organizationdesignforum.org/

This is the practitioner's Web site. It's a nonprofit membership group specifically for people who work in the organization design field. The Web site has limited information for nonmembers.

SUMMARY

Human resources is the function that works with senior and line management to provide the human talent necessary to execute the company's strategy. HR is charged with the care and feeding of most companies' critical assets.

HR comprises three different roles: administrative, specialist, and strategic. The administrative role is crucial to ensuring that people are paid properly and that all of their personal needs as employees are met. The specialist role is important in advising managers of particular legislation or benefits rules that could impact how the company does business and how it pays people. The strategic HR role is increasingly important today as line managers seek to improve the speed and efficiency of their organizations. The strategic HR professional partners with the business manager to provide advice and guidance.

10

Supply Chain

The well-run factory is a bore. It runs like clockwork. The poorly managed factory is a drama of crises.
>   —Richard F. Schmidt, Dun and Bradstreet (the information company)

Most skills and competencies needed to excel in logistics and supply chain management are the same skills and competencies needed to excel at disaster relief operations.
>   —Matt Waller, Associate professor of marketing and logistics, University of Arkansas

The factory of the future will have only two employees, a man and a dog. The man will be there to feed the dog. The dog will be there to keep the man from touching the equipment.
>   —Warren G. Bennis, Professor, University of Southern California

WHAT IS A SUPPLY CHAIN?

Back in the day when vertical integration (corporations control every stage of production) was the only way companies knew how to make stuff, raw materials would come in through one door and a finished product would pop out of the other. Procter & Gamble (P&G), for instance, used to make soap by crushing buckeyes and linseeds to produce oils that formed the basis of soap. The company owned forests where they'd grow their own trees to produce pulp for all of their paper products. In the 1880s P&G was the largest candle maker and one of the largest traders in animal fats in the United States. Back then P&G made as much money trading commodities as they did in selling soaps, their primary product. P&G has long since sold off its forests, pulp mills, and seed crushing operations. In fact, P&G doesn't even make its flagship Ivory soap brand—it's contracted out to another manufacturer.

In the past, the activities of what is now called "supply chain" were treated as separate functions and departments. These activities include raw materials sourcing and purchasing (also known as procurement), selection of partners (for component manufacturing and/or services outsourcing), production scheduling and planning, product manufacturing, assembly, testing, quality control, inventory management, spare parts, warehouse design and location, delivery fleet management, logistics and distribution management, order tracking, delivery, and customer returns. In other words, supply chain today encompasses all of the end-to-end processes from your supplier's supplier to your customer's customer. Supply chain does *not* include product development, sales and marketing (demand generation), research and development or certain elements of postdelivery customer support.

Supply chain management is the process of optimizing the creation and delivery of goods and/or services from the raw materials to the end user (final customer) at the lowest possible cost to the business and the highest possible value to the customer.

Supply Chain versus Value Chain

A supply chain is a component (albeit a large one) of the value chain. The value chain encompasses everything that a company does in order to turn a raw material into a final product or service that satisfies the end user's need at a price that is fairly valued. The value chain includes the activities of sales, marketing, post-sale customer service, product research and development, technical support, as well as strategic positioning and even the firm's core competencies and leadership, which if done properly, will show up in the final product or service.

WHY IS THE SUPPLY CHAIN IMPORTANT?

The notion of looking at the entire process of turning a raw material into a finished product, rather than treating each individual step along the way as a discrete event that is otherwise separate from the whole, comes from the following factors:

1. Competitive forces worldwide have led many companies to become more "customer-centric." This means that companies are forced to offer more variety in product features, associated services, and delivery options.
2. Global sourcing of materials as well as worldwide availability of manufacturing sites has enlarged the geographical reach of companies. This complicates the manufacturing planning process, but it also offers a rich variety of benefits (additional partners, wider supply of raw materials, and decreased manufacturing costs, to name a few).
3. New relationships on the factory floor and the focus on team-based decision making among all the players responsible for a product have lowered prior hierarchical barriers resulting in faster processing times. This means that more information can be handled more intelligently.
4. Software and manufacturing control technology has automated much of the verification and control activities.
5. The decline of the "command and control" method of management means that there are fewer managers planning and supervising. Thus

the workers must "self-manage" and simplify and/or eradicate cumbersome business processes.

6. As companies seek to simplify and reengineer their business processes, they have systematically reduced the number of suppliers, often giving entire chunks of a manufacturing process (such as the automobile interior) to a major supplier. This means that information on production scheduling, demand management, and raw materials sourcing must be shared more intensively between the company and its suppliers.

7. The current outsourcing trend (sometimes called "offshoring") has led companies to do only what they do best, and offload activities that other partners might be able to do better. But the cost of outsourcing means that more intensive communication has to occur between the company and its outsourcing partners.

8. Lean manufacturing (the compression of manufacturing time with reduced levels of inventory on hand) has meant that a product promotion launched by Sales and Marketing can wreak havoc on a production facility. Therefore, manufacturing needs to know in advance of a possible surge in product demand.

The combination of the factors listed above are forcing companies to look at the entire process of taking a raw material from start to finished product—even beyond their own customer all the way to the end user.

Partnering Along the Supply Chain

One of the most important skills for building a solid supply chain is the ability to choose and maintain relations with good partners. This is true whether a company is the one managing the whole chain or whether it is one of the partners contributing to someone else's supply chain. Choosing the right partner means doing your homework. It means learning about the partner company's strengths and weaknesses and how it responds in times of stress. Does the partner lay off all its workers, or does it try to find other work to fill in the slow period? What benefits can a partner bring to your company? Market access? Low cost manufacturing? A guaranteed supply of a crucial raw material? A group of skilled Muslim workers who are willing to work in Islamic countries? A large American financial services company went to Indonesia seeking a partner to help them break into the huge Indonesian market. The American company was presented with a list of potential partners. Since the Indonesian companies were listed in alphabetical order, the American company chose the one on the top of the list, without doing any homework on whether that company was a good fit for them. It turned out not to be the best marriage and the American company lost a pile of money and tarnished its otherwise good reputation in Indonesia. The Indonesians joke that Americans are "Friday Investors" because they fly in on Thursday night, do their business on Friday and then head to Bali (an Indonesian resort island) for the weekend.

The point here is that any company that is considering building a supply chain, which will probably involve either outsourcing parts of the chain entirely (see the section below on outsourcing) or partnering with another company, needs to handle the partner relationship very carefully and seriously.

PROCUREMENT OR PURCHASING

What Is Purchasing?

Purchasing, which is also known as procurement or spend management, is the function responsible for making sure that all the raw materials that are necessary for making a finished product are at the factory when they need to be there. But it's more than just buying iron ore, aluminum, partially assembled bumpers, widgets, and pencils. Purchasing in most large corporations has become a huge department that is charged with worrying about the entire supply chain, from everything that goes into the factory to everything that goes out and how it gets to the customer in the end.

Purchasing in a big company is divided into two separate areas: one is on direct spend, which is all the raw materials that are needed in the factory to produce the final manufactured widget (or output) of the company. People in this area used to be called 'commodity managers.' The second area is for maintenance, repair, and operations (MRO), also known as indirect spend, and includes things like office supplies, information technology expenses, negotiated airfare, hotel, and rental car rates.

Why Is Purchasing Important?

If you're a very small business with one or two employees and your primary output are some cool software programs, you probably don't spend a lot of time worrying about the kind of discount you can get on CDs, DVDs, labels, or even printed software boxes. But if you are General Electric, and your annual purchasing budget runs to about $42 billion—with a "b"—a penny here and a penny there really start to add up. That's why all large companies have someone, or more likely, a whole department of people who focus on saving money by buying in bulk and buying smarter.

Southwest Airlines claims to have saved nearly $300 million by hedging fuel contracts—that is, they bought jet fuel at an agreed upon price many months in advance, thus locking in the lower price as the price of oil headed for the stratosphere in 2005. Glaxo Smith Klein, one of the world's largest pharmaceutical companies, has an 800-person global procurement organization with a $12 billion annual budget. The company claims to have saved more than 20 percent on both direct and indirect spend using e-procurement technologies.

Purchasing is also important in choosing suppliers and outsourcing partners within the supply chain. Purchasing usually runs the e-procurement systems, which include e-commerce, B-to-B exchanges, auctions, and reverse auctions. These Internet-based systems enable fast and accurate cost comparisons among potential suppliers, as well as the ability to complete a transaction at high speed and very low cost.

But a good purchasing department is not just for getting the company the best deal at the lowest cost. Sometimes the higher cost supplier is better because their products are consistently free of defects, they deliver on time, and can incorporate special features relatively quickly. The purchasing function is also instrumental in business process reengineering efforts. These are initiatives that the company takes on in order to make its current work processes more efficient. For example, a manufacturer might analyze how a particular part is assembled in the factory and decide that some portions of that assembly flow are not cost effective to produce themselves. So they get a supplier to produce that part for them. Purchasing would likely get involved in both the analysis of the business process and vetting the new supplier.

Purchasing today is more aligned with the corporate strategy and values than it has been in past decades. As a result, purchasing managers' salaries and bonuses are increasing and reflect the value that they bring to the company.

Economies of Scale

Economies of scale is an economic term that refers to the decrease in the per unit cost of producing something—a widget, a loaf of bread, a cookie, a car, etc.—as more of those units are produced. Generally speaking, it's much more economical to bake an entire batch of 50 cookies than it is to make just one cookie. It involves the same amount of physical labor, the same amount of energy, the same amount of time (more or less), and the marginal cost of the ingredients for one cookie versus 50 cookies is minimal (besides, it's really hard to make a recipe with one-tenth of an egg). The same holds true for manufacturing stuff. So if you're a vendor selling steel to General Motors, you'd rather sell lots of steel rather than a couple of sheets. In order to get that business, you would probably pass on the cost savings you get from producing a huge amount of steel in order to get that big order.

In fact, this is a simplified example of economies of scale. Today, many big manufacturing companies are buying more than just steel from their suppliers. Johnson Controls is a company that used to specialize in car seats; that is, driver and passenger seats, not baby seats. Now it supplies complete automobile interiors for some of the major auto companies. Bosch used to supply spark plugs and now they provide entire antilock braking and traction control systems. These companies are part of a trend in manufacturing to reduce the number of suppliers to a company, but increase the importance of the remaining suppliers. So instead of giving Supplier A one or two parts of an automobile to manufacture, and Supplier B gets another few parts, the auto company gives Supplier A the automobile interior and Supplier B gets the audio system. Thus, the suppliers have more incentive to get things right from the standpoint of cost, quality, product features, lead time (the time it takes to make and deliver something after it is ordered), and delivery terms (when and where something will be delivered).

Leveraging Purchasing Power

For companies that have several divisions, business units or partnerships, leveraging their purchasing power is a way to use economies of scale to their advantage. In this way a group of companies band together to buy something from a supplier. The larger group represents a larger purchase (and larger economies of scale for the supplier). For example, a group of companies in a remote region, such as Summit County in Colorado, get together to jointly purchase health insurance, thus presenting a larger group of employees to an insurance company. Another example is Arsenal Capital Partners, a private equity firm that buys companies, turns them around, and sells them for a profit. Arsenal has a purchasing manager who created a purchasing council comprised of all the purchasing managers in all the companies they own. They collectively source goods and leverage their buying power to gain better prices and terms from suppliers.

B-2-B Exchanges

These are often Internet-based resources, also known as Internet exchange platforms and e-procurement systems that allow businesses to buy and sell from each other directly. It's kind of like an eBay for businesses only. One such exchange, Perfect Commerce (which acquired Commerce One in 2006), offers a suite of Supplier Relationship Management (SRM) programs that enable companies to source, procure, manage, finance, and analyze the raw materials and components necessary for their own operations. At the heart of the Perfect Commerce offering is an integrated network of "open suppliers." Perfect Commerce claims that it is the largest independent supplier group in the world comprising over 11,000 suppliers, 200,000 users, and 21 million SKUs (stock keeping units) of catalogued items, which resulted in more than 7 million transactions in 2005 alone. Citibank offers one of the components of the Perfect Commerce financing modules. When a company wants to buy supplies over the Perfect Commerce Internet site it registers information about which employees are authorized to transact the purchase along with the bank account from which the funds should be drawn. The buyer then clicks on the Citi Connect button to authorize payment to the seller. A message containing buyer information, purchase price, supplier information, the two banks involved, and when the payment should be transferred, is automatically sent to the settlement network and the transaction is completed. Since the whole transaction is automated, sellers claim to cut their settlement times (time is money) by 20–40 percent, and both buyers and sellers reduce settlement costs by 50–60 percent.[1]

Oddly enough, a 2005 survey of 650 manufacturing professionals found that nearly two-thirds of them did not use any kind of B-2-B electronic marketplace.[2] Apparently the trade exchanges are too much trouble to sort through for limited cost reductions.

Auctions and Reverse Auctions

Auctions are a process whereby a seller puts something up for sale — say, a Van Gogh painting, a camera, an automobile, etc. — and people bid a particular price indicating what they'll pay for the item. In a typical auction, the price usually goes up as more people compete to purchase a particular item. eBay is the Internet company most closely associated with auctions, and many businesses offer their products for sale on eBay.

A reverse auction is different. In a reverse auction a company indicates what kind of part, product or service it wants and then suppliers bid to deliver it. In a reverse auction the price usually goes down as more suppliers bid on the offering. General Electric and United Technologies popularized the reverse auction over the Internet in the late 1990s. Many companies claim that they have saved heaps of money by using this technique for finding suppliers. General Electric claims to have saved $600 million in 2001. Glaxo Smith Klein says that it saved between 5 and 35 percent on the 420,000 worldwide hotel rooms it pays for each year — and that's on an $80 million budget.

Critics of online reverse auctions say that the savings are a mirage. David Stec and M.L. Emiliani of the Center for Lean Business Management at Rensselaer Polytechnic Institute found that half of all the savings claimed in reverse auctions don't materialize because of errors in data from the supplier, negotiations between buyer and supplier after the auction, changes in quantities and/or specifications, poor quality, late deliveries, and failure of the supplier to perform.[3] Furthermore, the authors say that the divisive nature of reverse auctions work against building long-term and closely partnered supplier relationships, and might even be unethical.

OPERATIONS

What Is Operations?

Operations, also known as manufacturing, is where a company's product or service is made. For a company that makes stuff that you can touch, operations is usually called the factory. For a company that makes services, like hair cutting, management consulting, landscaping, or personal protection, operations is called service delivery. Service delivery is sometimes done in a fixed location (a barber shop) but more often the service gets delivered in a multitude of places.

Operations management, also called manufacturing planning and control (MPC), involves the following activities:

- planning plant capacity requirements and availability,
- determining the quantity and arrival time of materials needed,
- making sure that capital equipment and machinery is adequately utilized,
- managing inventory,
- scheduling production lines, including shift work and machine downtimes,
- tracking material, people, and customer orders,
- determining lead times for finished products and advising customers on any deviations in promised lead times,
- responding to and acting upon any unexpected problems,
- communicating up and down the supply chain (with purchasing, logistics, distribution) as well as senior management and other functions regarding work in process,
- determining capital investment decisions (whether to expand the plant, buy a new piece of equipment, etc.), and
- designing new and/or expanded facilities.

In many cases operations also participates in new product development projects with marketing and engineering.

Why Is the Operations Function Important?

Operations is the heart of the business—its reason for being. It's kind of like saying, "I produce, therefore I am." Some companies don't actually produce anything. They get other companies to produce everything, by outsourcing their manufacturing as well as most or all of the staff functions. These are often called "hollow corporations," "virtual corporations" or "networked organizations." But these types of organizations are unstable and do not tend to exist in the same form for very long. Nike, the athletic footwear and apparel company, is an exception. It outsources 100 percent of its manufacturing—that means that Nike, the footwear market leader, does not own any of the 830 independent factories that make Nike branded shoes, clothing, and sports equipment.

Most companies that make stuff have a factory somewhere, and they might even have lots of factories. Anything that you can touch had to be made somehow, somewhere. Operations is the function that is responsible for making a product at a quality and price that the company's target customers are willing to pay for, and in a time frame that will make profits for the company. Operations management is important because without it companies can find (1) that they have produced too many products for the market demand, (2) are stuck with a huge amount of inventory, (3) they have not utilized their employees or equipment properly, (4) their product quality has slipped, and/or (5) have annoyed their customers because products aren't delivered when promised. All of these miscalculations can cause serious problems including bankruptcy or even liquidation.

Here we'll discuss what the typical operations function does in a manufacturing company.

Mass Production, Mass Consumption, and the Disembodied Worker

Henry Ford is most often credited for creating in 1914 the first assembly line, which allowed him to produce automobiles in large quantities and at a relatively low cost. This is called mass production. Ford actually saw a "disassembly" line in a meat slaughterhouse where whole cows were loaded onto a conveyer belt and they were systematically disassembled (butchered) into the various cuts of meat. He took the conveyer belt idea and used it to assemble parts, which then got matched to other parts down the line and eventually a complete, functioning car came out of the other end. The concept of an assembly line depends on raw materials flowing from one end and being manipulated along the way such that they come out as a finished product that can be sold to consumers.

In Ford's assembly line, the whole process depended on low-skilled workers doing a multitude of individual jobs along the line. So for example, one worker would put a nut into a bolt and place the assembled part onto the conveyer belt. The next worker would take the nut/bolt assembly and combine it with another part to make yet a third subassembly. The work was excruciatingly boring and tedious. Workers did not repair their own tools (there were specialized repair people for that) nor did they clean their individual work areas (janitorial staff came in periodically to do that). All a worker was expected to do was his (and in those days they were mostly all men) individual job over and over again for 8 hours each day. Each job was clearly defined and standardized. Parts were designed such that everything fit perfectly together (standardization), thus eliminating any guesswork or rework in the process. Quality control was the job of specific workers at the end of the assembly line and rejects were set aside for later repair or discard. The time it took to complete each job on the assembly line was timed and documented such that everything moved at the optimum pace—this was the concept of "flow" that Ford introduced. Workers were punished for moving too fast or too slow. Ford distributed electric motors to drive machines that were placed along the assembly line rather than in one central location.

This increased throughput and dramatically raised productivity. Certain parts could now be made in parallel off the line and added to the automobile at strategic points on the assembly line. Workers were not expected to think, thus they became known as the "disembodied worker" who was there just for his physical labor (as in worker bees).

Ford soon discovered that even though he was making an automobile that sold for $360 (this was down from $780 in 1910), he found that the average worker still could not afford to buy his cars. So he doubled the pay rate for his assembly line workers to $5.00 per day. His main reason was to bribe his employees to do such tedious work. But at the same time, Ford created a middle class that could afford to purchase his automobiles. This is called mass consumption. Ford awakened a latent demand in a rapidly industrializing society for time and labor saving devices, starting with the automobile. Some people also call this process "Fordization", meaning to standardize a product and mass manufacture it at a price that is low enough for the common man to be able to afford. This is also where the term, mass production, comes from—as in "production for the masses."

Factors of Production

Factors of production are inputs or hard costs for things like capital (money tied up in assets like land, sophisticated machines, robots, and assembly lines), labor, and raw materials. All of these items contribute to producing a widget. Some economists add management skills as another factor of production (although several factory workers might question the notion that management adds anything to their ability to produce stuff). Other scholars add technology as an additional factor, but this could also be covered under the umbrella of "capital."

Economists like to use "long run" and "short run" when describing choices people make. In the long run, all of the factors of production can be increased or decreased depending on demand for a product. Some factors are fixed (like capital assets) and others are variable (like electricity, labor, and raw materials). In the short run, it is difficult to change the fixed factors of production (you can't expand a factory overnight), but it is easy to change a variable factor (you can add or subtract a shift of workers relatively quickly).

Manufacturing Planning and Control Systems

Manufacturing planning and control (MPC) systems are tools that help managers make decisions relative to the operations and production function. Many of these types of systems are now embedded in software, which is often embedded into sophisticated machinery. In this section, we'll list some of the most prevalent control systems and concepts in a manufacturing environment.

There are three major processes to building something in a factory. They are shown graphically in Figure 10.1. The first process is production scheduling. This involves predicting product demand in association with hopeful forecasts from marketing, a realistic production budget from finance, and product specifications from engineering. With these numbers in mind, the operations manager needs to verify that she has the capacity in her factory to produce the amount of product that marketing thinks it can sell. And she needs to develop a production

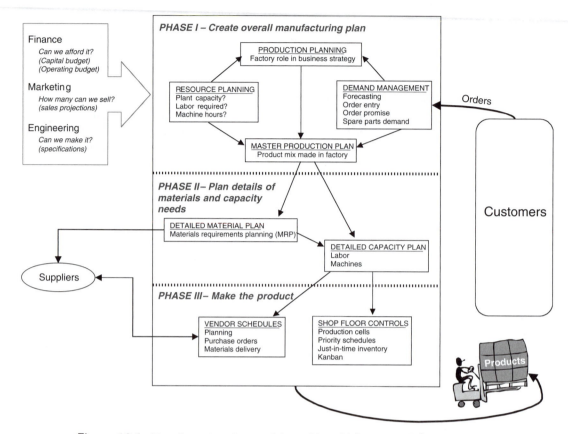

Figure 10.1. Manufacturing phases. (Adapted from Vollmann et al.)[4]

plan that sets forth how many units of product the factory will turn out and when they will be delivered. This is the top-down schedule for how things will get made.

The second stage in the process is planning in more detail which machines and assembly lines will produce what parts of the final product, how many workers, how many shifts, and the detailed breakdown of every screw, nut, bolt, and other raw materials that need to be ordered and when.

The final stage in the MPC process is actually making the product. This is an even more detailed description of what happens on the shop floor. It indicates which work centers will make what subassemblies and when. This plan sets forth production rules that describe what orders take priority at each work center. Products that go into similar parts or subassemblies get grouped together into production cells. This is also where the just-in-time (JIT) inventory system is implemented.

MRP and MRP-II

Material Requirements Planning (MRP) is a process for managing inventory and planning orders for parts and other materials that have demand generated from another item. The old term for MRP was "parts explosion." Think of how many little screws, nuts, bolts, washers, and various other parts might be needed to build a 747. That gives you an idea of the complexity involved in making sure that the factory's hardware store is amply supplied. MRP is a system that helps manage the inventory and automate (to some degree) the parts reorder process. It enables the folks on the shop floor to have the right part at the right time, without getting bogged down with wading through too much inventory. As a simple example, let's take a snowboard manufacturer. Each snowboard will need a finished plank and the binding assembly, consisting of two ratchets, two blocks, four buckles, two sets of toe and ankle straps, and two receptors. Now let's say that the manufacturer has received an order for 10 snowboards. He has to figure out how many parts he's got on hand (inventory status), how many parts are allocated to snowboards in process, what parts he had previously ordered and will arrive shortly, and which and how many parts he needs to finish the 10 snowboards. This process of disaggregating (or "exploding") the final product into its required parts is called MRP.

Where MRP concerns the inventory record keeping and ordering system for individual parts, MRP-II came about with the introduction of sophisticated computer systems and database management functions. MRP-II is known as "Manufacturing Resource Planning" or "big MRP" (the old MRP became known as "little MRP"). MRP-II allows the production manager to summarize the schedule of parts as they are needed in production, and see the bigger picture of when each finished unit would be produced. It also allows the manager to play complex "what if" scenarios with the production system (for example, "what if part A is delivered 2 weeks late. What effect will that have on subassembly D and what happens to the production schedule?"). Execution is now more predictable and this in turn, works as an accurate forecasting and control system.

Job Shops

Job shops are the short order cooks of the manufacturing world. They are usually small operations that make parts, subassemblies, or even finished products built to the specifications of a larger manufacturer or an end user. Since each order is either very different, or the operation gets batches of similar but small orders, the shop orders only the parts and raw materials necessary for the orders it has received. Job shop work is not typically a continuous flow process (like a food processing plant, oil refinery or a steel or textile mill), and certain tools or machinery might be unused for periods of time. Job shops are very common in the furniture industry, particularly for high-end furniture where the buyer wants special wood, fabrics, and finishes made to order, or an entire custom-built kitchen. Many job shops specialize in particular types of products and processes, like metal casting, centerless grinding, molding, ceramics, brazing, and soldering. Several Web sites enable a large manufacturer to find the specific service they're looking for. Most job shops that do business with the larger manufacturers are capable of delivering product to the manufacturer's receiving dock in a JIT manner and are certified in a number of manufacturing processes.

Mass Customization

Mass customization is the production, in very large quantities, of customized goods and services. Mass customization arose out of the failure of mass production to satisfy all customers all the time. Mass production relied on the following factors in order to deliver profits:

- Low cost and standardized products
- Homogeneous markets (the traditional American family with 2.2 kids, working father, and stay-at-home mother—think Mr. and Mrs. Cleaver in the TV show, *Leave it to Beaver*)
- Stable and predictable demand
- Long product life cycles
- Long product development cycles

Unfortunately for the mass producers of the old days (pre-1980) such as Ford, General Motors, McDonalds, your local bank, Procter & Gamble, and others, the world was changing. The United States and many other industrialized countries were experiencing massive inflows of people from overseas. The population became more heterogeneous with respect to social class, race, lifestyle, and national origin. In addition, the disparity in income widened so the rich people were now really rich and had much more disposable income than the really poor people. As people became richer, they did not want to have to accept the same quality of product that was being sold to the general public. In other words, they wanted a more customized product or service.

So now manufacturers had to figure out a way to produce things that had all sorts of new bells and whistles but still do so at a cost that would leave some profit for themselves. Several manufacturers redesigned their products and production processes so that the end product could be easily customizable, such as offering modules of options on a new car (if you wanted air conditioning, it usually came as part of a "luxury" package featuring a higher end stereo system, leather seats, and alloy wheels). Other manufacturers used software to help them manage the complexity in the production process. Lands' End, the catalog and online retailer, offers custom-fit pants. The customer enters their body shape, size, style, and fit preferences, and 2–4 weeks later, presto! Their pants arrive made to order. Behind the scenes, Lands' End computers compare the data entered by the customer to a huge database of body measurements, and then generate a prototype of the customer's body and weight distribution. The software also tells the machines at a contract manufacturer in Mexico exactly how to cut the fabric and how to stitch together the pieces, one pair of pants at a time.

Mass customization has revolutionized nearly every type of business. Now you have Coke in 20 different flavors (vanilla, cherry, lime, diet lime, Diet Coke with several types of sweeteners, New Coke, Classic Coke, Diet Coke with or without caffeine, and so on). You can get your McDonald's hamburger with or without pickles, onions, tomatoes, etc. Your bank probably offers an array of different checking and savings account options. In contrast to mass production, mass customization has the following characteristics:

- Low cost, high quality, and customized products
- Heterogeneous markets (there's a wide variety of ethnicity, income levels, tastes in food, tastes in clothing, service desires, etc.)
- Demand is unstable, fractured into different "flavors" of products (light beer, draft beer, fruit-flavored beer, dry beer, etc.)
- Product life cycles are short
- Product development cycles are short
- Product and process technology changes rapidly

So how does a company satisfy all these new demands for customized products and services? The next section on lean manufacturing will explain one of the key methods.

Lean Manufacturing

Does anybody want fat manufacturing? Lean manufacturing, also known as lean production, is sort of the opposite of mass production. Japanese manufacturers pioneered lean manufacturing, which is a management philosophy with the following principles:

- Elimination of the "seven wastes":
  - (a) Overproduction
  - (b) Waiting time
  - (c) Transportation (in excess of the minimum required)
  - (d) Overprocessing (too many people handling a component)
  - (e) Inventory
  - (f) Motion
  - (g) Scrap
- Get it right the first time (quality comes first, zero defects is the goal)
- Continuous improvement (learn from every process and work to make it better by reducing costs and increasing productivity)
- Pull processing—products are "pulled" through the assembly line by customer demand, rather than forecasts that 'push' products through
- Flexibility—many small lots of different types of products are produced, quick machine tool changeovers facilitate little or no down time on the assembly line.
- Close supplier relationships

When a true lean production line is put in place, product quality first tends to increase, costs decrease, and production time speeds up. Lean manufacturing uses many tools, including JIT inventory delivery, Kaizen (constant process analysis with a goal to improve the process), Kanban (see next section), self-organizing teams, and eliminating mistakes.

Lean production is lean because it uses less of everything: fewer workers, fewer factories, fewer (or no) inventory, fewer defects, less waste, less manufacturing space, less investment in tools and engineering hours, and less time to develop new products. But lean production does all this while offering a greater variety of products, at low cost, and fast delivery.

Fast Moving Teams by Dilbert
Dilbert: © Scott Adams/Dist. by United Feature Syndicate, Inc., Reprinted with permission.

The specialty truck manufacturer, Oshkosh Truck Corporation, in Wisconsin, has mastered the art of lean production (they call it flexible integrated manufacturing). The company produces almost every kind of heavy-duty truck for both the military and private sector commercial uses. They make concrete mixers, fire trucks, garbage trucks, wreckers, and snowplows among other equipment. On the same production line, they also make military transporters, heavy payload tactical trucks, and various other military logistic vehicles. Since demand for each type of truck isn't huge, the company has figured out how to manufacture each of these types of trucks with little or no stoppage in the production line. So you might see a fire truck coming down the line, followed by a military transporter, followed by a concrete pumping truck, and so on. They've gotten the cycle time for each station down to 22 minutes. Where they used to keep a week and a half's worth of engines on hand, now they only maintain a day-and-a-half's worth of inventory. In addition to higher productivity, higher quality, and faster delivery times, Oshkosh Truck has gained flexibility. The company can make last minute alterations to a truck if a customer decides that the trash trucks they ordered will be used in Savannah rather than Seattle, so they'll need air conditioning added.

Just-in-Time and Kanban

Just-in-time (JIT) is kind of like having your roommate show up with a six-pack of beer just as you've finished the last bottle in the fridge. In a factory, JIT is a relatively new concept in manufacturing. It's a key part of the famous Toyota production system. At its base level, JIT is a process by which parts arrive "just in time" to the particular shop area exactly where and when they are needed. But JIT actually embodies a wider set of principles including

- reduction of setup times and lot sizes,
- flexible manufacturing (ability to make several different types of products),
- elimination of waste (time, energy, material, labor),
- zero defects,
- a goal of continuous improvement (faster setups, more output, fewer defects), and
- the belief that workers should and can use their minds to better the manufacturing process.

In a true JIT plant, parts, subassemblies, and products flow through the operation with no long stops and starts. The concept of "flow" is key. The idea is to produce a little bit of everything on a continuous basis so that the factory turns out a constant flow of the different types of products or models. In traditional manufacturing, when an automobile plant wanted to shift production to a new model, the factory had to shut down for days or even weeks in order to change the dies (molds that make particular parts) and other machines for subassemblies and components. This is a costly procedure because the company still had to pay the workers who were idle waiting for the new shifts to start up again, and in the meantime, no product is coming down the line. In contrast, a plant running JIT will design the different automobile models *from the start* so that the component parts are similar and the dies and other machine tools can produce many different types of parts with minimal disruption to the production process. As part of this JIT philosophy, the entire process of how a product is made gets reengineered so that as many components as possible are made in small production cells, in small lots, and in parallel. This can mean that the shop floor might look like a small village with a front-end assembly cell, a back-end assembly cell, a paint cell, a chassis cell, and so on. Because product is flowing through the factory quickly, the amount of work in progress and the associated paperwork to keep track of it is minimal or nonexistent.

How does a production cell know when it needs to make more stuff? Kanban is a Japanese card system that indicates when a stock of parts needs to be replenished. In reality, any type of system can work, whether it's an empty container, a flag placed in an upright position, rolling a tennis ball to the cell that makes the particular part, or yelling, "Hey, make some more!" All of these methods signal a downstream need for a particular part, component, or subassembly, and authorize the upstream cell to make more of the component, usually in small lot sizes. In this manner, components are "pulled" through the system.

In a JIT system, the company's relationship with its suppliers takes on a new form, wherein suppliers are more tightly integrated into the product design and are responsible for delivering entire chunks of a product, such as an automobile interior, or a complete antilock braking system. Suppliers now deliver their piece of the product just as the component is needed on the assembly line. Such a new relationship requires a great deal of trust between the company and its suppliers. With JIT, the company doesn't have to maintain an expensive inventory of parts, components, and subassemblies. But if there is any interruption in supply (due to labor strike, raw material shortage, etc.), the impact is immediate.

When JIT Doesn't Work

Just-in-time manufacturing approaches are usually not useful for the following types of products/processes:

- **Job shop (batch manufacturing)**
- **Products with sporadic demand**
- **Custom products**

When JIT is properly implemented the benefits to a manufacturing plant are enormous: 20–90 percent reductions in cycle time, inventory, labor cost, space requirements, and material costs. At the same time, product quality increases dramatically. As you can imagine, all of these factors feed into the bottom line of the company's operating costs and show up as higher profits.

Quality, Six-Sigma, and ISO Certification

Total Quality Management (TQM) took off as a trend in business in the 1980s at about the same time that U.S. manufacturers realized that Japan was able to produce higher quality automobiles and electronics at much lower cost than American manufacturers could. The Japanese philosophy was to make something right the first time, eliminate waste, and constantly strive to improve a process. These are all components of lean manufacturing.

The irony about the quality movement is that it was an American, W. Edward Deming, who got the Japanese hooked on quality. Japanese manufacturing companies revered Dr. Deming as a god after a series of lectures he gave in 1950 (kind of like a demigod!) He told the Japanese not to copy the inefficient American manufacturing processes, but instead to embark on an entirely new philosophy that puts product quality first and meeting or exceeding customer expectations. Deming's prescriptions included eliminating waste in all forms (energy, manpower, production, etc.), treating workers as if they have a brain, preventing defective components from ever getting onto the production line, and building long-term, cooperative relationships with suppliers.

Six Sigma is a term that was popularized in the 1980s by Bill Smith, an engineer at Motorola. (In fact, Six Sigma is a registered trademark of Motorola.) It's a statistical approach to reducing manufacturing defects to less than 3.4 occurrences per million events. In layman's terms, Six Sigma is a tool that companies use to eliminate variation in a process outcome, with the ultimate goal of increasing profits. A company implementing Six Sigma can quickly measure the various parts of the manufacturing process and see where the opportunity for defects arises—and then fix the process. Obviously, the fewer defects (meaning anything that doesn't meet the customer's specifications) the higher the company's profits. General Electric figures that its own implementation of Six Sigma saved the company about $10 billion over the first five years it was in place.

The International Standards Organization (ISO) is a nongovernmental organization (NGO) comprising a network of the national standards institutes in 156 countries. It's the largest keeper, developer, and arbitrator of worldwide standards—mostly in the technical arena. ISO claims that standards are what make systems, machinery, and devices work well and ensure safety of the operators. Did you know that one of the ISO standards is A4 paper—the size commonly used in Europe and the rest of the world? It's a bit longer and skinnier than U.S. letter-sized paper. So why is ISO important? According to the ISO Web site:

> Without the standardized dimensions of freight containers, international trade would be slower and more expensive. Without the standardization of telephone and banking cards, life would be more complicated. A lack of standardization may even affect the quality of life itself: for the disabled, for example, when they are barred access to consumer products, public transport, and buildings because the dimensions of wheelchairs and entrances are not standardized.
>
> Standardized symbols provide danger warnings and information across linguistic frontiers. Consensus on grades of various materials give a common reference for suppliers and clients in business dealings.[5]

In reality ISO is important because it certifies companies and manufacturing processes under a long and complicated procedure. Companies will spend the large amounts of money that it usually takes to become certified because their own customers demand ISO certification. ISO certification guarantees that a company meets certain requirements for quality in the manufacturing and delivery of products and services.

OUTSOURCING

Outsourcing is the practice of contracting with another company to perform a specific job, function, service, or process. Offshoring is a similar type of outsourcing but it can be either to a foreign company, often on another continent, or to a foreign subsidiary of the home company. In 1990 General Electric made electronic components in Singapore, and in fact, was the biggest corporate employer there. Companies often outsource parts of their operations that they consider to be "non-core" meaning it is not proprietary or a key part of their competitive advantage. Examples include outsourcing the accounts payable and receivable functions, parts of the information technology function (usually routine IT tasks and data processing), the legal function, engineering (if it involves routine and/or fairly well-known calculations), computer-aided design, the transactional side of human resources (benefits, routine paperwork, etc.), and relatively predictable processing jobs. Today you can outsource almost anything, including air traffic control and online tutoring (see www.growingstars.com). Some enterprising college computer science students are even outsourcing their homework assignments (see www.rentacoder.com).[6] Many critics of outsourcing say that it will debilitate the American workforce by moving nearly all service sector jobs overseas.[7] In reality, it's hard to imagine that your morning café latte will ever be produced in India or China, much less that your garden in Berkeley can possibly tended from Santiago. In fact, what seems to be happening is that some service jobs (those that don't require specific local knowledge and can easily be done over the Internet) as well as high-level research and engineering jobs are indeed moving overseas.

WHY OUTSOURCE?

The main rationale for outsourcing a particular job is that a company realizes that it can't be good at everything, and it really wants to free up resources (people, money, lab space, server time, other non-monetary assets, etc.) to work on projects at which it truly excels. Therefore, the company pays someone else to do the non-core work that's necessary to help run the business. So to whom does the company give that work? So far, India and China seem to be the main beneficiaries of the outsourcing trend. In India's case it's in large part due to the high level of education of the Indian population and the fact that many of the people are taught in English, the de facto international language (much

Outsourcing Pseudonyms

- Fire and forget
- Run my mess for less

Outsourcing Pros and Cons

Pros:

- Enables a company to bring products & services to a local market
- A company can buy a particular service for lower cost than in the home market
- Outsourcing allows a company to reengineer or automate work that can be done better by someone else
- Companies can take advantage of highly educated people with foreign language skills
- Enables 24/7 support to all areas of the world
- Savings from transferring jobs overseas can allow a company to add more highly skilled jobs in the home country

Cons:

- Service can be a problem with some foreign workers (language skills, heavy accents, lack of service culture, etc.)
- Overseas infrastructure (roads, telecom networks, etc.) are often poor, resulting in higher costs than anticipated
- As more outsourcing to a particular geography increases, local wages rise and the initial cost advantages disappear
- 50% of outsourcing arrangements fail to live up to expectations
- Employee turnover at the overseas vendor is often high, resulting in unexpected costs.
- Some foreign countries do not have adequate protection for intellectual property rights, potentially jeopardizing the company's assets

to the annoyance of the French). In China's case it's the country with the world's largest population and it represents a huge and attractive market for companies to enter. In addition, China's universities turn out thousands of well-educated scientists and engineers, with skills that are dwindling in the United States, as college graduates pursue careers in less technical arenas. But China is more complex because products, services, and software all need to be tailored to the Chinese language and customs. Other emerging markets for technically skilled workers include the Philippines, Russia, Eastern Europe, Latin America, and South Africa. Fluor-Daniel, the giant American engineering and construction company, designs complex oil refineries using both U.S. and Philippine workers. In the evening when the American engineers go home, the drawings are beamed by satellite to the Philippines where engineers continue the work until the end of their business day and the process repeats on the other side of the Pacific. Dow Chemical is opening up a research center in Shanghai, which will house 600 technical workers. Dow expects to shift many of its 5,700 scientists to overseas locations, and alter the mix of nationalities it employs. Nike has long outsourced much of the manufacturing of lower-end athletic shoes and apparel to developing countries. Many call centers were moved to Ireland, India, The Philippines, and other English-speaking countries with lower labor costs. (However, several of those call centers are now coming back to the United States as service and quality have suffered.)

Outsourcing Functions by Dilbert
Dilbert: © Scott Adams/Dist. by United Feature Syndicate, Inc., Reprinted with permission.

LOGISTICS AND DISTRIBUTION

What Is Logistics?

The field of logistics, like many concepts in business, comes from military science. Military logistics involves the mathematical analysis and deployment of transportation and supply as well as troop movements. It means getting not only the soldiers out to the military theater, but also their vehicles, guns, ammunition, tents, beds, laundry facilities, dining halls, kitchens, hospitals, and all other support functions aligned and located in the same place and at the same time as the troops.

For a business, logistics is the function of planning, organizing and, controlling any and all activities involved in moving or storing goods or services required in the operation of a business. This includes goods acquired in raw material state, work-in-progress, parts inventory, and finished products that are destined for a customer's warehouse or retail store. Many of the activities that involve logistics often fall into other domains of a business. For example, there are logistics requirements in a factory as raw materials and subassemblies arrive on the loading dock for distribution into specific areas of the plant.

Just-in-time manufacturing has eliminated much of the need to keep track of work-in-progress as replacement parts get ordered automatically through a kanban type of system. But someone had to plan where all the JIT parts are put when they arrive. Similarly, the marketing function (see chapter 6) is mostly concerned with creating demand for the company's goods and services through product design, promotion, channel placement, and distribution to places where customers will buy the product. Logistics plays a role in getting the product from the factory to the store, whether it means contracting with overseas shipping companies, storage facilities, customs brokers, trucking companies, railroads and/or FedEx or UPS. In fact, most logistics professionals today would argue that they are intimately involved in all aspects of the entire supply chain. The primary responsibilities of the traditional logistics function in a large manufacturing company include the following:

- Transportation
  (a) Type of transportation and selection of service vendors
  (b) Carrier routing
  (c) Selection of vehicles and scheduling
  (d) Fleet maintenance
- Inventory management
  (a) Stocking policies of finished goods
  (b) Record keeping
  (c) Purchasing raw materials, parts, and supplies
  (d) Storage policies and facilities of in-route goods
- Order processing
  (a) Processing sales order information inside the factory
  (b) Collection, storage, and analysis of data (inventories, sales, material flow)
- Warehouse and materials handling
  (a) Determination of space requirements and warehouse configuration
  (b) Layout plan for stock placement and dock design
  (c) Design of order picking procedures
  (d) Stock storage and retrieval plan
  (e) Materials handling equipment selection and purchase
  (f) Development of warehouse equipment replacement policies

In a service business, like an airline, logistics is an enormously complex and important function. Imagine a big multinational airline with thousands of planes in the air at any given time. Now imagine a giant storm hitting Chicago and many of the planes destined to land at O'Hare are diverted to other airports across the Midwest. How does a company figure out how to get planes back on schedule after the storm passes? Even worse, how does the airline get its crews sorted out when they are now scattered all over the place and have worked the maximum number of hours permitted by the FAA? This is a job for linear programming.

Here we were in the boondocks. We didn't have distributors falling over themselves to serve us like our competitors did in larger towns. Our only alternative was to build our own warehouse so we could buy in volume at attractive prices and store the merchandise.

—Sam Walton, founder of Wal-Mart (quoted in *Forbes*)

Outsourcing Logistics?

UPS, the world's largest package delivery company, offers a host of 'supply chain solutions' for small to huge customers.

- Logistics and distribution (Nike shoes go from a factory in Asia to a UPS warehouse, where they are checked and shipped to individual customers by UPS employees)
- Transportation and freight services (ground, sea, air, rail)
- Freight forwarding (from one country to another)
- Consulting services (supply chain redesign and others)
- International trade management
- Customs brokerage
- Technical repair and configuration (UPS fixes Toshiba laptops)
- Returns management
- Supplier management
- International financing of cargo, equipment, real estate
- Business credit cards
- Cargo and credit insurance

Scheduling Algorithms (Linear Programming)

Scheduling algorithms, also known as linear optimization models, are mathematical equations that seek to optimize some sort of variable or outcome among many other variables (the most efficient delivery route, the best use of San Francisco-based flight attendants on a 3-day shift, the optimum number of distribution facilities servicing groupings of retail stores, etc.). Think of it as a *really* tricky word problem. Linear programming is one of the most commonly used types of algorithms, and today the equations are almost entirely run on computers. Several Web sites offer linear programming services and a few are listed at the end of this chapter.

What Is Distribution?

Distribution is the process by which finished goods move from the factory to the retailer. It can involve third party transportation companies, warehousing facilities, customs brokers (in the case of international distribution), and a host of other interim operators. Some companies, like Wal-Mart, create, maintain, and operate their own proprietary distribution system. Indeed, 85 percent of all of the products that arrive in a Wal-Mart store are brought there on Wal-Mart's trucks from a Wal-Mart distribution facility. The rest of the merchandise is delivered by the vendor to the stores. By contrast, most retailers run less than half of all merchandise through their own distribution centers, preferring to outsource the actual trucking function to a professional trucking company. Wal-Mart is now known as the standard of excellence in distribution. It operates its own six-channel satellite network. The network gathers real-time in-store data on sales, it handles credit card approvals at the register in 5 seconds or less, it tracks the company's vast and complex distribution system, it propagates employee-associate training videos, and it is the means by which headquarters officials communicate daily or even hourly with the various store managers and employee-associates.

Wal-Mart's gargantuan distribution centers (over a million square feet under a 28-acre roof) are strategically located as a hub for the stores such that each center can support about 150 stores. When Wal-Mart enters a new market, it opens a couple of stores followed by a distribution center and then it "backfills" the area to saturate the market with additional stores. Each center has state-of-the-art inventory control and materials handling technology. Goods coming in on trucks are offloaded onto an 11-mile-long conveyer belt system where they are laser-scanned and automatically routed to some 150 waiting Wal-Mart trucks. Every store gets a truckload of goods delivered every day. Very few humans staff these centers. The distribution centers get their instructions on what to load onto which truck from the satellite network. Barcode scanners at the checkout registers identify every product that is sold and transmit that information each night to Wal-Mart's headquarters in Bentonville, Arkansas as well as to the local distribution center. Buyers in Bentonville make sure that the distribution centers have enough product coming to them so that the stores are constantly replenished in a JIT manner. Wal-Mart's distribution costs are only about 1.3 percent of sales, compared to other retailers who pay between 3.5 and 5 percent for distribution costs.

The barcode scanner data also transmits critical real-time information about what products are selling. People at headquarters then analyze that data to discover, for example, that last year on Memorial Day, the start of the summer barbeque season, certain stores sold 18 pallets of charcoal, but also 6 pallets of beach umbrellas and canvas chairs. This information then helps the buyers plan for the upcoming summer season and they transmit that order information electronically to the vendors who make charcoal, beach umbrellas, and canvas chairs. This is an example of "pulling" merchandise through a supply chain, wherein demand from the customer dictates how much of what products are manufactured.

RFID

Radio frequency identification (RFID) tags are being used more frequently to help manufacturers keep track of where, exactly, their products are at any given moment. In a recent advertisement, an IBM help desk attendant sits at her desk in the middle of a road. A truck pulls up and stops in front of her. She walks up to the driver and tells him that he's lost, and explains how to get back on the right highway. He asks her how she knew that he was lost and she replies, "The boxes told me." To which the driver rather snidely responds, "Well why don't we let the boxes drive?"

RFID is actually an older technology that incorporates a microchipped tag with an antenna, and a reader with one or two antennae that use radio waves to capture the information stored on the tag. Some tags can hold up to 2 kilobytes of information, such as a product serial number, where and when it was manufactured, its sell-by date, and so on. Other high-end RFID tags allow the information on them to be changed or updated. As finished products roll out of the factory, antennae automatically read the tags on the product and transmit the data to the Internet so that the item (boxes, pallets, bottles, whatever) can be tracked through a secure computer network. Anyone with authorization to access that network can tell at a couple of clicks where a specific pallet of Diet

Coke is in the distribution system and when it was delivered to the customer's loading dock. Pfizer now ships Viagra bottles with RFID chips under the labels in an effort to control counterfeits. Pharmacists will scan the bottle with an RFID reader, which then transmits the product code to Pfizer's servers for verification. Cattle and other livestock are routinely fitted with ear tags that tell the rancher where each cow is.

Some people are concerned over the power of RFID to pinpoint people's locations a little too precisely, *à la* Big Brother is watching. One grade school in Northern California (Brittan Elementary School in Sutter) ordered all of its students to wear RFID badges so that it could make the attendance-taking process more efficient, and at the same time reduce vandalism and improve safety on campus. Many parents are outraged and are working to fight the new regime. And you thought *your* school treats you like a number!

RFID could be a dream come true for manufacturers and, in fact, most of the partners along the supply chain. So why isn't RFID use more widespread? It's sort of a chicken-and-egg situation. In early 2006 each tag cost between 20 and 40 cents, and most manufacturers say it's not economical until it becomes cheaper, to around 5 cents per tag. But the tags won't become cheaper until more companies use them, but more companies won't use them until they become cheaper. To that end, Wal-Mart mandated that as of January 2005, its top 100 suppliers must use RFID tags on everything that is delivered to Wal-Mart stores. In February 2006, Philips Research, the R&D function of Royal Philips Electronics, announced that it had developed a fully functional RFID tag completely made of plastic. This could go a long way to reducing the cost of the technology.

Another problem with RFID is that unlike barcode scanners, which only scan what is directly in front of them, the RFID scanners can read everything in range, such as *all* those boxes on the top shelf. In addition, RFID standards are not uniform and are still being developed worldwide. Boring old barcodes are standard everywhere, and probably will continue to be used for some time to come.

A DAY IN THE LIFE OF A SUPPLY CHAIN EXECUTIVE

Chris Barry
Senior Strategic Solutions Manager
FedEx

It seems I've always been involved in a distribution and logistics business. I was a paper boy when I was a kid in Pasadena, California. In the language of supply chain that is what we call the "Last Mile." When I ran out of money to fund my senior year at the University of California, Berkeley, I went and worked for 9 months for Flying Tigers, which was later (1989) purchased by FedEx. I found myself in the middle of the night, timing the unloading and loading of aircraft at Chicago's busy O'Hare airport. It was part of my wider responsibilities in the Terminal Planning group developing work standards, operations planning, and staffing. I graduated from UC Berkeley with a degree in industrial engineering and operations research. Building upon a senior project I did with Tigers and the U.S. Postal Service (USPS), I went to work for the USPS in their industrial engineering/management trainee program. I worked almost every job in the post office from mail processing clerk to acting postmaster in a town in Wyoming! I moved back to Pasadena and, while still doing engineering work for the Postal Service, got my MBA at the University of Southern California.

I joined Federal Express Corporation in 1990 as a "backroom engineer" doing industrial engineering work; setting up new operations/flights; internal logistics planning (called "system form"); then moving on to new product development; and strategic planning.

A typical project would be the introduction of a new aircraft type (new Airbus 300) or route to a market (direct flights to the Chicago ramp). We would plan how to load aircraft working back up to the point in which the courier picked up the package from the customer. We'd also plan the flow of packages across trucks, containers, conveyor belts, sorts, scans, and ground support equipment to the load position of the aircraft for an on-time departure. Then we'd plan the reverse flow with the final on-time delivery to the customer. Operating plans would be developed and communicated for these changes along with documentation on normal monthly changes. Operational impacts would be identified and measured and supporting operating budgets would be created.

FedEx has a number of companies within the corporation. We've got the original FedEx Express, plus we now have FedEx Ground, FedEx Freight (big, heavy stuff), FedEx Kinkos (print and ship, or send electronic documents for pickup at a Kinkos location), FedEx Trade Networks (customs clearance and freight forwarding), FedEx Custom Critical (fastest possible shipping for high value stuff with special handling requirements), and FedEx Services (sales, marketing, IT and supply chain services).

Today I work in the solutions group in the services organization, which supports all of the other FedEx companies in their quest to serve the customer. My primary role is consulting with customers with the support of our sales people. It means really understanding the customer's business, their strategy, and helping them improve how their products flow through their own supply chain. At a basic level supply chains are made up of three flows:

1. Material
2. Information
3. Money

We have to be conscious of how all of these components fit together, how they flow tactically, and whether the whole system supports the customer's strategy. For example, in shipping there's a big tradeoff between speed (transit time) and cost. If our customer promises delivery of its product to its own customers within a certain time frame, faster delivery time usually costs more. Can the customer's business model support that extra cost? In addition, there's a tradeoff between carrying inventories in a distribution warehouse so that product is on hand to ship immediately, or making a customer wait for a product because you have to make it first. Both choices will work and it's a business strategy decision on which way a company chooses to go.

Inventory is a key issue since it hits every financial statement. We look at the customer's inventory levels as well as their historical forecasts versus actual sales. In many cases we can propose solutions to reduce inventory, like shipping assembly parts directly from the manufacturer in Asia to a customer's assembly plant. Or we'll ship finished goods from a factory directly to a retail store in New York. You can think of actually using FedEx trucks and planes as a company's in-transit warehouses.

The best practices companies do not even assemble a product until they have an order and then they will pay their suppliers many days after receiving payment from the customer. By using FedEx and the information we provide as the order heads to their customer, these companies really get the most out of their cash cycle.

When we work with a customer the first phase of the engagement is Solution Definition and Design. We have a discovery discussion that may evolve into further meeting that is called a "Framing Session." We'll discuss their supply chain across six major functions—Source, Make, Sell, Fulfill, Ship, and Service.

Key activities in this first phase are

1. Evaluation and analysis of customer needs
2. A map of current state processes
3. A gap analysis (discovery of "pain points")
4. Design of future state recommendations
5. Identification of project timeline and resources required
6. A statement of work (SOW) and service agreement
7. A solution proposal with value proposition

The future state design may or may not involve FedEx service. If it doesn't we can provide resources (third party alliances) for the customer. If it does involve FedEx we become a "customer-centric representative" for the customer across the FedEx operating companies. We'll develop the business and functional requirements that can include local operating plans for both the customer and FedEx. We'll also make sure that the correct information technology (IT) and shipping automation gets installed. We can bring in our marketing folks if there is a co-branding and/or marketing effort required. If the customer is scattered globally we can arrange to have local FedEx personnel (sales and IT) contact the customer's local offices to implement solutions.

Some of our customers are new to FedEx. They come in and say that they're unhappy with our competitors and want a bid from us. So we look at their operation, analyze their shipping history over the past year and map it. Based upon their overall shipping strategy, we can tell them the best mix of our services to use for the particular types of shipments and destinations they have.

In other cases, an existing customer calls and says something like, "I don't really know what our warehouses do? Can you help me figure out if we've got our logistics and distribution process set up properly?" It's funny how things evolve in a company over time. One customer has something like 20 warehouses in various regions all over the United States. Back in the old days things were delivered by slow truck and rail, so in order to manage the tradeoff of inventory versus customer service, a company had to maintain warehouses all over the place. Today we can serve, by surface movement, most locations in the United States with 2-day delivery from just 3–4 warehouses nationwide.

We have one customer that has vendors and retail stores all over the country. This customer has its vendors supply the stores directly, which, by the way, is not a bad strategy as it reduces the requirement for warehouse space. But once we took a look at the customer's distribution to see if we could improve it, we found they were crossing the nation. I looked at their list of vendors and the vendor locations. In one case, a vendor in Washington was shipping product to Atlanta, and another vendor in Florida that supplied exactly the same product and was sending it to Oregon. It made no sense! So we suggested that the Washington vendor ship to the Pacific Northwest stores, while the Florida vendor service the Southeast stores. We point these things out even if it means that FedEx loses money (now that the Florida vendor isn't paying us to fly product to Oregon).

The usual process is that the sales person will call me in and I go with them for a visit to the customer. We'll ask the customer, "What are your pain points? What isn't working as well as you want it to work?" We look at their financial statements, inventory levels, distribution facilities, major markets, and so on. Some things are simple. One company we worked with had committed to ship every order on the same day it was placed. But when we looked at their operation we discovered that the call center is open until 10 PM Eastern time, but the distribution center (DC) closed at 5 PM Pacific time. So any orders that came in the evening would not get out that day. Sounds like a realignment of commitments or DC relocation.

This job is very different from any I've had before. First, it's a pure project management-based job. We get a problem from a customer and I work with all of our other groups within FedEx to provide a solution. It requires creativity and an ability to sometimes cajole other people in our organization to help me out. But we're all pulling for that customer's business. So I bring resources together to solve a puzzle and try to get it to work even better. Second, it requires a different kind of analytical approach. Before, I was doing very tactical analysis on plane loads, sort times, container sizes, work crew staffing, and all the details that have to come together with split-second precision to get the plane full of packages off on time. Now I'm looking at strategic issues, financial analysis, and the bigger picture of how a customer's supply chain flows.

What's the downside of this job? You spend a lot of time on the phone and doing e-mail. Travel can be a pain. You sometimes wonder if it is worth it sitting around a cold empty airport at 11 PM trying to get home. Unlike my former job, where you could see the impact of your planning instantly (either the plane took off on time or it didn't), in this job the implementation of our recommendations can take an extremely long time or sometimes they're never even followed. But the upside of the job far outweighs the downside. I'm always learning something different and the people I work with are great and very professional.

In order to succeed in this job you need a combination of skills:

- A strong engineering background—the understanding and ability to optimize or model situations
- Knowledge of finance—an understanding of financial statements and the customer's business
- A love of learning and problem solving
- Strong project management skills
- Some knowledge of geography
- Good people skills
- A good knowledge of FedEx companies' operations

Working in the solutions group is very interesting. There is always something new to learn or practice. On a more global basis, if you really think about what organizations have made major changes in the world today you really have to look at the positive impact of the FedEx Corporation. The whole Internet commerce industry exists because of and is sustained by the services provided by FedEx. We've changed the way products are held and sold. For many companies we've provided the "place" for their products and services to be marketed. The work we and others do on supply chains leads to the minimization of inventories, and smoothed out production cycles. Those two factors together have really reduced the impact of "boom and bust" pattern of recessions in our industrial societies. In developing countries that 5 years ago were unable to feed their people, today with the help of FedEx they can really participate in the global economy. The power of FedEx – how can you beat the excitement of that?

A day in the life of a supply chain executive:

7:30 AM	If not traveling to a customer site, I would be in my office reviewing the e-mails from the night before. I work with folks across many time zones. E-mail allows us to communicate and coordinate. I respond to inquiries by e-mail and phone. I also review my calendar for upcoming conference calls and project due dates.
8:00 AM	The first conference call. It's with a large customer based in the East Coast. Joining me on the call is the company's CFO and VP of Logistics. We discuss their three business units and our plans to undertake a network analysis on each. The result of the call will be a draft statement of work (SOW) that will form the basis of our service agreement with them.
9:30 AM	The conference call is over. I review my notes to make sure I have all the information I need to do the "minutes" of the call. I also make several follow-up calls. During our conversation, the VP mentioned that they were looking for a way to increase their delivery to USPS post office boxes. I make a call to my contact, Tim, in the FedEx SmartPost group. The FedEx Smartpost line hauls and processes parcels turning them over to the USPS for the "final mile" delivery (including PO boxes). I ask if they would like to be engaged in this project with this customer. I call Jeremy in Pittsburg about another customer we're working on. He's with FedEx Ground and can tell me about the analysis that he's done with their shipping data.
10:00 AM	Another conference call, but this time it's an internal one to review a customer presentation with some of my peers—John and Melissa. We're working with a spin-off company from a major electronics manufacturer. They took a vacant warehouse in Sacramento from the parent company and have been using it to kit and service their major markets in the East and Southeastern United States. We did a flow analysis of their products, which come from contract manufacturers (CM) in Asia and go to Mexico before entering the United States. We are going to suggest that they trade the California warehouse for one that's more central to their markets, such as in Kansas City. We also suggest that they look at moving the kitting material to forward locations servicing local markets directly from Asia. 11:00 AM The calls after the call again. This time I need to make a follow-up call to my FedEx customer integration solution person, Sunny, on a customer I talked with yesterday on our installation FedEx Ship Manager. The FedEx software will allow my customer, a large news organization, to monitor their field

	bureau's use of FedEx. Sunny has the answer to the customer's question and will follow-up directly with them. I will include this information in the documentation that I'll send out later this afternoon to the local FedEx sales force as a "Call to Action."
12:00 PM	Time flies and it's time for lunch. I continue my quest to explore all of the dive Mexican restaurants in East Los Angeles. I take my *birria burrito especial* to go. I eat in the break room while skimming through the *Wall Street Journal*. There is usually news on businesses we're working with or their competitors.
12:45 PM	I get a call from my boss, Dave. I'm usually working on anywhere from six to eight accounts at any given time. He has a question on an account that I closed out last week. He wants to make sure that the revenue for the account will be recorded in our web base project reporting system. He also asks, "What my bandwidth is?" ?? (AM/FM? Or how many things you can do at once?) I make a call to Michelle in our Customer Value Team (CVT). The CVT is part of our solutions group and is made up of writers and English majors. We run through a draft of request for quote (RFQ) we are working on for a major computer retailer. The document is the response to the questions from the company. We are competing with other vendors for this business. It takes a while, but it looks like we got most of it covered. She gently reminds me that I still need to work up the value quantification of the expected savings due to a reduction of inventory for the document and presentation. She also reminds me that I need to get the pricing of the Express component from the sales group. After I hang up, I make a call to Donna, the sales person to follow-up.
2:00 PM	I have some free time to run through some shipping data from another account I am working with. The financial analyst FedEx'd the data CD to me using a label created on FedEx.com and e-mailed to her. The data is a bit of a mess. There are 25 spreadsheets that I need to import into an Access database. Using some database files I have I am able to clean up the customer data and assign zones to the shipping records. I export summary data to some mapping software I use. I'm able to create a color-coded map showing the areas served by the customer's distribution centers. I then export the maps and additional data tables to a presentation that I'll review with her tomorrow. Donna calls back. She expects to get the pricing back in time to complete the RFQ. I type in an e-mail to Michelle to let her know.
3:30 PM	I pull up the presentation that I've been working on for the RFQ. It's based upon a model developed by my fellow solution managers and it creates a value proposition using financial and shipping data. I focus on the value driver involving the company's inventory level. I level set the data against financial documentation I have on the company. This includes information I got from my data analyst, Jennifer, and lists the company's performance and their close competitors. The report includes identification of the best in the group. I also re-read

	their annual report to incorporate their CEO's objectives. I'm pretty happy with the results and e-mail the draft to the rest of the team for their review.
4:30 PM	I punch up our web-based software that facilitates our "Call to Action." I focus on the news organization account. I'm checking the location data the customer has given to me. It's surprising (I guess to me because of my facilities background), but some customers have very poor information on their company's facilities locations. I have used Internet search engines in the past to correct addresses. This particular organization has very good information, but not in the format I need for our software. With the location information I can send an e-mail with information (background, pricing, strategy, automation, questions, etc.) on the account to the local FedEx sales person. The sales person has a target date to call on this location and cover the information. The sales person will use the software to let me know they made contact and communicate any issues we need to review. I check my e-mail one more time, cross items off my to do list, check on what's up for tomorrow then head out the door.
5:30 PM	I'm off to my UCLA Extension class. I'm going for my certification in project management. My motto: You can never stop learning!

Careers in Supply Chain Management

Some of the jobs in the supply chain function are listed below. For more detail, please visit JobGenie at www.stepfour.com/jobs. The site lists thousands of official job descriptions along with educational and other requirements. Here some examples:

Layout Worker

Industry: machine shop

Lays out metal stock or workpieces, such as castings, plates, or machine parts, to indicate location, dimensions, and tolerances necessary for further processing, such as machining, welding, or assembly, analyzing specifications and computing dimensions according to knowledge of the product, subsequent processing, shop mathematics, and layout procedures; studies blueprint, sketch, model, or other specifications and plans layout. Examines workpiece and verifies such requirements as dimensions and squareness, using rule, square, and straightedge. Lifts and positions workpiece in relation to surface plate manually or with hoist, using such work aids as shims, parallel blocks, and angle plates. Verifies position with measuring instruments, such as gauge blocks, height gauges, and dial indicators. Determines reference points and computes layout dimensions. Sets indicators on height gauge, protractor, or layout machine to computed dimensions, or projects dimensions by setting indicators to specified locations on model and moving instrument or machine so that indicators bear on corresponding locations on workpiece. Indents layout points, using prick punch, center punch, and hammer. Marks or scribes layout lines, using handtools and work aids, such as surface gauge, straightedge, compasses, templates, and scriber. Marks such data as dimensions, instructions, and part identification on workpiece. Works to tolerances as close as +0.001 inch. May position model in parallel relationship to workpiece. May apply pigment to layout surfaces using paint brush. May inspect machined parts to verify conformance to specifications. May add dimensional details to blueprints or prepare dimensional drawings to be followed by other workers. May layout sheet metal or plate steel, applying specialized knowledge of sheet metal layout geometry [Sheet-Metal Layout Worker (any industry)].

Supervisor, Electrical Assemblies

Industry: electrical equipment; machinery manufacturing

Supervises and coordinates activities of workers engaged in fabrication of subassemblies and assembly of electrical equipment, such as electric welding machines, conveyors, and other electrically powered machine tools. Confers with engineering and management staff to establish assembly procedures and production schedules. Interprets and modifies blueprints and wiring diagrams in accordance with assembly specifications. Inspects and tests assembled components and equipment, using oscilloscopes, voltmeters, ammeters, and other test instruments. Suggests design modifications to increase product efficiency and production output. Trains new workers and resolves personnel problems. Performs other duties as described under Supervisor (any industry) Master Title.

Logistics Engineer

Directs and coordinates program activities designed to provide subcontractors, management, and customers with logistics technology that ensures effective and economical support concerned for manufacturing or servicing of products, systems, or equipment. Analyzes contractual commitments, customer specifications, design changes, and other data to plan and develop logistic program activities from the conceptual stage through the lifecycle of the product. Develops and implements program activities, coordinates efforts of subcontractors, production departments, and field service personnel, and resolves problems in area of logistics to ensure meeting of contractual commitments. Develops and initiates preparation of handbooks, bulletins, and information systems to provide and supply logistics support. Compiles data on standardization and interchangeability of parts to expedite logistics activities. Determines logistic support sequences and time phasing, problems arising from location of operational area, and other factors, such as environmental and human factors affecting personnel. May perform special research or technical studies critical to logistic support functions. May utilize computer techniques for analysis, simulation or information systems, and documentation.

INTERNET RESOURCES

e-Procurement Tools

Perfect Commerce: www.perfect.com/home/index.html
Ariba: www.ariba.com
Emptoris: www.emptoris.com
Ketera: www.ketera.com
SciQuest: www.sciquest.com

Decision Analysis Services

Decision Analysis:	http://www.decisionanalysis.net/
AMPL:	http://www.ampl.com/TRYAMPL/
Kestrel:	http://www-neos.mcs.anl.gov/neos/kestrel.html
Best Possible Solutions:	http://www.bestpossible.com/LPServices.asp

Job Shops (precision parts contract manufacturing)

Jobshop.com:	http://www.jobshop.com/
GlobalSpec:	http://manufacturing-fabrication.globalspec.com/ ProductFinder/Manufacturing_Fabrication_Services
PFI Precision:	http://www.pfiprecision.com/ ?gclid=CPL_uc7fvoMCFTbdIgoddg77kQ

SUMMARY

The supply chain encompasses everything from purchasing raw materials, turning them into a product or service, and distributing the finished product to customers and/or the end user. In the past all these activities were separate and didn't communicate with each other. But today, with increasingly more demanding and global customers, the pressure to outsource activities at which a company is not "best in class," and tougher competition, it makes more sense for companies to integrate the entire process of turning a raw material into a saleable product or service.

In this chapter, we looked at the four main activities in the supply chain: purchasing, operations, logistics, and distribution. Purchasing as a function has increased in importance as companies seek to leverage their purchasing power and gain better pricing through economies of scale. The purchasing function also participates in selecting qualified vendors as partners in the supply chain. Operations is the function that makes the products and/or delivers the services that a company sells. Many companies now use lean manufacturing techniques and total quality processes to offer customized products at lower cost and higher quality than was the case as little as 25 years ago. Similarly, with the advent of lower cost and more powerful technologies, the logistics and distribution functions have become much more sophisticated and competitive. All of these factors benefit companies (through higher profits) and consumers (through higher quality, lower prices, and more customized products and services).

11

Research and Development

Invention is the process by which a new idea is discovered or created. In contrast, innovation occurs when a new idea is adopted.
> —Everett Rogers, author of *Diffusions of Innovations*

Our company has, indeed, stumbled onto some of its new products. But never forget that you can only stumble if you're moving.
> —Richard P. Carlton, former CEO of 3M

Ideas are a commodity. Execution of them is not.
> —Michael Dell, CEO of Dell Computer

WHAT IS RESEARCH & DEVELOPMENT?

Research and Development (R&D) is the process of discovering new ideas and technologies that can be turned into new products, services, processes, and business models. R&D is where science meets business, and where opportunity meets action.

R&D, also called "innovation," can take many forms depending on the kind of company you're discussing. The traditional R&D is a research lab in a big company that mixes chemicals or tinkers with bits of parts and electronics to come up with a really cool new product based on an entirely new technology. Some examples include General Electric's plastics labs, the former Bell Labs (now part of Lucent), most of the big pharmaceutical companies (Merck, Pfizer, Schering-Plough, Roche, Bayer, Novartis and others), and Hewlett-Packard's former instruments division, now called Agilent. All of these companies, at one point or another, invented something incredible that led to stunning growth in sales.

R&D can also take the form of new services (iTunes), new designs (IDEO created the Palm V and Leap chair), new ways to use an existing product

(Google, Procter & Gamble's Swiffer), new packaging materials (Procter & Gamble), new business models (eBay), new processes (Toyota), and creating entirely new and different markets by turning common assumptions upside down (Target—combined high style and design with discount retailing).

Most research activities take place in large corporations, universities, and state agencies. R&D is often perceived as hard to manage and very expensive because of the need to fund "experiments" and the search for as yet undiscovered technologies. There are two types of research: basic and applied. Basic research is pure science and the pursuit of knowledge. It takes a long time (years and decades) and a lot of money to fund basic research into things like string theory, nanotechnology, stem cell research, and the genome. Governments and universities are the main enablers of basic research.

Applied research is scientific inquiry (systematic and logical) to solve a problem or answer a question. Applied research delves into things like radar evading materials, lightweight and high strength metals, oil-eating bacteria, mathematical scheduling algorithms, cures for high cholesterol, pesticide-resistant corn, optical networking, and others. Applied research happens in a number of places and is funded by corporations, governments, and universities. Some of the premier research institutions are either wholly owned by corporations (Xerox's PARC, Lucent's Bell Labs, NTT's Basic Research Laboratories), government entities (DARPA, Los Alamos National Laboratory, Sandia National Laboratory), government-university partnerships (Lawrence Berkeley National Laboratory, Ames Laboratory, Johns Hopkins University Applied Physics Laboratory), government-corporate partnerships (RAND National Security Research Division), and corporate-university partnerships (Stanford Center for Magnetic Nanotechnology, Center for Effective Organizations at the University of Southern California).

The "development" part of R&D is when a company takes the knowledge gained from research and turns it into something that it can sell. It might be a new technology (putting a transistor on an ever-smaller silicon chip), a process (unloading, cleaning, and reloading a plane in 10 minutes or less), or a new business model (selling songs over the Internet). This is where marketing and sales meet science.

WHY IS RESEARCH & DEVELOPMENT IMPORTANT?

Research and Development (R&D) is vital to helping a company achieve significant growth in revenues. Almost every successful company has some component of increasing sales in its corporate strategy. But there are only a handful of ways in which a company can actually achieve higher revenues: expand the current market (sell to more people in more places), diversify (buy another company—either a competitor or someone that makes a complementary product) or create new products, services, and business models to open up entire new markets.

Companies that invest wisely in R&D and manage its propagation tend to perform better than those that don't. The Boston Consulting Group found that companies considered by their peers to be highly innovative generated higher shareholder returns than those that weren't innovative.[1] Among the companies considered to be the most innovative, the median return to shareholders was 14.3 percent per year over a 10-year period. That's significantly higher than

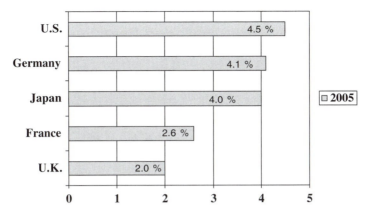

Figure 11.1. R&D as a percentage of sales in major industrialized countries.

the median 11.1 percent annual return of the S&P 1200 global stocks. And even more important, the innovative companies' median growth margin was 3.4 percent versus a measly 0.4 percent for the S&P global stocks. So R&D is important because it pays off in the long run.

R&D as a Percent of Total Sales (R&D Intensity)

Most companies in the United States spend about 3.5 percent of revenues on R&D.[2] In fact, U.S. companies lead the world in R&D intensity, which is R&D spending as a percentage of the sales. (See Figure 11.1)

Some industries are more R&D intensive than others. The pharmaceutical industry spends about 15 percent of sales on R&D, while the utility industry spends only 0.2 percent of sales on R&D. The top five R&D intensive industries are shown in Figure 11.2.

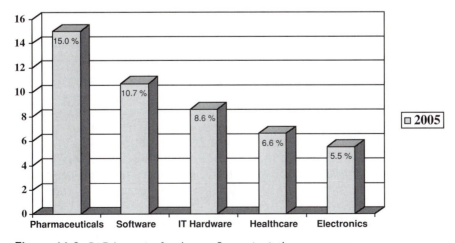

Figure 11.2. R&D Intensity for the top five major industry sectors.

R&D THROUGH THE GENERATIONS

Although corporate R&D labs existed before World War II, research and development with a specific purpose, began in earnest in the 1930s and 1940s as the U.S. government sought to gain military superiority. The list of successful inventions during and just after wartime is long: the atomic bomb, nuclear power, RADAR, the semiconductor, biological weapons agents, and supersonic air travel to name a few. During the years that followed, the nature of R&D changed. Here we'll look at how R&D management has adapted and become more professional in response to outside forces.

First Generation R&D

The purposeful management of science and technology began with a minimal management touch. This first generation R&D lasted until the 1970s. Both managers and scientists believed that science and scientists could not and should not be managed by outsiders. Management would only quash the scientists' creativity. So, about the only thing that managers could do was to select good people and decide how much to spend on science and technology. Scientists got to choose pretty much whatever they worked on. This minimalist approach worked fairly well. It was an opportunity-rich environment at that time. And the perception if not the reality was that science and scientists had played a key role in winning World War II and so why not leave them to work their magic during peacetime in corporate R&D labs?

During this period, public oversight of how managers spent corporate money wasn't as focused as it is today. (Only the incredibly rich bought stocks anyway, so the average Joe on the street didn't really care how well corporations were managing their assets.) Back then corporations could afford to dump piles of money into long-range R&D projects. But these long-range efforts were very uncertain and breakthroughs were very unpredictable. Therefore the belief was to develop the technology first then create the strategy to capitalize on it. It was a bottom-up process of development. The labs were quite separate from the users. The labs were organized around the various disciplines associated with the technologies, and measuring performance was not very explicit. Performance reviews focused on the technologies and developments that happened since the last review.

This time period was and still is viewed as the golden age of research. Money was available and there were few constraints on the scientists. But by the end of the 1960s and 70s the circumstances had changed.

Second Generation R&D

The second generation management of R&D began to link technology with the needs of the users. Imagine that! Doing research on something that people would actually want and need! Now R&D would be managed on a project-by-project basis. In the late 1960s time constraints became important and the resources became scarce.

Two factors led to the active management of R&D: The first was a commitment to put a man on the moon by 1970. Project managers inside and outside of government all began scheduling R&D work to meet this deadline. The scientists and engineers who had argued that you cannot schedule breakthroughs had to acquiesce and reluctantly fell into line. The days of bottom-up management had begun to decline.

The second factor was the relative scarcity of science and engineering talent. Airplane manufacturers, Boeing and McDonnell Douglas, struggled to attract people and supplies to meet the exploding demand for commercial jet aircraft. Aerospace companies competed for these same resources in order to support the space program. Defense firms also competed for scientists in order to support the expansion of the war in Vietnam. Managerially oriented leaders like Robert McNamara and James Webb moved into the top positions at the Department of Defense and NASA. They changed from cost plus contracting to fixed price, incentive contracts. Schedules and budgets became as important as technical performance. The scarcest resource of all became business-oriented project managers with technical backgrounds. It was during this period that a lot of project management tools like critical path scheduling were developed.

The project managers also discovered that in order to speed up development, they needed to have both the view of the technical disciplines and the focus of the specific project. So they created the project-function matrix organization, which is still used today as the model for organizing R&D. Second generation R&D spawned the discipline of project management. Professional societies like the Project Management Institute have grown and prospered.

In summary, the second generation R&D management attempted to link science and technology to the users on a project-by-project basis. It focused on project management and its place in matrix organizations. The second generation set the stage for the third generation.

Third Generation R&D

The resource constraints that began in the 1960s and 1970s continued in the 1980s. Companies faced increasing global competition. Governments faced budget deficits and aging populations. Leaders in both domains felt that they needed to be more careful with their funds and more selective in the programs that they supported. In addition, society began to question whether more scientific knowledge and technology development is always good. Increased pollution and the use of genetically modified organisms generated opposition and doubts. So in both the public and private sectors, leaders began to suggest that science is too important to be left to the scientists.

In third generation R&D, managers have more say in what the scientists work on and where they will take that research. This meant that management established more of a partnership with their R&D community. R&D began to be less isolated and more integrated into the corporate and business unit strategies. Management became much more active in funding and choosing projects. The funding was typically divided into short-, medium-, and long-term needs. The businesses were always active in funding and choosing the short-term (one year) product and process improvements. But now the businesses were also funding the medium term projects (1–3 years). R&D was becoming more accountable for results in the medium term. Managers evaluated R&D efforts against some of the same measures that they used for other investment decisions, like costs, benefits, risks, rewards, return on investment, how it supports the corporate strategy and so on. In addition, the new R&D projects were more closely linked to the business. Goals like reducing time-to-market became a priority. Long-term R&D projects (if they existed) were tied closely to corporate objectives and were less likely to be basic or speculative research. Now the scientists had bosses, targets and goals, and had to perform to standards like everyone else in the company.

Fourth Generation R&D

If scientists decided that they didn't like all this corporate bureaucracy stifling their creativity, they would leave. Thus began the age of R&D that took hold *outside* of the big corporate R&D labs. This era is called "fourth generation R&D" and some people also refer to it as "open innovation."

Four factors led to the decline of "closed innovation" in corporations. First, smart people became more mobile and didn't hesitate to move on to greener pastures. In addition, smart people were popping up all over the world: in India, China, Russia, and Europe. American corporations no longer held the best and the brightest paid serfs in their closed and proprietary labs. Second, customers became more demanding and wanted products with the latest technology available in stores yesterday. Time-to-market for new innovations became crucial, and a company just doesn't always have all of the requisite technology on the shelf and in-house. Third, in the early 1990s venture capitalists were making gazillionaires out of people who had brilliant ideas that could be turned into a cool new product. And fourth, when scientists left a corporate R&D lab (often for another corporate R&D lab or a Silicon Valley start-up) they usually took their brains and all the hard earned knowledge with them. This became a big problem for corporations (unless, of course, they were the ones doing the stealing).

What's a company to do? The big companies got smart fast. They decided that they would look outside their own labs to find out who was doing what and where. This often meant partnering with universities and small companies where your average rocket scientist was designing the next big thing. Procter & Gamble, one of the most secretive companies in terms of guarding its technology, developed an R&D program that they call "Connect and Develop." In connect and develop (C&D) a P&G scientist would put forth a request to a global network of people who tinkered either as hobbyists or were employed by a university or other research lab. For example, P&G wanted to print pictures and words onto each of its Pringles potato crisps, but it hadn't yet figured out the mechanics of how to do this (one team member even tried using the ink jet printer in her office). Rather than do all the research in-house, P&G sent out an inquiry to its network of innovators. The inquiry, what they call a technology brief, specified exactly what they were looking for. In the end, they found an Italian professor who ran a bakery on the side. He had invented a way to print edible pictures on cakes and cookies. P&G bought the professor's custom-manufactured baking equipment to produce the new line of printed Pringles. The whole process—from idea to production—took less than a year. Today P&G's goal is that half of all its new products emerge from outside the company's labs.

Companies have radically changed how they do R&D. In the past, big companies (25,000 or more employees) accounted for over 70 percent of all the industrial R&D, but today they generate only 40 percent.[3]

THE TREASURE HUNT

So how does a manager get people to produce good R&D? Does she lock a bunch of smart people into a room, throw money at them and tell them to "go be creative?" To some degree, that was the traditional way of getting R&D to happen, and it's how Lockheed developed things like its U2 spy plane and the Stealth Bomber in the 1960s and 1970s.

As we saw above, the whole approach to R&D has changed over the years. Nowadays managers have to point their innovative people to look outside the company for ideas. And they have to be able to control the technology they adopt either through joint ventures, partnerships or licensing agreements. The managers also have to figure out how to cut their losses on technologies that either don't work for the company or can't be adapted for products within the timeframe and/or cost constraints they require.

This section will outline some of the ways that managers are actively pushing and managing innovation.

Different Innovation Models

There are three main methods to innovate. One is to develop a new product based on new technology. Apple did this with its iPod. It figured out how to turn a hard disk into a personal juke box that allows the user to easily load, mix, and play whatever songs he wants. Similarly, Research in Motion, maker of the ubiquitous "BlackBerry," created a reliable wireless e-mail device that masquerades as a phone.

A second way to innovate is to introduce a new way of doing business or a new "business model." Apple did this again when it introduced its iTunes music store. Now you can buy a song rather than having to purchase an entire album, and you can own the song in seconds after downloading it to your computer. Virgin Group has created a brand based on a hip lifestyle, which the company applies to airlines, insurance, and banking. Dell turned the existing PC makers on their heads when it sold PCs directly to consumers through the Internet and telephone.

The third way to innovate is to develop new processes—a new way of doing something that's absolutely critical to fulfilling the company's strategy. Toyota revolutionized the manufacturing industry with its lean "Toyota Production System." Southwest consistently outsmarts its competitors by figuring out new

The World's Most Innovative Companies

Business Week and the Boston Consulting Group asked 1500 executives worldwide to rank the most innovative company outside their own industry. Here are the winners:

1. Apple
2. Google
3. 3M
4. Toyota
5. Microsoft
6. General Electric
7. Procter & Gamble
8. Nokia
9. Starbucks
10. IBM
11. Virgin
12. Samsung
13. Sony
14. Dell
15. IDEO
16. BMW
17. Intel
18. eBay
19. IKEA
20. Wal-Mart
21. Amazon
22. Target
23. Honda
24. Research In Motion
25. Southwest Airlines

Source: Business Week, April 24, 2006

ways to improve its operations—it was the first in the airline industry to turn planes around after only 10 minutes at the gate.

The Greenhouse Effect: Nurturing Good Ideas

In all of these cases, you have to start with a good idea and then figure out how to turn it into reality. Many companies have people who's job is to troll the networks of creative people, both inside and outside the firm, and stir the pot. These individuals, like John Gage at Sun Microsystems, keep their eyes on who's doing what, who they're talking to, and who they need to talk to. John Gage attends academic and industry conferences, wanders the halls of advanced computing universities and gets to know the key researchers, keeps up on the latest technologies like supercomputing and massively parallel computing, and visits all of Sun's internal R&D centers in Russia, Israel, the United Kingdom, Japan, India, China, Boston, and Silicon Valley to learn what they are up to. He's a one-man network hub. He brings together people who need to be working together.

Skunk Works

Another way of bringing people together is to physically locate them in a separate building, away from the rest of the organization. This is what Lockheed did with a small group of its top engineers and scientists in order to design, develop, and build the P-38 Lightning fighter jet, the U2 spy plane, the SR-71 Blackbird, and the F-117A Stealth fighter jet. In 1943 Kelly Johnson, a 33-year old engineer for Lockheed, created The "Skunk Works" under a rented circus tent next door to an odorous plastics factory in Burbank, California. The Skunk Works got its name from a cartoon strip that was popular at the time.

"Around the time Kelly's crew raised their circus tent, cartoonist Al Capp introduced Injun Joe and his backwoods still into his "L'il Abner" comic strip. Ol' Joe tossed worn shoes and dead skunk into his smoldering vat to make "kickapoo joy juice." Capp named the outdoor still 'the skonk works.' The connection was apparent to those inside Kelly's circus tent forced to suffer the plastic factory's stink. One day, one of the engineers showed up for work wearing a civil defense gas mask as a gag, and a designer named Irv Culver picked up a ringing phone and announced, 'Skonk Works.'[4] (Capp's publisher objected to the use of 'skonk works' so the group renamed it 'skunk works' and even trademarked the name.)

The main reason for creating a 'skunk works' or greenhouse incubator environment is to liberate a group of inventors from the constraints of the larger organization and let them do things differently. This is usually important when speed, creativity, and secrecy are in order. Secondly, by walling off the R&D group and giving them a fixed budget, the company can keep the costs and the financial risks low. A third reason is to prevent the managers from coming around and pulling up the new seedlings to see if they've grown any roots yet. Ideas take time to develop and creative types need to do so in an environment where failure is an option and it isn't a stigma to future career growth.

There are, however, some problems with creating a separate incubator to pursue new innovations. The main issue is that the outside group becomes so isolated from the main company that it no longer has any relevance to the company and can't leverage any of the parent company's technologies, processes, or other core attributes. The second issue is that without some guidance from the main company, the incubator develops products and technologies that are so vastly different from the core company that they are effectively useless. The incubator needs, therefore, to be distinct from the main company but not isolated.

Greatest Idea and Best Failure Awards

The old axiom is that you learn by making mistakes. At 3M the "No Guts, No Glory" award publicizes the most spectacular failures. The award goes to the engineer that made the best mistake – meaning the one that the other engineers learned the most from. It gets all the other engineers to talk about how truly exemplary the award winner's failure was. So in that respect, the engineer didn't fail at all. She succeeded in educating not only herself, but also her peers.

On the flip side, each year 3M awards "Genesis Grants" to 12–20 scientists who want to work on projects that are outside the scope of 3M's business. The grants range in value from $50,000–$100,000 each and the recipient can use it to buy equipment or hire staff. Nokia has a "Club 10" that honors researchers with ten or more patents to their name.

But how do you measure great ideas? What constitutes a success? *Business Week*'s survey of best innovators found that somewhere between 8 and 12 metrics, that are easy to understand and easy to measure, are what a company needs to focus on. Some examples are ratio of products that succeed, return on investment in new projects, percent of new products in the total portfolio, and time-to-market.

Customer Insights or Lead Customer R&D

Other than closing people up in an idea incubation room, how else does a company find new ideas for new products? How about asking a customer!

Lead customers are those who push the limits of what a product was designed to do. They often take matters into their own hands and jury-rig the product to satisfy a particular need they have. An example is Bose Corporation's small high fidelity speakers that were designed for home listening use. A Bose product development manager noticed that a Boston-area CD retailer (Strawberries) had suspended Bose speakers from the ceiling of the store so that they provided background music. The speakers hung precariously on flimsy metal straps. The retailer obviously wanted high quality sound for a large area, and at the time no ceiling-mounted speakers were available. Bose took this "lead" customer's hint and developed an entirely new market for commercial background music.[5]

Some companies actually go into peoples' homes and watch what they do with their products. This is how Intuit came up with its blockbuster software, Quickbooks. The company had originally designed Quicken to help the home user balance his or her checkbook and manage the budget. But then the company noticed that people who had small businesses were running their accounting operations using Quicken. As the Intuit marketing people looked on, the customer would apologetically say, "I'm sure that there's an easier way to do this ..." The customer's quest to find an easier way to manage a company's books spawned the creation of Quickbooks.

Companies can also learn to innovate by watching other companies. Mars (the maker of M&Ms) saw what Dell did for made-to-order computers and now offers customized M&M candies on their Web site (www.mms.com). You can order M&Ms with your own personalized messages in a range of 21 colors.

IF WE BUILD IT, WILL THEY BUY IT?

Most of this chapter has dealt with the "R" part of R&D. Once a company has a great idea, how does it turn that idea into a product or service that it can sell? Here we'll look at the "D" part of R&D and how products get developed.

The Design and Development Process

Originally product development was a process dominated by the scientists and engineers. Product specifications were agreed upon by management, marketing, and R&D, and then the scientists and engineers began designing and testing. The process was a sequential one. First, R&D designed the product, then manufacturing designed the process, and finally marketing and sales put together the launch plan. The process took place over many years, and changes to the original specifications were to be avoided.

Today just about everything in the development process has changed. The primary driver has been the desire to reduce the time to market. Indeed, reduced product development cycles have been both a cause and an effect of faster paced technology changes. Companies cannot take the risk of freezing a design and then taking years to develop it. In addition to reducing risk, shorter development cycles also reduce the cost of development. Managers understand that time is money. So there has been an all-out assault on the time to develop a new product or process platform.

One result has been to convert a sequential process measured in years to a simultaneous process measured in months. This means that the manufacturing engineers and product-marketing specialists join the scientists and engineers in the codevelopment of the product platform. The product development teams became larger, more interdisciplinary, and more interdependent. This increase in complexity required strong project managers and more complicated matrix organizations. The teams were measured not just on product technical performance but also on reducing time from project start to producing the product defect free at the desired volume.

Many products today are designed from the start to be "manufacturable" (easy to build at the lowest possible cost), recyclable, serviceable (easy to service), and have a low lifetime ownership cost. One way to achieve this is to use a platform and add modules on top to adapt to various country or market requirements. Hewlett-Packard, for example, makes the same printer for every market worldwide. Depending on the country and power source, a kanji software module or a 220-volt power adaptor is packaged into the box. All of these development initiatives mean that more people must be involved from the start of the product development process. It's a challenge for management, but it yields a far better product in the end.

Evaluating Product Development

How does a company know whether the great big idea it has will turn into a blockbuster product or a flop? One way is to build a couple of prototypes and go

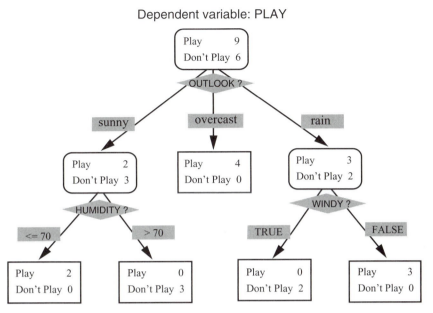

Dependent variable: PLAY

Figure 11.3. Decision tree for a golf club manager
Source: http://en.wikipedia.org/wiki/Decision_tree (downloaded on May 7, 2006).

test them with real customers. But if the company is Boeing and its product idea is for a new $150 million airplane, it's a little tough to go and build a sample plane. So the company uses a number of complex mathematical algorithms to evaluate the risk, and lots of marketing, finance, and supply chain brainpower to go with it.

Decision Trees

A decision tree is a logic-driven method for describing and testing the attributes of a particular problem. At each test junction (called a "node"), the answer to the particular question asked routes the analysis to another decision point. The end of a decision tree should point the analysis to a set of answers. Decision trees can get quite complex but when used correctly (in the hands of a trained professional) they can help people get their minds around a big hairy problem.

For example, a golf club manager is trying to get a sense of how many people come to play golf on any given day, so that he can staff the operations appropriately. After recording the weather variables (forecast, sun, rain, wind, humidity) he constructs the decision tree shown in Figure 11.3. The top box represents all of the decisions (how many people played or didn't play golf on a particular day in question). For three possible weather forecasts, sunny, cloudy or rainy, people would decide to play or not. If the weather forecast was for clouds, then all people played golf. But if the weather was sunny, a further variable came into question: humidity. More people refused to play golf if the humidity was more than 70 percent on a sunny day. In the case of rain, there were plenty of die-hard golfers who would play, but fewer of them wanted to go to the course if it was going to be a windy day. In this manner, the golf club manager was able to predict how many golfers would come to the course depending on the weather forecast.

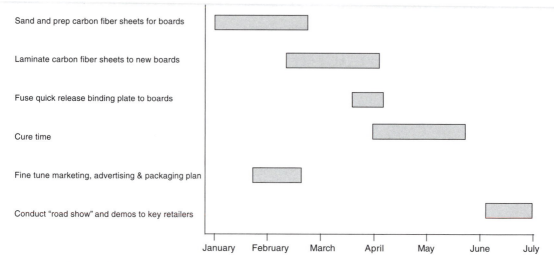

Figure 11.4. Gantt Chart for Joey's New Carbon Fiber Snowboard Project.

PERT and Gantt Charts

PERT and Gantt charts are tools used to track a project against time. Each project is broken down into its component parts, some of which can take place simultaneously and others have to wait until a subprocess is completed first. It's a very useful way to show visually how particular subtasks are dependent on each other and flow over time. Thus a manager can look at the chart and see whether a project is on schedule or falling behind. A sample Gantt chart is shown in Figure 11.4.

Gantt charts are useful for relatively simple projects, but when the project is hugely complex, such as a $100 million refinery construction project, the charts can have thousands of lines and run for hundreds of pages. For a better way to present project timelines see Edward Tufte's Web site (www.edwardtufte.com) or his famous books, *Envisioning Information* and *The Visual Display of Quantitative Information*.

A PERT network chart is similar to a Gantt chart but it shows project steps on a relative time scale as they are networked together (that is, they're not plotted against specific dates). It's a complex statistical technique to analyze the minimum amount of time necessary to complete the overall project. PERT stands for Program Evaluation and Review Technique and was invented by the U.S. Navy's Special Projects Office in 1958 during the development of the Polaris submarine.

Phased Process Evaluations

Most product development processes have some sort of evaluation built in at specific points in time. There are a number of names for these evaluations: "stage-gate process," targeting, critical path milestones, and so on. At each review point or "gate" the project is evaluated against a set of criteria that was agreed upon in advance. The project can only continue if all parties agree that it is ready to move to the next stage. Visually, the stage-wise evaluation looks like the one shown in Figure 11.5.

Most people agree that periodic reviews of product development projects are important. But critics of the "stage-gate" process say that the criteria that

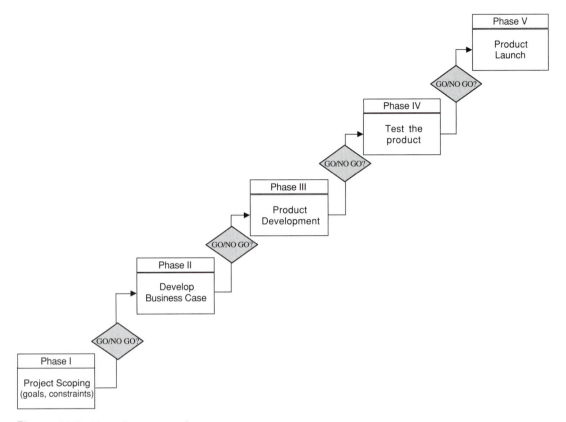

Figure 11.5. Phased project evaluation process.

are set in the beginning might not apply to a project once it's underway. In that case, a promising project can get derailed by a somewhat arbitrary "yes" or "no."

Metrics

Many companies use financial and other metrics to evaluate whether a development project is proceeding on time, on budget, and according to plan. Some of these metrics are listed in Table 11.1.

The point of using metrics to determine development potential is to give the process a logic-driven and systematic way to evaluate every product on the same important scale.

A DAY IN THE LIFE OF AN R&D MANAGER

Robert Niichel
Scientist and R&D Project Leader
Upsher-Smith Laboratories, Inc.

I grew up on a farm in Iowa. Our town had a railroad crossing, a grain elevator, and 2,000 people living in it. I went to the local Catholic high school and then attended Iowa State University, where I graduated with a bachelor's degree in finance and economics. I've always been intrigued by science, but my family really encouraged me to go into business. I did a bunch of job interviews

Table 11.1. Product development metrics

Metric	What it means
Time-to-market	Usually measured in days or months (shorter is usually better)
ROI	Return on investment
Product profitability (this generally can't be calculated until the product is on the market)	Cost to make product (not including development costs)÷revenues
Cost-to-market	A cumulative sum of total outlays before the first product is sold
NPV	Net present value of cash flows (including development budget and likely revenues)
Cost–Benefit analysis	What will this cost us (time, staff resources, lost opportunities, etc.) compared to the likely benefit (financial, brand name, presence in the market, etc.)?
Market risk	Do we understand this market? Do we currently sell into this market? Do we possess (or control) all of the value chain elements?
Technology risk	Can we produce this product? Do we really understand the technology involved?
User risk	What are the chances that this fabulous product is one that no one wants? (That is, did the engineers design this for their own amusement without taking into account the end user's desires?)

at the end of college and one of them took me to Pontiac, Michigan. I decided that I'd rather not live in Michigan.

In the mid- to late-1980s Colorado had a booming economy. My college roommate was living in Colorado and he told me to come for a visit. I did and quickly got a job with an investment bank doing research on other companies. The bank was looking to do IPOs (initial public offerings) for the various companies to help them raise capital. We worked with a lot of biotechnology and high-technology companies in the Denver area. I really liked working for the investment bank and was there for about six-and-a-half years. But then the company merged with another company and the atmosphere deteriorated. So I took the opportunity to go back to graduate school. I went to the University of Colorado and got a masters degree in biochemistry. You wouldn't necessarily expect it, but finance and chemistry are both driven by the same thought processes. Both use logic, mathematics, and analytical reasoning.

About a year before I graduated I got a job with Upsher-Smith. That was ten-and-a-half years ago! At that time the firm, then known as Rosemount Pharmaceuticals, was a subsidiary of a Dutch company called Akzo Nobel. But Upsher-Smith, a privately held corporation based in Minneapolis, bought Rosemount from Akzo Nobel in 2001.

Upsher-Smith is a relatively small company. We have about 125 employees here in Denver and 400 or so in Minneapolis. We make generic prescription drugs and sometimes we brand them as well. Those are called "branded generics." In the generics business, the goal is to produce a copy of a patented drug, like Vioxx(tm), Levitra(tm), or others, and have the generic version available for sale as soon as the patented drug's patent expires. We compete with a lot of very big generic pharmaceutical companies, like Teva (Israel), Barr (United States), and Ranbaxy (India). We also make what's known as "proprietary drugs" which are either brand new drugs or drugs that have a different delivery system. An example is an osteoporosis pill that we figured out how to put into a nasal spray. Our corporate strategy is to focus more on the proprietary market, so we're aiming to submit two new drug applications per year. To do this we either develop the new drugs and/or delivery systems in-house, or we partner with another small company that has a proprietary technology. Sometimes these are small start-ups or a professor at a university who has discovered a new molecule or technology that has promise as a new type of treatment.

When I joined Upsher-Smith, I started out in the laboratory doing routine testing, quality control, and some basic research. As I gained experience I took on bigger jobs. Now I'm part of the R&D group, which is about 40 people in total. R&D is comprised of the formulation group (10 people) and the laboratory (20 people). The laboratory people work on the methods to manufacture new products, do the testing and analysis, and they operate many of our sophisticated instruments. The formulation people figure out what exactly goes into the pill. That includes the active ingredient, the sugars, binders, dissolvents, and so on. Formulation is also responsible for making the early prototypes of the drug. My role is to represent both the lab and formulation on new product teams, help them move along to meet the project timeline, and to produce the required paperwork so we can file an application with the U.S. Food and Drug Administration (FDA).

Generally we start working on a new generic product about 2 years before a drug goes "off patent" (meaning the date that its patent is scheduled to expire). The process starts with our strategic planning folks in Minneapolis who decide which drug they want to target as a generic. Then they tell us in R&D to go make it! Well, it's not quite that simple. We form a new product development team, which has members from the laboratory, the formulation group, marketing, finance, regulatory support (the people who talk to the FDA), and production (the factory). I represent the lab and the formulation groups on these teams.

The first thing we do is seek out three to four active product ingredient (API) suppliers. The active ingredient is crucially important (it's what makes the drug do its job). Very few API vendors are U.S.-based. Most of them operate in South Africa, France, Italy, Spain, and India. That's because making the API can be toxic and dangerous. You often have toxic wastes and work under highly sensitive conditions where plants occasionally explode. So after we identify a suitable active ingredient we go and buy some of it. The API is usually really expensive. For one drug we're currently working on, the API costs $130,000 per kilogram (2.2 pounds)—that's almost $4,000 per ounce!

After we get the API we start trying to make the tablets or capsules. I work with the formulation group to figure out what mix of sugars, dissolvents, API, and other ingredients go into the pill and how we'll make it. When we have a pill, we test it in the laboratory. This can be a pretty involved process. We do "assays" which are tests to make sure that each pill has the 10 milligrams (or whatever dose) it's supposed to have in order to be effective. Sometimes you lose part of the active ingredient in the manufacturing process. So we have to figure out why and devise a better method of making the pills. Humidity in the air and any number of other factors can cause you to lose API. We also do a dissolution test. For this test we fill six flasks with a solution that mimics the environment found in the human gastrointestinal tract. We stick a pill in each flask and measure at specific time intervals (10, 20, 30, and 60 minutes) to see how much of the pill has dissolved. You generally want a tablet to fully dissolve in 60 minutes. Ten minutes might be too soon. If we don't get the right dissolution period then we go back and tweak the formula.

After we think we have the right formula and method, which is basically a recipe detailing exactly how to make the pill, we take it into the laboratory and make bigger batches and test those. We test all along the process to make sure that our recipe is bulletproof and can be repeated by anyone who follows the procedure.

At the moment we've got five projects under development. As the project leader representing the laboratory, I go to all the project meetings and later instruct people in the laboratory and formulation groups what to do based on our project team discussions. I make sure that we're operating under "Good Manufacturing Practices" mandated by the FDA. It's a code of manufacturing practices that ensures we follow standard operating procedures. I also do Internet research (on things like active ingredients, new sugars, dissolvents, and other related issues). I write up reports on meetings, methods, tests, and formulations. I'm responsible for making sure that all the proper documentation is in order so that we can submit our product to the FDA for approval. I also work with the formulation people to help them figure out exactly which components we'll put into our tablet or capsule. That often involves me going into the lab and working on the equipment (doing initial research, formulation tests, and so forth). I also set up the project on Microsoft Project, which involves establishing the project timelines, contingency dates, and all the details required to track the project. Much of our test equipment is software driven, so I also get involved in doing the periodic software upgrades in the lab.

A lot of our work is organization and planning. For example, we have four controlled substances in the Denver lab and these are highly regulated by the Drug Enforcement Agency (DEA). They're locked up in an alarmed vault. In order to use them you have to submit to a background check and be authorized to work with these narcotics. You check them out in the morning and the product can't be left unattended for even a second. So it means that if we have an experiment that requires one of these regulated substances, we have to plan ahead and make sure that everything is ready at the precise moment that we need to use the substance. The DEA checks our procedures quarterly. It's serious business because if the DEA finds any faults with how we've handled these products, someone can end up in jail.

To do this job you need a specific combination of skills. First you have to have a degree in science, such as chemistry or biology. You can get a starting position with a bachelor's degree, but a master's or Ph.D. is more useful. Experience in a lab is also helpful. An entry-level position here would start in the laboratory doing quality control and basic testing. You also need a mindset that is detail-oriented and rule-driven. Here it's imperative that we document everything. We're in a regulated industry so you can't "finesse" things the way you could in, say, a sales job. We have to follow standard operating procedures—it's the law. We also need team players. Yes, we have some older scientists who don't really want to be part of a team. They're functional experts and they're certainly congenial, but they really just want to plow their head into their work and not be bothered with other issues.

I'm very involved in the hiring process. HR usually does the initial screen of an applicant. If they pass that, the candidate will talk to a couple of people at a time in three to four different groups in the company. Sometimes HR sends him or her to our Minneapolis operation to talk to some of the senior executives. If successful, the applicant will take a personality test. During the interviews with the candidate I usually ask a mix of technical and personality questions. I ask them what instruments and products they've worked on, or I'll give them a scenario and ask them to design a methodology to test something in the scenario. I try to determine how organized a person is by asking how they document reports, how they fill out their notebooks and I try to assess their ability to plan ahead. Toward the end of the interview I ask the candidate things about their ability to work on teams, and personal issues like hobbies or if they like to ski.

This is a really neat job and industry to be in. It's not geeky or nerdy or anything like that. I get to work with a lot of interesting people. It challenges your brain and forces you to be creative. I think it's a job that actually makes you more intelligent over time because you're using your brain all the time.

Working at a small company like Upsher-Smith is great. I get to wear a lot of different hats and my days are always different. I like the challenge here of the entrepreneurial spirit. We're all in this together and if we come up against a problem, we all roll up our sleeves and say, "Let's go figure it out." This company is also very flexible and focused on balance. I get a lot of work done in the short hours of a day, so I can work around my wife's busy work schedule. I have the flexibility to go and pick up our kids from day care if I need to. At the big R&D and biotechnology firms that's not always possible.

There really aren't many downsides to my job. I have to gently nudge people, especially scientists, to keep them on track and keep the project moving on schedule. In a scientific project it's sometimes tough to diplomatically encourage scientists to think in business terms. As a scientist and businessperson, I have to plan ahead, make commitments, and hit the milestones. I also have to get the scientists to stop analyzing and reworking a formula to get it perfect—a formula that's "good enough" will do the job and meet our deadline. One negative side of my job is the resource constraints we sometimes face. It can be difficult to convince the powers that be that we need a piece of new equipment or a special product. My perspective is that we need to invest a dollar today in order to reap $10 tomorrow.

The best part of working in this industry is that I get to work on products that will help people live a better life. That's incredibly rewarding. I get to work on some really cool stuff—not just the products, but the instruments and software too. It's exciting to think that by doing what I like to do, I can actually change the world a little bit for the better.

A typical day:

8:00 AM	I get to my office and check e-mails and phone messages.
8:15 AM	Telephone call to our regulatory affairs group. I have to follow-up on some of the remaining documents that are required for a new product filing with the FDA.
8:30 AM	I go to the laboratory to continue working on a solubility study of a new drug we're developing for schizophrenia.
9:30 AM	The MIS group is installing a new upgrade to our Empower^2 software program. They're having some problems with it, and asked me to help them work through the cause.

10:00 AM	Another quick check of e-mails. One of them is a note from our regulatory affairs group. The FDA has identified a deficiency in an anabolic steroid drug we're developing. We schedule a rush meeting for 1:00 PM tomorrow to discuss how we'll respond to the FDA and correct the deficiency. It shouldn't be too big of a problem to fix. We just need to run another dissolution test using the parameters that the FDA has specified.
10:20 AM	I do some quick research online to look for some appropriate buffers for our solubility study. I need something in the range of pH 4.5–7.0 with specific properties that will work within the parameters we've set. I prepare a list of additional buffer solutions that we'll need to procure for the remaining solubility tests we'll conduct. We'll use a variety of pHs and temperatures to see the effects on residual salts.
10:30 AM	Back to the laboratory to continue the solubility study on the schizophrenia drug.
11:00 AM	Begin training a new employee in the lab. We work on quality control procedures and residual solvent testing. I show her how to prepare the write-ups of the results.
12:00 noon	I grab a quick bite to eat and then head to a group member's office. We discuss the residual solvent analysis results, and plan tomorrow's test runs.
12:45 PM	I review the trainee's write-up of our quality control procedures from the morning, and forward the results onward.
1:00 PM	Weekly conference call and staff meeting. We discuss current projects, the status of assays, and provide updates on financial issues and other administrative details.
2:00 PM	Work with the validation manager from the IT department regarding our Empower^2 upgrade. We discuss performance qualification issues.
3:00 PM	Prepare my portion of tomorrow's meeting with the directors and vice presidents from our corporate office. I'll be giving an update on where we stand on the five projects I'm working on.
3:30 PM	Another check of e-mails and voice messages. I read the advance preparatory material for the Office of Generic Drugs Webcast, which will take place in two days. They're changing the format for how generic filings will be conducted starting next January. I jot down some questions I have.
4:00 PM	Meet with our engineering department. We discuss the lab expansion plans.
4:30 PM	Back to the lab. I start a final quality control run that will go overnight.
4:50 PM	I'm out of here. Got to go and pick up the kids at daycare.

INTERNET RESOURCES

MIT's OpenCourseWare: http://ocw.mit.edu/index.html

This is a free educational site for anyone who is interested. OpenCourse-Ware is a project jointly funded by the William & Flora Hewlett Foundation, MIT, and the Andrew Mellon Foundation. It offers hundreds of courses and thousands of articles available for download. While it doesn't have a specific

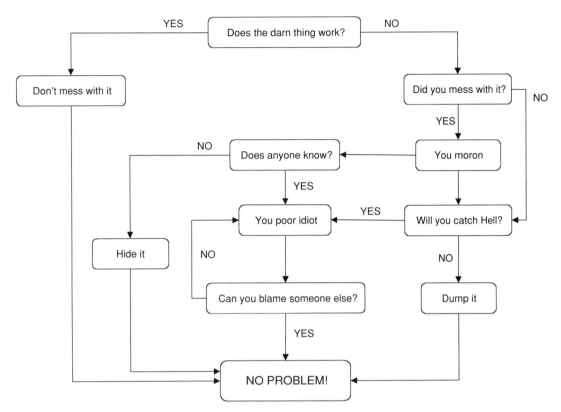

Figure 11.6. A problem-solving flowchart. Adapted from a flowchart that was circulating over the internet in 1995 and 1996.

area dedicated to R&D, it's a good place to find out about different fields that do research. It also offers links to other open courses in China, Japan, France, Vietnam, and the United States.

UK Department of Trade and Industry: http://www.innovation.gov.uk
This site offers a comprehensive view of R&D efforts of companies mostly in the United Kingdom, but also among industrialized countries.

R&D Magazine: www.rdmag.com
For the truly scientifically inclined, this site has free articles on all sorts of obscure technologies. This is also the sponsor and creator of the prestigious "R&D 100" awards.

Decision trees: http://www.aaai.org/aitopics/html/trees.html
This is an excellent Web site sponsored by the American Association for Artificial Intelligence that points people to other links about decision trees.

Edward Tufte: www.edwardtufte.com
Edward Tufte is a genius when it comes to presenting complex information in an easy to understand fashion. (The New York Times calls Tufte the "Leonardo da Vinci of data.") This is his Web site and it offers discussion forums, information on his books, and other fascinating tidbits.

Columbia University's former project management site: www.projectreference.com

This has an enormous amount of practical and free information on project management, how to get a job in project management, and innumerable other resources.

Project Management Institute: www.pmi.org
This is the largest membership organization for project managers. It offers a certification program, research into best practices, surveys, publications, courses, and many other resources for members.

SUMMARY

Research and development is one of the primary methods that companies have to increase revenues. Companies that invest intelligently in R&D tend to be more profitable than those that don't. R&D has changed significantly through the ages. Where before R&D was mostly done inside secretive corporate labs with almost limitless funding, today R&D is done in smaller start-ups and through network partnerships. Professional project managers actively manage R&D, often through a matrix-type of organizational structure.

New innovations can manifest themselves as new products, new processes, and new business models. Customers often provide much of the inspiration to marketers and researchers looking for new ideas.

As the push to reduce new product time-to-market cycle times intensifies, the new product development process has also changed. In the old days it was a linear process that took years. Today the development process has been significantly shortened as multifunctional teams of specialists cooperate to design new products from idea to manufacturability. R&D is a function that is resurgent today as more people from inside and outside of corporations work together to open up entirely new technologies and markets.

12

Other Staff Functions

What's the difference between a dead lawyer in the road and a dead snake in the road?
There are skid marks in front of the snake!

I have observed that newspaper publicity is usually followed by a jail sentence.
—Nick the Greek, gambling handicapper

I don't want to hire a lawyer to tell me what I cannot do; I hire him to tell me how to do what I want to do.
—J. Pierpont Morgan, found of the bank JP Morgan.

In addition to all the functions described in the other chapters, there are a number of "staff" jobs that have varying importance depending on the type of business a company is in. A large legal department is often necessary for a company that operates in a heavily regulated environment, such as a utility company (telephone, gas, electricity), a pharmaceutical company, or a cigarette company (with lots of lawsuits). Many of these same types of companies also need sizeable lobbying groups to work with government and state regulators and politicians in an effort to influence rulings and laws in their own interests. This chapter will describe some of the other staff functions that companies often employ in the course of doing business.

LEGAL

The legal department of a company is, not surprisingly, usually full of lawyers. These folks are known as "corporate lawyers" because they are "in-house" (i.e., they are employed by the company) and work exclusively on the company's business. The corporate lawyers are different from external attorneys, who usually work for an independent law firm that services many different clients. Many in-house attorneys used to work for independent law firms and for a variety of reasons, take jobs with corporate legal departments. Some of them prefer the (usually) more relaxed pace of work as a corporate attorney and other prefer to immerse themselves in a particular type of industry or company rather than taking on a variety of cases in independent firms.

What Does the Legal Department Do?

Contracts

A corporate legal department creates, reviews, and/or approves all legal documents and contracts that come into or go out of a business. If a company decides to open a new branch office in another country, for example, the legal department will be involved in the contractual arrangements to which the businesspeople commit. Similarly, if a company hires an independent management consultant or a training company to work with them, the legal department will most likely draft up (or at the least approve) the contract that specifies the kind of work the company will get for the amount of money it will pay.

Intellectual Property Protection

As more and more product value resides in software and high-technology components and/or processes, companies have to find ways to protect their competitive advantage over rivals. This is another arena where corporate attorneys are involved. Many companies find that they cannot go it alone anymore and have to take on partners to produce an end product, or sell in a particular geography. But in order to do so, they often need to share proprietary information with the partners. Corporate attorneys will draft up agreements that specify the kind of information partners or third parties will have access to, and how that information is to be protected.

Microsoft, Napster, and Apple all have taken big companies and even the little guy to court to protect their intellectual property. The corporate legal department usually spearheads these efforts and works with outside counsel to pursue their claims in court.

Legal Defense

In today's litigious society, it's an unfortunate fact that the chances of landing in court due to some sort of legal challenge are higher now than they were 50 years ago. Some of the lawsuits brought against companies, particularly the large and publicly visible ones, are "frivolous" and can be dismissed quickly. But even the nonsense legal issues have to be handled by someone. The more serious challenges, such as claims that a product malfunctioned and caused bodily harm, can be a huge drain on a company's time, assets, and reputation. The legal department is a key player in dealing with every legal claim against the company.

Public Documents

All publicly traded companies in the United States must be extra careful with what they say (in print or verbally) to their investors. This has become even more important in the wake of the Sarbanes-Oxley bill that stipulates yet more legal compliance on the part of corporate officers. For example, an officer of a publicly traded corporation cannot cavalierly say that business looks good and he thinks earnings will be increasing. Such a statement can be taken as a fact by the market and will probably drive people to buy more of the company's stock thus bidding up the price. If the company's business lives up to the market's expectations, then all is well. But what happens if there is a downturn in the company's business and it turns out that not only are earnings not rising, but actually falling? Investors will be angry and may sue the company for portraying a false or misleading earnings picture. The corporate legal department is charged with ensuring that executives don't say or write stupid things that could come back to bite them later.

Public corporations have a massive amount of legal documents that must be produced to satisfy regulators and government agencies, in addition to investors. The legal department is intimately involved with producing the annual report, quarterly reports, 10K forms, and the mountain of other paper required. In each case, a corporate lawyer must review what gets written and published in print form and on the company's Web site.

Many companies host what is known as "conference calls" with analysts. These are investment experts who usually work for a big bank or mutual fund and are charged with understanding every detail of the specific companies that they track. In many cases, the company's CFO or CEO or both host a conference call to discuss the status of the company's business and their views of the future. You can bet that the corporate lawyers have discussed the details of these calls with the executives beforehand.

Senior Management Counsel

A good legal team will help the CEO and her senior management team to make decisions based on the business logic of a situation, but also with guidance from a legal perspective. Many companies in their quest to expand internationally choose to take on joint venture partners in new and unfamiliar geographies, like Indonesia. The legal team can help the company structure a partnership agreement that is beneficial to both parties. Or if the company prefers to license the technology they have in order to gain faster market share, the legal department is usually involved in the negotiation of the licensing agreements.

Why Is the Legal Department Important?

Many businesspeople see the legal department as a "cover-your-butt" type of necessary evil. To some degree that's an old-fashioned view. The more progressive corporate legal departments are partners with the businesspeople, and often report directly to the head of the business unit and sit on the management team. As such, they provide the following services:

- Advice on proposed business transactions *before* the deal is finalized
- Credibility and a comfort level that certain decisions are sound

- Assistance in crafting joint venture, franchising, and licensing agreements
- Safeguards for intellectual property, trademarks, and copyrights
- Legal defense against lawsuits
- Business-savvy negotiating skills when dealing with industry regulators, government agencies, and lawyers from other companies
- Education on the limits of what the executives can do or say in particularly touchy situations
- Protect the businesspeople from doing stupid things

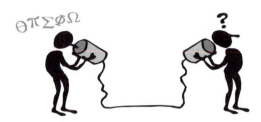

COMMUNICATIONS

The communications function has two sides: internal and external. We'll take a look at both of those functions later in this section. Large companies usually have a dedicated communications function that reports to the CEO or COO depending on how important this job is for the company's business. In some companies, the communications function resides in different staff departments, like the legal department, the human resources department, or the investor relations group. In small companies, the communications function might reside in one or two people who are entirely dedicated to that job, or also do other jobs. In today's wired world, the communications function also gets involved in designing and providing content for the company's external Internet site as well as the internal Intranet.

Internal Communications

The internal communications function is focused on getting messages out to the employees, suppliers, and other partner organizations. The messages vary widely and can consist of newsletters, the corporate mission statement, corporate value and strategy statements, new policies, new products, new initiatives, new partnership arrangements, e-mails, video- or webcasts from the CEO, internal training opportunities, job postings, and other notifications.

Internal communications are important because they set the tone of an organization and have a huge role to play in the company's culture. And internal communications are an efficient way to let people know what is going on outside of their own particular department.

External Communications

The external communications function—also known as Public Relations or Corporate Relations—focuses on stakeholders outside of the company, such as investors, environmentalists, the government, the community, and the media. The external communication function is charged with projecting the public face of the company, its values and reason for being, to interested outsiders. So when *60 Minutes* shows up at the CEO's door wanting to know why his company polluted a particular waterway, he needs someone to help coach him on the appropriate and most effective way to answer those questions.

External communications are important in shaping public perceptions of what the company does and equally, does not do. The giant oil companies are spending heaps of money advertising how they love the environment and are working hard to protect it. In a somewhat perverse twist (brought on as a result of many lawsuits) the big tobacco companies are spending loads of money trying to convince people not to smoke.

INVESTOR RELATIONS

The Investor Relations department is responsible for disseminating information that's required to meet regulatory statutes (like the annual report, the 10K, and other legal financial documents). It also sends out the proxy and meeting notices to all investors. If the company has a dividend reinvestment program, the Investor Relations department coordinates it. The investor relations group also sets up quarterly "analyst conference calls" wherein the CEO or CFO talk to the financial analysts to explain current events in the company and the prognosis for future profits.

Corporate Governance

Another task that the investor relations group sometimes takes on is telling the world about the company's corporate governance policies (or in some cases trying to explain why the CEO's salary is so high). Corporate governance also includes communicating the company's code of conduct and ethics policies, the articles of incorporation and bylaws, and the policy on board member terms and how they're elected.

Corporate Social Responsibility

Depending on the size of the company, Investor Relations might also be responsible for clarifying the company's corporate social responsibility policy and actions. This includes publishing documents explaining what it is doing to reduce noxious emissions (carbon dioxide, nitrous oxide, etc.) from its factories and how it is helping to control greenhouse gases (it runs its fleet vehicles on biodiesel). IBM, for example, has an innovative program that seeks to ameliorate the shortage of math and science teachers by helping departing IBM employees become teachers. But if a company is particularly large, this corporate social responsibility program might reside in the Health, Safety, and Environment function, the Public Affairs function, or in the Corporate Communications function.

PUBLIC AFFAIRS

This group has a wide variety of names including Corporate Affairs, Government Affairs, External Affairs, and Governmental Programs. The main responsibility of the public affairs department is twofold: first, the group represents the company's views to members of the government with a view to influencing policy discussions and proposed laws, and second, it brings the range of public opinions toward the company and its actions to the forefront of senior management's radar screen. The range of topics that the public affairs department focuses on is wide:

- Government legislation and regulation (proposed, existing, and in the process of being modified)
- Current events, such as being asked to testify in front of the Congress on a particular issue (like corporate governance, immigration issues, or a policy to self-censor in China)
- Security—crime, computer networks, military defense, civil defense, disaster preparedness, etc.
- Public health
- Pollution, emission control, trading of development rights
- Intellectual property rights
- Tax policy
- Tariff legislation and implementation, trade restrictions, foreign market access

As you can imagine, the public affairs department of a large corporation has many lobbyists working in the corridors of political power. But the group also produces "whitepapers," which are documents stating the company's position on any number of issues. These are usually available for download from the company's Web sites.

HEALTH, SAFETY, AND ENVIRONMENT

This is a big arena that covers a diverse array of topics. Depending on the size of the company and its industry, it may have all or none of these functions. And some of the functions, like health and safety are often found under the operations or manufacturing domain. Environment can be a big issue (if you're an airport operator like BAA or an oil company), a midsized issue or even nonexistent. IBM has an extensive Environment group that determines policy for the company (for example recycling components) and establishes a benchmark to help ease the company's impact on climate change.

The health and safety group usually focuses on workplace issues and promotes the cognizance of hazards to employee health and prevent accidents. People in this group work on a lot more than preventing paper cuts or factory accidents. They also develop safety guidelines that every vendor must adopt and agree to abide by if they want to sell anything to the company.

QUALITY

Quality is a topic that gained momentum in the 1980s with the Total Quality Management movement and the Toyota Production System. Many companies realized that they could not only save lots of money by building things right the first time and following quality standards in the product design and development, but that high quality also really pleased their customers. So many companies established a "quality" group that sought to learn best practices from other companies and propagate the "quality-in-all-we-do" mantra throughout the organization.

The Quality department develops standards by which the company's vendors are held to when delivering their products. These are often called things like supplier quality management systems and/or a quality information network. Vendors must usually agree to follow the rules and processes set forth in the documents produced by these quality systems before they are approved as a supplier.

Depending on the size of the company and the importance placed on quality, the quality function might report directly to the CEO, to a staff function or it might report to an operating unit, such as manufacturing.

CUSTOMER ADVOCACY

Have you ever gotten frustrated after getting lost in a big company's "customer support" phone maze? Sometimes you just want what appears to be a simple answer to a common problem. And sometimes you want to talk to a real human rather than press a series of buttons on your telephone. Customer Advocacy (also sometimes called "customer care") is a relatively recent invention. It's designed to look at how customers view doing business with the company from the customer's point of view. Customer advocacy seems like it shouldn't be necessary, but in the rush of doing business, many big companies lost focus on why they are in business. Customer advocates are there to represent the customer to senior management, improve customer satisfaction by building products and services that the customer will use and value, and earn loyalty through honesty and transparency. Sun Computers has a Chief Customer Advocate who's responsibility is to "amplify the voice of the customer across the company, while driving sustained processes that add a strong customer-first ethic to Sun's leadership in entrepreneurship and networked computing technology innovation."[1]

A DAY IN THE LIFE OF A CORPORATE AFFAIRS EXECUTIVE

Kathleen Linehan
Vice President (Retired)
Corporate Affairs – Central and Eastern Europe, Middle East and Africa
Philip Morris International, Altria Group

I was at the top of my game when I was asked to move from Washington, D.C., to Lausanne, Switzerland. At the time, I ran the Washington, D.C., office and was in charge of all of Philip Morris' federal lobbying efforts for its food, beer, and tobacco companies. My job was to be the eyes and ears for our company regarding what was going on inside Washington politics. I had to keep our headquarters in New York informed about current political trends and act as a window for the executives on the public mood. But I also had to thoroughly understand the businesses, their future, and what legislation our operating executives needed to understand and either support, oppose or urge modification. I was one of few women heading the Washington offices for a Fortune 25 company. I loved the intensity of working the Hill, assembling the team to work out a legislative strategy, engaging the company's management in the process, identifying the players, our opponents, allies, and working for the votes. Our office had worked hard to gain the respect of our senior management, which is fundamental to the success of any Washington office. We spoke regularly with them and often brought them to Washington to meet with the Administration and the Congress.

I grew up and went to school in the Washington, D.C., area. I've always loved international travel and learning about other cultures. I was an exchange student in Brazil during high school and I spent my junior year of college at the University of Madrid in Spain. I also worked as a maid in a resort hotel in Switzerland during my sophomore year, and served cocktails, ironically, at the Montreux Palace hotel. It was in this hotel, just next to that bar, where−25 years later−I was introduced as the new corporate affairs manager at Philip Morris. It's funny how life cycles around!

After I finished my law degree, I went to work on Capitol Hill and later I became a lobbyist for a major oil company. Then I signed on with Philip Morris and worked my way up the ranks to eventually running the Washington, D.C., office.

However, while heading a Washington office for a high profile company was often difficult and challenging, the position in Europe was, by far, more complex and interesting to me. I'm glad that I was lured to Europe for such an unusual job−especially for an American not knowing just how different this experience would be!

When I arrived in Switzerland, the corporate affairs function was not well integrated with the business units. Its priorities were not aligned with the businesses and the whole function was in need of reorganization. My responsibility was to run corporate affairs for all of Central and Eastern Europe, the Middle East and Africa. There were 30 major markets (countries) in my region. I had to ensure that each country team was on top of the laws, legislative, and regulatory actions. As in Washington, I was in charge of bringing the public view of Philip Morris−and especially the public attitudes toward tobacco−to our senior management team in Lausanne and each major market.

It was a fascinating job but it had an unbelievable learning curve! While I had traveled a lot through Europe and studied overseas, nothing would really prepare me for the cultural "transition" I would have to make. When I left the United States in 1995, tobacco companies were facing huge class action lawsuits, countless House and Senate hearings leading to a big legislative battle in the Senate, and very damaging press reports. (Remember all those tobacco executives publicly swearing that smoking was not addictive?) President Clinton had targeted tobacco companies for increased taxes and regulatory control.

I arrived in Europe a few years after the Berlin Wall fell. The initial attitude of most of our European managers was, "Europe is different, the United States has all those lawyers who stir up trouble. The American problems won't happen here because we Europeans are so much more pragmatic." Frankly, if I had been part of that management I might have felt the same way. But the "perfect storm" created by the media, the politics, and the trial lawyers over 'youth smoking' unleashed public fury. Moreover, the industry's total inability to understand these public attitudes and bring its positions and practices in sync just added fuel to the fire.

However, the negative public opinions were not going to be isolated to the United States. Health consciousness does not stop at some real or imaginary border. My responsibility was to point out that these issues are global and they should be addressed sooner rather than later. Europeans believe that the state should not dictate 'personal freedoms' the way it does in the 'nanny state' of the United States. Furthermore, Europeans are not 'litigious' societies. They viewed Americans as having lost a sense of personal responsibility for their actions.

The industry's tendency had been to fight everything—any marketing and advertising restrictions, smoking restrictions, and tax increases. But the firestorm of the 1990s woke up the industry (as many 'firestorms' have done for other industries such as oil) in the United States and forced it to face the public scrutiny and be realistic. The new approach had to be global. It had to accommodate the public's need for smoking restrictions, as well as marketing and advertising restrictions to prevent youth smoking. The European managers listened; they understood the concept of getting ahead of the curve and actively addressing the public's concerns. But still it was easy to blame the U.S. trial lawyers and political system for all this trouble.

The job required a good deal of travel – about 50% of the time. I was working in countries like Poland, Russia, and the Czech Republic that had just opened up to Western ways of doing business. We had a number of young workers who were eager to learn. We trained them on topics like issues management, public affairs strategy, and communication. It was our goal to develop the most sophisticated corporate affairs staffs in every country where we did business. We developed a corporate affairs group that not only understood what their public and opinion elite felt about our company and its products, but also worked with management to translate the public's concerns into action.

In the beginning, we showed video footage of antitobacco rallies and debates from the United States. The managers didn't believe that this would come to a city near them until they saw similar antismoking campaigns across Europe on their own televisions. Then the European Union started to take action along with its member countries. This was important. With the break up of the Soviet Union, Central and Eastern European countries had no real laws on advertising and marketing. Now these countries, which wanted to be members of the EU, looked west for future trends and eventually had to conform their laws to those of the EU for entry. The Middle East was also sensitive to the antismoking trends.

We started to do public opinion surveys on smoking in our major markets. We found similar attitudes to those of the U.S. public. To the surprise of some of us in the company, these populations also stated that smoking is addictive, that there should be smoking restrictions or bans in public places, that marketing to youth should be banned, and that countries should enact and enforce minimum age laws. So the average guy in the street in Budapest, Moscow, or Tel Aviv generally agreed with the average guy in Cleveland. Bingo!

Philip Morris is a bit unique because we're the only American tobacco company with operations outside the United States (everyone else sold off their foreign subsidiaries). Moreover, our main competitors overseas are either national tobacco companies or other Europe-based multinationals, like BAT (British American Tobacco). Most of our competition overseas had not experienced the U.S. class action lawsuits or scathing media campaigns. It was still normal business practice to hand out sample packets of cigarettes at rock concerts. Philip Morris supported a global ban on "sampling" (the free cigarette giveaways) because they sometimes made their way into the hands of underage kids. While it was a competitive disadvantage to take steps like that unilaterally, we always hoped that the competition would soon also understand that it was not smart business practice and counter to public views.

We have really extraordinarily smart management overseas. They are used to constant change in the business environment, and those same intellectual skills helped them deal with the "U.S.-focused" issues here. They came to understand that the U.S. issue was a global social issue spilling over into their countries and the European Union. Perhaps the most important activity we did with our management was to provide them with extensive briefings on our detailed in-country opinion surveys on smoking, and then having them watch focus groups that always confirmed the survey findings (much to my amazement)! These techniques were akin to marketing research and analysis, so line management could relate well to them.

Change is hard—there's lots of resistance in any business. But seeing change up close and personal in the form of a freewheeling focus group means more than mountains of data or endless corporate affairs presentations! Even I was sometimes astonished to see the health threats of smoking so well articulated and intensely felt by the man in the street overseas. We emerged from these meetings with a 2- to 3-year strategic plan to ameliorate public opinion and agreement on Philip Morris' priorities for what should be done on future legislation. The end result was action by management. We identified what should be done to meet these concerns, such as supporting smoking restrictions or bans, and enforcing corporate policy not to pursue certain types of marketing and advertising that might reach the underage crowd.

You have to be very responsive to your management's needs, work to keep good relationships during "changing" times, maintain the professionalism of the corporate affairs staffs through training, and ensure that they focus on what's important in their markets. We do this with the same intensity as that of the line management when pushing its brand managers to build growth. Responding to a changing corporate environment is the responsibility of management and it tests a lot of boundaries—cultural, geopolitical, and ethical.

To get a job in a corporate affairs role you need the following attributes:

- Excellent communication skills—writing, speaking, and especially *listening*. You must be clear and precise in both writing and speaking
- Knowledge of the legislative and regulatory processes
- Good diplomatic and "people" skills
- Focus, drive, energy, and adaptability
- Good time management and organizational skills; ability to delegate
- Ability to think strategically
- Initiative and perseverance
- Stamina for the many social events helps too

All in all, this job was a humbling experience. It taught me that the typical American style and business practices might not work overseas. Foreign managers often have more to teach you than vice versa! It's best to listen and keenly observe for a good 6–8 months before you even begin to understand that! You learn that every country has its own political culture and ways of doing things. And you absolutely must respect and defer to your in-country management. Furthermore, you must treat each country individually even if there are regional similarities. You can't take the easy route and just say that all of Central Europe is the same. I certainly made my share of mistakes and hope that I learned from them. It was very rewarding to have worked through it and then see such positive results.

A typical day:

7:00 AM	Driving in to work I put in a call to our Tel Aviv office. I want to reach my head of corporate affairs there before she hops on a plane to Paris later this morning.
7:30 AM	I'm at my desk and checking the e-mails that came in overnight from our New York and Washington offices. I had asked them for details of legislation and voter referendums on a number of total smoking bans being enacted in several cities across the United States.
8:00 AM	Our weekly staff meeting. We review important legislative action in our major markets and what our in-country teams are doing in response. We also review the agenda for the upcoming media training for corporate affairs market heads. We must start to prepare for the annual presentation to the CEO.
10:00 AM	Conference call with our operations in Morocco. We're hosting a women's literacy event to bring attention to the fact that not all women in lower income countries are able to attend school. We contribute to special causes in all our markets because we want to give back to the community.
10:30 AM	Meet with the Vice President in charge of the Middle Eastern region who is at headquarters for a few days. I have a few of my Lausanne staff with me to go over specific legislative issues in his area, and some public affairs programs that he might want to adapt for his markets. We bring him up to date on the latest issues in the United States.
12:00 noon	Lunch with our corporate lawyer from New York. He and I discuss current litigation issues and how they will impact the company down the road.
1:30 PM	Meet with the VP of Marketing from our Lausanne office on the youth smoking issue. It's picking up steam here. He wants me to make a presentation to his annual regional marketing conference and include some videos on the new European antismoking campaigns.
2:30 PM	Meet with my boss who runs the Region. He taught me a lot about making presentations to management: be ultra focused, very clear, and to the point. I need to get my budget numbers in and be less reliant on carrying over money that was budgeted last year but not spent! We have to be extra careful in how we spend our funds. My boss, like many in line management, views corporate affairs as a 'cost center' and therefore, he demands that we add value to their business. We are doing that but when you don't bring in money and you are carrying messages people don't want to hear, such as 'we must give up certain types of marketing,' it takes time. But his healthy skepticism helps us pay attention to what's important to management and to try to engage management in understanding how the policy issues impact their business in the long term.

3:30 PM	Conference call with our team in Prague. They've launched a public affairs program at a few select downtown bars where they set up some unique nonsmoking and smoking sections. We're doing these programs to show bar owners that they won't lose clientele if they separate the smokers, and in fact, some of them find they gain more nonsmokers.
4:00 PM	Meet with my communications director to review our crisis management training sessions. We'll be holding these sessions for the senior management in 14 markets. We've created a generic and simple four-page crisis management guide. It outlines step-by-step what you have to do in a crisis, and can be easily translated for our factory personnel. It will be used as the basis of the role playing exercises in our training program. We've already had to deal with "crisis management" in a few of our Eastern European countries and these incidents (which, thankfully, all turned out okay) prompted us to "institutionalize" the process for headquarters and management in the various markets.
5:00 PM	I jump in my car for the 40-minute drive to the Geneva airport. I'm off to Bucharest to meet with the management teams from Romania, Hungary, the Czech Republic, and Poland. My group has a half-day session with each country over the next several days to go over what we found from market surveys and local focus groups. It should be very interesting to see their reactions!

SUMMARY

In addition to all the functions described in the other chapters, most businesses have some other staff functions that are important for running the company. The legal department is usually the biggest staff function. Legal is responsible for keeping the company and its officers out of trouble. But legal also has a role to play in guarding proprietary technology, intellectual property, and defending the company from legal claims against it. Legal also works with the investor relations department as well as the communications group to coordinate the messages that are conveyed to investors and outside stakeholders.

Several other staff roles may be present in businesses depending on the industry they're in, the environment in which they operate, and the size and focus of the company. These can include Health, Safety, and Environment, Consumer Advocacy, Public Affairs, Quality and others.

Each of these staff roles is important in helping a business succeed at its primary goal: delighting customers and making profits.

Appendix: Job/Career Training and Preparation Resources

Entire libraries of books have been published about careers, career guides, and how to go about finding a job. This section is not designed to be comprehensive by any means. The purpose of this section is to give you a general idea of what you need to think about when pursuing a career in business, how to go about finding a job and where to look on the Internet for additional information.

SELF-ASSESSMENT

So you've decided you want to go into business, eh? Are you sure that this is the right place for you? Do you have an analytical and logical mind? Are you extroverted? Can you make ruthless decisions quickly and not lose sleep over them? Are you a whiz with numbers? Are you greedy for money and power? If you answered "no" to any or all of these questions, don't worry, be happy. You don't need to be any particular type of person to get into business. But in order to succeed, you will need to work hard, know your own strengths and weaknesses (yes, those are important too) and learn to enjoy working with all types of people (if you don't already). It also helps to be a very good listener and communicator, both in writing and orally. And finally, a great education helps you get a leg up on your competition.

Beyond those general guidelines, you should think about what kinds of things you really enjoy. If you like mathematics and problem solving, perhaps accounting or finance would be good to pursue. If you like problem solving and have a creative bent, you might want to think about R&D. If you *really* like people and are particularly gregarious and outgoing, sales might be a good spot to look into. If you like strategizing over how to get people to buy stuff, then maybe marketing would appeal. If you have an analytical mind and like to

Top 25 Undergraduate Business Programs

1. Pennsylvania (Wharton)—Philadelphia, PA
2. Virginia (McIntire)—Charlottesville, VA
3. Notre Dame (Mendoza)—South Bend, IN
4. MIT (Sloan)—Cambridge, MA
5. Emory (Goizueta)—Atlanta, GA
6. Michigan (Ross)—Ann Arbor, MI
7. NYU (Stern)—New York
8. Brigham Young (Marriott)—Provo, UT
9. Texas (McCombs)—Austin
10. Indiana (Kelley)—Bloomington, IN
11. North Carolina (Kenan-Flagler)—Chapel Hill, NC
12. UC Berkeley (Haas)—Berkeley, CA
13. Georgetown (McDonough)—Washington, DC
14. Cornell—Ithaca, NY
15. Washington University (Olin)—St. Louis, MO
16. Carnegie Mellon—Pittsburgh, PA
17. Miami University (Farmer)-Oxford, OH
18. Lehigh—Bethlehem, PA
19. Villanova—Villanova, PA
20. SMU (Cox)—Dallas, TX
21. USC (Marshall)—Los Angeles
22. Illinois—Urbana-Champaign, IL
23. Boston College (Carroll)—Boston
24. Wake Forest (Calloway)—Winston-Salem, NC
25. Richmond (Robins)—Richmond, VA

Source: Business Week, May 8, 2006

write, try the legal department. If you like to work behind the scenes but enjoy seeing your "fingerprints" on everything you touch, then human resources might be a place to go. If you are a natural born leader, then you will still have to work your way up an organization to get to the top, but getting into a good company with a management training program is a great way to start.

There are numerous resources and questionnaires you can look into to find out to where you should direct your interests. Career centers at most high schools and colleges can start you out. There are also Internet questionnaires to consider. Some are better than others, some are free but require registration first, and some require an upfront payment. Several are listed below.

Career Key: http://www.careerkey.org/
This site offers a comprehensive, professional quality test that helps people decide what careers to investigate.

Quest Career Center: http://www.questcareer.com/career_assessment_resources.html

Career test: http://www.careertest.us/

Which Career.com: http://whichcareer.eak/>com/cgi-bin-wc/from.pl?from=GO23

GENERAL OCCUPATION INFORMATION

Still not sure that you should be an accountant as the questionnaire suggested? (After all, you *do* have a sense of humor!) Then look around on some of the Web sites listed below for information about particular jobs, where they're most plentiful, the work involved in each type of job, what careers will be in high demand in the future, how much you can earn, and the kind of working conditions you can expect.

The Place to Start

Bureau of Labor Statistics: http://www.bls.gov/oco/
On this site you'll find the occupational outlook handbook. It has a wealth of information about different types of jobs in virtually all areas of business. It describes

what qualifications are best for a particular job, what the job entails, how much growth and demand is predicted for the field, what the average salaries are, and even the kind of working conditions you should expect to find.

Try These Next

Vault: www.vault.com
This is a huge site with a ton of information about careers, salaries, jobs, interview resources, and much more. Most of the information is free but some require a membership to the site. There is an entire section called "A Day in the Life..." which features hundreds of profiles of people holding various jobs. You learn the nitty gritty details about what people actually do all day long.

Montana State University career center: http://www.montana.edu/~wwwcp/tips.html
This site offers many free tips and resources for job searches, interview pointers, etiquette, and so forth. Some of the links direct you to job placement company Web sites where they hope to entice you to pay them to help you out.

U.S. Department of Labor: www.dol.gov
This is a big and free site with heaps of information on jobs, pay rates, rules, etc. The problem can be finding what you're after.

America's Career InfoNet: www.acinet.org
This is a component of Career One Stop, which is sponsored by the U.S. Department of Labor. This site is very user-friendly and offers information on local and national job data. It has many tools and offers a section for students to find out about workforce credentials, federal training programs, videos of people doing their jobs, and so on.

One Stop Coach: www.onestopcoach.org
Part of Career One Stop, you can post your resume online, look for organizations in a particular field, look at salary data, find out about high-growth industries, research knowledge and skills requirements, and much more.

Job profiles: www.jobprofiles.org
This is a Web site set up by a nonprofit organization dedicated to providing "career exploration and inspiration...where experienced workers share their motivations, basic skills and advice with those just entering the career field." You'll find questionnaires completed by a variety of people who work in a particular job. They describe their jobs, the benefits and downsides, and what motivates them to come to work. Although the site does not get updated often, the profiles are still valid.

JOB TRYOUTS

Another way to investigate particular jobs or fields of industry is to try a job on for size. There are several ways to go about this. Any kind of summer job that does not require experience is likely to be an entry-level position offering little discretion in how you do the job, and it probably provides few opportunities to develop additional skills. However, you can make the most of the situation you've got. You can ask questions (being careful, of course, not to annoy everyone around you). Try to learn about what other people in your workplace do, what they like about their job, what they dislike, and what kinds of skills are necessary to do the job. Equally important to finding a job you like, is figuring out what kinds of jobs you don't want. Maybe your passion is fly-fishing. There are jobs as fly fishing guides or running a fly fishing shop in a town that has lots of good rivers and lakes. The sections below describe some additional ways to learn about particular jobs.

Internships

If you're lucky enough to land a job as an intern in a field that interests you, you can use that opportunity to learn by doing. Many companies offer summer internships, and some of them even help you transition to management. Some schools partner with companies to help recruit talented students for jobs. The downside of taking a job as an intern is that very often these positions do not pay any money (or very little). Internships are often advertised as a way to learn about a career and prove yourself to the future employer, but occasionally they are a ploy to get slave labor for a short period of time.

Listed below are some Web sites that offer to connect students with companies looking for interns.

Rising Star Internships: www.rsinternships.com
This site has a number of internship positions listed in a wide variety of fields. Some are with companies and others are with nonprofit and political foundations. On this site you can post your resume, amend or change it and set up contacts with companies seeking interns.

National Internships Online: www.internships.com
This site says that it's the world's largest internship site. It sells guidebooks online. In order to access the site you have to be a student at one of the colleges that is affiliated with the site.

Internships-USA: www.internships-usa.com
Internships-USA claims to be the largest internship resource site in the United States. Much of it requires a password to access, but it is available through many colleges and law schools.

Internship Programs: http://internships.wetfeet.com
Internjobs.com: www.internjobs.com
This is a subsidiary of aboutjobs.com.

University of California Irvine: www.cie.uci.edu/iop/internsh.html
This has a number of links to other sites for internships and studies abroad. It's a good place to start if your aspirations include international business. However, they offer no assistance to people who are not affiliated with UC Irvine.

Intern Abroad: www.internabroad.com
This site is packed with information not only about internships abroad, but also educational opportunities, language schools, teaching abroad, eco-tourism, and practical travel tips.

Job Shadowing

Job shadowing is a form of learning by watching others. When you shadow someone, you are in effect, being their shadow. You follow them around all day, watch what they do, listen to how they interact with others, see the challenges they face and how they handle them, and learn many of the subtleties of the job your shadow person does. The best way to shadow someone is to ask a person you know if you could accompany him or her to work one day. It's a great way to learn about a job, and if you like the job and the company, you can see what it takes to be hired there. Some tips on job shadowing:

1. Be creative. You can job shadow any number of jobs. Does your mother's friend own a florist or an interior design business? Does your uncle work in an architectural firm? Do you have a zoo or a theater group in your town? Give people a call and ask. Most people are interested in helping students get jobs. After all, the worst they can say is "no."
2. Dress appropriately. Don't show up in a t-shirt and jeans if you'll be in an office setting. Dress in the same fashion as the people on the job (suit or business casual). However, if your shadow person is in equine management, then you probably do want to show up prepared to muck out a horse stall. When in doubt, ask.
3. Be on time. The person you're shadowing is doing you a favor, don't make them wait for you.
4. Bring a notebook and pen to take notes.
5. Send a thank-you note afterward (preferably one that's hand written and sent via snail mail). It lets people know that you care, it keeps a line of communication open (especially if you think you want a job there) and it's a great habit to get into.

The Web sites shown below offer information about job shadowing.

Virtual Job Shadow: www.virtualjobshadow.com

Yahoo! Shadow jobs: http://hotjobs.yahoo.com/jobs/VA/Shadow/Internet-New-Media-jobs

Quintessential Careers: www.quintcareers.com/job_shadowing.html

Informational Interviews

Informational interviews are another way of learning about a job. They are less involved than job shadowing in that you request a 30- to 60-minute interview with a person to ask them questions about their job. You can ask anyone if they would be willing to talk to you about their job. Many busy executives are just too swamped to do this, but some of them will make time for an interview if you can show that you've done some research on the business, the job, and the industry. The same tips apply to informational interviews as do to the job shadow. Be polite and very conscious of the person's time. Ask intelligent questions. Don't waste your interviewee's time by asking things that you could learn from the company Web site. Ask the interviewee what brought them to the position they're in, what they like about it, what they don't like about it, what challenges they face, and what kind of skills you need to get into this kind of job. And, of course, after the interview, send a thank-you note.

MENTORS AND NETWORKS

Many studies have shown that executives who have had mentors in their lives do much better in business than those who have never had a mentor. A mentor is a person who "takes you under her or his wing" and shows you the ropes. She or he gives you advice, counseling, coaching, and helps you see the bigger picture so you can deal with day-to-day issues more coherently. You're never too old or too young to have a mentor. The best mentor–mentee relationships are those that are voluntary and become established over time through the mutual interest of both people. The benefits for a mentee (no, that's not a typo for 'manatee;' a mentee is the person being mentored) are enormous. The mentee gains the experience of the mentor, a broader perspective on life and work in general, and the coaching and advice of a trusted advisor on numerous challenges in life and work. The mentor often feels rewarded by the fact that someone trusts her/him enough to seek her/his advice, and she/he can feel good about helping a younger person gain from her/his experience.

Mutual trust and respect are the hallmarks of a good mentor relationship. To find a mentor, start with some of the adults you know. Look at people who have been through a lot in life already, who have worked in a field that interests you, and who might be willing to share their experiences with you. Mentoring takes time and effort, so choose a mentor carefully. You might start by getting to know the person and asking them questions about their job and the challenges they've faced. Good mentors will help you in both your career and personal life. Then build the relationship over time.

Mentors can also help you build networks. Professional and social networks are like computer networks. They help connect people. There is some truth to the old adage, "It's who you know" when you're looking for a new job. Networks are indispensable tools for job hunting, and indeed, for working in business. (Many executive women have neglected to build personal networks, which often hampers their ability to climb the corporate ladder.) A personal introduction to a business person who is looking for a new employee or some other favor is always more powerful than a cover letter from a stranger. (How do you think this author got all the interviews with the "Day in the Life" contributors?)

There are formal networks that can help you develop mentor relationships. While the formal mentor–mentee relationships tend to be more difficult to sustain, they can help you build a network of people in the business and/or industry you want to get into.

Listed below are a number of mentoring and networking Web sites.

Mentors Inc.: www.mentorsinc.org
This is primarily a Washington, D.C., based organization.

The Mentoring Group: www.mentoringgroup.com

Mentor Net: www.mentornet.net
This site is specifically targeted to people in the science and engineering domains.

Menttium: www.menttium.com
Menttium is an organization founded primarily to help business women connect with suitable mentors in their own and other companies.

Oregon Mentors: www.ormentors.org
DECA: www.deca.org

DECA is an association of high school and college students interested in careers in marketing, management, and entrepreneurship. It was founded 56 years ago with the goal to improve education and career opportunities for students. The organization has chapters in all U.S. states plus Canada, Germany, Puerto Rico, and the Virgin Islands. It offers programs in leadership, and hosts several conferences each year.

GETTING THE JOB

Once you've figured out where you think you would like to work, then it's up to you to make sure you have (or are developing) the skills needed to go after the job you want. Mountains of books have been written on the topics of résumé writing, cover letters, interview skills, and other job search essentials. We won't spend a lot of time on those details here. Your school's career center can provide you with many tools and coaching on how to polish your résumé and write an appropriate cover letter. Here we'll define what these essential bits of paper are and steer you to some Web sites that offer some initial advice and tips.

Résumé Writing

A résumé is a one-page summary of your education and work-related experience. It should list in a very concise form, what you have accomplished. A résumé is usually split into three general categories: educational history, work history, and personal data. A sample résumé is shown below:

MARY QUITE CONTRARY
28 SHEPHERD'S GLEN
LAMBSWOOL, MONTANA
TEL: (970) 043-0XXX
E-MAIL: MARYLAMB@XYZIP.NET

EDUCATION

Bozeman High School, Bozeman, Montana
Diploma awarded in June 2000

Sheepherding University, Melbourne, Australia
Bachelor's degree in sheepherding awarded June 2005

PROFESSIONAL HISTORY

March-April 2005   KIWI TEXTILES, Cloudy Bay, New Zealand

Yield Analyst (cooperative work/study program)

Calculated effective yields from local shearing operations. Developed profit metrics and program to increase wool output from same shearing base. Analyzed local soil fertilization capacity and recommended rotation strategy for sheep herds.

Summer 2004	AUSSIE WOOL ENTERPRISES, Melbourne, Australia
	Assistant chief shearer

Salaried position as second-in-command in herding and shearing operation for the Brighton Grange pasture. Supervised and rotated a herd of 1800 sheep through a 20 square mile ranch. Responsible for ongoing training of Australian shepherd dogs, ordering supplies and preparation of camp meals. Culled lambs for transport to shearing yards. Trained interns.

Summer 2003	AUSSIE WOOL ENTERPRISES, Melbourne, Australia
	Shepherd intern

Learned about Australian shearing and herding methods. Assisted in periodic shearing. Worked with dog trainers and learned voice and whistle commands. Worked on shearing spreadsheets and calculated annual returns and profit margins.

March 1998	WALKER'S SHEEP SHEARING, Sheeptown, Montana

Assisted with the annual shearing of sheep and lambs. Held sheep down for shearing, changed and sharpened blades.

AWARDS

August 1995	First Place, Junior Handler's competition in sheepherding, 4-H Club Montana
June 1993	Second Place, Best Lamb competition, 4-H Club Montana

PERSONAL

Born February 1984 in Lambswool, Montana

Interests in rollerblading, snowboarding, dog training and textile weaving.

Listed below are several Web sites that will help you understand more about résumés and how to write one.

http://content.monster.com/basics/

http://hotjobs.yahoo.com/careertools

http://www.jobweb.com/Resumes_Interviews/default.htm

http://owl.english.purdue.edu/workshops/hypertext/ResumeW/

http://channels.netscape.com/careers/resume.jsp

http://www.bc.edu/offices/careers/skills/resumes/

Interview Skills

An interview is a question and answer session designed to give you a taste of what the job is about, and to give the interviewer a chance to find out about you and develop an initial sense of whether you will "fit" with the organization. The quickest way not to get a job is to blow the interview. Like it or not, you have only a few minutes before a person will develop an impression of you. Your best bet is to make a good impression and learn how to answer the questions thrown at you during an interview. Most interviewers are not "out to get you" or trap you into saying something stupid. Most interviewers genuinely want to learn about who you are, what you've done, and why you want the job.

Some types of jobs are harder to interview for than others. In part, it depends on the competitiveness of the industry. You're unlikely to find a starting position as an investment banker. However, you might find a way to get into an investment bank in an entry-level position. The culture of the industry and the organization will affect what kinds of things (skills, talents, social etiquette and background, personality, etc.) the company is looking for. Here are some tips to succeeding at the interview:

1. Do your homework! Learn about the company and the industry that you're applying with. Go to the company's Web site and look at their products and services, learn about their history and where they operate. Download the annual report and at least read the letter from the CEO and the first section that discusses the company's products, services, brands, and geographic operations. (You can also get a lot of information in the "notes to the financial statements" about what kinds of lawsuits and other strategic issues face the company.) Ask your librarian to help you find information about the industry, the players (competitors), if there are substitute products and services, the business model (that is, the value chain, how the companies in the industry make money), and the strategic threats and opportunities to the industry. If you know someone who works for or with the company, ask him or her about the company.
2. Think about questions you'd like to ask the interviewer. (Salary shouldn't be the first one . . . or perhaps even the last one on the initial interview.) Ask about the work you'll be expected to perform, the kind of people who work there, the company culture, values, and mission (but only if you didn't find this information on the company's Web site).
3. Find out from others what kinds of questions you're likely to face. Consulting companies are famous for giving the applicant a business problem to solve in 10 minutes or less (called a "case study interview"). If you have friends who have interviewed with the same company, try to learn what they were asked.
4. Be prepared with an answer for those tough questions, like, "Tell me about a time you failed at something" or "What do you consider to be your personal weakness?" The answer is not, "I've never failed" or "I am perfect." You should be able to describe a challenge you've faced, how you dealt with it and what you learned from it.
5. Look at some of the Web sites listed below. There is a wealth of information here that will give you an idea of what an interview is and even what kinds of questions the interviewer might ask.
6. Be on time (or a little early) for your appointment!

7. Dress the part. No one wants to hire someone who just rolled out of bed and "threw something on." When in doubt, overdress. Leave the flip-flops, t-shirts, and halter tops at home.

8. You have two ears and one mouth. Use them proportionately. That means, don't spend the entire time talking... do a lot of listening as well. This is your opportunity to find out if you want to work there.

See the following Web sites for additional interview tips:

http://interview.monster.com/

http://jobsearch.about.com/od/interviewsnetworking/a/wininterview.htm

http://www.western.edu/career/interview/Interview_skills.htm

http://www.bc.edu/offices/careers/skills/interview/

HR Guide: http://www.hr-guide.com/
HR Guide is a site designed for the HR professional, but can aid the student look-ing for information and hints—go to the "tough questions" section [http://www.hr-guide.com/data/G353.htm] for a preview of some interview questions that will really make you squirm.

References

You should be prepared to give an interviewer a list of three references. References are people who know you, your work and/or accomplishments, your skills and personality, and who can provide a positive (we hope) recommendation to an employer. Do not include references in your résumé. They should be listed on a separate piece of paper and given to an employer if they ask. People who are good candidates to be your reference include a teacher or professor, a former boss, or someone who knows you and your work from another aspect (a volunteer program, your church, etc.). A current boss is a great reference as long as you both understand that you're looking for a new job. Don't ask any close relatives to be a reference for you. The one exception might be if you are working for your Uncle Al's business and Al can provide a candid view of your performance. The best combination of references is one personal reference (someone who can vouch that you aren't an axe murderer) and two business references (people who can attest to the quality and professionalism of your work, as well as your skills). Always check with the people who you'd like to list as references *before* you put their names and contact information on your reference sheet.

Cover Letters and Thank-You Notes

A cover letter is the letter you write to the company you'd like to interview with. It is a cover letter because it goes on top of your résumé. A cover letter explains why you want the job that's advertised, why you think you would be a good fit with that particular company, and how you can help the company. Here are some cover letter tips:

1. NO TYPOS! You are on that page. Make sure that your spelling and grammar are absolutely correct. Companies get hundreds (or thousands)

of résumés per year so you have to make sure that yours won't hit the trash bin because you can't spell (or are too lazy to run the spell checker).

2. Don't address your letter to "Dear Sir or Madam." Find the name (and correct spelling) of the person in charge of the initial interview screening process. You have to get past the gatekeeper first.

3. Show that you know what you're applying for. Do some research on the company and the industry. Indicate why you really want to work for this particular company. (This means, don't just take the same letter and change the name and address. People will see through that ploy.)

4. Show some enthusiasm, creativity, and wit. Tell the company why you'd be a good fit and do so in your own words.

5. If you're answering an advertisement, make sure that you indicate how you measure up to the stated requirements of the position.

A thank-you note is an essential tool in the job interview process. Even if you don't want the job, it's polite and proper to write a thank-you note after you've had an interview. If you do want the job, it's your opportunity to communicate again with the company and reiterate why you think you would be the best candidate. The purpose of the thank-you note is to (1) thank the person for their time in interviewing you and (2) state what you like about the job and company and why you really want to work there. Show your energy and enthusiasm for the job. Make yourself stand out in a positive manner. Ideally, thank-you notes should be typewritten or neatly handwritten and sent via snail mail to each individual you spoke with. If you talked to 5 people during a morning at a company, you need to write 5 thank-you notes. If you talked to 15 people, you've got a lot of writing to do. Or you can be creative. Some people send bagels and cream cheese or donuts the next morning to everyone in an office along with a note addressed to the group. If there is a head person (decision maker) at the group or office, address a separate note to her or him. Use the thank-you note to show that you were paying attention during the interview. If you noticed that the interviewer had photos of dogs in her office, then find a card with a dog picture, or mention something you discussed during the interview. In any case, be quick with thank-you notes. Get them out immediately following your interview.

Listed below are some Web sites that will help you with cover letters and thank-you notes.

Strunk & White *Elements of Style*: http://www.bartleby.com/141/strunk3.html
This particular link is an online guide to commonly misused words and terms. It comes from the original Strunk and White's Elements of Style book (published in 1914) and is still useful today.

Job Star: http://jobstar.org/tools/resume/index.php
This Web site has some great tips on writing cover letters and résumés.

Career Lab: www.careerlab.com/letters/default.htm
This link is part of Career Lab, a job resource site. The letter section provides sample cover letters and thank-you notes. To access all of the letters you will have to pay a subscription fee.

ADDITIONAL EDUCATION

If you find that you want to look into other fields, but don't want to make a huge commitment yet, there are a number of ways to learn about other fields. One of the biggest is MIT's Open Course Ware program. You can take courses online for free (you won't earn any college credits for them, however). You can also download most of the papers and presentations used in the university courses for free.

MIT's OpenCourseWare: http://ocw.mit.edu/index.html

This is a free educational site for anyone who is interested. OpenCourseWare is a project jointly funded by the William & Flora Hewlett Foundation, MIT and the Andrew Mellon Foundation. It offers hundreds of courses and thousands of articles available for download. While it doesn't have a specific area dedicated to R&D, it's a good place to find out about different fields that do research. It also offers links to other open courses in China, Japan, France, Vietnam, and the United States.

SUMMARY

This appendix presented several ways to go about finding out the kind of job that might interest you and how to learn more about the jobs that are available. We've also provided you with a brief summary of job search tools, like résumés, cover letters, and thank-you tips. This section is not meant to be an all-inclusive or an exhaustive treatment of career options and job search techniques, but it should give you a start. Continue the journey by visiting your career guidance center and talking to as many people in business as you can find. Good luck in your search and your career!

Glossary

Absenteeism A measure of work hours lost due to unscheduled job absence divided by the actual hours worked (per employee).

Accounting The function of gathering, measuring, reporting, and analyzing quantitative and financial information about a particular economic activity, usually a business.

Accounts payable The total amount of bills that a company has outstanding (has not yet paid) to suppliers. It can also refer to the department inside a company that's responsible for paying the company's bills.

Accounts receivable The total amount of invoices that are owed to a company. It also means the department that's responsible for collecting receivables (outstanding invoices due to be paid to the company).

Activity-based costing system A management accounting system that assigns a cost to indirect and support services so that managers can get a better idea of what a particular process or activity truly costs. Examples include expenses associated with after-sales service, materials handling, and customer service calls.

Agile manufacturing Tools, techniques, and initiatives that enable a plant to respond rapidly to changing conditions, whether brought on by competitive forces, technical surprises, or changes in demand.

Assembly line A factory conveyer belt system that was first designed and implemented by Henry Ford. It moves parts, components, and subassemblies (i.e. things that go into final products) on a moving mechanical line from one station to the next. At each station, a worker has to do something to the part to build on to it. At the end of the assembly line, a finished product (like a car) emerges.

Asset turnover   A measure of how well a company is using its assets to produce sales. It refers to how fast the company is selling its products. The
ratio = net sales ÷ average total assets.

Auditor   A person who verifies that a company's accounts are true. An auditor
checks that the financial statements reflect the actual numbers reported
and the true value of the particular assets and liabilities. It can often mean
physically counting inventory and equipment.

B-2-B   Business-to-business. It usually refers to marketing or selling between
two businesses.

B-2-C   Business-to-consumer. This refers to a business selling products or services to an individual end user.

Balance sheet   A snapshot of a company's financial position at the close of
business on a particular date. It shows the company's assets, liabilities, and
owner's equity.

Benchmarking   A method of comparing how a best-in-class company performs a certain task (management processes, customer or supplier relationships, production methodologies, R&D management, etc.) to another
company that wants to learn (usually from a noncompeting firm). Visits are
often arranged to acquaint managers with each other and exchange best
practices.

Bond   A debt security, or loan that is secured by something—usually the assets
of a company. In the case of bonds issued by the U.S. Government, bonds
are secured by "the full faith and credit of the US Government."

Bondholder   A person or entity that buys a bond.

Brand   The name, look, logo, symbol, design, slogan, character, and/or packaging that uniquely identifies a particular product or service and differentiates
it from its competitors.

Brand equity   The value of a brand to a company.

Business model   A company's formula for winning—the way it does business.
At its heart is the value proposition to the customer. A business model incorporates the company's cost structure, its value chain, distribution channels,
margins, pricing, and the market segments in which it operates.

Business portfolio   The products and services that a company sells. It's also
the grouping of business units and/or strategic business units that make up
the company.

Business process engineering   A method of reviewing and analyzing the various subprocesses and tasks in a larger business process (like order fulfillment or new product development). The goal is to eliminate useless work
and streamline the flow of work so that the entire process works faster and
more efficiently. Information technology is often used to enable the flow of
information in the new process.

Business unit   A separate grouping of products and/or services that have some sort of commonality, like a common technology, a shared group of customers, or a similar geographic region. This separate grouping usually enables the managers to "get their arms around" a more self-sustaining business and run it like a smaller company within a larger corporation. It often enables the managers to focus more clearly on the specific goals of the business independent from the rest of the company's operations.

Cash cows   A marketing term for products or services that are hugely profitable for a company. They are usually low-growth but have a high market share and help the company pay its bills.

Cellular manufacturing   Equipment and workstations are arranged in smaller, more localized zones to enable small-lot, continuous-flow production. A "cell" is usually a self-contained setting where everything necessary to produce a component or subassembly is within reach and can be made quickly. Workers in cells are usually cross-trained to work on a variety of machines and tasks. A cell is the opposite of an assembly line.

Changeover   The process of modifying a workstation in a manufacturing operation (for example, installation of new dies for a different automobile model).

Channel   A method of bringing goods and services to market. Distribution or sales channels can include door-to-door sales, retail stores, catalogues, and the Internet.

C-Level   An executive at the top level of the organization. This person usually has a title that starts with "Chief..." and she or he generally reports to the Chief Executive Officer. It's also sometimes called "C-Suite."

Commodity   Anything that is produced or exchanged. In business it often refers to a raw material (cotton, soy, sugar) that's used in its raw form. It can also mean something that is cheap, homogeneous, and relatively easy to obtain.

Computer-aided design (CAD)   Computer software and hardware systems that together facilitate the design and development of products and systems. (Some examples are floor plan layouts, complex hydrochemical plants, automobiles, airplane wiring diagrams, and factory tooling systems.) CAD systems incorporate many analytical analysis tools that allow for "what if" types of modifications.

Computer-aided manufacturing (CAM)   Similar to CAD, these systems allow managers to download manufacturing instructions to robots or operator workstations.

Concurrent engineering   A cross-functional and team-based approach to designing a product at the same time (that is, in parallel rather than sequentially) with other groups working on the same product. The aim is to design the product right the first time.

Core competency   A process, function, technology, specific expertise or activity that is central to a company's competitive advantage.

Corporate culture A belief and value system that's shared (often unconsciously) by the people who make up an organization. It's an unwritten "rule book" that guides how people behave and respond to specific situations and challenges.

Coupon The interest payment on a bond.

Cows See cash cows.

Credit rating A grade given to a company by one of the several "rating agencies" like Standard and Poors or Moody's Investor Services. It indicates how likely a company will be able to pay back its debts and is based on an analysis of the company, its markets, customers, assets, liabilities, and other financial data.

Cross-functional team A group of people (usually employees, but can also include outside suppliers or even customers) that represent different functional disciplines necessary to solve a particular business or product issue.

Cross-training The process of training people in different types of skills necessary for getting a particular job done. This is usually done to increase workforce flexibility.

Culture See corporate culture.

Customer-centric A term developed by Jay R. Galbraith meaning an orientation toward the total satisfaction of a company's customers. It entails not just selling whatever combination of products or services (regardless of whether the company actually makes them) are necessary to fulfill a customer demand, but also restructuring the company's systems, processes, compensation programs, and people practices to support a customer (rather than product) mindset. IBM in 2006 is a good example of a customer-centric company.

Customer Relationship Management A cross-functional business process that aligns the interactions between a company's customers and all of the interfaces in the company with the end goal of enhancing customer loyalty and profitability. It usually involves assessing who the most valuable and profitable customers are and devising ways to enhance those customer relationships. Information technology is often used to gather and disseminate crucial information about customers. Many companies offer prepackaged CRM software. CRM is enabled by technology—not driven by it.

Cycle time Usually refers to the time required to manufacture a product from raw material to finished good. It can also refer to service contracts and other processes within an organization. It's also called "lead time."

Data mining A process of systematically extracting information from large databases and identifying patterns. It's used to put various bits of seemingly unrelated data together with other data to produce a useful picture of an individual. For example a retailer can see from their own scanner database that you frequently buy diapers, a disposable camera, dog food, Fruit Loops® cereal, and cat litter. Then putting that data together with demographic information on neighborhood incomes, the retailer develops a profile of you as a middle class consumer with young kids, a dog, and a cat.

Days of inventory   Average inventory on hand ÷ average daily inventory usage. From a financial analysis perspective, a smaller number is better. From a customer service perspective, a larger number is often better.

Decision tree   A logic-driven method for describing and testing the attributes of a particular problem.

Derivative   A financial security that has an underlying value based upon something else, like a basket of stocks, bonds, interest rates, Mexican copper, Congolese diamonds, or mortgages.

Design for assembly   A process by which a product is designed from the start for easy and low cost assembly.

Design for manufacturability   A process by which a product is designed from the start for easy, low-cost, and high-quality manufacturing.

Development   The process of turning an idea into a product, new business model, or process that can either save the company loads of money or bring in new sources of revenues. It's the "D" part of R&D.

Diversification   A strategy that a company employs to increase the variety in its product and/or service offerings—usually with the goal to increase revenues. Diversification often means that a company is trying to buy up other companies to increase the number of product/services it has. But it also can mean expanding sales into other markets (industries, consumer groups, etc.).

Dogs   A marketing term for products (or services) that don't generate much profit. They have low-growth and low market share and might generate enough cash to support themselves, but they do not have a promising future in a company's business portfolio.

EBITDA   Earnings Before Interest, Taxes, Depreciation and Amortization (or Earnings Before I Tricked the Dumb Auditor). This is a controversial financial metric that the financial analysts use to calculate a company's true profitability. It strips out the noncash effects (like depreciation and taxes) on a company's earnings and theoretically gives a truer picture of a company's profit potential. Critics say that these noncash expenses actually do come home to roost (like the cost to repair broken machines, or the fact that the equipment is old and doesn't produce as much or as cost-effectively as a similar new model.)

Electronic data interchange (EDI)   A method of exchanging instructions and documents between companies and/or individuals through electronic means. It's a quick and virtually fail-safe method of transferring information.

Enterprise resource planning (ERP)   This combination of software and hardware was originally an extension of MRP II manufacturing software systems. ERP systems attempt to connect and integrate several parts of the organization, like supply chain, production, sales, marketing, human resources, finance, distribution, and accounting. The idea is to make information move seamlessly across the organization.

Exchange   An organization or corporation that facilitates the trading of stocks, bonds, or commodities. Some examples are the New York Stock Exchange, the NASDAQ, the Chicago Mercantile Exchange, and the London International Financial Futures and Options Exchange (LIFFE).

Expert systems   Software that mimics and reproduces the knowledge and experience of experts in a given field so that less skilled people can use it to make decisions.

Extranet   An Internet-like connection that enables customers and suppliers to access a corporate network for information. It is outside of the company's own network, or "intranet."

Face value   See 'par.'

Finance   The provision of capital (money) when and where it's needed. It is also the act of managing tangible assets (machinery, equipment, factories, offices), intangible assets (trademarks, patents, technical expertise, brands), debt, and capital budgets.

Financial accounting   The collection, reporting, and analysis of the traditional accounting information that a business needs to present to its bankers, investors, the government, and stakeholders *outside* the company.

Focus groups   A group of people assembled for a session during which they're asked to respond to a variety of questions. It's usually designed to get live, real time reactions from people considered to be representative of the consumer population of interest.

Fourth generation R&D   The process of using external partnerships and networks along with internal R&D organizations to facilitate faster and more productive innovations.

Functional organization   The basic organization type. It features clear role separations so that people can specialize in a particular function, or operation, of a firm, such as sales, manufacturing, accounting, and distribution.

Future value   The value of an amount of money that you'll receive (or own) at some point in the future. It takes into account the time value of money.

Gantt chart   A planning and control method of laying out the various tasks and subtasks in a project along a timeline. Henry L. Gantt, a mechanical engineer and management consultant who worked with Frederick Taylor at Bethlehem Steel, invented it in 1910.

Geographic organization   Also called "regional organization," it's an organization that separates certain functions or business units into geographic or regional focus areas. The sales function is almost always separated into geographically defined domains of responsibility.

Gross margin percentage   A financial ratio determined by dividing gross margin (revenue minus cost of goods sold) by the sales revenues and multiplying the result by 100. A higher number indicates that the manufacturer is more efficient at turning raw materials into income.

Gross revenues   See gross sales.

Gross sales   The total amount of goods and/or services that a company sells in a given period of time (before any deductions are taken for rebates, discounts, refunds, etc.). Another word is "gross revenues."

Hoshin Kanri   A Japanese term for a planning process that involves the Deming principles of Plan-Do-Check-Act. It's a system of forms and rules that help people to look at a situation, figure out how to improve it, check to make sure that the improvements are doing what they're supposed to, and if not, change the system. It's used extensively at Hewlett-Packard and Xerox.

Income statement   A financial statement showing whether a company is making money or losing money. The income statement shows revenues from sales, less expenses to produce those revenues, and any other business-related deductions to produce the bottom-line of net income or net loss.

Information systems   See Information technology.

Information technology   The combination of computerized hardware, software, networks, routers, telecommunications infrastructure, and people that together power the systems that let data flow from one area to another.

Innovation   The act of introducing new methods or ideas. In business it's the process of discovering new ideas and technologies that can be turned into new products, services, processes, and business models.

Internet   The Internet is a worldwide network of computers and servers that use a common language (protocol) to talk to each other. It was originally created by the Advanced Research Projects Agency (ARPA) as ARPANET and grew into the Internet. The Internet is now the de facto method of communication in business and commerce, as well as in its original sphere of academia. (If you haven't heard of the Internet, we're all wondering what cave you've been living in.)

Internet marketing   A method of selling goods and services using the Internet.

Intranet   A secure, internal, Internet-based computer network for corporations, their employees, and trusted outsiders.

ISO 9000   A certification and auditing program developed by the International Standards Organization in Geneva, Switzerland. Certification provides assurance of quality processes in manufacturing.

ISO 14000   Similar to ISO 9000 but it pertains to environmental management systems.

Just-in-time (JIT)   Also known as continuous-flow production. JIT uses "pull" signals such as Kanban cards to initiate production. Intermediate parts get delivered "just in time" as they are needed in the manufacturing process. JIT reduces lot sizes, setup times, waste, work-in-progress inventory, manufacturing cycle time, and other non-value-added activities.

Kaizen   A Japanese term for a systematic and organized program of continuous process improvement.

Kanban   A Japanese term for the system of signaling suppliers or upstream production cells that it's time to replenish stocks of components or subassemblies in a just-in-time production system. Kanban cards were originally used, but now any signal (empty containers, "hey you" or computer-driven lights) is called Kanban.

Laddering process   A market analysis tactic that attempts to connect product attributes with certain core values held by consumers. It's also called benefit laddering, means-end chain, argument mapping, and cognitive linking.

Lead time   The time it takes from ordering a product until it is delivered to the customer.

Leverage   The use of debt to free up capital that can be put to more productive ends. If a company can borrow money at an interest rate that is lower than its own return on capital, then it has used leverage to the benefit of the shareholders. However, a high degree of leverage can also bring on added risk (the inability of the company to pay back the debt if economic conditions change).

Management accounting   The collection, reporting, and analysis of quantitative information that is useful to people *inside* the company to help them make better decisions.

Manufacturing cost   An accounting term that includes direct and indirect labor, quality-related costs, machine time, manufacturing support and overhead, equipment repair, and other costs directly related to the cost of producing a finished good. It doesn't include purchased materials costs or any other nonmanufacturing expenses (sales, marketing, etc.).

Manufacturing planning and control systems   Tools that help managers make decisions relative to the operations and production function, usually in a factory. Many of these types of systems are now embedded in software, which is often embedded into sophisticated machinery.

Marketing   The process (and function) by which a company gets the word out about its products and services. It involves figuring out who its customers are and how to communicate with them.

Market penetration   A growth strategy that involves selling products/services into a new or existing market with a company's current (unmodified) products. Usually a company does this at the expense of its competitors in that market, but it can also mean convincing new customers to try the product or getting current customers to buy more.

Market positioning   How a company features its product (versus the competing products) in the minds of the people it thinks will buy that product.

Market segment   A group of customers who can be lumped together based on some outside criteria. The criteria can range from age groupings, religion, sexual preference, smoking preference, hobbies, national/cultural characteristics, financial risk tolerance, lifestyle, and any number and combination of other divisions. In the high-technology industry this is often called "market space" and can carry an additional connotation of how people use the product or service.

Market space   See market segment.

Mass customization   The use of flexible manufacturing processes to develop and sell a product that is easily customized (personalized) to a wide group of people.

Mass marketing   The act of selling one product to the widest possible group of buyers. No effort is made to differentiate the product (customize) or the group to which it is addressed.

Mission statement   A short summary of what the company does—why it's in business. It's a call to action to tell employees what the company's main purpose is. The mission statement usually includes specific goals for growth, quality, customer satisfaction, and so on.

MRP II   Manufacturing Resources Planning. A software-based system that translates sales forecasts into master production schedules, which drive work orders for each step in the production, inventory requirements, materials purchases, financial reports and heaps of other information depending on the specific requirements of the factory.

NAICS   North American Industry Classification System that identifies to which industry sector a business belongs. It replaces the SIC (Standard Industrial Classification) codes.

Natural work team   A bunch of employees who share the same general space and are responsible for a particular process.

Net present value   The value today of a series of cash flows (both positive and negative) that have been discounted to allow for the time value of money.

Open innovation   See fourth generation R&D.

Overhead   The base cost of running a business. This usually refers to the cost to heat and light the physical building(s) where the company operates. But it can also include a number of other expenses, like the secretary salaries, maintenance contracts on the copiers and other machines, telephone fees, office supplies, and so on. Overhead is usually charged as an additional expense in the form of a percentage cost of whatever the company sells.

Par   The "face value" of something. For a bond it's the principal amount owed (or borrowed). For a stock, it's the issue price.

PERT network   A planning and control method for managing large, nonrecurring projects. It's a complex statistical technique to analyze the minimum amount of time necessary to complete the overall project.

Poka-yoke   A manufacturing technique to eliminate errors as early in the production process as possible in order to prevent rework. An example is designing openings for components that are only big enough for them to pass through (if the part is too big it's rejected and alerts operators to an error).

Present value   The sum of a series of cash flows in the future that have been discounted by an appropriate interest rate to account for the time value of money. The concept is that money in your hand today is worth more than money you will receive tomorrow, next week, or next year. It's a way of comparing all those cash values in the future to the value of money held today.

Process manufacturing   A manufacturing operation that makes things in batches rather than individual (discrete) units. Process manufacturing usually applies to end products like chemicals, gasoline, beverages, liquid cosmetics (lotions, cleansers, etc.), and food. It often involves heating, cooling, pressurizing, and other time consuming operations to produce the final batch.

Product-centric   The mindset of most companies in the past 200 years. It refers to a company's propensity to develop products and/or services that will satisfy a specific (and narrowly defined) need without regard to the overall job that the customer needs to have accomplished. Most companies make products to sell (push) to a variety of customers. Product-centric is the opposite of customer-centric. Pharmaceutical companies are a good example of product-centric companies.

Product development   The action of modifying or creating new products from a new idea, or creating a new use for an old product into something tangible that a company can sell.

Product development cycle   The time it takes to bring a product from its initial idea (glimmer of hope) to when it is actually sold in stores or online. It's sometimes called "time to market."

Product organization   An organization structure that is divided into product lines. The primary focus of this organization is to develop and sell as many products as it possibly can to as many possible customers.

Profit and Loss   The term, also called "P and L," describes a function or business unit that is expected to stand on its own and hopefully generate profits (income) and not losses. When someone is said to have P+L experience, it means that she has been responsible for running a business and has general management experience.

Profit margin   A financial ratio that indicates the percentage of sales that goes to profit. It's determined by dividing net income by the sales revenue and multiplying by 100. A high profit margin is good. A low profit margin may indicate that a company isn't pricing its product effectively, that there is heavy competition or substitutes, or that a company is having difficulty managing its expenses.

Proxy   A piece of paper allowing a person to mail in his or her vote on shareholder issues at an annual meeting in lieu of physically attending the meeting and voting in person.

Pull system   Used in manufacturing, the flow of component parts is "pulled" through the assembly process by signals downstream such as Kanban cards. This way a product is only made as it is needed. The opposite is a "push" system where forecasts dictate what products are to be made and when.

Question marks   A marketing term for products or services that have low market share but are in high-growth markets (or have the potential to be in high-growth markets). They usually require a lot of cash to nurture their development but their future is uncertain.

Relationship marketing   A type of marketing that attempts to build loyalty with existing customers by providing products and services that the particular customer wants and needs.

Research and development (R&D)   The process of discovering new ideas and technologies that can be turned into new products, services, processes, and business models. R&D also refers to the function within a business that is charged with innovating.

R&D intensity   Total R&D spending as a percentage of sales. It's a ratio produced by dividing total R&D outlays by total sales and multiplying by 100.

Return on assets   A financial ratio that indicates how well a business is using its assets to generate profits. ROA is calculated by dividing net income by total assets and multiplying by 100. A high number is better than a low number.

Return on investment   A financial ratio that shows profit as a percentage of total shareholder's equity. ROI is calculated by dividing net income by total shareholders equity and multiplying by 100. A high number is better than a low number.

Return on invested capital   See Return on investment.

Risk   Exposure to something, the outcome of which you're uncertain. In finance, risk often refers to the volatility of financial assets, such as an unexpected increase or decrease in the value of a stock or bond. In credit terms, risk means the probability that the lender will be fully repaid by the borrower.

Sarbanes-Oxley Act of 2002   The U.S. Congress passed this act in the wake of several high profile corporate accounting scandals. The act requires more financial disclosure from corporations, and higher responsibility and accountability on the part of senior managers. Sox or SarbOx, as the act is also known, establishes a public accounting oversight board, auditor independence, and numerous other reporting and data security requirements.

Shareholder   See stockholder.

Six Sigma   This is a quality improvement program that was pioneered at Motorola. The goal is to continuously improve a process (manufacturing, sales, product development, purchasing) in large part by reducing defects to nearly zero—3.4 defects per million "opportunities" or 99.99966% good "outcomes." Six sigma refers to the statistical concept of "six sigmas" out on the extremities of a bell curve.

Space   See market segment.

Stakeholders   The group of people who have an interest in a company and how it behaves. These can include employees, shareholders, debtors, creditors, suppliers, customers, the government, the community a business operates in, and so on.

Stars   A marketing term for products or services that are in high-growth markets and have a large share of the market. They are often the whiz-bang high-technology stuff that makes executives' and customers' eyes pop. They typically need a lot of cash to sustain their high-flying market position.

Stock   A claim of ownership on the assets of a company. In the United States, a stock is a piece of paper that grants the holder title to an equivalent share of a company.

Stockholder   A person or entity that owns stock in a company. Also known as shareholder.

Strategic business unit (SBU)   It's also known as a business unit, but the adjective "strategic" implies that it's crucial to the company's future. An SBU is a sort of "company within a company" that has its own mission and goals. It's often very independent from the other businesses of the company and is managed separately. An example is the many SBUs of General Electric: Aircraft Engines, Medical, Lighting, Power Generation, and so on.

Strategic planning   The process of identifying and developing a conceptual fit between an organization's capabilities and goals, and the wider arena of where it does business and who it competes against. It also means developing an action plan for how a company will pursue its goals.

Supply chain   In this book we consider supply chain to include the functions of purchasing, manufacturing (operations), distribution, and logistics. Other uses of the term, supply chain, limit it to distribution and logistics only—that is, the physical movement of goods from one point to another and the accompanying information on the goods' whereabouts.

Supply chain management   Software and hardware networks that help manufacturing operations keep track of their inventory, production schedules and work flow.

Supplier partnerships   These are joint operating agreements between a buyer and a seller that specify at a base level what a supplier will deliver and when. In return the supplier usually gets a guarantee of business over a specific period of time. Supplier partnerships can involve a high degree of cooperation where buyer and seller share a lot of operational information and even develop products together.

SWOT analysis   A method used in marketing and strategic planning to identify strengths, weaknesses, opportunities, and threats to a company. It forces a logic-driven comparison of the external environment and a company's internal attributes and capabilities.

Time value of money   A dollar held in your hand today is worth more than that same dollar tomorrow (or next week or next year). This is because money can work and earn interest.

Total Quality Management   This is a big, multidimensional, company-wide approach to improving quality and customer service. It's a way to wake up everyone in the company and point to ways that they can do their job better by such actions as eliminating waste and wasteful activities, preventing equipment from breaking down (maintenance), responding quicker and nicer to customers, and a wide array of other problem-solving techniques.

Turnover   Europeans and Asians use this term to refer to gross sales or gross revenues. It can also mean asset turnover. The higher the turnover, the better for the company.

Unique selling proposition A concept used in marketing that defines what *exactly* the product will do for you, and why it is very different from competing products or services.

Value added This is a concept that looks at the core value of an item (for example a nut or bolt that comes into a manufacturing operation) and adds to that item the value or cost of any additional work done to it to turn it into a more valuable and thus, more profitable product. The term can be applied to almost anything, including raw lumber, which, with value-adding activities can turn it into plywood, a chair, or even a prefabricated house.

Value-added reseller A company that adds an additional component to a product it buys and then sells it to the end user. It can be as simple as embroidering or embellishing a plain t-shirt to resell to teenage girls, or as complex as packaging sophisticated software to a bundle of hardware (like a trading floor or a paint station in an auto manufacturing plant) and selling it to the company that will use the system.

Value chain A model that explains how a business takes raw materials, and through various processes, converts those materials into products and/or services to sell to customers. An example is Joey taking his lemons and turning them into lemonade by adding sugar, water, ice, and other ingredients and then selling the beverage to customers. Joey can further expand his value chain by delivering lemonade to his customers' home or office.

Value stream mapping A process that identifies how and how much value is added to a product or service as it moves through the company (or manufacturing line).

Vertical integration A process by which a company controls the entire value chain, from raw materials to the finished product. Procter & Gamble used to crush buckeyes to make soap base, which they then turned into things like Ivory® soap.

Work in progress A manufacturing term for the amount of product that is moving through the factory. It's stuff that is not yet finished goods. From an accounting standpoint, it's the value of all the bits of parts that are lying around on an assembly line waiting to be finished. It's valued at cost, meaning what the company paid for it, including the overhead (costs to keep the building lit and heated) and direct labor (salary) costs.

Yield curve A graph that shows the market return (interest rate) of bonds against their maturity dates.

Notes

Chapter 1. Introduction

1. *American College Dictionary*, 17th ed., s.v. "commerce." New York: Random House, 1963.

2. William Clarence Webster, *A General History of Commerce*, vol. 1, p. 3. Boston, MA: Ginn & Company, 1903.

3. University of Pennsylvania Museum of Archeology and Anthropology. Taken from http://www.museum.upenn.edu/new/exhibits/online_exhibits/wine/ on June 14, 2005.

4. Webster, *General History of Commerce*, p. 34.

5. Ibid., p. 50.

Chapter 3. Business Strategy

1. Michael E. Porter, *Competitive Strategy: Techniques for Analyzing Industries and Competitors*, New York: The Free Press, 1980.

2. See W. Chan Kim and Renée Mauborgne, "Blue Ocean Strategy," *Harvard Business Review*, October 2004, pp. 76–84.

3. C.K. Prahalad and G. Hamel, "The Core Competence of the Corporation," *Harvard Business Review*, May 1, 1990, pp. 79–91.

Chapter 4. Leadership

1. D.C. McClelland and D.H. Burnham, "Power Is the Great Motivator," *Harvard Business Review*, January 2003, pp. 117–126.

2. A.S. Tannenbaum, *Control in Organizations*, New York: McGraw-Hill, 1968.

3. L.A. Hill, "Exercising Influence," Harvard Business School case study #9-494-080, May 31, 1994.

4. R.M. Kanter, *Men and Women of the Corporation*, New York: Basic Books, 1977.

5. J. Welch with S. Welch, *Winning*, New York: HarperCollins, 2005, p. 63.

6. Institute for Policy Studies/United for a Fair Economy, "Executive Excess 2005," pp. 13–15. CEO salary numbers are based on *Business Week*'s annual compensation survey. Paper was downloaded from www.faireconomy.org/press/2005/EE2005_pr.html on December 23, 2005.

7. M. Kroll, "CEO Pay Rates: U.S. vs. Foreign Nations," November 17, 2005. Paper was downloaded from www.cab.latech.edu/~mkroll/ 510_papers/fall_05/Group6.pdf on December 23, 2005.

8. E. Dash, "Off to the Races Again, Leaving Many Behind: Executive Pay, A Special Report," *New York Times*, Sunday Business. Data is from a survey by compensation consultants Pearl Meyer & Partners.

9. "Executive Pay: Too Many Turkeys," *The Economist*, November 26, 2005, pp. 75–76.

Chapter 5. Finance and Accounting

1. G.A. Holton, "Defining Risk," *Financial Analysts Journal*, 60(6), 2004.

Chapter 6. Marketing

1. American Marketing Association definition taken from http://www.marketingpower.com/mg-dictionary-view1862.php on March 12, 2006.

2. P. Kotler and G. Armstrong, *Marketing: An Introduction*, Englewood Cliffs, NJ: Prentice-Hall, 1987, p. 4.

3. G. Bannock et al., *Dictionary of Business*, London: Profile Books, 2003, p. 215.

4. P. Drucker, *Management: Tasks, Responsibilities, Practices*, New York: Harper & Row, 1973, pp. 64–65.

5. Definition from the Chartered Institute of Marketing as cited on Wikipedia on March 14, 2006.

6. C. M. Christensen, S. Cook, and T. Hall, "Marketing Malpractice: The Cause and the Cure," *Harvard Business Review*, December, 2005, pp. 74–83.

7. A. Dragoon, "How to Do Customer Segmentation Right," *CIO Magazine*, October 15, 2005. Taken from http://www.cio.com/archive/100105/cus_segment.html on March 15, 2006.

8. B. Langer, "Unlocking the Value of Your CRM Initiative: The Strategy Plus Technology Dynamic," Peppers & Rogers Group, 2003. Downloaded on March 27, 2006 from http://www.peppersandrogers.com/view.aspx?ItemID=611.

9. Gartner Group research cited in D.K. Rigby, F.F. Reichheld, and P. Schefter, "Avoid the Four Perils of CRM," *Harvard Business Review*, February 2002, pp. 101–109.

10. T. Kretschmer, "DeBeers and Beyond: The History of the International Diamond Cartel," London Business School, 1998.

Chapter 7. Sales

1. Source is CNW Marketing Research, Inc. cited in J. Saranow, "Car Dealers Recruit Saleswomen at the Mall," *Wall Street Journal*, April 12, 2006.

2. M. Barletta, *Marketing to Women: How to Understand, Reach and Increase Your Share of the World's Largest Market Segment*, 2nd edn., Kaplan Business, 2006.

3. S. Miller, *ProActive Selling: Control the Process—Win the Sale*, New York: Amacom, 2003, pp. 46–56.

Chapter 8. Management of Information Systems

1. N. Gibson, *Essential Finance*, The Economist, 2003, London edition.

2. See A.P. McAfee, *"Managing Information Technology: Course Overview Note for Instructors,"* Harvard Business School Press #5-603-026.

3. *"Why Today's IT Organization Won't Work Tomorrow,"* a study by A.T. Kearney, 2005. Downloaded from: http://www.atkearney.com/main.taf?p=5,9,2,8 on February 9, 2006.

4. Source: www.coldhardfootballfacts.com.

5. See J.W. Ross and P. Weill, "Six IT Decisions Your IT People Shouldn't Make," *Harvard Business Review*, November 2002.

6. I. Limbach, "A Fresh Way of Using Data for Enhancing Customer Experience," *Financial Times*, January 25, 2006.

Chapter 9. Human Resources

1. D. Ulrich, *Human Resource Champions: The Next Agenda for Adding Value and Delivering Results*, Boston, MA: Harvard Business School Press, 1997.

2. J. Welch, with S. Welch, *Winning*, New York: HarperCollins, 2005, p. 102.

3. R. E. Stross, *The Microsoft Way: The Real Story of How the Company Outsmarts its Competition*, Reading, MA: Addison-Wesley, 1996, p. 41.

4. K. Freiberg and J. Freiberg, *Nuts: Southwest Airlines' Crazy Recipe for Business and Personal Success*, Austin, TX: Bard Press, 1996, p. 67.

5. Circulated on the Internet, fall 1997. Taken from H. Ehrlich, *The Wiley Book of Business Quotations*, New York: John Wiley, 1998, p. 318.

Chapter 10. Supply Chain

1. J. Hagel III and J. Seely Brown, "Your Next IT Strategy," *Harvard Business Review*, October 2001.

2. T. Vinas, "Industry Week Value-Chain Survey: A Map of the World," *Industry Week*, September 1, 2005.

3. M. L. Emiliani and D. J. Stec, "Realizing Savings from Online Reverse Auctions," *Supply Chain Management: An International Journal*, 7(1), 2002, pp. 12–23. Downloaded from www.theclbm.com/research.html on February 19, 2006.

4. T. E. Vollmann, W. L. Berry, and D.C. Whybark, *Manufacturing Planning and Control Systems*, 4th ed. Boston: Irwin McGraw-Hill, 1997.

5. ISO Web site, "Overview of the ISO System" taken from http://www.iso.org/iso/en/aboutiso/introduction/index.html on March 1, 2006.

6. See Lee Gomes, *Wall Street Journal*, January 18, 2006.

7. Stephen Roach, Managing Director and Chief Economist at Morgan Stanley, quoted in E. Kinetz, "Who Wins and Who Loses as Jobs Move Overseas?" *New York Times*, December 7, 2003, and R. Hira and A. Hira, *Outsourcing America: What's Behind our National Crisis and How We Can Reclaim American Jobs.* New York: American Management Association, 2005.

Chapter 11. Research and Development

1. "The World's Most Innovative Companies," *Business Week*, April 24, 2006.

2. All data in this section are from the United Kingdom Department of Trade and Industry, "The 2005 R&D Scoreboard" downloaded from http://www.innovation.gov.uk/rd_scoreboard/downloads.asp on May 2, 2006.

3. H. Chesbrough, "The New Rules of R&D," *Harvard Management Update*. Article reprint No. U0305D, 2003.

4. B. R. Rich and L. Janos, *Skunk Works: A Personal Memoir of My Years at Lockheed.* New York: Little, Brown and Company, 1994, pp. 111–112.

5. Example is from E. von Hipple, J. Churchill, and M. Sonnack, *Breakthrough Products and Services with Lead User Research*, cited in "Note on Lead User Research," Havard Business School Case No. 9-699-014, 1998.

Chapter 12. Other Staff Functions

1. Marissa Peterson quoted in a Sun Computer press release dated July 31, 2002. (Available from http://www.sun.com/smi/Press/sunflash/2002-07/sunflash. 20020731.4.xml)

Annotated Bibliography

Ballou, R.H. *Business Logistics Management*. Englewood Cliffs, NJ: Prentice Hall, 1973.

Chesbrough, Henry. *Open Innovation: The New Imperative for Creating and Profiting from Technology*. Boston, MA: Harvard Business School Press, 2003. Presents the logic for fourth generation R&D and gives a number of examples.

Davila, Tony, Marc J. Epstein and Robert Shelton. *Making Innovation Work: How to Manage It, Measure It, and Profit from It*. Upper Saddle River, NJ: Pearson Education, 2006. This book deals with the organizational aspects of managing innovation. It gives practical advice for how to set up structures, reward systems, metrics, and processes to foster consistent innovation.

Freiberg, Kevin and Jackie Freiberg. *Nuts! Southwest Airlines' Crazy Recipe for Business and Personal Success*. Austin, TX: Bard Press, 1996. The Freibergs describe the torturous start of the airline and add many humorous stories about Herb Kelleher and other senior executives. They also present Southwest's somewhat unorthodox method of managing.

Galbraith, Jay R. *Designing Organizations: An Executive Guide to Strategy, Structure and Process*. San Francisco: Jossey-Bass, 2002. Written by the world's leading expert on organization design, this book is an excellent primer for anyone who wants to learn more about organization design, what it is, and how to do it.

Gitomer, Jeffrey. *The Little Red Book of Selling: 12.5 Principles of Sales Greatness*. Austin, TX: Bard Press, 2004.

Gitomer, Jeffrey. *Little Red Book of Sales Answers: 99.5 Real World Answers That Make Sense, Make Sales and Make Money*. Upper Saddle River, NJ: Prentice Hall. 2006. Both of these books written by Gitomer, a former sales guy and now a consultant and journalist, are quick "how to" reads on selling. Much of the advice he gives is designed to build self-confidence in the sales person.

Lawler, Edward E. III. *From the Ground Up: Six Principles for Building the New Logic Corporation*. San Francisco: Jossey-Bass, 1996. Ed Lawler is the unquestioned authority on pay-and-reward systems. In this book he describes what companies need to do from a human resources perspective in order to compete effectively in an environment where good talent is hard to find.

Pine, B.J. II. *Mass Customization: The New Frontier in Business Competition*. Boston, MA: Harvard Business School Press, 1993.

Porter, Michael E. *Competitive Strategy: Techniques for Analyzing Industries and Competitors*. New York: The Free Press, 1980. Porter is the leading authority on top-down analysis of strategy from the industry level. For years this book has been required reading for anyone interested in learning about strategy.

Rich, Ben R. and Leo Janos. *Skunk Works: A Personal Memoir of My Years at Lockheed*. New York: Little, Brown and Company, 1994. A fascinating description of the genesis of the Lockheed Skunk Works that describes in vivid terms some of the real challenges faced by a group of people charged with developing cutting-edge aviation technology under pressure.

Roussel, Philip A., Kamal N. Saad and Tamara J. Erickson. *Third Generation R&D: Managing the Link to Corporate Strategy*. Boston, MA: Harvard Business School Press, 1991. This book provides a good summary of the history of R&D throughout the various generations of R&D management. It's written primarily for the manager who has to get the most out of the company's R&D investments. Latter chapters give many concrete examples.

Tufte, Edward R. *The Visual Display of Quantitative Information*. Cheshire, CT: Graphics Press. 1983.

Tufte, Edward R. *Envisioning Information*. Cheshire, CT: Graphics Press. 1990. All of the Tufte books (there are more than we've listed here) are works of art in themselves. They have logical, forthright discussions and pictures of how to display information so that the user gains a fast and more comprehensive understanding of what's being presented.

Vollman, Thomas E., William L. Berry and D. Clay Whybark. *Manufacturing, Planning and Control Systems*, 4th ed. Boston, MA: Irwin McGraw-Hill, 1997. Everything you ever wanted to know about running and managing a factory.

Welch, Jack and Suzy Welch. *Winning*. New York: Harper Collins, 2005. In this autobiography of sorts, written with his third wife, Jack Welch talks about his 40 years at General Electric. It's packed with Welch's no-nonsense views on managing, reward systems, strategy, and just about anything else you ever wanted to know about leadership and running a business.

Womack, J.P., D. T. Jones and D. Roos. *The Machine That Changed the World*. New York: Rawson Associates/Macmillan Publishing, 1990.

Index

About the Author

SASHA GALBRAITH is a Partner in Jay R. Galbraith Management Consultants, Ltd., managing a variety of functions, including marketing, information technology, contract negotiations, human resources, and accounting, and with research specialties in joint venture management and women in business. She has served as an Adjunct Research Associate at IMD, the International Institute for Management Development, conducting educational seminars for senior executives, and in management positions at Karsten Realty Advisors and Wells Fargo Bank.